The New
Baby
Name
Survey

The New Baby Name Survey

Bruce Lansky

Meadowbrook Press
Distributed by Simon & Schuster
New York

Library of Congress Cataloging-in-Publication Data

Lansky, Bruce.
  The new baby name survey / by Bruce Lansky.
    p. cm.
  Summary: An alphabetical listing of 1,800 baby names, their origins and meanings, the perceived images of people with these names, and their famous namesakes.
  ISBN10 0-88166-493-6, ISBN13 978-0-88166-493-5 (Meadowbrook);
  ISBN10 0-684-03164-7, ISBN13 978-0-684-03164-4 (Simon & Schuster)

  1. Names, Personal—Dictionaries. I. Title.
CS2377.L3736 2007
929.4'4—dc22

                        2007020262

Editorial Coordinator: Megan McGinnis
Data Coordinator and Analyist: Alicia Ester
Copywriter: Angela Wiechmann
Researcher: Maureen Burns
"First Impressions" Index: Beverlee Day
Production Manager: Paul Woods
Graphic Design Manager: Tamara Peterson
Cover Photos: © Corbis, Getty Images, Veer

Published by Meadowbrook Press, 5451 Smetana Drive, Minnetonka, Minnesota 55343

www.meadowbrookpress.com

BOOK TRADE DISTRIBUTION by Simon and Schuster, a division of Simon and Schuster, Inc., 1230 Avenue of the Americas, New York, New York 10020

10 09 08 07 10 9 8 7 6 5 4 3 2 1

Printed in the United States of America

Dedication

I dedicate this book to expecting parents who are considering lots of names but need some help whittling down the list and making the final choice. Especially if you've received strong naming suggestions from family or friends, you'll appreciate an objective resource that helps explain to them why names like Igor or Elmer, Bambi or Bertha, may not be in your child's best interest. (Look them up; you'll see what I mean.)

I also dedicate this book to parents who believe picking a unique name will help their child become a unique person. After looking at the uncommon or off-the-wall names in this book (like Dorcas, Baba, Gwidon, and many of the notorious celebrity baby names sprinkled throughout the book) and discovering the first impressions they make on others, I hope you'll realize that unique names can often make strange or negative first impressions.

Acknowledgments

Meadowbrook Press extends its grateful thanks to Meredith Corporation and to www.americanbaby.com for conducting the baby name survey that provided the image data for the names included in this book.

Contents

Introduction

The New Baby Name Survey, the third edition of our successful baby name survey book, may be the most helpful guide ever written for parents who want to select a name that will give their child a head start in life.

A person's name often influences our first impressions of him or her. Because we're exposed to many of the same movies, TV shows, books, magazines, newspaper headlines, comic strips, and other forms of mass culture, we share many of the same images and stereotypes about names.

For example, most people would match the personality traits and names listed below in the same way:

Personality Traits	Girls' Names	Boys' Names
ditzy/dumb	Barbie	Bud
intelligent	Amelia	Barack
funny	Fran	Nathan
beautiful/handsome	Alyssa	Fabio

Most of us associate the names listed above with the real and fictional people whose images have shaped our perceptions of those names: Barbie (doll) and character Bud Bundy (*Married…with Children*), aviator Amelia Earhart and politician Barack Obama, actress Fran Drescher (*The Nanny*) and actor Nathan Lane (*The Producers*), actress Alyssa Milano and model Fabio Lanzoni.

When the names are uncommon, like Waylon or Gwyneth, it's almost impossible to think of them without thinking of their most famous namesakes, country singer Waylon Jennings and blond actress Gwyneth Paltrow. Other uncommon names that bring to mind clear mental pictures that most of us share are Madonna, Cher, Bambi, Elton, Rudolph, and Rocky.

But the images of many names don't remain static; time allows new images to emerge. With the help of a well-known parenting website, which conducted a massive survey that polled thousands of respondents, this edition has been completely updated with all-new images.

For example, in the second edition of this book (published in 1998), Angelina was pictured as a delicate, angelic woman who just stepped out of an Italian Renaissance painting. In this edition, Angelina calls to mind someone wild and glamorous, like actress Angelina Jolie. Previously, Dora was viewed as a swinging "Dumb Dora." Now she's pictured as a spunky, adventurous Latina, like Dora the Explorer.

When thinking of names for your baby, you may remember how cruel teasing can be during childhood—and you may shy away from names that will give bullies a reason to tease your child. You want your child to be accepted by his or her peers and have a good self image. One step in that direction is to give your child a name that's perceived positively. As you consider various names, you'll realize that you don't have as clear an image of, say, John as you do of Rocky. And, unfortunately, you probably won't know how others perceive the names you like best.

For example, as you think about the name Elizabeth, you may picture Queen Elizabeth, actress Elizabeth Taylor, actress Elizabeth Montgomery (*Bewitched*), or poet Elizabeth Barrett Browning. You may think of Elizabeth as regal, glamorous, magical, or romantic. But how do others think of Elizabeth?

This book is designed to help you answer that question for nearly two thousand popular and uncommon names. It's organized into two main sections to make selecting a great name for your baby easy and fun.

The first section, First Impressions, contains a list of adjectives and nouns that describe physical traits, personality, life style, and other attributes (for example, freckled, funny, French, or farmer). Under each adjective or noun, you'll find the boys' or girls' names people most often associate with it. You can use this list as follows:

1. Ask yourself what traits you admire. Look up those traits and see what names are associated with them.

2. Scan the lists. You'll find other traits that appeal to you. See what names are associated with them.

3. Finally, make a list of the names that reflect the traits that appeal to you. These are names worth considering further.

Next, turn to the second section, Images, which contains an alphabetical list of girls' and boys' names complete with origins, meanings, and famous namesakes. Most important, each listing also contains an image profile of the name based on the opinions of numerous survey respondents. This unique information gives you a more complete picture of each name, particularly of how other people view it. Use this list in the following way:

1. Look up the names you selected when reading the First Impressions section, to gain a better picture of the image associated with each name.

2. Think about your own impressions of the names you're considering, as well as other people's impressions.

3. List the pros and cons of each name you're considering.

4. Finally, pick the names that sound good, look good, feel good, and make sense as a "label" that will last a lifetime.

I hope you'll agree that by considering the impressions that names make on people, you'll be able to make a wiser final choice.

I also hope you'll enjoy reading this new edition, which contains several improvements over the previous editions. In it, we:

• Included fun image profiles of the names of several celebrity babies, like Rumer, Suri, and Apple.

• Designed the First Impressions section like an index so it's more complete and useful.

• Wrote the image profiles with more focus and punch. Each profile provides a clearer picture and is more fun to read.

• Listed only the famous namesakes that are most likely to have shaped people's perceptions of the names. Don't be surprised if we've left out a namesake here and there!

Lastly, I hope that the process of naming your baby will be a pleasure for you.

Bruce Lansky

Bruce Lansky

First Impressions of Girls' Names

First Impressions

Admirable
Kay

Adorable
Evie
Molly

Adventurous
Penelope

Affectionate
Abira
Daphne
Pauline

African American
Aaliyah
Janae
Kenya
Latonya
Latoya
Yolanda
Zahara

Ambitious
Octavia
Roma
Suzanne
Vanessa

Angelic
Alyson
Angelina
Chastity
Gabriela
Isabel

Antisocial
Urania

Approachable
Anastasia
Charlene
Julie

Arrogant
Chris
Francesca
Kirsten
Mariah
Phyllis
Sheila
Sondra

Articulate
Arlene
Yasmine

Arty/Artistic
see also Creative
Dena
Frida
Gillian
Mia

Asian
Kameko

Assertive
Candra
Tyne

Athletic
see also Basketball player; Sporty
Martina

Attention seeking
Delphine
Lisa

Attentive
Carlen
Mya

Attractive
see also Beautiful; Cute; Pretty
Claire
Jillian
Kali
Lilah
Michaela
Racquel
Sydney

Awkward
Flannery

Backstabber
Glory

Bad attitude
Juanita

Bashful
see also Shy
Colleen
Mariel

Basketball player
Jordan

Battler
Tracy
Zena

Beautiful
see also Attractive
Alyssa
Bonita
Chaya
Clara
Ebony
Ella
Estelle
Gabriella
Harmony
Jolie
Mallory
Morgan
Selena
Stella

Big
Olga

Big-boned
Alberta
Hedda

Big-haired
Bunny

Bitter
Hortense

Black-haired
see also Dark-haired
Demi

Blond
Blythe
Caitlin
Cassidy
Nicolette

Boisterous
Jolene

Bold
Gwen
Taka

Bombshell
Naomi

Bossy
Elena
Lucinda
Nellie
Tanya
Yvonne

Bouncy
Betty
Haley

Brainy
Stacey
Uriana

Brash
Liz
Rue

Brassy
Joan

Brave
Athena

Bright
Larissa

Brilliant
see also Intelligent; Smart
Eldora
Iris
Sierra

Brown-eyed
Brooke

Brunette
Hazel
Sonya

Brutish
Helga

Bubbly
Ashley
Christa
Cicely
Cynthia
Dani
Judy
Kanika
Marilyn
Suzette
Suzie
Taffy
Tierney
Tina
Trish

Calm
Charlotte
Patricia
Serena

Carefree
Jade
Kylie

Caring
Aimee
Amaya
Benita
Delilah
Florence
Gracie
Guadalupe
Harriet
Honora
Lyla
Mackenzie
Margaret
Marlo
Maya

Melody
Nessa
Oprah
Pearl
Ricki
Rochelle
Rosemary
Shakila
Wendy

Charismatic
Babette
Darla
Dianne

Charitable
Alma
Charity

Charming
Alissa
Charisma

Chatty
see also Talkative
Destiny

Cheerful
Autumn
Betsy
Florida
Lulu
Stormy
Summer
Sunshine
Taylor
Terri

Cheery
Emma

Chestnut-haired
see also Dark-haired
Lea

Chipper
Amanda
Dottie

Chubby
Roseanne

Classy
Kimberly

Clever
Barbara

Cliquish
Brittany

Cockiness
Starr

Cold
Margaux
Portia
Winter

Comical
Bridget

Compassionate
Breena
Elizabeth
Gavin
Grace
Maire
Maxine
Rhiannon
Thea
Virginia

Competitive
Annika

Conceited
Desiree
Scarlett

Confident
see also Self-assured
Andrea
Antonia
Ava
Camryn
Judith
Koren
Lonna
Michelle

Reese
Regina

Conscientious
Noel

Conservative
Edna

Considerate
Vicki

Country girl
Billie

Courageous
Storm

Coy
Modesty

Crabby
Sharon

Cranky
Doreen
Fleta
Myrna
Prudence

Creative
see also Arty/Artistic
Jenay
Lia
Odera
Taryn
Veda
Zola

Cruel
Natasha

Cuddly
Elsie

Cultured
Sophie

Cunning
Pandita

Curly-haired
Peggy

First Impressions

Cute
Alice
Brenna
Katelyn
Katy
Mindy

Cynical
Randi

Dainty
Jena
Nerissa

Dark-haired
see also Black-
haired; Brunette
Alexandria
Carmen
Jocelyn
Phylicia

Daydreamer
Felicity

Delicate
see also Dainty
Lacy

Demure
Camilla
Catherine
Violet

Dense
see also Dumb
Pamela

Dependable
Consuelo

Depressed
Sylvia

Determined
Greta
Hanna
Iman
Ingrid
Jaclyn
Josephine

Katherine
Sarina

Devout
Magdalen

Dimwitted
Candi
Crystal
Tiffany

Distrusting
Sharlene

Ditzy
Bambi
Barbie

Dorky
see also Nerdy
Moira

Dramatic
Georgia

Dreamy
Esperanza

Droll
Renee

Dull
Pat
Velma

Dumb
see also Dimwitted;
Ditzy
Adena
Mitzi
Orella
Theresa

Earthy
Gemma
Oceana

Easygoing
see also Happy-
go-lucky
Linda

Eccentric
Cyndi
Isi
Lois
Yoko

Educated
Constance

Elderly
see also Old
Ada
Agatha
Ester
Mabel
Odele

Elegant
Audrey
Cora
Eleanor
Helene
Julianne
Katarina
Verena

Empathetic
Eva

Energetic
Candida
Melissa
Patti
Shari

Entertaining
Madison

Enthusiastic
Nikki

Exciting
Electra

Exotic
Alana
Asia
Hasana
Sheba

Extroverted
Brenda

Fair-haired
see also Blond
Natalie

Family oriented
Oletha

Fashionable
Yvette

Fast talking
Tanith

Fearless
Savannah
Torrance

Feisty
Kendall
Sabra
Zaida

Flamboyant
Lola

Flighty
Posy

Flirtatious
Jessica
Kristina

Focused
Joni

Fragile
Sybil

Free spirited
Anika
Dawn
Journey
Liberty
Lucie
Mansi

Friendly
Adelaide
Akiko
Amy
Becky
Capri
Carina
Danica
Dee Dee
Denise
Dolly
Jaime
Jasmine
Jelena
Kari
Katina
Lauren
Lindsey
Lynn
Maisie
Marcy
Nadia
Norell
Rita
Savanna
Sophia
Sue
Susannah

Frumpy
Gladys

Full figured
Georgina

Fun
Christy
Laurie
Tara
Tess
Whitney

Fun-loving
Aileen
Gabrielle
Hayley
Lori
Muriel
Paris
Tessa

Funny
Angie
Celeste
Fran

Fussy
Kelsey

Gawky
Geraldine

Generous
Cheri
Heidi
Nanette
Sandy
Zaza

Gentle
Belinda
Iolanthe
Lynette
Patrice
Rosalyn

Gifted
Marley

Giggly
Dixie

Giving
Aurora
Carlotta

Gloomy
Sasha

"Good girl"
Ashlyn

Goodhearted
Hope
Kessie

Good-humored
Paz

Good-natured
Danielle
Joyce

Good person
Blaine

Good-willed
Brianna

Goofy
Kimmy

Gorgeous
see also Beautiful
Tyra

Goth
Calantha

Grandmother
Ethel

Gregarious
Andreana

Grumpy
Rhea

Happy
see also Jolly/Jovial;
Joyful
Bliss
Cheyenne
Doris
Glenda
Lila
Olivia
Shirley
Sunny

Happy-go-lucky
see also Easygoing
Jessie
Kerry
Kristin
Marissa

Harsh
Mae

Headstrong
Rori

Heartfelt
Hallie

Heartless
Jezebel

Heavyset
see also Overweight
Baba
Poria

Hefty
Angus

Helpful
Bella
Glenna
Janet
Lane
Ruth

High spirited
Carolina

Hilarious
Janine

Homely
Huberta
Maud

Honest
Letitia

Horrible
Ursula

Hurtful
Angelica

Imaginative
Fantasia

In-charge
Gina

Independent
Ariana
Kendra
Kiara
Shauna

First Impressions

Innocent
Ariel
Janie
Kishi
Millie

Insecure
Roxanna

Insightful
Mara

Intelligent
see also **Brilliant;**
   Smart
Amelia
Jean
Jennifer
Justine
Lina
Marit
Nyssa
Tatiana
Therese

Introverted
Agnes
Henrietta
Nola

Italian
Giovana

Jealous
Tonya

Joker
Carol

Jolly/Jovial
Olive

Joyful
Joy
Marjorie
Montana

Kind
Abigail
Angela
Anna

Aubrey
Bernadette
Beth
Britta
Chavi
Christina
Claudia
Deirdre
Della
Dominique
Dorothy
Francine
Hermosa
Irene
Ivy
Janna
Juliana
Kacey
Kathleen
Kona
Marietta
Megan
Mimi
Miriam
Rosa
Shelly
Siobhan
Tisha

Kindhearted
Ali
Annette
Caley
Eve
Karen
Serenity

Laid-back
Eartha

Lanky
Stevie

Large
see also **Heavyset;**
   Overweight
Wilhelmina

Latino
Maria

Levelheaded
Marcella

Liberal
Berkley

Librarian
Lenora

Light
June

Likable
Lorraine
Matilda
Reagan

Limber
Kala

Lithe
Fiona

Lively
Bailey
Caprice
Kate
Lupita

Logical
Caroline

Lonely
Eunice
Noreen

Loud
Carla
Carlene
Kitra
Krystal
Lindsay
Marcia
Mercedes
Nidia
Priscilla
Rachael
Wanda

Lovable
Charisse
Corrina

Lovely
Leilani
Theone

Loving
Ivory
Marie
Melanie
Opal
Pennie
Sara

Loyal
Diane

Malicious
Millicent

Manipulative
Selina

Matronly
Laverne

Mean
Brandy
Dana
Lorna
Meryl

Meek
Carey
Fawn
Maggie

Middle Eastern
Samara

Mischievous
Cori
Katrina
Ramona

Model
Breanna

Moody
Donata
Jeanette

Mopey
Doria

Motherly
Bess
Martha

Motivated
Shonda

Mousy
Blinda
Cathy
Darcy

Muscular
Olympia

Mysterious
Cecelia
Laila
Lydia
Raven

Naïve
Gretel

Narcissistic
Narcissa

Nerdy
Adele
Eliza

Nervous
Melinda

Nice
Bonnie

Nurturing
Mary
Tammy

Obese
see also Overweight
Bertha

Observant
Nyx

Old
see also Elderly
Agatha
Beatrice
Bernice
Beverly
Blanche
Edith
Heloise
Irma
Maureen
Winifred

Olive-skinned
Malana
Modesta
Tamara

Opinionated
Hilary
Rhonda

Optimistic
Cristy

Organized
Jayne

Outcast
Carrie

Outgoing
Addie
Bree
Charmaine
Deborah
Krista
Lakeisha
Rae
Tia
Zephyr

Outrageous
Esmeralda

Outspoken
Roberta

Overbearing
Audra

Overweight
see also Heavyset
Laveda

Pale
Blanca

Passionate
Anya

Patient
Genevieve

Peace-loving
Onella

Peppy
Polly

Perceptive
Erin

Perky
Allie
Katie
Kelly
Stephanie
Tasha

Personable
Chelsea

Pessimistic
Pythia

Petite
Ann
Georgette
Kimi
Lilac
Minnie
Nina

Playful
Astra
Lolly
Lucy
Minka
Mona

Pleasant
Christine
Kora
May

Plump
see also Overweight
Libby

Poised
Felice
Jacqueline

Polite
Giselle
Kaya
Lily
Paige
Reilly

Popular
Alicia
Candace
Casey
Jackie
Kaylee
Mandy
Shanna
Sheena
Tricia
Winona

Practical
Linnea
Verna

Preacher's daughter
Eden

Pretty
see also Attractive;
    Lovely
Alisha
Chantal
Jana
Kayla
Maddie
Nailah

First Impressions

Prim
Isabella

Prissy
Alexandra
Angelique
Blair
Kristen

Proper
Rose

Proud
Sagara

Prudish
Marsha
Norma

Pure hearted
Juliet

Quick-tempered
Alena
Joanna

Quick-thinking
Sandra

Quick-witted
Delta

Quiet
Bette
Clementine
Ela
Gwendolyn
Helen
Jody
Laurel
Rhoda
Riona
Romola
Sylvana

Rambunctious
Cassie

Raspy voiced
Dina

Rebellious
Cara

Redheaded
Ginger
Reba

Regal/Royal
Antoinette

Reserved
India
Jane
Marlene

Resilient
Phaedra

Responsible
Lara

Rich
see also Wealthy
Caitlyn
Evelyn
Monique

Rough
Darlene

Rude
Gwyneth
Veronica

Sassy
Roseanna
Tawny

Scandinavian
Inga

Scary
Drusilla

Self-assured
see also Confident
Bianca
Maura
Tatum
Torie

Self-centered
Thomasina

Self-sufficient
Robyn

Sensitive
Abby
Julia
Mary Beth

Sexy
Alexis
Brigitte
Chloe
Lana
Simone

Shallow
Kristine

Short
see also Petite
Dora
Missy

Short-tempered
see Quick-tempered

Shy
see also Bashful
Akina
Aubrey
Donna
Emily
Gail
Ghita
Kalare
Lizina
Marta
Mauve
Mead
Myra
Nadine
Nia
Nora
Othelia
Patience
Qadira

Silly
Mickie
Sherry
Zizi
Zoe

Sincere
Susan

Singer
Celine

Skinny
see also Thin
Tegan

Slow
Winda

Small
see also Petite; Short
Trina

Smart
see also Intelligent
Cathleen
Clare
Eileen
Gretchen
Kass
Nancy
Nevaeh
Paula
Paulette
Trinity

Smart mouthed
Germaine

Snippy
Maira

Snobby
Anais
Delia
Erica
Italia
Jessamine
Meredith

Snooty
Buffy
Margot

Sociable
Cindy
Miranda
Rosalie
Sally
Samantha

Soft
April

Softhearted
Kathy

Soft-spoken
Amber
Aolani
Cordelia
Enid
Lillian
Meka
Sofia

Sophisticated
Vera

Spirited
Jenna
Tameka

Spiteful
Leona

Spoiled
Alexa
Celia
Clarissa
Diamond
Fifi
Kelby
Sapphire
Vanna

Sporty
see also Athletic
Callie
Jodi
Nike

Spunky
Annie
Brittney
Chika
Felicia
Jada
Josie
Rebecca

Stand-up girl
Reanna

Storyteller
Lainey

Stout
Hedwig

Strange
Tova

Strong
Aretha
Lilith
Pavla
Thema
Zelia

Strong-minded
Rachel

Stuck-up
Heather
Nicole
Valarie

Studious
Ilene
Mireille

Stunning
Anezka
Leila

Stylish
Chanel

Sunny
Becca
Britany
Daisy

Jenny
Toni

Sweet
Adora
Adrienne
Allison
Baka
Belle
Bethany
Briana
Callidora
Camille
Cheryl
Corinne
Diana
Ellen
Ellie
Faith
Ginny
Hannah
Holly
Jill
Kyla
Kyra
Leandra
Louisa
Natalia
Petula
Sabina
Shelby

Talented
Aria

Talkative
Carly
Chiara
Gaby
Kalinda
Kaliska
Kristi
Lawanda
Mary Ellen

Tall
Ana
Nikita

Sabrina
Skye
Stacy
Svetlana

Tease, a
Courtney

Temperamental
Collette

Thin
see also Skinny
Laura

Timid
Eugenia
Pansy

Tomboy
Dakota
Jo

Tough
Lorena

Traditional
Elaine

Trampy
Misty

Troubled
Delores

Type A
Katharine

Understanding
Lacey

Unique
Cai
Luna

Unpopular geek
Gloria

Unusual
Phoebe

First Impressions

Upbeat
Allegra
Carissa
Janelle

Uppity
Victoria

Upstanding
Frances

Uptight
Adeline

Vain
Monica

Vibrant
Trista

Vivacious
Jeri
Kim
Piper
Vivian

Vulnerable
Guinevere
Ophelia

Waiflike
Willow

Waitress
Louise

Warm
Anita
Imogene
Leah
Lucia
Shakira

Warmhearted
Kira
Milly

Weak
Connie

Wealthy
Leigh
Madeline
Sable

Well bred
Greer

Well educated
Marguerite

Well liked
Cadence
Shoshana

Well mannered
Stockard

Well read
Tabitha

Well traveled
Elise

Whiny
Marnie
Sissy

White-haired
Mildred

Wholesome
Sarah

Wide-eyed
Regan

Wild
Avril
Chiquita
Janis
Liza
Loretta
Margarita
Sage
Shannon
Stacia

Willowy
Neena

Wise
Cassandra

Wispy
Brie

Witty
Lucille

Wrinkly
Ida

Young
McKayla
Trudy

First Impressions of Boys' Names

First Impressions

Accommodating
Porter

Adventurous
Doyle
Logan
Mario
Ranger

African American
Jamal
Jermaine
Terrell
Terrence
Tyree

Aggressive
Troy

Aloof
Akeem

Ambitious
Garrett
Raheem

Annoying
Clifford
Curtis
Jerry

Arrogant
Chet
Randolph
Simon
Stefan

Arsonist
Arsen

Articulate
Connor
Perry

Arty/Artistic
see also Creative
Dominic

Asian
Vijay

Athletic
see also Basketball player; Football player; Soccer star; Sporty
Chad
Jerome
Tommy

Attractive
see also Cute; Good-looking; Handsome
Braden
Nigel

Authoritative
Frederick
Stanley

Average
Bob
Ryan

Awkward
Ed
Harvey
Myron

Basketball player
Tyrel

Bawdy
Rollo

Beefy
Mitch

Beer guzzling
Homer

Bespectacled
Arnold

Big
Barry
Butch
Christian
Lars
Rock
Xavier

Blond
Ken
Tyler

Blowhard
Rush

Bold
Slade

Book smart
Elliot
Royce

Bookish
Edwin
Graham
Milton
Sherrod
Wendall

Boorish
Don

Brainy
Ignatius
Milt
Norton
Schuyler

Brave
Wyatt

Bright
Emery

Brilliant
see also Intelligent; Smart
Charles
Kadar
Myles

Brown-eyed
Shawn

Bubbly
Jules

Buff
Julius

Bulky
Brent

Burly
Argus
Boris
Gunther
Jarl
Mack

Carefree
Benny
Jordan
Riley

Caring
Adrian
Alexander
Clark
Dave
Eli
Habib
Ira
Isaiah
Jeriah
Joel
Manuel
Matthew
Roy
Sylvester

Charismatic
Gabe
Julian
Omar

Charming
Hayden
Nicholas
Oliver
Rhett
Rodrigo
Steven
Thaddeus

Chatty
Carlos

Cheeky
Danny

Cheerful
Dylan
Kelly

Chubby
Marty
Otto

Class clown
Alex

Clever
Guy

Clumsy
Gomer

Cocky
Bond

Cold
Reynold

Coldhearted
Ford

Colorful
Alejandro

Compassionate
Bryson
Gavin
Hunter
Jonah

Computer geek
Alvin

Conceited
Ferguson

Condescending
Ashton

Confident
see also Self-assured
Carson
Simba

Congenial
Derek
Jeffrey

Conniving
Conrad

Considerate
Benjamin
Brett
Jonathan
Kris

Controlling
Emilio

Cool
Griffin
Sidney
Silas

Corrupt
Hussein

Country boy
Garth

Country singer
Waylon

Courageous
Malik

Courteous
Orlando

Cowboy
Laramie
Sadler
Travis

Cranky
Leroy

Creative
see also Arty/Artistic
August
Timothy

Criminal genius
Lex

Cruel
Adolf

Cultured
Dante

Cute
Cory

Dainty
Auden

Dark-featured
Joey
Julio
Raul
Roberto
Salvador

Dark-haired
Arturo
Santos
Sergio
Vince

Dark-skinned
Kale

Debonair
Miles

Dedicated
Caleb
Quincy

Defiant
Wade

Demonic
Damian

Dependable
Joseph

Determined
Vladimir

Dictator
Fidel

Dimwitted
Cletus
Dwight
Elmer

Dirty
Coty
Dusty
Wiley

Distant
Shavar

Distinguished
Godfrey

Doofy
Clarence

Dopey
Kurt

Dorky
see also Nerdy
Eugene
Freddie
Rhys

Driven
Douglas
Lamar
Lane

Dumb
see also Dimwitted
Bud
Darryl

Easygoing
Kevin
Shepherd
Tan

Eccentric
Xerxes

Educated
Christopher
Stephen

Egotistical
Jock

Elegant
Alden

First Impressions

Energetic
Brooklyn
Jesse
Sean

Energized
Chase

Ethnic
Louis

Evil
Deman

Faithful
Muhammed
Nathaniel

Fast paced
Craig

Fearful
Herman

Feisty
Kendall

Fisherman
Marlon

Flashy
Rolando

Flirtatious
Greg

Football player
Payton
Tyrel

Footloose
Darrius

Forgiving
Jesus

Formidable
Tyson

Forthright
Baul

Frail
Arlen

Freewheeling
Donovan

French
Jacques
Pierre

Friendly
Adriel
Brant
Breck
Casper
Duncan
Kenley
Kenneth
Leon
Lonnie
Lyle
Ty
Will

Fun
Jake
Kieran
Tad

Fun-loving
Johnny
Reese
Ringo
Shane
Zeno

Funny
Alec
Asher
Hilario
Hugo
Leif
Nathan
Terry
Vaughn

Gangly
George
Karl

Geeky
see also Übergeek;
    Unpopular geek
Albert
Dennis
Gideon
Kenny
Preston
Ross

Generous
Bill
Kelvin
Moses

Gentle
Austin

Gentlemanly
Johann

Genuine
Addison

Gifted
Forrest

God-fearing
Josiah

Good person
Blaine

Goodhearted
Trent

Good-humored
Leo

Good-looking
see also Attractive
Devin
Jackson
Nick

Good-natured
Desmond
Paddy
Ricky

Good-tempered
Cyrus

Goofy
Archie
Carl
Chandler
Corey
Darren
Eddie
Gordon
Luis
Poni

Goofy-looking
Ernest

Gorgeous
Fabian
Josh
Kyle

Gracious
Ellis

Gray-haired
Willis

Gregarious
Carlo
Finnegan

Grouchy
Wilson

Gruff
Harley
Winston

Grumpy
Grover
Wayne

Handsome
Antoine
Brian
Collin
Evan
Fabio
Jason
Raphael
Taylor
Tristan

Happy
see also Jolly/Jovial
Dustin
Ramon
Sam
Tanner

Hardworking
Benett
Glen
Harrison
Keene
Rudy

Harsh
Ezra

Heartless
Jamie

Heavy metal musician
Duff

Heavyset
see also Overweight
Ruben

Hefty
Angus

Helpful
Gabriel
Mark
Ottokar

Heroic
Antonio

Hick
Billy

High-strung
Raymond

Hilarious
Monty

Hillbilly
Jed
Purdy

Hippie
Denver

Honest
Jamison

Huggable
Teddy

Humorous
Wilbert
Humphrey

Hunky
Zane

Imaginative
Lee

Immature
Denny

Indian
Vijay

Inquisitive
Walter

Intellectual
Clayton
Fergus
Jefferson
Mathias
Trayton

Intelligent
see also Brilliant;
   Smart
Abraham
Armen
Avery
Barak
Brady
Carter
Colin
Constantine
Deangelo
Donald
Garrison
Lionel
Lloyd
Marion
Maxwell
Noel
Owen
Phineas
Rashad
Sebastian
Soloman
Theodore
Wood

Introspective
Jude
Xander

Introverted
Dexter
Leonard

Inviting
Dakota

Irish
Seamus

Italian
Tony

Jolly/Jovial
Bobby
Jack
Ted

Kind
Adon
Charlie
Carmel
Chris
Eric
Jimmy
Lorne
Mateo
Paul
Reggie
Robert
Rodney
Stevie
Trevor

Kindhearted
Daryl
Fred
Jay
Joe

Laid-back
Israel
Rusty

Lanky
Dwayne
Jeremiah
Kareem
Quentin

Large
see also Heavyset;
   Overweight
Trey

Latino
Alberto
Eduardo
Javier
Jose
Miguel
Pablo
Santiago

Leader
Aurek
Bryce
Grant
Malcolm
Octavius
Victor

Levelheaded
John

Liar
Richard

Literate
Virgil

Lively
Bailey

Logical
Seth

Lonely
Byron
Ernie

First Impressions

Loner
Alfred
Murray
Rufus

Loony
Llewellyn

Loud
Geraldo
Jan
Jibril
Randy
Regis
Steve
Tom
Zeke

Loving
Jorge
Kellan
Toby

Loyal
Harmon
Tobias

Lumbering
Clyde

Macho
Alfonso
Fernando
Rocky
Steel

Magnetic
Dimitri

Manipulative
Cody

Manly
Hector

Masculine
Beau

Mature
Thomas

Mean
Baron
Dick

Mechanic
Lowell

Meek
Carey
Chester
Lester
Willard

Melancholy
Edgar

Merry
Patrick

Middle Eastern
Ittamar

Mild-mannered
Herschel
Navin
Yoshi

Mischievous
Jeff
Lucas

Miserly
Grimshaw

Model
Bjorn

Moody
Gene
Orien

Moral
Abel
Elijah

Mousy
Sarngin

Muscular
Caesar
Luke
Samson

Titus
Tyrone

Musician
Clay

Mysterious
Sterling

Naïve
Tate

Nasty
Ajay

Neat
Keaton

Needy
Bane

Nerdy
Arnie
Bart
Cornelius
Elvin
Flynn
Larry
Marvin
Melvin
Norman
Oswald
Quintin
Stuart
Warren
Wilbur

Nervous
Holden

Nice
Herbert
Jacob
Kohana
Rei

Noble
Lance
Noah

Nomad
Giuseppe

Nordic
Hans
Skyler

Novelist
Ewan

Obnoxious
Gerald

Old
Dan
Earl
Eldon
Lincoln
Maurice
Orson
Otis
Roger
Senior

Old-fashioned
Sawyer

Only child
Landon

Opinionated
Dalton

Optimistic
Kirk

Ordinary
see also Average
Morris

Outcast
Berk

Outdoorsy
Wilfred

Outgoing
Bo
Keenan
Zephyr

Outspoken
Saburo

Overweight
see also Heavyset
Bert
Obert

Pale
Lister

Passionate
Armando

Patient
Joshua
Robin

Personable
Jasper

Philosophical
Curt

Physically fit
Adam

Physician
Cliff

Piggish
Ham

Playful
Tevin

Polite
Amos
Andrew
Darius
Ivan
Quinn
Reilly

Pompous
Alistair

Popular
Andre
Dale
Jayden
Jeremy
King
Mike
Scott

Portly
Sharif

Powerful
Lyndon
Maximilian
Merlin
Vito

Preppy
Brayden
Reid

Pudgy
Ronnie

Quick-witted
Ian

Quiet
Bern
Fletcher
Harold
Hubert
Ike
Kim
Mandek
Nodin
Peter
Sullivan
Tariq
Trenton
Zedekiah

Quirky
Ervin

Rancher
Houston

Raunchy
Prince

Rebellious
Jagger

Refined
Benson
Grayson

Regal/Royal
William

Reliable
Keith
Martin

Religious
Ezekiel
Jonas

Renaissance man
Robbie

Reserved
Bram
Ethan
Fritz
Morton

Respectful
Alfredo
Roland
Samuel

Responsible
Stanislav
Theo

Rich
see also Wealthy
Allen
Bartholomew
Beaman
Gilbert
Mason
Parker

Robust
Charlton
Rolando

Romantic
Anthony
Enrique

Rough
Blade
Judd
Max
Ruskin

Rowdy
Chance

Rude
Gwidon
Philip
Rex
Russell
Vic

Rugged
Clint

Russian
Mikhail
Yakov

Scholarly
Henry

Scrawny
Pete
Timmy
Willie

Self-absorbed
Vance

Self-assured
see also Confident
Abram
Hugh

Self-confident
Rico

Selfish
Frick

Selfless
Angel
Leslie

Self-sufficient
Ronald

Sensitive
Aidan
Dudley

Serene
Emmanuel

First Impressions

Serious
Diego
Ennis
Mitchell

Sexy
Brad
Marc
Paolo

Short
Kermit
Pedro

Shrewd
Lawrence

Shy
Chuck
Elton
Lenny
Marcel
Skipper
Tymon

Silly
Elmo
Ollie
Sammy

Simple-minded
Hank

Sincere
Grady
Pat

Skinny
see also Thin
Cecil
Nelson
Vernon

Slick
Clinton

Sloppy
Frank

Slow
Floyd

Sly
Aladdin

Smarmy
Brock

Smart
see also Intelligent
Aaron
Barton
Franklin
Harry
Irving
Isaac
Kane
Keelan
Mervin
Neal
Rick
Sheldon
Todd

Smart aleck
Humphrey

Smooth talking
Juan

Snobby
Ballard
Barrett
Brandon
Kipp
Palmer
Percy
Pierce
Scotty

Snooty
Alcott
Basil
Edmund
Thornton
Upton

Soccer star
Gareth

Sociable
Kerry

Softhearted
Matt

Soft-spoken
Fynn

Sophisticated
Campbell

Spiteful
Cain

Spoiled
Blake
Drake

Sporty
see also Athletic
Carrick

Spunky
Tracy

Standoffish
Claude

Strange
Dorcas
Elias

Strict
Jedidiah

Strong
Darrion
Gage
Heath
Kent
Kiros
Lorenzo

Strong-minded
Marco

Strong-willed
Ali
Casey

Stubborn
Bilal

Studious
Arthur

Bennett
Dirk
Emil
Lewis
Montgomery
Wallace

Stuffy
Colby
Pryor

Stylish
Jaden

Suave
Anders
Luc
Ricardo
Rudolph

Successful
Caden
Roosevelt

Supportive
Horace

Surfer
Levi

Sweet
Ace
Aubrey
Ben
Bruce
Buddy
Drew
Francis
Justin
Luther
Michael
Ralph
Tim
Tomlin
Tucker

Talented
Elvis
Ephraim
Marcus
Marshall
Pascale

Tall
Amir
Bentley
Bradford
Calvin
Cameron
Daniel
David
Dorian
Howard
Roman
Stefano
Tremaine

Temperamental
Gino

Tender
Vincent

Thick
Og

Thin
see also Skinny
Jared

Thug
Hakim

Timid
Pin

Tiny
Quinlan

Tough
Angelo
Axel
Nolan
Roscoe
Sherman
Vinny

Troublemaker
Thanos

Übergeek
Darby

Unattractive
Alphonse
Armand

Unhappy
Jim

Unique
Bernard
Oz

Unpopular geek
Bradley

Unruly
Kelsey

Unsure
Maynard

Untrustworthy
Bryan
Devlin

Unusual
Dunn

Upper-class
Ferdinand
Reginald

Upstanding
Spencer

Used-car salesman
Ray

Vibrant
Morgan
Wesley

Violent
Rocco
Slater

Warm
Aron
Gary
Sundeep
Zachary

Warmhearted
Brendan
James

Wealthy
Edward
Park
Sinclair
Sutherland
Weston

Well educated
Carlton

Well read
Emerson

Well traveled
Ansel

Whiny
Oscar

Wholesome
Corbin

Wild
Cole
Cooper
Gerard

Willful
Serge

Wimpy
Andy
Gaylord

Wise
Augustus
Gregory
Ulysses
Zachariah

Wisecracker
Saul

Withdrawn
Reynard

Witty
Cedric
Ron
Shakir

Woodsy naturalist
Adler

Worldly
Liam

Young
Ahmad
Emmett

Images
of Girls'
Names

Girls

Aaliyah

(Hebrew) a form of Aliya.

Image: When they hear this name, people overwhelmingly picture Aaliyah, the late R&B star. They describe Aaliyah as an African American singer with long hair and a willowy frame. People also imagine she's motivated and assertive, but in her own shy, soft-spoken, and sweet way.

Famous Namesakes: Singer Aaliyah Haughton

Abby

(Hebrew) a familiar form of Abigail.

Image: When you need a friend, Abby is happy to lend an ear. She strikes people as a sensitive and understanding girl. People say she's pretty, cheerful, bright, and great at listening and giving advice—perhaps a reference to advice columnist Abigail "Dear Abby" Van Buren.

Famous Namesakes: Advice columnist Abigail "Abby" Van Buren; character Abby Lockhart (*ER*)

Abigail

(Hebrew) father's joy.

Image: Abigail is a tender lass with humble talents. She's described as kind, gentle, and humble, not to mention pretty. She's most likely intelligent and artistic, enjoying reading, painting, and music. Some people, however, say she's high maintenance and snooty.

Famous Namesakes: First lady Abigail Adams; columnist Abigail Van Buren; actress Abigail Breslin

Abira

(Hebrew) my strength.

Image: Abira's beauty is only rivaled by her kindness. She's said to be an affectionate and sweet woman with a pretty smile and exotic, perhaps Arabian, looks. She also comes across as graceful, quiet, and intelligent, although she may be a bit spoiled.

Famous Namesakes: None

Ada

(German) a short form of Adelaide. (English) prosperous; happy. (Hebrew) a form of Adah.

Image: Like a fine wine, Ada improves with age. She's imagined as an older woman who's stunningly beautiful and elegant. People suspect she's wise, witty, and charming, but often quiet.

Famous Namesakes: Writer Ada Louise Huxtable; character Ada Monroe (*Cold Mountain*)

Addie

(Greek, German) a familiar form of Adelaide, Adrienne.

Image: People use -*y* words to describe Addie: *bubbly*, *witty*, and *spunky*. She's said to be an outgoing, playful gal with a big smile. She also comes across as funny, clever, and sharp with a curious moxie about her.

Famous Namesakes: Activist Addie Mae Collins; character Addie (*American Girl* series)

Adelaide

(German) noble and serene.

Image: Adelaide is the perfect hostess. People say she's friendly, pleasant, and eager to make you feel right at home. She's known for her spirited and funny conversation. Physically, she may be heavyset, freckled, and—thanks to the city of Adelaide—Australian.

Famous Namesakes: Character Miss Adelaide (*Guys and Dolls*)

Adele

(English) a short form of Adelaide, Adeline.

Image: Adele may be a wallflower, but look a little closer, and you'll see a smile on her face. People say Adele is nerdy, shy, and not very pretty. Below the surface, however, she's most likely quite sweet.

Famous Namesakes: Character Adele (*Die Fledermaus*); character Adele (*Jane Eyre*)

Adeline

(English) a form of Adelaide.

Image: Adeline is always home in time for town curfew, but that's easy to do if you never go out. She's described as an uptight and conservative small-town girl. People believe she's shy and polite, but boring.

Famous Namesakes: Actress Adeline Blondieau

Adena

(Hebrew) noble; adorned.

Image: Adena isn't the brightest bulb, but there's never a dull moment when you're around her. People think she's a dummy, but she's sweet, well liked, and the life of the party. She's said to be crazy and wild, but she does know when to stop—which perhaps means she's smarter than she lets on.

Famous Namesakes: Singer Adena Howard

Adora

(Latin) beloved.

Image: Adora may be adorable in many ways, but she's also odd. People say she's a sweet girl with a precious, cherublike face. As adorable as she may be, she's known to dress in odd, strange clothes that make her seem dorky—and thus make her unpopular.

Famous Namesakes: Character Princess Adora (*She-Ra: Princess of Power*)

Adrienne

(Greek) rich. (Latin) dark.

Image: Adrienne thinks of others, even at her own expense. She's described as a sweet, caring woman who's always there for her loved ones, making them happy when they're upset. She's considered to be quiet and shy, which is perhaps why some people take advantage of her kindness.

Famous Namesakes: Poet Adrienne Rich; designer Adrienne Vittadini

Agatha

(Greek) good, kind.

Image: Pity the poor soul who marries into Agatha's family. She's pictured as an old, wrinkled mother-in-law who's an opinionated, know-it-all nag, not to mention a cranky, witchy priss. A few think instead of Agatha Christie and say this name reminds them of a detective novelist who's curious and perhaps shy.

Famous Namesakes: Author Agatha Christie; Saint Agatha

Agnes

(Greek) pure.

Image: Agnes is an unpleasant lady. People think she's introverted and nerdy with glasses and a matronly, homely appearance. Some believe she's kind, but others find her to be conservative, bullheaded, and sad.

Famous Namesakes: Dancer Agnes de Mille; actress Agnes Moorhead

Aileen

(Scottish) light bearer. (Irish) a form of Helen.

Image: Aileen is a perfect balance of personality and intellect. She's thought to be fun-loving and bubbly, but she's also insightful and intelligent. She may be a linguist or librarian. People picture her as naturally pretty, and they find her to be caring and even inspiring.

Famous Namesakes: Infamous killer Aileen Wuornos

Aimee

(Latin) a form of Amy. (French) loved.

Image: Aimee is sweetheart—and spunky to boot. People believe Aimee is caring, charming, and cute. With such a bright personality, it's no wonder she's known to be a social butterfly with a lot of friends.

Famous Namesakes: Singer Aimee Mann; actress Amy Irving; singer Amy Grant; singer Amy Winehouse; actress Amy Adams; actress Amy Sedaris; actress Amy Brennemen; comedian Amy Poehler; novelist Amy Tan

Akiko

(Japanese) bright light.

Image: Akiko is as light as an ocean breeze. People think of Akiko as a friendly and sweet free spirit of Japanese or Hawaiian descent. She's most likely happiest when she's telling jokes and collecting shells.

Famous Namesakes: Actress Akiko Wakabayashi; comic book character Akiko

Akina

(Japanese) spring flower.

Image: It's not clear if Akina lets life slide by or if she meets it head on. Some people imagine she's a shy, submissive lady who's intelligent but timid. Then again, others say she's bubbly, confident, and downright spunky. Either way, she's very pretty with dark brown or red hair.

Famous Namesakes: Singer Akina Nakamori

Alana

(Irish) attractive; peaceful. (Hawaiian) offering.

Image: Alana turns heads wherever she goes. People regard her as an exotic and glamorous woman whom men can't help but find attractive. She's thought to be lively and fun—perhaps even wild—as well as upper-class. There are those, however, who say she's a standoffish snob.

Famous Namesakes: Model Alana Stewart; actress Alana De La Garza

Alberta

(German, French) noble and bright.

Image: Alberta, Canada, is often envisioned as a cold, hard region, and this name's image draws from that vision. Alberta is described as a big-boned, plain, older woman who's cold, unfriendly, and conservative. She's most likely dull and proper, but some people imagine she's aggressive.

Famous Namesakes: Blues singer Alberta Hunter; actress Alberta Watson

Alena

(Russian) a form of Helen.

Image: Consider this a warning: Alena has a short fuse. She's thought to have a nasty and wicked temper that flares up on short notice. When her mood is in check, she seems to be quiet, sly, and even a little flirtatious with her shy, beautiful smile.

Famous Namesakes: Model Alena Seredova

Alexa

(Greek) a short form of Alexandra.

Image: Alexa lives a pampered life. This name gives the impression of a spoiled rich girl with a sports car, cell phone, and free ride to a fancy college. She's thought to be cute and perfectly manicured. People also imagine she's confident (that is, *self-centered*) and savvy (that is, *scheming*).

Famous Namesakes: Politican Alexa McDonough; star kid Alexa Ray Joel; actress Alexa Vega

Alexandra

(Greek) a form of Alexander.

Image: Alexandra carries herself like royalty—and expects others to regard her as such. People think she's prissy, stuffy, and snobby. This beautiful, thin woman is most likely rich and sophisticated. People say she was a spoiled daddy's girl as a child, and to this day, she still wants to be treated like a queen.

Famous Namesakes: Actress Alexandra Paul; empress Alexandra Fyodorovna

Alexandria

(Greek) a form of Alexandra.

Image: Alexandria has posh possessions to go with her posh personality. People think of her as a dark-haired and dark-skinned looker. She comes across as a materialistic and snobby sophisticate, and she may even be royal. Some see her in a more positive light, saying she's sweet and caring.

Famous Namesakes: Star kid Alexandria Zahra Bowie

Alexis

(Greek) a short form of Alexandra.

Image: This name is hard to separate from *Dynasty* vixen Alexis Carrington. Alexis is thought of as a sexy and seductive knockout. She's known for her outgoing charm and sharp thinking, but she can also be jealous, selfish, and bossy.

Famous Namesakes: Actress Alexis Bledel; actress Alexis Arquette

Ali

(Greek) a familiar form of Alice, Alicia, Alisha, Alison.

Image: Being Ali means never having to say you're sorry. People say Ali is a kindhearted, unselfish, and well-liked girl. Like *Love Story* actress Ali MacGraw, she's pictured with long, dark hair and long, dark eyelashes.

Famous Namesakes: Actress Ali MacGraw; actress Ally Sheedy; television character Ally McBeal; actress Ali Larter

Alice

(Greek) truthful. (German) noble.

Image: Like the girl in *Alice's Adventures in Wonderland*, this Alice is looking for an exciting new experience to shake up her quiet life. People say Alice is a cute, slim blond who's kind and meek, but eager to have a wonderful adventure.

Famous Namesakes: Character Alice (*Alice's Adventures in Wonderland*); author Alice Walker; character Alice Nelson (*The Brady Bunch*); character Alice Hyatt (*Alice*); writer Alice B. Toklas

Alicia

(English) a form of Alice.

Image: Alicia has confidence at the clubs and at work. She's believed to be a popular, confident, and perky party girl. While she may be a lot of fun, she's also said to be smart, driven, and no-nonsense. People tend to picture Alicia as a pretty long-haired blond who's a bit curvy.

Famous Namesakes: Actress Alicia Silverstone; singer Alicia Keys; actress Alicia Witt

Alisha

(Greek) truthful. (German) noble. (English) a form of Alicia.

Image: There seems to be some disagreement about Alisha. People agree she's pretty, but they aren't sure whether she's friendly, cuddly, and helpful or bossy, whiny, and stubborn. Either way, she may be a determined, goal-oriented dancer.

Famous Namesakes: Singer Alicia Keys; actress Alicia Silverstone; actress Alicia Witt

Alissa

(Greek) a form of Alice, Alyssa.

Image: Don't let Alissa's innocent looks fool you. She's thought to be charming, outgoing, and playful. People say she's adorable and naïvely beautiful, but she's quite an alluring flirt.

Famous Namesakes: Actress Alyssa Milano

Allegra

(Latin) cheerful.

Image: People say Allegra is a dark beauty with hippie-like, freewheeling tendencies. She's known to be upbeat and cheerful, and she comes from a big, close family. Because she shares her name with a brand-name antihistamine, some people even imagine Allegra suffers from allergies.

Famous Namesakes: Heiress Allegra Versace; ballerina Allegra Kent

Allie

(Greek) a familiar form of Alice, Alicia, Alisha, Alison.

Image: That Allie, she'll pull your leg. This name calls to mind a perky and cheerful girl who loves to kid around. In addition to being comical, she's imagined as easygoing, lovable, and cute with red or brown hair.

Famous Namesakes: Actress Ally Sheedy; television character Ally McBeal; actress Ali MacGraw; actress Ali Larter

Allison

(English) a form of Alison.

Image: Allison is the definition of *friendly*. She's described as a sweet and personable woman who's helpful, full of compliments, and eager to make others happy. Most people see her as a pretty, blue-eyed blond. She's also imagined to be creative and energetic, lovingly making handmade gifts for family and friends.

Famous Namesakes: Actress Allison Munn; actress Allison Janney; singer Alison Moorer; musician Allison Kraus

Alma

(Arabic) learned. (Latin) soul.

Image: It's only fitting that Alma means "soul" in Latin. People say she's a charitable, sincere, and soulful Latina who's spiritually and emotionally strong. She's also thought to be quite wise.

Famous Namesakes: Prophet Alma the Younger

Alyson

(English) a form of Alison.

Image: There are conflicting ideas about Alyson. Some people say she's angelic and kindhearted, but others say she's controlling and spoiled. Some believe she's an outgoing cheerleader, but others believe she's shy and boring. No one can agree about her looks, either: Some say she's pale with big feet and teeth; others find her pretty, fair, and petite.

Famous Namesakes: Actress Alyson Hannigan; actress Allison Munn; actress Allison Janney; singer Allison Moorer; musician Allison Kraus

Alyssa

(Greek) rational.

Image: Actress Alyssa Milano shapes many people's image of this name. People picture Alyssa as a beautiful, dainty woman with dark features and so much confidence, she borders on being arrogant and temperamental.

Famous Namesakes: Actress Alyssa Milano

Amanda

(Latin) lovable.

Image: Amanda will smile to your face, but watch out when you turn your back. Most people believe she's chipper, bubbly, and smiley, but others sense she's backstabbing, gossipy, and judgmental. Regardless, she's said to be a smart, strong-willed risk taker, especially when it comes to activities like cheerleading and gymnastics.

Famous Namesakes: Swimmer Amanda Beard; actress Amanda Peet; actress Amanda Bynes; gymnast Amanda Borden; actress Amanda Plummer

Amaya

(Japanese) night rain.

Image: Amaya is a laid-back dreamer—as long as you pick up after yourself. She's regarded as a caring sweetheart who's dreamy and peaceful. She may be Japanese or Latino, and she's known for her pretty smile. She's generally thought to be cheerful and calm, but she can be an uptight neat freak from time to time.

Famous Namesakes: Journalist Amaya Brecher

Amber

(French) amber.

Image: Amber has only a few close friends, but she's well liked by everyone. Most people see her as a soft-spoken and shy girl who's quietly popular. She's known to have a kind heart and sweet personality. Other people imagine she's vivacious, free spirited, and spunky. Interestingly, people see her with any combination of eye color, hair color, and body build.

Famous Namesakes: Actress Amber Tamblyn; actress Amber Benson; model Amber Valletta

Amelia

(German) hardworking. (Latin) a form of Emily.

Image: For decades, Amelia Earhart has been a popular feminist figure, and she may still influence this name's image. People say Amelia is an intelligent, independent, successful, and very classy woman. She's pictured as lean and pretty with a quiet confidence.

Famous Namesakes: Aviator Amelia Earhart; children's book character Amelia Bedelia; beauty queen Amelia Vega

Amy

(Latin) beloved.

Image: Is it any wonder Amy means "beloved"? She's viewed by most as a friendly and perky gal who loves to join in the fun. She can be thoughtful and sensitive as well. Physically, she's thought to be pretty but a little stocky.

Famous Namesakes: Actress Amy Irving; singer Amy Grant; singer Amy Winehouse; actress Amy Adams; actress Amy Sedaris; singer Aimee Mann; actress Amy Brennemen; comedian Amy Poehler; novelist Amy Tan

Ana

(Hawaiian, Spanish) a form of Hannah.

Image: Ana is quite content. The name calls to mind a tall, thin woman who's pretty, happy, compassionate, and full of life. People envision she's brilliant and funny, and occasionally she enjoys some quiet time with a good book.

Famous Namesakes: Comedian Ana Gasteyer; singer Ana Johnsson; poet Ana Castillo

Anais

(Hebrew) gracious.

Image: Anais is too cool for you. People envision her as snobby, judgmental, and the center of the arty, popular crowd. With her dark hair and eyes and waiflike good looks, she may be strong-willed and overbearing, but some people maintain she's nice.

Famous Namesakes: Writer Anaïs Nin

Anastasia

(Greek) resurrection.

Image: Anastasia is as kind as she is pretty. People think she's an approachable, cheery, and warmhearted woman. She may be a tall Russian with high cheekbones and fine bone structure. While she's known to be loyal and upbeat, some say she's naïve.

Famous Namesakes: Grand duchess Anastasia of Russia; singer Anastacia

Andrea

(Greek) strong; courageous.

Image: Andrea is an inspiration. She comes across as a confident and intelligent achiever. People imagine she's optimistic, sophisticated, caring, and even happy-go-lucky at times.

Famous Namesakes: Journalist Andrea Mitchell; character Andrea Zuckerman (*Beverly Hills, 90210*); comedian Andrea Martin; actress Andrea Thompson; singer Andrea Corr

Andreana

(Greek) a form of Andrea.

Image: Andreana will win you over with her outgoing wit—but then she'll turn nasty. People say she's a gregarious and witty woman with a fun smile, but she has a mean, self-centered side. She's pictured as small with wild, curly hair.

Famous Namesakes: None

Anezka

(Czech) a form of Hannah.

Image: Anezka is beautiful and worldly inside and out. She's believed to be as stunning and exotic as a model with her tribal art tattoos and traditional clothing. Her appearance seems to match her personality—she's a philosophical and worldly hippie with loads of creativity. People imagine she's either African American or Russian.

Famous Namesakes: None

Girls

Angela

(Greek) angel; messenger.

Image: Angela seems like a contradiction: She tells it like it is, but she does so politely. She's envisioned as a kind and polite woman who surprises you with her street smarts and straightforward honesty. Even though people say she's outgoing and loud, they maintain that she's always well behaved.

Famous Namesakes: Actress Angela Lansbury; actress Angela Bassett; chancellor Angela Merkel; activist Angela Davis

Angelica

(Greek) a form of Angela.

Image: Angelica Pickles is a manipulative toddler on the cartoon series *Rugrats*, and she influences this name's image in many ways. People imagine Angelica is a hurtful, conniving girl who's spoiled, bratty, and used to things going her way. She's most often viewed as petite, blond, and cute—but not as cute as she thinks she is.

Famous Namesakes: Actress Angelica Huston; character Angelica Pickles (*Rugrats*)

Angelina

(Russian) a form of Angela.

Image: Actress Angelina Jolie is known for her humanitarian work as well as her wild celebrity antics, so this name's image shares that duality. People see Angelina as an angelic, sympathetic, and giving woman who can also be fiery and spontaneous. She's thought to be beautiful and slim with dark hair.

Famous Namesakes: Actress Angelina Jolie; abolitionist Angelina Grimke; character Angelina Johnson (*Harry Potter* series)

Angelique

(French) a form of Angela.

Image: Either there are two sides to Angelique, or her true self dominates her image. Many people think she's prissy, mean, and pampered, with sexy looks and fashionable clothes. Others see a more vulnerable Angelique, saying she's delicate, sweet, and gentle.

Famous Namesakes: Singer Angelique Kidjo

Angie

(Greek) a familiar form of Angela.

Image: Angie dishes the latest scoop with plenty of laughs. She strikes people as a funny, happy-go-lucky, and popular gal. They describe her as vibrant and loud, and she loves to gossip. She's pictured as gangly and a bit uncoordinated.

Famous Namesakes: Actress Angie Dickinson; actress Angie Harmon; model Angie Everheart; singer Angie Stone; rapper Angie Martinez

Anika

(Czech) a familiar form of Anna.

Image: Anika is a creative soul. People describe her as a free spirit who's expressive, artistic, and sensitive. She's most likely African American, beautiful, and fond of dramatic clothing. Some people, however, think her "uniqueness" is over the top.

Famous Namesakes: Actress Anika Noni Rose

Anita

(Spanish) a form of Ann, Anna.

Image: Anita speaks her mind out of love. She's regarded as a warm and friendly woman who's often brave with her sharp tongue. Although she's outspoken, she's generally seen as smart, witty, and bighearted. Physically, she may be a heavyset, plain Latina.

Famous Namesakes: Singer Anita Bryant; singer Anita Baker; character Anita (*West Side Story*); actress Anita Ekberg

Ann

(English) gracious.

Image: Ann carries herself with well-mannered poise. People think she's a petite woman who's responsible, sensible, and polite. She's also regarded as generous and kind as well as educated and sophisticated. As if that weren't enough, she's most likely beautiful.

Famous Namesakes: Columnist Ann Landers; actress Ann-Margaret; singer Anne Murray; writer Ann Coulter; politician Ann Richards; diarist Anne Frank; comedian Anne Meara; actress Ann Bancroft; author Anne Rice

Anna

(German, Italian, Czech, Swedish) gracious.

Image: Anna has so much to offer—personality, brains, looks, and more. People imagine her as a kindly and outgoing woman with a charming sense of humor. Slim, blond, and pretty, she's thought to be intelligent and dependable as well.

Famous Namesakes: Actress Anna Paquin; model Anna Nicole Smith; tennis player Anna Kournikova; columnist Anna Quindlin; actress Anna Faris; designer Anna Sui; editor Anna Wintour

Annette

(French) a form of Ann.

Image: Annette is the high-school band majorette. She's thought to be a kindhearted girl who's a good friend but a little geeky, especially when it comes to music. People also describe her as bright and bubbly.

Famous Namesakes: Actress Annette Bening; actress Annette Funicello

Annie

(English) a familiar form of Ann.

Image: The spirit of Annie "Little Sure Shot" Oakley is alive and well in this name's image. People say Annie is spunky, brave, quirky, energetic, and joyful. In addition, she's helpful, loyal, and eager to look after others. Some people believe she may be hot-tempered and out of control, but others just call her sassy.

Famous Namesakes: Comic strip character Little Orphan Annie; cowgirl Annie Oakley; singer Annie Lennox; photographer Annie Leibovitz; writer Annie Proulx

Annika

(Russian) a form of Ann. (Swedish) a form of Anneka.

Image: Annika Sörenstam is known as one of the world's best female golfers, so naturally she affects this name's image. People describe Annika as a competitive and athletic woman with a blond, Scandinavian appearance. She's most likely energetic and outgoing, although some people imagine she's shy.

Famous Namesakes: Golfer Annika Sörenstam; character Annika Hansen (*Star Trek: Voyager*)

Antoinette

(French) a form of Antonia.

Image: Antoinette can be described in different ways. Some people think she's regal, classy, and wealthy—no doubt because of Marie Antoinette—but others say she's snobby, pompous, and prissy. Some imagine she's fun, flirtatious, and bold, but others describe her as brash, loud, and opinionated.

Famous Namesakes: Queen Marie Antoinette; minister Antoinette Blackwell

Girls

Antonia

(Greek) flourishing. (Latin) praiseworthy.

Image: Antonia is a natural leader. She's imagined as a confident and commanding woman with great leadership qualities. She's pictured as a striking and tall brunette from Europe. People consider her to be determined, intuitive, and refined.

Famous Namesakes: Poet Antonia Byatt; character Antonia Shimerda (*My Antonia*); author Antonia Fraser; film director Antonia Bird

Anya

(Russian) a form of Anna.

Image: Anya is a strong character who believes in herself. She's considered to be passionate, determined, and focused on her goals. With her willowy, lithe figure, she's most likely a dancer or gymnast. People imagine she's sweet and spunky in addition to being deeply dedicated to her art.

Famous Namesakes: Character Anya (*Buffy the Vampire Slayer*)

Aolani

(Hawaiian) heavenly cloud.

Image: The image for this Hawaiian name is as beautiful as sunbeams dancing on the ocean. Aolani is said to be a soft-spoken woman who's warm, peaceful, and fond of golden sunsets viewed from the beach. Perhaps she's too nice, though, because she's easy to take advantage of.

Famous Namesakes: None

April

(Latin) opening.

Image: April is as gentle and pleasant as a spring shower. She's described as soft and sweet, but still outgoing, fun, and popular. People imagine her with blue eyes and freckles. In addition, she's most likely smart, honest, and giving.

Famous Namesakes: Character April O'Neil (*Teenage Mutant Ninja Turtles*); actress April Grace

 **Star Kids**

Apple Blythe Alison

Apple Blythe Alison is as pleasant and pure as the fruit she's named after. People think she's a sweet, thoughtful, and innocent woman who's a writer or musician. She's also said to be deeply spiritual. People imagine her with a petite frame, strawberry-blond hair, red cheeks, and blue eyes. Truth be told, this image probably perfectly describes Apple Blythe Alison, daughter of actress Gwyneth Paltrow and Coldplay frontman Chris Martin.

Aretha

(Greek) virtuous.

Image: If you share a name with Aretha Franklin, the Queen of Soul, you'll get some R-E-S-P-E-C-T. People see Aretha as a strong, gifted, and loud African American singer. She's most likely a full-figured woman with an independent streak.

Famous Namesakes: Singer Aretha Franklin

Aria

(Hebrew) a form of Ariel.

Image: If you're as inventive and gifted as Aria, you're probably a wee bit unusual, too. People think Aria is a talented and intelligent woman who's creative, charming, and a little eccentric. She's imagined with long brown hair, brown eyes, and a big smile.

Famous Namesakes: None

Ariana

(Greek) holy.

Image: Which Ariana will it be? She may be independent, stubborn, and self-centered, or she may be compassionate, sensitive, and helpful. Whichever way, most people picture her as pretty and petite.

Famous Namesakes: Columnist Arianna Huffington

Ariel

(Hebrew) lioness of God.

Image: This name's image will forever reflect a certain little mermaid. Most people think of Ariel as an innocent (perhaps naïve) princess who often has her head in the clouds. They say she's not content to just dream, however, so she reaches for her goals with a surprisingly feisty and independent stubbornness. Appropriately, she's described as pretty and slim with long red hair.

Famous Namesakes: Character Ariel (*The Tempest*); character Princess Ariel (*The Little Mermaid*)

Arlene

(Irish) pledge.

Image: Arlene's friends always look to her for advice—but not when it comes to fashion. People see her as a bravely articulate woman who, with her warm heart and gentle sensitivity, is a friend to many. Although she may be brave when she speaks her mind, she's quite conservative with her old, frumpy clothes.

Famous Namesakes: Actress Arlene Dahl; television personality Arlene Francis

Ashley

(English) ash-tree meadow.

Image: Ashley's cheery act fools a lot of people—but not all. Most people think of Ashley as a bubbly and popular cheerleader who's innocent and sweet. She's most likely tall with curly, blond hair. But a lot of people argue that this rich girl is actually a picky and bossy snob.

Famous Namesakes: Actress Ashley Olsen; singer Ashlee Simpson; actress Ashley Judd; singer Ashley Tisdale

Ashlyn

(English) ash-tree pool. (Irish) vision, dream.

Image: Ashlyn may seem like an ordinary girl, but she's quite special. She's imagined as a "good girl" who's tender, gracious, and a little naïve. She comes across as charming, joyous, beautiful, and youthful. People feel there's something unique and special about her, even if they can't explain why.

Famous Namesakes: None

Asia

(Greek) resurrection. (English) eastern sunrise. (Swahili) a form of Aisha.

Image: In appearance and personality, Asia is intriguing. She's thought of as an exotic and mysterious woman. People contend she's intelligent and well traveled, and she has beautiful eyes and complexion, thanks to her ethnically diverse heritage.

Famous Namesakes: Actress Asia Argento

Astra

(Greek) star.

Image: It's hard to pinpoint Astra. People perceive Astra as a playful, free-spirited flirt; a warm mother; or a mysterious and bashful introvert. Physically, she's thought to be big-boned but very feminine with long, dark hair.

Famous Namesakes: Comic book character Astra; character Princess Astra (*Dr. Who*)

Athena

(Greek) wise.

Image: Athena is the Greek goddess of wisdom and war, and this name's image shares her qualities. Athena is thought of as a brave heroine with a statuesque and sculpted physique. People imagine she's daring, intelligent, regal, and determined.

Famous Namesakes: Mythological figure Athena; heiress Athina Onassis de Miranda

Aubrey

(German) noble; bearlike. (French) blond ruler; elf ruler.

Image: Aubrey may be shy or flirty, but either way, she's a loving soul. She's thought to be kind, generous, and thoughtful. This willowy brunette is most likely smart as well. While some people imagine she's friendly, flirtatious, and quick to smile, others say she's shy and serious.

Famous Namesakes: Singer Aubrey O'Day; artist Aubrey Beardsley

Audra

(French) a form of Audrey.

Image: Audra may be a lot of things: She may be an overbearing, ritzy eccentric who's stuck-up and rude. She also may be a thoughtful and good-natured soul who loves both kids and animals. Then again, she may also be a depressed and quiet bore.

Famous Namesakes: Actress Audra Lindley; actress Audra McDonald

Audrey

(English) noble strength.

Image: It's no surprise this name evokes Audrey Hepburn, one of Hollywood's most memorable icons. Audrey makes people think of an elegant, graceful, sweet, and beautiful woman. She's most likely intelligent and understated as well as petite, brunette, and big-eyed.

Famous Namesakes: Actress Audrey Hepburn; actress Audrey Tautou

Aurora

(Latin) dawn.

Image: Aurora has a strong sense of self and a stronger presence. People believe Aurora has an inner strength that allows her to be giving, happy, and bold. She's very likely beautiful enough to be a supermodel, and she's always the center of attention—even with the "in" crowd.

Famous Namesakes: Goddess Aurora; character Princess Aurora (*Sleeping Beauty*)

Autumn

(Latin) autumn.

Image: There are two Autumns, each at opposite ends of the personality spectrum. Some people say Autumn is cheerful, energetic, colorful, and talkative. Others say she's uppity, reserved, well behaved, and quiet. People do agree that she reminds them of fall foliage, with her freckles and red hair.

Famous Namesakes: Actress Autumn Reeser

Ava

(Greek) a form of Eva.

Image: Much like silver-screen siren Ava Gardner, this Ava is a bombshell. She comes across as a confident and fun-loving girly girl who's hyper. People suspect she's trendy and glamorous, maybe even spoiled, but she's sweet overall. Physically, she's imagined to be beautiful, tall, and voluptuous.

Famous Namesakes: Actress Ava Gardner; country singer Ava Barber

Avril

(French) a form of April.

Image: Pop sensation Avril Lavigne has a sassy attitude and style. Perhaps thinking of her, people say this Avril is a wild and opinionated rock star with lots of creativity and spunk. At the same time, she's known to be as petite and pretty as the girl next door.

Famous Namesakes: Singer Avril Lavigne

Baba

(African) born on Thursday.

Image: Baba may be the "black sheep" of her family. People imagine Baba as an heavyset simpleton who's immature and shy. Consciously or not, people also picture her as hairy or woolly.

Famous Namesakes: Character Ali Baba (*The Book of One Thousand and One Nights*)

Babette

(French, German) a familiar form of Barbara.

Image: Babette is one chic chick. People think she's a charismatic, confident, and stylish blond who's quite attractive and fashionably thin. She may be polite, but underneath her good manners, she's most likely a shallow, materialistic airhead.

Famous Namesakes: Character Babette (*Babette's Feast*)

Bailey

(English) bailiff.

Image: A unisex name like this leaves people guessing, so this image works for a girl or a boy. People imagine Bailey as lively, playful, charming, happy, and loving. This youngster most likely has a small build, brown hair, and an adorable smile. Still, a few people imagine Bailey may be a cranky and stubborn dullard without any creativity or intelligence.

Famous Namesakes: Character Miranda Bailey (*Grey's Anatomy*); singer Corinne Bailey Rae

Baka

(Hindi) crane.

Image: It doesn't take Baka long to warm up to a new friend. Baka is thought of as a sweet, kind foreigner who's pudgy but strong. People imagine she's very shy at first, but when she's comfortable with someone, she can be quite talkative.

Famous Namesakes: Deity Baka Brahma

Bambi

(Italian) child.

Image: Disney's Bambi was an innocent fawn, but a woman with this name is probably far from innocent. People think of Bambi as a ditzy and bubbly bimbo who has bleached-blond hair and about 38DD's worth of jiggle. It's most likely a stage name for a hooker or stripper.

Famous Namesakes: Film character Bambi

Barbara

(Latin) stranger, foreigner.

Image: Barbara is probably a wit, but she may be a grouch or a doormat. This name makes most people think of a clever, talkative, and funny woman who's always kind and pleasant. That said, other people envision her as a grouchy complainer or a submissive 1950s homemaker.

Famous Namesakes: Journalist Barbara Walters; singer Barbra Streisand; actress Barbara Stanwyck; singer Barbara Mandrell; author Barbara Kingsolver; senator Barbara Boxer; first lady Barbara Bush; actress Barbara Hershey

Barbie

(American) a familiar form of Barbara.

Image: As the name of one of the most popular toys, Barbie has quite a reputation. Most people see Barbie as a ditzy drama queen who's as conceited, attention starved, and unlikable as she is dumb. Naturally, she's described as blond, tall, impossibly thin, fashionable, and chesty. Perhaps this is why several people think Barbie is popular with men.

Famous Namesakes: Famous doll Barbie; centerfold Barbie Benton

Beatrice

(Latin) blessed; happy; bringer of joy.

Image: Visiting Beatrice is not a fun experience, to say the least. She's regarded as old, matronly, and plump, as well as grouchy and rude. People imagine she's prim and proper in an old-fashioned, stubborn way, and she can be deceptively shrewd.

Famous Namesakes: Actress Beatrice Arthur; character Beatrice (*Much Ado about Nothing*); character Beatrice Portinari (*The Divine Comedy*); actress Beatrice Strait; princess Beatrice of York

Becca

(Hebrew) a short form of Rebecca.

Image: Becca is a ray of sunshine. People overwhelmingly think of Becca as sunny, sweet, demure, and honest. They say she's the perfect best friend. A few people suspect her one fault is that she's something of a gossip. Physically, she's described as a brunette who's cute and wholesome.

Famous Namesakes: None

Becky

(American) a familiar form of Rebecca.

Image: Becky is positively perky and popular. She's thought to be friendly, fun, and cheery, which no doubt makes her the center of attention. She's most likely blond with freckles and a nice smile. A few people, unfortunately, see her as spoiled.

Famous Namesakes: Character Becky Sharp (*Vanity Fair*); character Becky Thatcher (*The Adventures of Tom Sawyer*); actress Becky Ann Baker; character Becky Conner (*Roseanne*)

Belinda

(Spanish) beautiful.

Image: Belinda's loved ones don't care what she looks like, because it's what's on the inside that counts. People say she's a gentle and sensitive girl who happens to be full-figured and dumpy with braces and stringy hair. Looks aside, she's most likely kind, soft-spoken, and well loved.

Famous Namesakes: Singer Belinda Carlisle

Bella

(Latin) beautiful.

Image: Bella's personality is as beautiful as her name suggests. She's described as a helpful and caring woman who's gentle with animals and sweet with her friends. She's likely beautiful and graceful, and she can often be spirited and fun-loving. People believe she's of Italian descent.

Famous Namesakes: Feminist Bella Abzug

Belle

(French) beautiful.

Image: Belle fits her name perfectly. She's overwhelmingly envisioned as a sweet, angelic woman who's sensitive, affectionate, and caring. She's also thought to be stunningly attractive with blue eyes. And because this name is often used to describe women down in Dixie, people view her as a charming and genteel Southern *belle*.

Famous Namesakes: Character Belle (*Beauty and the Beast*); character Belle Black (*Days of Our Lives*)

Benita

(Spanish) a form of Benedicta.

Image: Benita knows when to work and when to play. She's said to be a caring and helpful heavyset Latina with olive skin. People imagine she's diligent and serious at times, and other times she's cheerful and playful.

Famous Namesakes: Athlete Benita Fitzgerald Mosley; singer Benita Hill; novelist Benita Brown

Berkley

(Scottish, English) birch-tree meadow.

Image: The University of California, Berkeley, is renowned for its activism in the '60s and '70s, and that radical spirit lives on in this name's image. Berkley is imagined as a liberal, hippie activist who's well educated and strong-minded. A Californian, she's also thought to be sunny and fun with blond hair and blue eyes behind smart-looking glasses.

Famous Namesakes: Choreographer Busby Berkeley

Bernadette

(French) a form of Bernadine.

Image: Most people imagine Bernadette lives a quiet, simple life. She's thought to be a kind, honest, and hardworking older woman. Many believe she's solemn, shy, and plain. But some disagree, saying she's annoyingly talkative and full of unwanted advice.

Famous Namesakes: Actress Bernadette Peters

Bernice

(Greek) bringer of victory.

Image: Bernice has one image if she's old and another if she's young. She's primarily described as an older homemaker who wears headscarves outside and house slippers inside. Like most traditional women of her era, she's thought to be a great cook. Others imagine her as a young woman who's smart but fidgety, introverted, and decidedly geeky.

Famous Namesakes: Songwriter Bernice Williams

Bertha

(German) bright; illustrious; brilliant ruler.

Image: The Germans called their heavy WWII howitzer "Big Bertha" for good reason. Bertha is described first and foremost as obese, but she's also thought to be unfriendly, rude, and slow. People envision her as an old maid with sloppy gray hair, and she's slathered in stinky arthritis ointment.

Famous Namesakes: Tennis player Bertha Townsend

Bess

(Hebrew) a short form of Bessie.

Image: C'mon over to Bess's—she'll have some fresh-baked cookies cooling on the counter. She's regarded as a motherly, caring woman with laughing eyes and a wide smile. She's pictured to be pleasantly plump and short, and she enjoys her simple, small-town life.

Famous Namesakes: First lady Bess Wallace Truman; character Bess (*Porgy & Bess*); actress Bess Armstrong

Beth

(Hebrew, Aramaic) house of God. A short form of Bethany, Elizabeth.

Image: It's hard for anyone not to think of gentle Beth March from *Little Women* when hearing this name. Beth is thought to be a kind, sensitive, and sincere young woman who's meek and shy. She's known to have a real talent for playing the piano.

Famous Namesakes: Character Beth March (*Little Women*); playwright Beth Henley; comedian Beth Littleford

Bethany

(Aramaic) house of figs.

Image: Bethany is typically imagined as a quiet girl, but others believe she has some pep. For many people, she comes across as sweet, loving, and demure. Because Bethany is a biblical place name, some believe she's religious as well. Physically, she's pictured as pretty and slim. A few people see Bethany in a livelier light, saying she's fiery, passionate, peppy, and even sassy.

Famous Namesakes: Surfer Bethany Hamilton; actress Bethany Joy Lenz

Betsy

(American) a familiar form of Elizabeth.

Image: Betsy is off-the-wall. People say she's a cheerful woman who's wacky, silly, wild, and loud. Some say she's ditzy, although others classify her as bubbly. Then again, a few believe her energetic antics are nothing more than attention-getting ploys.

Famous Namesakes: Flag maker Betsy Ross; designer Betsy Johnson

Bette

(French) a form of Betty.

Image: Bette is the one with a lock of curls shyly hiding her eyes. This name evokes the image of a quiet, serious, and compassionate girl with curly, brown hair and a pretty face. People also say she's hardworking and smart.

Famous Namesakes: Entertainer Bette Midler; actress Bette Davis

Betty

(Hebrew) consecrated to God. (English) a familiar form of Elizabeth.

Image: With so many famous Bettys—from Betty Boop to Betty Crocker—this name has competing images. For some people, Betty seems like a bouncy and perky woman with a big, friendly smile and a petite frame. Other people imagine Betty as the nurturing, motherly kind with conservative clothes and granny glasses.

Famous Namesakes: Actress Betty White; feminist Betty Friedan; cartoon character Betty Boop; actress Betty Grable; character Betty (*Archie* comic book series); first lady Betty Ford; character Betty Rubble (*The Flintstones*); character Betty Suarez (*Ugly Betty*)

Beverly

(English) beaver field.

Image: Beverly is either perpetually disapproving or perpetually fun. Most people think she's an older mother who's hard to please and doesn't realize she's critical and insensitive. Others think she's a people-person and loads of fun to hang around.

Famous Namesakes: Actress Beverly D'Angelo; author Beverly Cleary; actress Beverly Mitchell; opera singer Beverly Sills

Bianca

(Italian) white.

Image: When the work day is done, Bianca trades her smart pantsuit for a little black dress. Bianca is envisioned as a self-assured, bold, and successful businesswoman. People also state she's intelligent, worldly, and articulate. Outside of work, she's a passionate, mercurial, and pampered seductress, using her dark European beauty to its full power.

Famous Namesakes: Character Bianca (*Othello*); character Bianca (*The Taming of the Shrew*); jetsetter Bianca Jagger

Billie

(English) strong willed. (German, French) a familiar form of Belle, Wilhelmina.

Image: Billie likes to have a good ol' time. She's imagined as a country girl who's unsophisticated and uneducated but a lot of fun. People believe she's goofy and mischievous, and she likes to knock back the beers at the honky-tonk. As for her looks, she's pictured as leggy, blond, and a little scruffy.

Famous Namesakes: Actress Billie Piper; tennis player Billie Jean King; singer Billie Holliday; actress Billie Burke

Blair

(Scottish) plains dweller.

Image: Blair was the pretty, snobby girl on TV's *The Facts of Life*, and maybe that image has stuck. Most people think of Blair as a prissy and stuck-up preppy who's easily angered. She's likely a tall and thin blond. A few people have a lighter view, thinking of her as funny and kind.

Famous Namesakes: Character Blair Warner (*The Facts of Life*); prime minister Tony Blair

Blanca

(Italian) a form of Bianca.

Image: Everyone who's anyone attends Blanca's fundraising galas each year. She's described as a pale and blue-eyed society matron who's famous for her work with children's charities. In many ways, Blanca is said to be as elegant as she is powerful. Most people believe she's an eloquent speaker, but a few imagine she's quiet and shy despite her prestigious position.

Famous Namesakes: Actress Blanca Portillo

Blanche

(French) a form of Bianca.

Image: For this name, the character Blanche from TV's *The Golden Girls* is on most people's minds. For this reason, they say Blanche is an older woman who's flamboyant, confident, attractive, and still man-hungry. Others consider her to be gentle and motherly. Finally, literary types think of Blanche DuBois from the play *A Streetcar Named Desire*, saying she's outright crazy.

Famous Namesakes: Character Blanche DuBois (*A Streetcar Named Desire*); jazz singer Blanche Calloway; character Blanche Devareaux (*The Golden Girls*)

Blinda

(American) a short form of Belinda.

Image: Urban slang defines a *blinda* as an annoying roommate with no social skills. Perhaps for this reason, Blinda is thought of as a mousy and often bullied pushover who lacks self-esteem. She's said to be mad at the world, a neat freak, and quite unattractive.

Famous Namesakes: None

Bliss

(English) blissful, joyful.

Image: What more do you expect from a woman named Bliss? People understandably think she's happy, sweet, and quiet—she's a pleasure to be around. She's believed to be charmingly naïve and unaware of her great beauty.

Famous Namesakes: Poet Bliss Carman

Blythe

(English) happy, cheerful.

Image: Blythe is either the classiest woman in the arty crowd or the artiest woman in the classy crowd. To most people, she's a blond but rather plain-looking sophisticate with an artistic, creative flair. Rich and elegant, she's sometimes thought to be pretentious and snobby.

Famous Namesakes: Actress Blythe Danner

★ Star Kids

Bluebell Madonna

Bluebell Madonna is bubbly but not brainy. She comes across as a loud, bouncy, and chatty cutie with blue eyes and curly, blond hair. She's most likely innocent and provincial, not to mention dimwitted. It's doubtful this image describes the one that former Spice Girl Geri Halliwell predicts for her daughter, Bluebell Madonna.

Bonita

(Spanish) pretty.

Image: If your name means "pretty," how can you *not* be vain? Bonita is described as a beautiful, black-haired Spanish woman with big brown eyes. She can be outgoing and spunky at times, but people say she's rude because she's so obsessed with her looks.

Famous Namesakes: Actress Bonita Granville

Bonnie

(English, Scottish) beautiful, pretty. (Spanish) a familiar form of Bonita.

Image: Be careful if you sit by Bonnie—she'll talk your ear off. She's most often described as a nice but annoying chatterbox who can be a little too wild and fun. She's probably nosy as well. People picture her as cute and small.

Famous Namesakes: Bank robber Bonnie Parker; singer Bonnie Raitt; actress Bonnie Hunt

Brandy

(Dutch) an after-dinner drink made from distilled wine.

Image: You're probably asking yourself, why in the world is Brandy so popular? People see her as mean and self-centered, yet she's popular. She's suspected to be unintelligent and even trashy, with bleached-blond hair that doesn't hide her dark roots.

Famous Namesakes: Singer Brandy Norwood; basketball player Brandy Reed; singer Brandi Carlile

Breanna

(Irish) a form of Briana.

Image: Breanna likes herself a lot more than other people like her. She's considered to be an aspiring model who's vainly beautiful and self-absorbed. People see her as spoiled, witchy, and petulant—not to mention ditzy. On the plus side, a few folks say she's friendly every now and then.

Famous Namesakes: Reporter Brianna Keilar

Bree

(English) broth. (Irish) a short form of Breann.

Image: Bree won't talk to just *anyone*. She's imagined as an outgoing but snobby blond fashionista who's friendly to the popular crowd, but fake and rude to everyone else. Wealthy and spoiled, she's considered to be a rambunctious free spirit.

Famous Namesakes: Character Bree Van De Kamp (*Desperate Housewives*)

Breena

(Irish) fairy palace.

Image: One Breena will take you by the hand; the other will push you out of the way. Some people imagine Breena as a compassionate, loving girl who listens to friends' concerns and is altogether great to be around. In a stark contrast, other people believe she's headstrong, bossy, self-absorbed, and always willing to do whatever it takes to get what she wants.

Famous Namesakes: Author Breena Clarke

Brenda

(Irish) little raven. (English) sword.

Image: Brenda is the person you want working for your company. She's described as an extroverted and confident woman who's hardworking, capable, and assertive. At times, she may be somewhat self-absorbed and bullheaded, but people contend she's loyal and trustworthy.

Famous Namesakes: Comic strip character Brenda Starr; actress Brenda Fricker; actress Brenda Strong; character Brenda Walsh (*Beverly Hills, 90210*); singer Brenda Lee

Brenna

(Irish) a form of Brenda.

Image: Brenna may be on the pep squad, but she's no ditz. People picture her as a cute and confident cheerleader. Fittingly, she's said to be peppy and very popular (especially with boys), but she's also intelligent and ambitious.

Famous Namesakes: Singer Brenna Gethers

Briana

(Irish) strong; virtuous, honorable.

Image: Briana is a great person—she just has her not-so-great moments now and then. She's seen as a sweet, cheery, and dependable woman with raven hair and feminine features. From time to time, she can be whiny and bossy, but she's usually mature and dependable.

Famous Namesakes: Reporter Brianna Keilar

Brianna

(Irish) a form of Briana.

Image: Brianna is a sweetheart. People say she's good-willed and bighearted. In addition, she's said to be easygoing and sweetly shy. As for her looks, people imagine she's a petite thing with big eyes and smiles.

Famous Namesakes: Reporter Brianna Keilar

Bridget

(Irish) strong.

Image: Blame it on Bridget Jones: People envision Bridget as a comical and sometimes flighty Englishwoman who's blond and just a little plump. She's said to be kind and well liked, but her obsession with finding love and losing weight gets her into many mishaps.

Famous Namesakes: Actress Bridget Fonda; actress Bridgette Wilson-Sampras; character Bridget Jones (*Bridget Jones' Diary*); actress Bridget Moynahan

Brie

(French) a type of cheese.

Image: Like any diva, Brie is famous for her mood swings. She's probably a wispy, pretty thing who can be funny and flirty, but also mean and moody. This wealthy socialite doesn't seem short on confidence, but sometimes she can be reserved. A few people, perhaps thinking on an empty stomach, say she loves cheese.

Famous Namesakes: Character Bree Van De Kamp (*Desperate Housewives*)

Brigitte

(French) a form of Bridget.

Image: With namesakes like Brigitte Bardot and Brigitte Nielsen, it's only fitting that this image is full of sex appeal. People agree that Brigitte is a sexy and long-legged European who's ambitious and in charge. What they disagree on is whether she's good-natured and helpful or cold and stubborn.

Famous Namesakes: Actress Brigitte Nielsen; actress Brigitte Bardot

Britany

(English) from Britain.

Image: Britany sure seems adorable, but this girl's got sass. She's said to have a sunny disposition, blond locks, and a head full of air. Sometimes her bubbly nature can give way to cattiness, and many people find her to be a cheeky, sassy floozy.

Famous Namesakes: Actress Brittany Snow; actress Brittany Murphy; singer Britney Spears; actress Brittney Powell

Britta

(Swedish) strong. (Latin) a short form of Britany.

Image: Britta lives for fundraising dinners and charity balls. This name calls to mind a kind, classy, and beautiful woman who's completely comfortable and confident at social gatherings. People marvel at how elegant and well dressed she is, not to mention how feminine.

Famous Namesakes: Saint Britta

Brittany

(English) from Britain.

Image: Doesn't everyone remember someone like Brittany from high school? She's believed to be a cliquish and snobby teen who's self-absorbed, shallow, and mean. She's pictured as a blond cutie, but she's so vain, she's constantly looking in the mirror. People also say she's very ditzy.

Famous Namesakes: Actress Brittany Snow; actress Brittany Murphy; singer Britney Spears; actress Brittney Powell

Brittney

(English) a form of Britany.

Image: Of all the alternate spellings, this one is closest to Britney Spears's—and its image matches her personality. People think of Brittney as a spunky and bubbly blond who loves parties and clubs, but happens to be a bit spacey. According to some, she's a snob, but others think she's the ultimate best friend.

Famous Namesakes: Actress Brittany Snow; actress Brittany Murphy; singer Britney Spears; actress Brittney Powell

Brooke

(English) brook, stream.

Image: Most people see Brooke as carefree, fun spirited, and talkative. Like Brooke Shields, she's pictured as a brown-eyed brunette. At times, she comes across as a smart bookworm, but she's also known to be a confident and sexy sophisticate.

Famous Namesakes: Model Brooke Shields; model Brooke Burke; actress Brooke Burns; singer Brooke Hogan

Buffy

(American) buffalo; from the plains.

Image: For years, Buffy was, like, a total ditz, but thanks to TV's *Buffy the Vampire Slayer*, there's a whole new twist to her image. When some people hear this name, they still think of a snooty, spoiled, and selective blond Valley girl. But others picture a cheerleader who kills immortal, bloodsucking vampires in her spare time.

Famous Namesakes: Character Buffy Summers (*Buffy the Vampire Slayer*); singer-songwriter Buffy Sainte-Marie

Bunny

(Greek) a familiar form of Bernice. (English) little rabbit.

Image: *Playboy* magazine is famous for its bunny logo and the Bunny waitresses at its clubs. For that reason, people think Bunny is a big-haired and dimwitted blonde who models for *Playboy*—or at least has the *va va voom* to do so. Some people even imagine she's a stripper or prostitute.

Famous Namesakes: Character Bunny Lake (*Bunny Lake Is Missing!*); character Bunny Lebowski (*The Big Lebowski*); character Bunny MacDougal (*Sex and the City*)

Cadence

(Latin) rhythm.

Image: Cadence lives life with a strong rhythm. She's imagined as a well-liked and joyful young girl. She's spunky and peppy, but she's also a smart deep thinker. People depict her as cute with fair hair and skin.

Famous Namesakes: None

Cai

(Vietnamese) feminine.

Image: Cai has the one-of-a-kind blend of looks, kindness, and drive. People think of her as a unique and interesting woman who may be Chinese or Hawaiian with dark hair, bright eyes, and distinct features. She's most likely loving and sweet, but she's also disciplined, strong-willed, and tireless when it comes to achieving her goals.

Famous Namesakes: Inventor Cai Lun

Caitlin

(Irish) pure.

Image: Yes, Caitlin is well-to-do, but she's not well thought of. She's described as a blond woman from a privileged, upper-middle-class family. Not surprisingly, people also imagine she's egocentric, snobby, and spoiled, although she may be perky and bubbly.

Famous Namesakes: Figure skater Caitlyn "Kitty" Carruthers; swimmer Kaitlin Sandeno; character Caitlin Cooper (*The O.C.*)

Caitlyn

(Irish) a form of Caitlin, Kaitlan.

Image: Caitlyn may be misunderstood simply because of her upper-class standing. People see her as a rich preppy who's motivated, caring, and popular. Some may say she's *too* popular, not to mention spoiled, but others maintain that she's loving.

Famous Namesakes: Figure skater Caitlyn "Kitty" Carruthers; swimmer Kaitlin Sandeno; character Caitlin Cooper (*The O.C.*)

Calantha

(Greek) beautiful blossom.

Image: There are two Calanthas, and they probably couldn't tolerate each other. Some people imagine Calantha is a weird goth who's intelligent but also moody and even a little scary. Others see her in a completely different light, saying she's lively and energetic with moments of ditziness now and then. Either way, she's pictured as big-boned and unattractive.

Famous Namesakes: None

Caley

(American) a form of Caeley.

Image: Caley has strong morals, even if she comes across as a bore. She's thought to be a kindhearted and positive goody-goody with a comforting smile. Some people feel she's popular and fun, but others say she seems a bit dull because she always does what's right and moral.

Famous Namesakes: None

Callidora

(Greek) gift of beauty.

Image: There are two drastically different images of Callidora and her career. People see her as either a sweet, quiet, and old-fashioned woman who works with kids (as a teacher or a pediatrician) or a lively, colorful, and no-nonsense woman who works in the entertainment industry (as a singer or a movie star).

Famous Namesakes: Character Callidora Black (*Harry Potter* series)

Callie

(Greek, Arabic) a familiar form of Cala, Calista.

Image: Callie loves the thrill of mountain biking with her friends. She's pictured as a sporty, energetic gal who's cheery, funny, sweet-natured, and popular. She may even be reckless when it comes to adventurous sports. Some people, however, imagine this blond cutie as shy and timid.

Famous Namesakes: Screenwriter Callie Khouri; character Callie Torres (*Grey's Anatomy*)

Camilla

(Italian) a form of Camille.

Image: It's likely that people associate this with name Camilla, the Duchess of Cornwall and second wife of Prince Charles. They say that although Camilla appears demure and ladylike with her thin figure, she's actually stuck-up, stiff, and adulterous.

Famous Namesakes: Duchess Camilla Parker-Bowles; actress Camilla Belle

Camille

(French) young ceremonial attendant.

Image: Camille is blessed with elegance and many talents. She comes across as a sweet, stylish, and sophisticated beauty. She's also known to have an intelligent mind; a creative, artistic side; and an entertaining wit.

Famous Namesakes: Composer Camille Saint-Saëns; author Camille Paglia

Camryn

(American) a form of Cameron.

Image: Camryn is a lovable mischief maker. She's pictured as a confident woman who's good at everything she does. She seems to have a cheeky, cocky knack for making mischief, but people understand it's all in good fun. Camryn is said to be sweet and warm, and it's no wonder some people peg her as a cruise director.

Famous Namesakes: Actress Camryn Manheim; actress Cameron Diaz

Candace

(Greek) glittering white; glowing.

Image: It's recommended that you take Candace in small doses. People see her as a popular, fun, and perky cheerleader, but they imagine her nonstop pep and ditziness get annoying quickly. Some even say she seems sweet, but is actually obnoxious when you get to know her.

Famous Namesakes: Actress Candice Bergen; actress Candace Cameron; wrestler Candice Michelle

Candi

(American) a familiar form of Candace, Candice, Candida.

Image: With a name like Candi, people easily assume they know her occupation. She's pictured as an dimwitted bimbo who most likely enjoys her work as an exotic dancer. Aptly, she's also imagined as flirty, loose, perky, and wild—not to mention blond, buxom, and leggy. Some people fear she's selfish and two-faced as well.

Famous Namesakes: Singer Candi Staton; drag queen Candy Darling; actress Candy Clark

Candida

(Latin) bright white.

Image: For Candida, it's all about personality. People picture her as an energetic and vibrant woman. She's also thought to be sweet and compassionate as well as funny, mischievous, and always smiling. She may or may not be pretty, but she's too happy to care either way.

Famous Namesakes: Novelist Candida Crewe

Candra

(Latin) glowing.

Image: Candra is a strong woman, but she has to be careful not to seem *too* strong at times. She's said to be an assertive, self-assured, and outgoing woman with a polite demeanor. From time to time, however, people feel she comes across as a little snooty. She's probably attractive and tall, perhaps even athletic.

Famous Namesakes: Emperor Candra Gupta I

Capri

(Italian) a short form of Caprice.

Image: Follow Capri, and you'll find yourself in a fun, playful escapade in no time. She's seen as a friendly, innocent, and lighthearted pixie who loves to go on adventures. People believe she's short, thin, beautiful, and as perky as can be.

Famous Namesakes: Senator Capri Cafaro

Caprice

(Italian) fanciful.

Image: With her sexy looks and wild personality, supermodel Caprice gives this name's image some flash. People imagine Caprice as a lively, fun-loving, and strong-willed party girl. She's thought to be charismatic, flashy, and, of course, capricious. In addition, she's pictured as tall, tan, sexy, and blond.

Famous Namesakes: Model Caprice Bourret

Cara

(Latin) dear. (Irish) friend.

Image: Cara is a rebel with a cause—but perhaps at a cost. She's known to have a rebellious, wild side that expresses her independence, outspokenness, and opinions. Some people also suspect she's kindhearted and caring. Others, however, can't get beyond her strident antics, saying she's mean, stuck-up, and flaky.

Famous Namesakes: Actress Irene Cara; actress Cara Buono

Carey

(Welsh) a familiar form of Cara, Caroline, Karen, Katherine.

Image: Carey's unisex name leaves a lot of folks wondering. First, people aren't sure if Carey is a girl or a boy. They're also unsure whether to describe Carey as a meek and smart bookworm or an outgoing and upbeat joker. Whatever the case, Carey most likely has pale skin and blue eyes.

Famous Namesakes: Actress Carey Lowell; character Carrie White (*Carrie*); character Carrie Bradshaw (*Sex and the City*); actress Carrie Fisher; actress Carrie-Anne Moss; actress Kerry Washington; actress Kari Wührer; actress Keri Russell

Carina

(Italian) dear little one. (Greek) a familiar form of Cora. (Swedish) a form of Karen.

Image: Carina may surprise you with her wild side. She strikes people as a friendly woman with a sweet disposition. Some imagine she's the shy, sensitive type, but others see through to her mischievous zest for life. They say she's even wild and flirtatious at times. Many people describe her as a sultry Latina, but others say she has fair hair and skin.

Famous Namesakes: Actress Carina Lau

Carissa

(Greek) beloved.

Image: Carissa is proof that not everyone in the popular crowd is a snob. She's said to be upbeat, fun, cool, and well liked. People assert she's friendly and pleasant, not to mention smart. She's pictured with perfect teeth, a petite frame, and fair features.

Famous Namesakes: Surfer Carissa Moore

Carla

(German) farmer. (English) strong. (Latin) a form of Carol, Caroline.

Image: *Cheers* was one of TV's best-loved sitcoms, and Carla, the wisecracking waitress, was one of its best-loved characters. For this reason, Carla is described as a loud and lively woman full of sarcasm, spunk, and wit. With dark hair and a short build, she's also known to be honest, loyal, and a good friend.

Famous Namesakes: Actress Carla Gugino; model Carla Bruni; character Carla Tortelli (*Cheers*)

Carlen

(English) a form of Caroline.

Image: Carlen may just be the perfect boss. People see her as an attentive, diplomatic, and outgoing leader who's a strong communicator and genuinely concerned for the well-being of others. She's also said to be sophisticated, creative, and hardworking. It's no wonder she's so popular.

Famous Namesakes: Country singer Carlene Carter

Carlene

(English) a form of Caroline.

Image: Carlene's attitude is as brassy as her hair. She's depicted as a loud and brash gal who's tough but friendly. People may even call this redhead trashy, but they can't ignore her big smile.

Famous Namesakes: Country singer Carlene Carter

Carlotta

(Italian) a form of Charlotte.

Image: Carlotta has a lotta charm. People envision her as a giving and thoughtful Latina with a ton of charm and a ton of friends. Although she may be sensitive, she's a strong personality who sticks up for herself. People imagine her as beautiful with dark hair and complexion.

Famous Namesakes: Journalist Carlotta Gall; ballerina Carlotta Grisi

Carly

(English) a familiar form of Caroline, Charlotte.

Image: It's so easy to like Carly. This name makes people think of a talkative, carefree, and sometimes silly woman. She's most likely popular, due to her good-natured, friendly personality. As for her looks, she's portrayed as a lanky redhead who's cute in a mousy way.

Famous Namesakes: Musician Carly Simon; gymnast Carly Patterson

Carmen

(Latin) song.

Image: With the fiery gypsy protagonist of the opera *Carmen* and sultry actress Carmen Electra in mind, people definitely have something to say about this name's image. Carmen is imagined as a dark-haired, dark-eyed beauty who's passionate and full of life, but is sometimes arrogant. People clearly see her as a flirt, if not a stripper or exotic dancer.

Famous Namesakes: Opera character Carmen; actress Carmen Electra; character Carmen Sandiego (*Where in the World Is Carmen Sandiego?*)

Carol

(German) farmer. (French) song of joy. (English) strong.

Image: Carol is a card. She's thought to be a friendly joker who wins people over with her honesty, wry sense of humor (thanks to Carol Burnett, perhaps), and big smile. People consider her to be enthusiastically full of life as well as successful and determined.

Famous Namesakes: Comedian Carol Burnett; actress Carole Lombard; actress Carol Channing

Carolina

(Italian) a form of Caroline.

Image: Carolina has both the skills and motivation to succeed. She's regarded as a high-spirited and vibrant charmer with talent, drive, and ambition. Sometimes she can be loud, and other times she can be calm and quiet. People believe she has a lovely face and dark hair, and she may of Latino or Mediterranean heritage.

Famous Namesakes: Designer Carolina Herrera

Caroline

(French) little and strong.

Image: Caroline usually keeps her head down in a book. She strikes people as a logical and practical bookworm who's timid, a little boring, but sweet nonetheless.

Famous Namesakes: First daughter Caroline Kennedy Schlossberg; princess Caroline of Monaco; comedian Caroline Rhea

Carrie

(English) a familiar form of Carol, Caroline.

Image: Apparently, booklovers and moviegoers can't get Stephen King's *Carrie* out of their minds. Many people think Carrie is an awkward outcast who uses her telekinetic powers in a rampage. Those who aren't familiar with the work (or are trying to mentally block it) see Carrie as sweet, gentle, pretty, and full of life.

Famous Namesakes: Character Carrie White (*Carrie*); character Carrie Bradshaw (*Sex and the City*); actress Carrie Fisher; actress Carrie-Anne Moss; actress Kerry Washington; actress Kari Wührer; actress Keri Russell; actress Carey Lowell

Casey

(Irish) brave. (Greek) a familiar form of Acacia.

Image: Casey is everybody's friend. She's described as a popular, friendly, and good-humored gal. With certain people, she may be hyper and loud, but with others she may be well mannered and sweet. In either case, everyone seems to think she's sweet.

Famous Namesakes: Singer Kasey Chambers; actor Casey Affleck; radio personality Casey Kasem

Cassandra

(Greek) helper of men.

Image: Shy or outgoing, Cassandra is an upstanding woman. Most people view her as wise and sophisticated with a kind heart and graceful elegance. Some think she's extroverted and self-assured; others see her as shy and dreamy. Physically, she's believed to be a beautiful and tall blond.

Famous Namesakes: Author Cassandra King; mythological figure Cassandra

Cassidy

(Irish) clever.

Image: Cassidy either has a free spirit or a costly lifestyle. While people agree she's a blond, they aren't sure if she's a bubbly and charming sprite or a well-mannered yet snobby rich girl. She's most likely intelligent and confident either way.

Famous Namesakes: Actress Cassidy Rae; rapper Cassidy

Cassie

(Greek) a familiar form of Cassandra, Catherine.

Image: Cassie will tell it to ya straight. She's pictured as a rambunctious, chatty, and loyal working-class hero. People say she's direct, if not brash. Physically, she's depicted as a good-looking, big-haired blond who wears a little too much makeup.

Famous Namesakes: R&B singer Cassie

Catherine

(Greek) pure. (English) a form of Katherine.

Image: Catherine was taught that manners are everything. She's portrayed as a demure girl with classy, traditional manners. People suspect she's upper-class and well educated, but she's sweet and friendly. They see her as a beauty with long dark hair and an olive complexion—perhaps a nod to actress Catherine Zeta-Jones.

Famous Namesakes: Actress Catherine Zeta-Jones; actress Catherine O'Hara; singer Katherine McPhee; actress Catherine Bell; empress Catherine the Great; actress Catherine Deneuve; actress Katharine Hepburn; publisher Katharine Graham; actress Katherine Heigl

Cathleen

(Irish) a form of Catherine.

Image: Cathleen doesn't make friends, because that means leaving her comfort zone. People say she's a smart, avid reader, but they also feel she's dull and afraid to take risks. For these reasons, she's seen as a shy loner. Those who see beyond the shyness believe she's a kind Catholic.

Famous Namesakes: Actress Kathleen Turner; actress Cathleen Nesbitt; actress Kathleen Robertson

Cathy

(Greek) a familiar form of Catherine, Cathleen.

Image: There are a lot of vivid images of Cathy. She may be a mousy and book-smart introvert with no friends but her cats. She may be a kind and even-tempered soul who doesn't smoke, drink, curse—or do anything remotely fun. Or she may be a "chatty Cathy" secretary who's witty and energetic but always capable.

Famous Namesakes: Comic strip character Cathy; actress Kathy Bates; model Kathy Ireland; cartoonist Cathy Guisewite; television host Kathie Lee Gifford

Cecelia

(Latin) a form of Cecilia.

Image: Most find Cecelia to be an enigma. People say she's a mysterious woman who's so shy and strange, she's hard to read. She may be religious. She's envisioned as a small, beautiful Latina with thick, curly hair. Having a different view, others say she's sweet, vivacious, and quick-witted.

Famous Namesakes: Saint Cecilia; opera singer Cecilia Bartoli; artist Cecilia Rodhe

Celeste

(Latin) celestial, heavenly.

Image: Celeste is a hoot, no matter what she looks like. She's believed to be funny, crazy, and always ready for good-natured fun. Unfortunately, some find her zaniness annoying. People have a hard time agreeing about her looks, envisioning her with dark or light skin, black or blond or red hair, and brown or green eyes.

Famous Namesakes: Actress Celeste Holm; author Celeste Bradley

Celia

(Latin) a short form of Cecilia.

Image: Celia is a fun person—too bad she hangs out only with her stuck-up friends. She's pictured as a spoiled and snobby preppy with long dark hair and a long, willowy body. She has lots of snooty friends, and they find her to be spunky and clever.

Famous Namesakes: Singer Celia Cruz; actress Celia Weston

Celine

(Greek) a form of Celena.

Image: With one of the greatest voices in pop music, Canadian chanteuse Celine Dion certainly influences this name's image. People say Celine is a singer with a beautiful voice, beautiful face, but emaciated figure. She's known to be composed and sophisticated, which leads some to suggest she's snooty, pretentious, and insipid. Others argue that she's outgoing and compassionate.

Famous Namesakes: Singer Celine Dion

Girls

Chanel

(English) channel.

Image: Chanel is one of the world's most renowned fashion houses, giving this name's image its glamour. People feel this name fits a stylish, trendy, and sophisticated blond model with classic beauty. She's most likely a bubbly and outgoing partier who loves to have fun, but she's probably high maintenance and rather snobby as well.

Famous Namesakes: Designer Coco Chanel; model Chanel Iman

Chantal

(French) song.

Image: Chantal has her finger on the pulse of style. People agree she's a pretty woman with an elegant, sophisticated fashion sense, which makes her a great fashion magazine writer. She's thought to be charming and humorous, but she can also be demanding and blunt when need be.

Famous Namesakes: Singer Chantal Kreviazuk; singer Chantal Goya

Charisma

(Greek) the gift of leadership.

Image: Charisma's name seems to announce her personality. People imagine she's a charming, magnetic, and likable woman. They also find her to be energetic, boisterous, and outgoing. She's likely a beautiful African American, and she may be a singer or dancer. Interestingly, a few people have an ironic view and say Charisma is shy and soft-spoken.

Famous Namesakes: Actress Charisma Carpenter

Charisse

(Greek) a form of Charity.

Image: It's impossible for anyone to resist Charisse's charms. She evokes the image of a lovable, affable, and desirable French charmer. Her sweet disposition, easy smile, and feminine curves seem irresistible to men, but women also find her to be a great friend.

Famous Namesakes: Actress Cyd Charisse

Charity

(Latin) charity, kindness.

Image: Charity lives up to her name. People naturally think she's charitable, describing her as helpful, kind, and always wanting to make a difference. She's most likely outgoing and well liked. Some people imagine she comes from a religious, wealthy family who obviously believes charity is an important part of life.

Famous Namesakes: Character Charity Standish (*Passions*)

Charlene

(English) a form of Caroline.

Image: Like any Southern woman, Charlene is full of charm. People think she's an approachable, congenial woman with a funny wit and a friendly laugh. She may be a Southern belle with average but curvaceous looks. Some people imagine she's smart, but a few say she's a touch gullible.

Famous Namesakes: Actress Charlene Tilton; fitness guru Charlene Prickett; singer Sharlene Spiteri

Charlotte

(French) a form of Caroline.

Image: Charlotte is an alluring woman for many reasons. People get the impression she's a calm and collected thinker with sexy allure. She comes across as strong and determined, and she's charming as well. Perhaps because of Charlotte York's character in *Sex and the City*, she's viewed as a conservative and rich woman with an artistic background.

Famous Namesakes: Character Charlotte York (*Sex and the City*); author Charlotte Bronte; author Charlotte Perkins Gilman; singer Charlotte Church; actress Charlotte Rae; actress Charlotte d'Amboise; actress Charlotte Gainsbourg

Charmaine

(French) a form of Carmen.

Image: Charmaine has attitude—and that may or may not be a good thing. People think she's an outgoing and outspoken woman who's fun-loving and loud. Some suspect she also has a stuck-up attitude and quick temper. She's pictured as a beautiful African American with striking eyes.

Famous Namesakes: Character Charmaine Bucco (*The Sopranos*); singer Charmaine Neville

Chastity

(Latin) pure.

Image: A name like Chastity says a lot. Most people imagine she's an angelic, compassionate, and virginal girl. She's likely pretty with a sweet smile, but she's so shy and quiet, she hides behind her glasses. Others have a distinctly ironic view, saying that Chastity is a perky, trailer-trash stripper.

Famous Namesakes: Activist Chastity Bono

Chavi

(Gypsy) girl.

Image: Being so quiet makes Chavi seem even tinier—or is it the other way around? She's said to be kind, caring, and so small that she's affectionately called a pipsqueak. She seems to be well liked by everyone, but this Latina is most likely quiet and a little insecure.

Famous Namesakes: Actress Chavi Mittal

Chaya

(Hebrew) life; living.

Image: Chaya is unique, but the world can use more people like her. She's imagined to be a beautiful and friendly African American woman who's a fun people-person. People say she's outgoing, funny, caring, creative, and one-of-a-kind.

Famous Namesakes: Composer Chaya Arbel

Chelsea

(English) seaport.

Image: Chelsea is a great friend—probably. She's described by most as a personable, popular, and sunny girl who's true to her friends. Others see her as a jealous and mean snob. She's pictured much like Chelsea Clinton: fair, tall, and red-haired.

Famous Namesakes: First daughter Chelsea Clinton; actress Chelsea Noble; actress Chelsea Handler

Cheri

(French) a familiar form of Cher.

Image: Cheri's happy disposition is perfect for someone who looks after others. She's imagined as an extremely generous and helpful woman who's a great caretaker. Most people describe her as a bubbly, outgoing, and fun redhead, but others say she's ditzy and perhaps a little *too* eager to please others, especially men.

Famous Namesakes: Comedian Cheri Oteri; actress Sherry Stringfield; actress Shari Belafonte

Cheryl

(French) beloved.

Image: People can't quite agree about Cheryl. She may be a sweet and feminine woman who favors frilly clothes. Or she may be a cranky and sarcastic barmaid who likes to smoke. Or she may be a smart and organized leader who enjoys bossing people around.

Famous Namesakes: Actress Cheryl Hines; model Cheryl Tiegs; singer Sheryl Crow; actress Cheryl Ladd

Cheyenne

(Cheyenne) a tribal name.

Image: Cheyenne is a good person with a bad attitude every now and then. She's thought to be a happy, popular girl who's responsible and caring. She's perhaps a bit arrogant and self-centered at times, but she's very sweet more often than not. Most people think of her as a blond with dark skin.

Famous Namesakes: Singer Cheyenne Kimball

Girls

Chiara

(Italian) a form of Clara.

Image: If you feel your ears burning, that's just Chiara talking behind your back. She's described as a talkative, if not big-mouthed, gossiper who's sometimes sweet and sometimes backstabbing. People picture her as big-boned and beautiful, although heavily made-up. At best, they say she's full of life.

Famous Namesakes: Actress Chiara Caselli

Chika

(Japanese) near and dear.

Image: It doesn't take long to understand why Chika gets so much attention. People say she's spunky, which means she's opinionated, outspoken, and often the center of attention. Her friends are fine with that, because she's also known to be friendly, happy, and hilarious.

Famous Namesakes: Author Chika Unigwe

Chiquita

(Spanish) little one.

Image: Everyone knows the logo on Chiquita bananas. So when people hear this name, they think of a wild and colorful Latino dancer who's fun, flamboyant, and a little saucy. Looking deeper, some people say she's warmhearted and flighty, but others sense she has an attitude.

Famous Namesakes: Banana mascot Miss Chiquita

Chloe

(Greek) blooming, verdant.

Image: People agree on Chloe's looks, but there's no end to the personalities she may have. There's a clear-cut image of her as a sexy, willowy blond with feminine features. But she may be a sweet-natured and friendly charmer, an arrogant and shallow fashionista, a weak and timid follower, or a worldly intellectual.

Famous Namesakes: Actress Chloe Sevigny; character Chloe O'Brian (*24*)

Chris

(Greek) a short form of Christopher, Christina.

Image: Compared to names like Christina or Christy, this name has a harsher sound, which may explain its harsher image. Chris is imagined as an arrogant, obnoxious dullard. She's most likely overachieving and overbearing with an average build and average looks. That said, a few people find her to be caring and affectionate.

Famous Namesakes: Tennis player Chris Evert

Christa

(German) a short form of Christina.

Image: Christa is a wild child. This name makes people think of a bubbly and outgoing party girl. She may be known to be a lot of fun, but she's also known to be loud, obnoxious, attention grabbing, and typically out of control. People don't see her as college material, with her short attention span and dislike of school. She's most likely a blond who always seems to need to touch up her roots.

Famous Namesakes: Teacher Christa McAuliffe; actress Christa Miller; actress Krista Allen

Christina

(Greek) Christian; anointed.

Image: There are two images of Christina—one of them is warm and one is cold. Some people say Christina may be kind, friendly, and soft-spoken. But others argue she may be snobby, immature, and bratty. Thanks in part to pop star Christina Aguilera and actress Christina Applegate, she's portrayed as a pretty and tall blond with style and talent.

Famous Namesakes: Singer Christina Aguilera; actress Christina Applegate; actress Christina Ricci; singer Christina Milian; character Christina Yang (*Grey's Anatomy*)

Christine

(French, English) a form of Christina.

Image: Christine gives dinner with friends the same importance as lunch with clients. She's regarded as a pleasant, good-humored, and hospitable woman. She's most likely strong-willed and career minded with a scholarly education, high energy, and a crazy schedule.

Famous Namesakes: Actress Christine Taylor; actress Christine Lahti; actress Christine Baranski; speed skater Kristine Holzer

Christy

(English) a short form of Christina, Christine.

Image: Although her name is spelled differently, supermodel Christie Brinkley conjures up sunny images for this name. Most people think of Christy as a fun and flirty party girl who's cheerful and sweet. Some people, however, think of her as a snobby model or actress with a big ego. Not surprisingly, she's described as a tall, slender, and good-looking blond.

Famous Namesakes: Model Christie Brinkley; model Christy Turlington; actress Kristy McNichol; actress Kristy Swanson; figure skater Kristi Yamaguchi; singer Cristy Lane

Cicely

(English) a form of Cecilia.

Image: Cicely keeps people laughing and having fun. She's thought to be a bubbly and adventurous girl who's flirty and funny. People also consider her to be smart and kindhearted. As for her looks, she probably has dark hair, and she may be Native American.

Famous Namesakes: Actress Cicely Tyson; illustrator Cicely Mary Barker

Cindy

(Greek) moon. (Latin) a familiar form of Cynthia.

Image: Perky, bossy, or snobby—Cindy's personality runs the gamut. Many people say Cindy is a sociable and flirty girly girl with light hair and a ditzy demeanor. Others assert she's a strong-willed go-getter who speaks her mind and bosses others around. Lastly, a few picture her as a superficial and immature snob.

Famous Namesakes: Model Cindy Crawford; character Cindy Brady (*The Brady Bunch*); singer Cyndi Lauper

Claire

(French) a form of Clair.

Image: Claire is the type of woman you might envy, if only she weren't so kind. She's envisioned as attractive, sweet, and perfect in every way: She has perfect hair, perfect clothes, and a perfect boyfriend. In addition, she's thought to be smart and humorous, although a few people find her to be snobby.

Famous Namesakes: Actress Claire Danes; actress Claire Bloom; character Claire Bennett (*Heroes*); saint Clare of Assisi; playwright Clare Boothe Luce

Clara

(Latin) clear; bright.

Image: The years have been good to Clara. She's thought to be a beautiful and dainty old woman. People regard her as kind, charming, and graceful. One thing isn't so clear about Clara: She may be quiet and shy, or she may be no-nonsense and straightforward.

Famous Namesakes: Nurse Clara Barton; character Clara (*The Nutcracker*)

Girls

★ Star Kids

Coco Riley

People simply think of Coco Chanel when they hear the name Coco Riley. For this reason, they say she's a wild and colorful fashionista who's charming, rebellious, and well dressed. She's said to have black hair, olive skin, and a beautiful body. One may think that actors Courteney Cox and David Arquette had Chanel in mind when they chose this signature name for their daughter, but Coco is actually a nickname for Courteney's mother.

Clare

(English) a form of Clara.

Image: The most intriguing thing about Clare is her mind. She's imagined as a smart and sophisticated scholar who's introspective and serious. In addition, people suspect she's caring and nice, and she doesn't like to gossip. She's pictured with a svelte, athletic figure.

Famous Namesakes: Saint Clare of Assisi; playwright Clare Boothe Luce; actress Claire Danes; actress Claire Bloom; character Claire Bennett (*Heroes*)

Clarissa

(Greek) brilliant. (Italian) a form of Clara.

Image: Clarissa needs a lot of attention. Most people picture her as a spoiled brat who's highbrow, prim, and artistic. Some people say she's unfriendly, but others say she's outgoing. Either way, she likes being the center of attention. Physically, she's thought to be a slender and well-groomed blond.

Famous Namesakes: Character Clarissa Darling (*Clarissa Explains It All*); character Clarissa Dalloway (*Mrs. Dalloway*); character Clarissa Harlowe (*Clarissa*)

Claudia

(Latin) a form of Claude.

Image: There are a trio of images for Claudia. People think Claudia may be 1) a kind, honest, and smart bookworm; 2) an uptight, conservative, stern, and standoffish prude; or 3) a bold, powerful, rich, and spoiled diva. She has a trio of physical descriptions, too. She may be sexy, plain, or dowdy.

Famous Namesakes: Model Claudia Schiffer; character Claudia Salazar (*24*)

Clementine

(Latin) merciful.

Image: In the old folksong, Clementine is "lost and gone forever," which perhaps gives this name its lonely image. Clementine is thought to be quiet, shy, dull, and stodgy. She's most likely homely, old, and large. Clearly, she's said to be a sad, lonely woman.

Famous Namesakes: Character Clementine Kruczynski (*Eternal Sunshine of the Spotless Mind*); baroness Clementine Spencer-Churchill

Colleen

(Irish) girl.

Image: Colleen is a shy lass—at first. She strikes people as bashful and bookish, but once she comes out of her shell, she's sweet and playful. With a strong Irish name like this, it's no surprise people picture her as pretty and feminine with red hair and green eyes.

Famous Namesakes: Actress Colleen Dewhurst

Collette

(Greek, French) a familiar form of Nicole.

Image: Collette uses her shy flirting as a cover. She's imagined as a temperamental and sometimes snobby woman with a small build. She comes across as coy and coquettish, but this Southern socialite also has a stubborn side that causes a lot of trouble.

Famous Namesakes: Actress Toni Colette; designer Collette Dinnigan

Connie

(Latin) a familiar form of Constance.

Image: If you cross paths with Connie, she'll either barely register on your radar, or she'll draw you right in. Some people say she's the weak, mousy type who blends into the background. Others believe she's a perky and outgoing optimist with lots of self-assurance. Everyone seems to agree that she's a short, older woman with a full figure, a kind heart, and a sharp mind.

Famous Namesakes: Actress Connie Britton; news anchor Connie Chung; singer Connie Frances; actress Connie Selleca; singer Connie Stevens; actress Connie Nielsen

Constance

(Latin) constant; firm.

Image: Constance seems aloof, although perhaps she doesn't mean to come across that way. She's described as an educated woman who's serious, reserved, and shy. She may be ambitious and confident when it comes to her career, but her discomfort in social situations makes her seem unfriendly and prudish—perhaps even ornery.

Famous Namesakes: Actress Constance Towers; actress Constance Marie

Consuelo

(Spanish) consolation.

Image: Consuelo's smile is as pleasant as she is. She's regarded as a dependable, loyal, and easygoing Latina with black hair, olive skin, and a pretty smile. People can't agree on whether she's debonair or coarse, but she seems to be likable.

Famous Namesakes: Aristocrat Consuelo Vanderbilt

Cora

(Greek) maiden.

Image: Cora may be classy, but that doesn't stop her from being difficult. She's pictured as an elegant and graceful European woman who's bossy and always in charge. People envision her as lithe and beautiful with red hair. Sometimes she's said to be smiling and friendly, but she's more likely to be mean and demanding.

Famous Namesakes: Actress Cora Witherspoon

Cordelia

(Latin) warmhearted. (Welsh) sea jewel.

Image: Cordelia is a gentle creature. She's described as a soft-spoken, passive, and wholesome woman. She's most likely old-fashioned, but she has a generous heart. People also say she's a beautiful brunette with snow-white skin and long eyelashes.

Famous Namesakes: Character Queen Cordelia (*King Lear*); character Cordelia Chase (*Buffy the Vampire Slayer*)

Cori

(Irish) a form of Corey.

Image: Cori is an unisex name, which may explain why its image has a tomboyish spirit. People describe Cori as a mischievous and fun-loving tomboy with red hair and freckles. She's probably energetic, happy, and always hangin' with the boys.

Famous Namesakes: Model Cory Kennedy

Corinne

(Greek) maiden.

Image: Corinne will either help you find a book or she'll invite your over for mint juleps. She's imagined as either a sweet, helpful, and shy librarian or a graceful and outgoing Southerner. She's thought to have fair skin and red hair, and perhaps she's of Irish descent.

Famous Namesakes: Singer Corinne Bailey Rae

Corrina

(Greek) a form of Corinne.

Image: Corrina is kooky. People say she's lovable, boisterous, and sometimes silly. She's famous for being an eccentric artist, and she has an unconventional type of beauty as well with her black hair and tall, thin physique.

Famous Namesakes: Ancient poet Corinna

Girls

Courtney

(English) from the court.

Image: Quite a contrast here: Some think Courtney is a tease, and others think she's a goody-goody. Most people describe her as a wild and crazy flirt who's loud, talkative, and always popular with guys. But others think she's a snobby and prissy preacher's daughter. Either way, she's imagined as short and slim.

Famous Namesakes: Singer Courtney Love; actress Courteney Cox

Cristy

(English) a familiar form of Cristina.

Image: Cristy is optimism at its finest. People feel Cristy always looks on the bright side of life and always radiates good feelings. They say she's a helpful problem solver as well—a trait her many close friends appreciate. Lastly, she seems to be spunky and adventurous, but down-to-earth.

Famous Namesakes: Singer Cristy Lane; figure skater Kristi Yamaguchi; model Christie Brinkley; model Christy Turlington; actress Kristy McNichol; actress Kristy Swanson

Crystal

(Latin) clear, brilliant glass.

Image: Crystal may be nice, but honestly, she's trashy. People tend to see Crystal as a dimwitted bimbo who's friendly and giggly people-pleaser. She's thought to be a bleached blond who lives in a trailer, works in a bar, and shops for clothes at Wal-Mart.

Famous Namesakes: Actress Krystal Bernard; singer Crystal Gayle; gospel singer Crystal Lewis

Cyndi

(Greek) a form of Cindy.

Image: Most of the image for this name traces back to pop star Cyndi Lauper. Cyndi is considered to be an eccentric, wild, opinionated, and boyish punk. That said, people imagine she's self-important, cunning, and not friend material.

Famous Namesakes: Singer Cyndi Lauper; model Cindy Crawford; character Cindy Brady (*The Brady Bunch*)

Cynthia

(Greek) moon.

Image: No one sees eye to eye about Cynthia. Some people think she's bubbly and cheery, but just as many think she's stiff and snooty. And just as many more people say she's shy and boring. At least people agree she's a skinny blond with blue eyes.

Famous Namesakes: Designer Cynthia Rowley; actress Cynthia Nixon; actress Cynthia Watros

Daisy

(English) day's eye.

Image: The inspiration for this name's image likely stems from a certain flower. Daisy is thought to be sunny, sociable, and happy-go-lucky. That said, she's probably not known for having a high IQ or behaving seriously. People feel this cute, petite blond may be a hippie.

Famous Namesakes: Character Daisy Buchanan (*The Great Gatsby*); fiction character Daisy Miller; character Daisy Duke (*The Dukes of Hazzard*); Disney character Daisy Duck

Dakota

(Dakota) a tribal name.

Image: You'll find Dakota over at the park, laughing and playing kickball with her friends. She's thought of as a tomboy who loves sports and the outdoors and who's always nice to other children. People say she's precocious and spunky. Having a tribal namesake, she's also imagined as a pretty Native American with dark hair and skin.

Famous Namesakes: Actress Dakota Fanning

Dana

(English) from Denmark; bright as day.

Image: Dana has two images, and luckily for her, one is a bit better than the other. To some, Dana is pictured as a mean, sad, and insecure brunette. Others disagree, believing instead she's lively and strong-minded—but still annoying.

Famous Namesakes: Character Dana Scully (*The X-Files*); actress Dana Delaney; actress Dana Reeve; actress Dana "Queen Latifah" Owens

 **Star Kids**

Daisy Boo

Daisy Boo is the stripper—or hillbilly—with a heart of gold. She strikes people as a strawberry-blond beauty who's dumb as a post, but flirty, friendly, and popular. (Her job as a pole dancer no doubt helps her popularity.) A few people also suspect she's a ditzy Southern country gal, perhaps like TV character Daisy Duke. While being *friendly* is an admirable goal, perhaps TV's Naked Chef, Jamie Oliver, has more in mind for his daughter Daisy Boo.

Dani

(Hebrew) a familiar form of Danielle.

Image: Dani is a feminine twist on a masculine name, which may help explain this image. Dani reminds people of a bubbly, active sports nut—maybe even a tomboy. She's most likely blond and cute, and she's assertive, strong-willed, but always happy.

Famous Namesakes: Character Dani Beck (*Law & Order: Special Victims Unit*)

Danica

(Slavic) morning star. (Hebrew) a form of Danielle.

Image: Danica is bursting with life—and chatter. She's regarded as a friendly, talkative, and dramatic girl who loves life. People suspect she's a little short on common sense, but she's not short on smiles. A few have a different view, saying she's a smart girl who's nerdy, shy, and dull. Like racecar driver Danica Patrick, she's usually pictured with brown hair and a pretty face.

Famous Namesakes: Racecar driver Danica Patrick; actress Danica McKellar

Danielle

(Hebrew, French) God is my judge.

Image: Danielle is a woman with great qualities. She's imagined as good-natured, helpful, and funny. She also may have a quiet, sensitive side. But then again, others say she's a disliked snob.

Famous Namesakes: Novelist Danielle Steel; model Danielle Evans

Daphne

(Greek) laurel tree.

Image: Tell Daphne all your worries—she's a good listener. She's described as an affectionate and nonjudgmental confidante who has tall, model-like looks and lots of patience. She's also said to be a hard worker and very smart. Some think she's a tomboy, and still others think she's an unpopular nerd.

Famous Namesakes: Actress Daphne Zuniga; character Daphne Blake (*Scooby Doo*); actress Daphne Maxwell Reid; actress Daphne Ashbrook

Darcy

(Irish) dark. (French) fortress.

Image: These two images of Darcy are as different as night from day. Some see Darcy as a mousy and lonely nerd, but some see her as a perky and out-of-control wild girl. Either way, she's probably sweet and intelligent. She's also thought to have brown hair and eyes.

Famous Namesakes: Musician D'arcy Wretzky

Darla

(English) a short form of Darlene.

Image: Darla is a winsome thing. People think Darla is charismatic, affectionate, cheerful, and quite popular. People gush that she's an adorable youth with black curls, a button nose, and dimples. Adding to her charm, she's said to be smart and talented.

Famous Namesakes: Character Darla (*Buffy the Vampire Slayer*); character Darla (*The Little Rascals*)

Girls

Darlene

(French) little darling.

Image: Perhaps Darlene Conner of TV's *Roseanne* is an inspiration for this name's image. Darlene is pictured as a rough, rude, and uncultured loudmouth with lots to say and lots of spunk. People depict her with dark hair, a husky build, and a messy style.

Famous Namesakes: Singer Darlene Love; character Darlene Conner (*Roseanne*); tennis player Darlene Hard

Dawn

(English) sunrise, dawn.

Image: Dawn's luminous name gives her a sunny image. Most people picture Dawn as a free-spirited hippie. She's said to be bubbly, gentle, and sweet. Others, however, think of her as lonely and reserved or obnoxious and rebellious. Like a true California girl, Dawn is blond.

Famous Namesakes: Actress Dawn French

Deborah

(Hebrew) bee.

Image: Although she's very social, Deborah isn't easy to get along with. Deborah is imagined as an outgoing girl who loves gossiping as much as she loves picking up guys. People say she's pushy and judgmental, not to mention a little slow. A few people, however, argue that she's sweet and nice. She's described as a chubby and tall brunette with an outdated hairdo.

Famous Namesakes: Actress Debra Winger; singer Deborah Gibson; journalist Deborah Norville; actress Deborah Kerr; singer Deborah Harry; singer Deborah Cox

Dee Dee

(Welsh) black, dark.

Image: Dee Dee loves to be around people, but do they love to be around her? Dee Dee is described as friendly, playful, and outspoken, even though she's something of an airhead. Perhaps it's no wonder some say she's annoying, if not obnoxious, and childish.

Famous Namesakes: Radio personality Dee Dee Bridgewater

Deirdre

(Irish) sorrowful; wanderer.

Image: Deirdre isn't always talkative, but she's always a good friend. People describe Deirdre as a kind companion with a big heart and a desire to please. Sometimes she can be introverted; other times, she can be extroverted. People imagine this middle-aged woman is interested in the arts as either a dancer or a writer.

Famous Namesakes: Actress Deirdre Hall; author Deirdre Coleman Imus

Delia

(Greek) visible; from Delos, Greece. (German, Welsh) a short form of Adelaide, Cordelia.

Image: Delia may very well be an ice queen. Most people describe her as snobby, aloof, self-centered, and greedy. Physically, she's pictured as pretty and dainty with light brown hair. A few people warm her up a bit, calling her caring, sweet, and funny.

Famous Namesakes: Journalist Delia Gallagher; television chef Delia Smith

Delilah

(Hebrew) brooder.

Image: Want your next bash to be a success? Make sure you invite Delilah. Caring, friendly, and humorous, she's said to be the life of the party. She's most likely intelligent, and while most people say she's trustworthy, a few find her to be a bit sly. As for her looks, she's thought to be a sleek brunette with a snappy wardrobe.

Famous Namesakes: Biblical figure Delilah; radio personality Delilah

Della

(English) a short form of Adelaide, Cordelia, Delaney.

Image: You may have to tell Della more than once to hold the mayo on your BLT. People think of Della as a kind but ditzy and distracted waitress. People say she wears a lot of makeup and has no problem filling out the top half of her uniform.

Famous Namesakes: Actress Della Reese

Delores

(Spanish) a form of Dolores.

Image: Delores is a form of Dolores, which aptly means "suffering." Most people think of Delores as a troubled, unhappy, and lonely woman who's been disappointed and hurt throughout her life. Now in her twilight years, she's described as frumpy and homely. Others, however, have a brighter view, imagining she's a hardworking and confident woman who's a gossip queen.

Famous Namesakes: Fiction character Dolores Claiborne; character Dolores Umbridge (*Harry Potter* series)

Delphine

(Greek) from Delphi, Greece.

Image: If you want the world to know your business, tell Delphine. She's imagined as an attention-seeking motor mouth who loves to gossip. Her nosiness may make her seem rude, but she seems to have a sweet side, too. Some people say she's interesting, perhaps because she has a lot of juicy stories to dish.

Famous Namesakes: Businesswoman Delphine Arnault; actress Delphine Seyrig

Delta

(Greek) door.

Image: Delta Burke has a reputation as a Southern belle, especially from her days on TV's *Designing Women*. People imagine Delta as a quick-witted social butterfly with Southern charm. She may be haughty from time to time, but she's usually nice. Physically, she's portrayed as a tall, full-figured woman.

Famous Namesakes: Singer Delta Goodrem; actress Delta Burke

Demi

(French) half. (Greek) a short form of Demetria.

Image: When hearing the name Demi, people picture a singular physical image, but they depict very different images of her personality. Nearly everyone describes Demi as black-haired, slender, and sexy—very likely a nod to actress Demi Moore. But people said she may be funny, well liked, and cheerful; spoiled, rich, and self-involved; or mysterious, independent, and confident.

Famous Namesakes: Actress Demi Moore

Girls

Dena

(English, Native American) valley. (Hebrew) a form of Dinah.

Image: Dena is no soccer mom. She's pictured as an artistic, energetic, and free-spirited woman who, despite her eccentricities, is a kind and caring mother. People consider her to be attractive, funny, and full of life (although her kids find her to be a little annoying now and then).

Famous Namesakes: Basketball player Dena Head

Denise

(French) follower of Dionysus, the god of wine.

Image: These two images of Denise register on opposite ends of the sociability scale. Many people feel Denise is a friendly and outspoken busybody who's cheerful, spunky, and well liked by everyone. Others contend she's a bashful wallflower who's dull, underachieving, and easily persuaded. In either case, she's probably a plump African American.

Famous Namesakes: Actress Denise Richards; singer Denise Williams; fitness guru Denise Austin; character Denise Huxtable (*The Cosby Show*)

Desiree

(French) desired, longed for.

Image: Desiree's looks may be desirable, but some say her personality is not. Desiree comes across as either conceited and rude or caring and quiet. Physically, she's pictured with dark hair, a slim figure, and feminine beauty.

Famous Namesakes: Singer Desiree

Destiny

(French) fate.

Image: True to her name, Destiny lives to meet her fate—or at least dream about it. Destiny is pictured as a chatty and vivacious go-getter, but she also has a sweet, dreamy side. Some people think Destiny is smart and witty, but others see her as an airhead. As for her looks, Destiny is portrayed as tall and slender.

Famous Namesakes: Actress Destiny (Miley) Cyrus

Diamond

(Latin) precious gem.

Image: Diamonds may be precious jewels, but they're also hard—and so is this name's image. People describe Diamond as spoiled, vain, demanding, and as elegant as her name suggests. Sometimes she seems serious and quiet, and other times she seems outgoing and loud. Most people imagine she's a big-boned and buxom brunette.

Famous Namesakes: Singer Neil Diamond; actor Lou Diamond Phillips

Diana

(Latin) divine.

Image: This name will forever be associated with the late Princess of Wales. Diana is described as a sweet, generous, and poised princess who's beautiful, slender, and radiant. She's also described as a tender mother.

Famous Namesakes: Princess Diana; singer Diana Ross; actress Diana Rigg; musician Diana Krall

Diane

(Latin) a short form of Diana.

Image: Diane is full of confidence, but sometimes she seems a little too self-assured. Most people view her as a loyal, nice, and smart achiever. But at times she comes across as overly sophisticated and haughty. She's pictured as a waiflike older blond.

Famous Namesakes: Actress Dianne Wiest; actress Diane Keaton; speed skater Dianne Holum; actress Diane Lane; zoologist Dian Fossey; actress Diane Ladd; journalist Diane Sawyer; designer Diane von Furstenberg; senator Diane Feinstein

Dianne

(Latin) a short form of Diana.

Image: Diana is a goddess in Roman mythology, but it's Dianne who's described as an idol. People say she's a charismatic but determined woman with statuesque, goddesslike beauty. She's also thought to be intelligent, graceful, focused, and quite popular.

Famous Namesakes: Actress Dianne Wiest; actress Diane Keaton; speed skater Dianne Holum; actress Diane Lane; zoologist Dian Fossey; actress Diane Ladd; journalist Diane Sawyer; designer Diane von Furstenberg

Dina

(Hebrew) a form of Dinah.

Image: There are two images of Dina—one has fun, and the other has manners. Most people describe Dina as a raspy-voiced woman who loves to drink, smoke, flirt, and have a wild time. They also say she's spunky and outspoken. Others see her as demure, ladylike, and sweet. Either way, she's attractive, petite, and fair.

Famous Namesakes: Actress Dina Meyer; singer Dinah Shore; politician Dina Powell; actress Dinah Manhoff; singer Dinah Washington

Dixie

(French) tenth. (English) wall; dike.

Image: This gal sure is whistlin' Dixie. People say Dixie is a giggly, chatty, and ditzy Southerner. Sweet and outgoing, this country girl seems as rowdy as the boys. She's also thought to have blond pigtails, long legs, and cute freckles.

Famous Namesakes: Actress Dixie Carter

Dolly

(American) a short form of Dolores, Dorothy.

Image: Not surprisingly, people associate this name with country singer Dolly Parton. They say Dolly is a friendly, vivacious, and cheerful country girl. She's most likely successful and talented, and she's pictured with blond hair, blue eyes, and—of course—bountiful bosoms.

Famous Namesakes: First lady Dolly Madison; singer Dolly Parton

Dominique

(French) a form of Dominica.

Image: No single image of Dominique is dominant. Dominique is thought to be kind, faithful, and sweet; temperamental, conceited, and unreasonable; or funny, confident, and playful. There's some consensus about her looks: Everyone gushes that she's a beautiful dark-featured girl, but they can't decide if she's African American, Italian, or Latino.

Famous Namesakes: Actress Dominique Swain; gymnast Dominique Dawes; gymnast Dominique Moceanu

Donata

(Latin) gift.

Image: How many positive qualities does Donata have? *Nada.* People see her as a moody and dull nag with a bad attitude. She's said to be lazy and unsuccessful, unintelligent and oafish, and self-righteous and narrow-minded.

Famous Namesakes: None

Girls

Donna

(Italian) lady.

Image: There's very little consensus about Donna. People say Donna may be shy and reserved, loud and outgoing, mean and sarcastic, smart and sensible, loyal and nice, impatient and short-tempered, or perhaps ditzy and weird. When it comes to looks, people agree she's tall, but she may be pretty, plain, or homely.

Famous Namesakes: Actress Donna Reed; singer Donna Summer; designer Donna Karan; singer Donna Lewis; character Donna Martin (*Beverly Hills, 90210*)

Dora

(Greek) gift.

Image: Most people think Dora is like cartoon character Dora the Explorer: She's described as a short munchkin who's kind, intelligent, pleasant, and adventurous. She's likely Mexican with black hair and tan skin. Thinking of the real world, some people say Dora is meek, childish, and two-faced.

Famous Namesakes: Television character Dora the Explorer

Doreen

(Irish) moody, sullen. (French) golden. (Greek) a form of Dora.

Image: Doreen is a negative person, which makes sense because there are few positives about her. Doreen is imagined as a cranky grump who's brainy but boring and introverted. She probably has a squeaky voice. People say her looks are a downer, too: They describe her as homely with frizzy dark hair and a frumpy style.

Famous Namesakes: Author Doreen Cronin

Doria

(Greek) a form of Dorian.

Image: Every night, poor Doria microwaves her dinner for one. People see Doria as a mopey wallflower who's unpopular and unsocial, and who lives alone with her cats. She's known to be very brainy and responsible, but she has self-esteem issues, which may stem her appearance: She's described as frumpy, big-nosed, and bespectacled.

Famous Namesakes: None

Doris

(Greek) sea.

Image: Everybody wants a grandma like Doris. She's thought to be a happy old lady who bakes cookies and knits garments for her beloved family. After years of raising children and grandchildren, she's known to have an authoritative side, but she's usually quite attentive. People picture her in a polyester housedress.

Famous Namesakes: Actress Doris Day; actress Doris Roberts; author Doris Kearns Goodwin; heiress Doris Duke

Dorothy

(Greek) gift of God.

Image: The most famous Dorothy wanted to be somewhere over the rainbow, but she inspires only one of this name's images. Most people describe Dorothy as a kind, forgiving, and hospitable friend who's honest and hardworking. Thanks to the lead character in *The Wizard of Oz*, some believe she's brave, adventurous, and independent. Still others find her to be a pushy and overbearing older woman.

Famous Namesakes: Character Dorothy Gale (*The Wizard of Oz*); model Dorothy Stratten; character Dorothy Zbornak (*The Golden Girls*); writer Dorothy Parker; actress Dorothy Dandridge; figure skater Dorothy Hamill

Dottie

(Greek) a familiar form of Dorothy.

Image: Dottie is still upbeat after all these years. She's described as a chipper and talkative older woman who's sort of round, very sweet, and not really hip. Some may say she's easily distracted and ditzy, but others say that's just how she expresses her silliness.

Famous Namesakes: Country singer Dottie West; golfer Dottie Pepper

Drusilla

(Latin) descendant of Drusus, the strong one.

Image: Something wicked this way comes: This name's image bears resemblance to Drusilla, a vampire from TV's *Buffy the Vampire Slayer*. People think Drusilla is scary, evil, and witchy. Even when using less wicked words, people still imagine she's calculating, cold, moody, and unfriendly.

Famous Namesakes: Character Drusilla (*Buffy the Vampire Slayer*)

Eartha

(English) earthy.

Image: People take this name literally, it seems. They describe Eartha as a laid-back and earthy nature lover. Most people say she's simple and maybe even boring, but a few describe her as an opinionated environmentalist. It's also fitting that she's pictured with plain, natural looks.

Famous Namesakes: Actress Eartha Kitt

Ebony

(Greek) a hard, dark wood.

Image: Ebony is a strong beauty and strong personality. She's pictured as a beautiful African American model with high cheekbones, clear skin, and long, silky black hair. She's driven, passionate, and confident. At times, she seems caring and helpful, but at other times, she seems haughty and harsh. Either way, people say she's always smart and outspoken.

Famous Namesakes: Actress Ebony Thomas

Eden

(Babylonian) a plain. (Hebrew) delightful.

Image: Eden sounds like a heavenly girl—right? At first glance, Eden is perceived as a preacher's daughter who seems innocent and angelic. But at second glance, people say she's quite deceiving: She's much more worldly, flirty, and naughty than her daddy realizes.

Famous Namesakes: Actress Eden Riegel

Edith

(English) rich gift.

Image: Having tea with Edith may be pleasant, but it also may be painful. People agree Edith is an old grandmother, but they can't decide on her personality. She may be a soft-spoken and secluded wallflower with a caring heart, or a snippy and impatient grouch with a stern face. Either way, she's old-fashioned, tiny, and frumpy.

Famous Namesakes: Character Edith Bunker (*All in the Family*); designer Edith Head; author Edith Wharton

Edna

(Hebrew) rejuvenation.

Image: Neighborhood folks can feel Edna's glare through her windows as they walk by her house. She's thought to be a conservative and mean old spinster who wears horn-rimmed glasses, frumpy cardigans, and a permanent scowl. She's known to dislike children and, basically, all people in general.

Famous Namesakes: Poet Edna St. Vincent Millay; television host Dame Edna Everage; character Edna Krabappel (*The Simpsons*)

Eileen

(Irish) a form of Helen.

Image: Eileen is a good worker and a good person. Most people see her as a smart, book-ish woman who can be serious, strict, and well organized when it comes to her work. Outside the office, she's seen as a loyal, sweet, and even bubbly person. She most likely comes from a middle-class background.

Famous Namesakes: Modeling agency founder Eileen Ford; actress Eileen Atkins; actress Eileen Davidson; designer Eileen Gray

Ela

(Polish) a form of Adelaide.

Image: Ela pours herself into making her home-made goodies. She's imagined as a quiet, elderly lady who lives in an old-fashioned country home where she enjoys reading and baking. People say she's as nice and sweet as the cookies she makes.

Famous Namesakes: Singer Ella Fitzgerald; activist Ella Baker

Elaine

(French) a form of Helen.

Image: Dealing with a personality like Elaine's, a lot of butlers and servants burn out. Elaine strikes people as a traditional, rigid woman who's critical, loud, and demanding. This brunette most likely comes from a classy, rich background. A perfectionist, she's always complaining about something.

Famous Namesakes: Character Elaine Benes (*Seinfeld*); comedian Elayne Boosler; actress Elaine Stritch

Eldora

(Spanish) golden, gilded.

Image: Eldora is a bold but peculiar character. She strikes people as a brilliant yet pretentious Greek woman. She seems to be a little eccentric with her creative, imaginative thinking, but she's also described as classy and graceful with dark hair and features.

Famous Namesakes: None

Eleanor

(Greek) light.

Image: Eleanor is full of intelligent thoughts, but she keeps them to herself. She's pictured as an elegant, refined, and brilliant thinker with an introverted, reserved nature that dislikes sharing her ideas with others. Physically, most people see her as matronly and small.

Famous Namesakes: First lady Eleanor Roosevelt; queen Eleanor of Aquitaine

Electra

(Greek) shining; brilliant.

Image: With comic book heroine Elektra and sex symbol Carmen Electra as namesakes, it's no great mystery where this name's image comes from. People think Electra sounds like an exciting, daring, and electrifying woman. She may very well be a racy exotic dancer or a model. She comes across as bratty and even mean at times, but she can also be a lot of mischievous fun.

Famous Namesakes: Actress Carmen Electra; mythological figure Electra; comic book character Elektra

Elena

(Greek) a form of Eleanor. (Italian) a form of Helen.

Image: Elena has her good side and her bad. On one hand, people see as her bossy and over-bearing. On the other hand, they say she's family oriented, faithful, and sometimes even sweet. She's described as a lovely and exotic woman, and she probably comes from a tradi-tional Latino family.

Famous Namesakes: Opera singer Elena Gerhardt

Elise

(French, English) a short form of Elizabeth, Elysia.

Image: Elise is a jet setter. She's pictured as a well-traveled and smart sophisticate who can be sullen and needy at times, but funny and personable at others. Some see her as a spoiled snob. Physically, she's pictured as a beautiful and slender blond who puts a lot of time (maybe too much) into maintaining her appearance.

Famous Namesakes: Actress Elise Neal

Eliza

(Hebrew) a short form of Elizabeth.

Image: Eliza knows the Dewey Decimal System inside and out. She's thought of as a nerdy and dorky bookworm, and she may just be a librarian. Some describe her as funny and nice, but others call her goofy. She's pictured with a skinny face and even skinnier figure.

Famous Namesakes: Actress Eliza Dushku; character Eliza Doolittle (*My Fair Lady*)

Elizabeth

(Hebrew) consecrated to God.

Image: The image for Elizabeth is only partly influenced by the current British monarch. Many people describe Elizabeth as compassionate, sweet, and demure with plenty of smiles to go around. Those most likely thinking of Queen Elizabeth II, however, say she comes across as superior, guarded, and a bit snobby.

Famous Namesakes: Queens Elizabeth I and II; actress Elizabeth Taylor; actress Elizabeth Hurley; activist Elizabeth Cady Stanton; actress Elizabeth Mitchell; actress Elizabeth Berkley; senator Elizabeth Dole

Ella

(English) elfin; beautiful fairy-woman. (Greek) a short form of Eleanor.

Image: How can anyone not like Ella? This name reminds people of a beautiful, good-natured, and well-liked woman. She's said to be caring, tender, fashionable, and graceful. She may also have a quick, funny wit.

Famous Namesakes: Singer Ella Fitzgerald; activist Ella Baker

Ellen

(English) a form of Eleanor, Helen.

Image: Most people think of Ellen as a timid and mousy booklover. When she opens up, she's considered a great friend because she's sweet, caring, and nurturing. She's also known to be tidy and organized, perhaps making her a perfect bookkeeper, secretary, PTA president, or homemaker. People think she looks a lot like comedian and talk show host Ellen DeGeneres: wiry and tall with short blond hair.

Famous Namesakes: Comedian Ellen DeGeneres; actress Ellen Pompeo; actress Ellen Barkin

Ellie

(English) a short form of Eleanor, Ella, Ellen.

Image: Although her name is spelled differently, Elly May Clampett of TV's *The Beverly Hillbillies* heavily influences this name's image. Ellie is imagined as an overwhelmingly sweet and adorable Southern girl who's bubbly and playful. She's also thought to be an attractive and petite redhead or blond with freckles.

Famous Namesakes: Character Elly May Clampett (*The Beverly Hillbillies*)

Elsie

(German) a familiar form of Elsa, Helsa.

Image: Try to keep from smiling around Elsie—it's not easy! Elsie is pictured as a cuddly, loving, and happy girl with plenty of smiles and giggles. In a bovine connection, she's thought to be pleasantly plump and not very smart, like Elsie the Cow, mascot of Borden Milk Products. But people also say she's quite cute.

Famous Namesakes: Dairy mascot Elsie the Cow

Emily

(Latin) flatterer. (German) industrious.

Image: This name's image takes on a great deal of poet Emily Dickinson's qualities. People describe Emily as shy, soft-spoken, and poetic. Some say this sweet-faced girl is likable and fun when she opens up, and she's always well mannered.

Famous Namesakes: Author Emily Bronte; etiquette expert Emily Post; poet Emily Dickinson; actress Emily VanCamp; actress Emily Blunt

Emma

(German) a short form of Emily.

Image: Emma is a beam of happiness and sweetness. Most people picture her as a cheery and optimistic sprite with a large smile and a kind heart. She comes across as quite intelligent and helpful as well. At times, she can be shy and wistful—perhaps even romantic.

Famous Namesakes: Character Emma Woodhouse (*Emma*); actress Emma Thompson; actress Emma Samms; actress Emma Watson; singer Emma Bunton; actress Emma Roberts

Enid

(Welsh) life; spirit.

Image: Enid is a victim of her own shyness. People say she's soft-spoken, shy, and sometimes fearful. For these reasons, she comes across as unfriendly and stern, which makes this bony, homely girl rather unpopular. Some suspect she's intelligent, but others say she's not very bright.

Famous Namesakes: Author Enid Blyton; author Enid Bagnold

Erica

(Scandinavian) ruler of all. (English) brave ruler.

Image: Erica proves that being successful doesn't always mean being nice. People believe Erica is a snob who's vain, proud, disloyal, and demanding. That said, they also believe she's strong, aggressive, and confident in business. Tall, brunette, slim, and attractive, Erica is most likely a man-eater, and she can be chatty and fun in the right situations.

Famous Namesakes: Actress Erica Durance; character Erica Kane (*All My Children*); singer Erykah Badu

Erin

(Irish) peace.

Image: Erin Brockovich spearheaded a major lawsuit and became a household name when she was portrayed in a hit movie. For these reasons, Erin is seen as a perceptive and clever woman with good instincts, lots of compassion, and a bubbly personality. Full of sex appeal, she's described as a leggy, slim blonde.

Famous Namesakes: Activist Erin Brockovich; actress Erin Moran

Esmeralda

(Greek, Spanish) a form of Emerald.

Image: Esmeralda's qualities seem to contradict one another, but somehow they come together. She's envisioned as an outrageous woman who's caring but bossy, wise but goofy. Described as attractive, classy, bone thin, and tall, she may be a ballet instructor.

Famous Namesakes: Character Esmeralda (*The Hunchback of Notre Dame*); character Esmeralda (*Bewitched*)

Esperanza

(Spanish) hope.

Image: The name Esperanza means "hope," and that's a beautiful way to describe this girl. People envision Esperanza as dreamy and hopeful, optimistic and inspirational, caring and faithful. She's said to be a dark-haired and petite Latino beauty with a secretive, romantic side that waits for her dreams to come true.

Famous Namesakes: Jazz musician Esperanza Spalding

Estelle

(French) a form of Esther.

Image: Estelle has it all. When people hear this name, they think of a beautiful, charismatic, and interesting woman with poise, grace, intelligence, and a warm heart. She's most likely a brunette, and she may be older.

Famous Namesakes: Actress Estelle Getty; actress Estelle Harris

Ester

(Persian) a form of Esther.

Image: Much of Ester's abrasive personality is simply due to her age. She's said to be an elderly woman who's reserved and grouchy. Being old, she's no doubt old-fashioned, conventional, and sedate. A few people have a more positive view, saying she can be friendly and smart in certain situations.

Famous Namesakes: Biblical figure Esther

Ethel

(English) noble.

Image: Ethel may be a sweet granny or an old grump. Everyone pictures her as a grandmother with gray hair, wrinkles, and a chunky figure. For some, she's friendly and nice, and she keeps her mind sharp with books and crossword puzzles. But others say she's a stubborn and sour prude who's constantly grumpy.

Famous Namesakes: Socialite Ethel Kennedy; singer Ethel Merman; character Ethel Mertz (*I Love Lucy*); alleged spy Ethel Rosenberg

Eugenia

(Greek) born to nobility.

Image: Eugenia never has to worry about her social life interfering with her homework. She's regarded as a timid, nerdy math wiz with average, mousy looks and thick glasses. She may be endearing if you get to know her, but many people find her to be dull.

Famous Namesakes: Model Eugenia Silva

Eunice

(Greek) happy; victorious.

Image: Eunice doesn't belong to any social circle. Instead, she's said to be a lonely and nerdy outcast. People have different theories for her exile: Some say she's shy, others say she's aloof; some believe she's prudish, others say she's meddlesome. They all describe her as old and unattractive with a hook nose.

Famous Namesakes: Socialite Eunice Kennedy Shriver; character Eunice (*A Streetcar Named Desire*)

Eva

(Greek) a short form of Evangelina. (Hebrew) a form of Eve.

Image: Eva is a woman of strong character. People say she's empathetic, kind, and even-tempered. She's likely quiet and reserved, but she's also wise and deeply spiritual.

Famous Namesakes: Actress Eva Longoria; actress Eva Gabor; actress Eva Mendes; actress Eva Green; first lady Eva Peron

Eve

(Hebrew) life.

Image: Several images are all about Eve: She may be a kindhearted and polite sweetie, a wild and mischievous rebel, a smart and strong-willed leader, or a sporty and cool tomboy. At least people agree that she's tall with an hourglass figure.

Famous Namesakes: Rapper Eve; biblical figure Eve; actress Eve Arden; actress Eve Plumb

Evelyn

(English) hazelnut.

Image: Evelyn exemplifies the upside and the downside of the upper-class. People say she's rich, spoiled, and snobbish, but she's also stingy with money. Her lavish upbringing seems to have given her a certain amount of grace, sophistication, and smarts, but many people still find her to be rude.

Famous Namesakes: Actress Evelyn Keyes; singer Evelyn Champagne King

Evie

(Hungarian) a form of Eve.

Image: Evie has her head in the clouds. People think Evie is an adorable girl who's good-humored, positive, and smart, but she's also absent-minded and late for everything. Her friends don't mind, though, because she's so sweet and fun.

Famous Namesakes: None

Faith

(English) faithful; fidelity.

Image: Have a little faith in this name's image. People describe Faith as a sweet, angelic, and, of course, faithful woman. She's likely a good mother, she may be shy at times, and she's said to be very smart. Many people can't help but think of country star Faith Hill, saying she's a gorgeous blond with great singing talent.

Famous Namesakes: Singer Faith Hill; actress Faith Ford; singer Faith Evans

Fantasia

(Greek) imagination.

Image: *American Idol*–winner Fantasia Barrino had a fantastical rise to stardom. Similarly, people think this Fantasia is an imaginative and joyful waitress who struggles to make her way as a singer. She's pictured as a slim African American who's most likely bubbly and a little flighty. But she's also artistic, using her voice as a painter uses brushstrokes.

Famous Namesakes: Singer Fantasia Barrino

Fawn

(French) young deer.

Image: One image of Fawn is as innocent as a baby deer, but another image is not so pure. Most people say Fawn is meek, shy, gentle, and sweet. Physically, she's most likely small, delicate, and cute. But other people say she's a bubbly, low-class airhead from a trailer park. She may be slovenly and dirty, or she may be a stripper.

Famous Namesakes: Infamous secretary Fawn Hall

Felice

(Latin) a short form of Felicia.

Image: Felice has many wonderful qualities, but she's afraid to show them. People say she's poised, ladylike, and mature, not to mention highly intelligent. Unfortunately, though, she's most likely timid and shy, keeping her gifts to herself.

Famous Namesakes: None

Felicia

(Latin) fortunate; happy.

Image: Felicia is high energy and high class. She's described as a spunky and sassy people-person. She seems to have two distinct sides: Sometimes she may be classy and elegant, and other times she may be athletic and outdoorsy. She's pictured as a tall, slender, and beautiful African American woman.

Famous Namesakes: Character Felicia Forrester (*The Bold and the Beautiful*); actress Phylicia Rashad

Felicity

(English) a form of Felicia.

Image: This name's image is inspired by the title character from TV's *Felicity*, who was most famous for her tresses. Felicity is imagined as a daydreaming, gentle, and spontaneous girl who always follows her heart. She's pictured as a curly-haired brunette with a pretty face and eyes.

Famous Namesakes: Actress Felicity Huffman; character Felicity Porter (*Felicity*); character Felicity (*American Girl* series)

Fifi

(French) a familiar form of Josephine.

Image: Fittingly, Fifi is a name often given to pampered French poodles. When most people hear this name, they envision a spoiled and self-involved French airhead who thinks she's better than everyone else. She's pictured with curly, fluffy hair that may resemble poodle fur. And like a high-strung pooch, she's probably silly and bursting with nervous excitement.

Famous Namesakes: Character Fifi Le Fume (*Looney Tunes*); star kid Fifi Trixibelle Geldof

Fiona

(Irish) fair, white.

Image: Singer Fiona Apple is famed for her songwriting talent, waiflike looks, and strong will. Because of this, people say Fiona is a lithe and gangly girl with a poetic, creative spirit. She's known to be withdrawn, stubborn, and perhaps pretentious.

Famous Namesakes: Character Princess Fiona (*Shrek*); singer Fiona Apple; actress Fiona Shaw

Flannery

(Irish) redhead.

Image: People think Flannery is a socially awkward and quiet loner with a frail figure, glasses, and knobby knees. Under the nerdy exterior, she's most likely kind, respectful, and smart. She may be a soft-spoken teacher.

Famous Namesakes: Author Flannery O'Connor

Fleta

(English) swift, fast.

Image: Is Fleta a grump because she's withdrawn, or is she just downright mean? People find Fleta to be a cranky and harsh old lady who wears glasses and frumpy dresses. She's said to be lonely and depressed, and people wonder if that's because she's shy or because her grumpiness chases visitors away. In addition, it's unclear whether she's a smart bookworm or an easily confused dimwit.

Famous Namesakes: None

 **Star Kids**

Fifi Trixibelle

No matter how silly she may be, Fifi Trixibelle is still a diva. Most people imagine she's a goofy, sappy, and ditzy supermodel who loves to spill secrets. She's pictured with curly blond hair, like a poodle. In fact, some people even guess she *is* a poodle. That must be an image Fifi Trixibelle, daughter of late British TV personality Paula Yates and political activist Bob Geldof, *loves* to hear.

Florence

(Latin) blooming; flowery; prosperous.

Image: Florence is well loved and well read. She's imagined as a caring and happy woman who's loved by everyone. People believe she's an intelligent, avid reader, and she's straight-laced and moral as well. She's most often pictured with dark skin and elegant beauty.

Famous Namesakes: Actress Florence Henderson; nurse Florence Nightingale

Florida

(Spanish) a form of Florence.

Image: Florida is the Sunshine State, so this name's image must be sunny as well. People claim Florida is a cheerful and bright blond who's talkative, flirty, but perhaps a bit ditzy. She's known to love flowers and beaches as well as parties, where she tends to be a little mischievous.

Famous Namesakes: Character Florida Evans (*Good Times*)

Fran

(Latin) a short form of Frances.

Image: Fran Drescher of TV's *The Nanny* has brassy personality. Therefore, most people think of Fran as funny, loud, and cheerful—but bordering on obnoxious. Some people have a different view, saying Fran is old-fashioned and loving as well as plump and mousy.

Famous Namesakes: Comedian Fran Drescher; author Fran Leibowitz

Frances

(Latin) free; from France.

Image: Frances is a no-frills kind of girl. She's thought of as an upstanding, smart, and quiet straight shooter. She may be too utilitarian, however, because she comes across as a dull and nerdy loner to many people.

Famous Namesakes: Actress Frances Farmer; actress Frances Bavier; actress Frances McDormand

Francesca

(Italian) a form of Frances.

Image: Francesca has high self-esteem, but that's the problem. She's described as an arrogant and bossy woman with beautiful bone structure and a dainty physique, and who's of Italian heritage. She may be proper and well read, but many people find this beauty to be a snob.

Famous Namesakes: Actress Francesca Annis

Francine

(French) a form of Frances.

Image: Francine is an odd old lady. People say she's a kind, quiet, and happy elderly woman. She's envisioned as mousy and fragile, and many people find her to be a little weird.

Famous Namesakes: Character Francine Frensky (*Arthur*)

Frida

(German) a short form of Alfreda, Elfrida, Frederica, Sigfreda.

Image: Whether calm or fiery, Frida is passionate about her art. Many people imagine she's a visual artist, like Mexican painter Frida Kahlo, but some believe her art is dance. Some folks describe her as calm, strong, smart, and unflappable. Others, however, imagine her to be a hotheaded and outspoken extrovert.

Famous Namesakes: Artist Frida Kahlo

Gabriela

(Italian) a form of Gabrielle.

Image: Gabriela is a quiet charmer. People think she's completely angelic and sincere. They also find her to be carefree, charming, and bubbly in an unassuming way. She's described as a leggy, pretty brunette with a dark complexion.

Famous Namesakes: Poet Gabriela Mistral; tennis player Gabriela Sabatini

Gabriella

(Italian) a form of Gabriela.

Image: With so many upsides, Gabriella is allowed one downside. She's envisioned as a beautiful woman who's warm, confident, elegant, and intelligent. It seems the only shortcoming for this petite brunette is her tendency to be snobby at times. Many people picture her as a lawyer.

Famous Namesakes: Poet Gabriela Mistral; tennis player Gabriela Sabatini

Gabrielle

(French) devoted to God.

Image: Gabrielle is a one-woman show. She's pictured as a fun-loving charmer who enjoys singing, dancing, and telling jokes, which people find wildly entertaining. People also find her to be wildly attractive, as well as sweet and confident. Physically, she's imagined as attractive and tan with a small waist, long hair, and beautiful eyes.

Famous Namesakes: Character Gabrielle Solis (*Desperate Housewives*); model Gabrielle Reese; actress Gabrielle Carteris; actress Gabrielle Union; actress Gabrielle Anwar

Gaby

(French) a familiar form of Gabrielle.

Image: Gaby, it seems, is true to her name. She's said to be a very talkative, vivacious, and creative girl. People believe she likes to have a good time and show off her great smile.

Famous Namesakes: Actress Gaby Hoffmann

Gail

(English) merry, lively. (Hebrew) a short form of Abigail.

Image: It takes Gail a little while to warm up. People say she's shy and soft-spoken when you first meet her, but you quickly discover she's a sweet and devoted family woman. This average-looking brunette is known to enjoy a good read, and she's often funny in her own quiet way.

Famous Namesakes: Runner Gail Devers

Gemma

(Latin, Italian) jewel, precious stone.

Image: Gemma is the sweetest girl in the commune. She's described as an earthy flower child who's sweet, caring, and free spirited. People picture her with very long hair and a natural beauty.

Famous Namesakes: Model Gemma Ward; singer Gemma Hayes

Genevieve

(German, French) a form of Guinevere.

Image: Whether in days of yore or today, Genevieve is a magnetic damsel. She's said to be a patient, respectful, and gentle woman who's bright and jovial. People are drawn to her wit, love of life, and willowy beauty. Some people see her as a regal—if not royal—snob; others see a distressed damsel from medieval times.

Famous Namesakes: Actress Genevieve Bujold; television host Genevieve Gorder

Georgette

(French) a form of Georgia.

Image: Georgette's personality can be interpreted many different ways. People agree Georgette is a petite and pretty blonde with freckles and a shapely figure. Many say she's vivacious and bubbly, but others believe she's desperate for attention. Some imagine she's from the South, but others say she's a hillbilly. A few describe her as sweet and fun, but others suspect she's ditzy.

Famous Namesakes: Actress Georgette Harvey; character Georgette Franklin (*The Mary Tyler Moore Show*)

Georgia

(Greek) farmer.

Image: Georgia is a peach—as long as she's in charge. Georgia is described as a dramatic and independent woman whose temper and bossiness are sometimes hard to handle. In calmer times, though, she comes across as a friendly and gracious Southern belle with curly brown hair and feminine beauty.

Famous Namesakes: Actress Georgia Bright Engel; artist Georgia O'Keeffe; actress Jorja Fox

Georgina

(English) a form of Georgia.

Image: Georgina paints the town as red as her hair. People say Georgina is a full-figured redhead who's gregarious, fun-loving, and always ready for a night on the town. She most likely has a quick wit to boot.

Famous Namesakes: Author Georgina Gentry

Geraldine

(German) mighty with a spear.

Image: Geraldine remembers being picked on so many years ago. This name makes people think of a gawky, geeky, and lonely old lady. In her youth, she may have been the brunt of bullies' jokes with her glasses and buckteeth. Those who give her a chance quickly learn she's a gracious and inviting soul.

Famous Namesakes: Actress Geraldine Sue Page; politician Geraldine Ferraro

Germaine

(French) from Germany.

Image: Germaine comes on strong. She's imagined as a smart-mouthed and enthusiastic African American woman with big brown eyes. Some find her to be rude and aggressive, but others say she's exciting and fun.

Famous Namesakes: Writer Germaine Greer

Ghita

(Italian) pearly.

Image: Ghita enjoys a night of family fun after she finishes her homework. She's imagined as a shy and unassuming schoolgirl who's studious and friendly in her own quiet way. Pretty and diminutive, she most likely comes from a close-knit Italian family.

Famous Namesakes: Actress Ghita Norby

Gillian

(Latin) a form of Jillian.

Image: Gillian's art exhibits get better—and weirder—each year. People envision Gillian as an artist with a wild, far-out imagination. She's most likely energetic and strong-willed when it comes to her career, but she's also a friendly person in general. Like Gillian Anderson of TV's *The X-Files*, she's pictured as a small, lovely redhead.

Famous Namesakes: Actress Gillian Anderson; singer Gillian Welch; actress Jillian Barberie

Gina

(Italian) a short form of Angelina, Eugenia, Regina, Virginia.

Image: Gina is a powerhouse. She's pictured as an in-charge and outspoken woman who's sure of herself. People also find her to be kind-hearted, perky, and well liked. Strong and fit, she may channel her energy as a cheerleader or aerobics instructor. No matter what, she's most likely the center of attention.

Famous Namesakes: Actress Gina Lollabridga; actress Geena Davis; actress Gina Gershon; actress Gina Rowlands

Ginger

(Latin) flower; spice.

Image: For the most part, Ginger leaves 'em guessing. Everyone agrees she's a redhead with pale, freckled skin. As for her personality, she may be a shy, hesitant follower; a bitter, bratty snob; or a wild, rebellious dropout.

Famous Namesakes: Dancer Ginger Rogers

Ginny

(English) a familiar form of Ginger, Virginia.

Image: Ginny is in touch with her inner child. She's thought to be sweet, playful, fun, and unfailingly optimistic. People best sum her up by saying she's filled with childlike wonder, but they also admit she's a bit naïve at times.

Famous Namesakes: Character Ginny Weasley (*Harry Potter* series)

Giovana

(Italian) a form of Jane.

Image: Not many waitresses can write Petrarchan sonnets like Giovana can. She's most often imagined as an Italian woman with a warm personality and a beautiful face. People imagine she's a lighthearted and capricious waitress by night, but she's a diligent college student studying poetry by day.

Famous Namesakes: Actress Giovanna Antonelli

Giselle

(German) pledge; hostage.

Image: Giselle is a nice girl who's easy to misread. Most people think Giselle is polite, quiet, and intelligent. She seems to have a slight arrogance about her, although that's most likely due to being so tight lipped. She's pictured a lot like supermodel Gisele Bündchen: pretty and skinny with chestnut hair and fair skin.

Famous Namesakes: Model Gisele Bündchen

Gladys

(Latin) small sword. (Irish) princess. (Welsh) a form of Claudia.

Image: Hear that? It's Gladys either complaining or gossiping. Gladys strikes people as a frumpy and frail grandma who's cranky, strict, and always complaining. She's most likely a busybody, full of mean gossip. Then again, a few people see a more lighthearted side to her, saying she's a funny and sweet lady (even if she does gripe now and then).

Famous Namesakes: Singer Gladys Knight; actress Gladys Cooper

Glenda

(Welsh) a form of Glenna.

Image: The first thing you notice is Glenda's smile. People say Glenda is a happy and sweet woman who's always smiling. And she seems to have a lot to be joyful about: She's said to be rich, elegant, and smart.

Famous Namesakes: Actress Glenda May Jackson

Glenna

(Irish) valley, glen.

Image: It's a tossup: Glenna may be kind, dull, or high class. Some believe she has a helpful, cheerful attitude and plenty of smiles. Others imagine she's prudish and quiet, if not boring. And a few suspect she's a smart and motivated socialite. In the end, though, everyone agrees she's blond, fit, and feminine.

Famous Namesakes: None

Gloria

(Latin) glory.

Image: Gloria is totally psyched about her entry in the Young Inventors Fair. People believe she loves school and particularly science, which means she's an unpopular geek. But that doesn't seem to stop her from being happy, hyperactive, and nice to whomever she meets. She's most often pictured as a Latina with dark hair and homely looks.

Famous Namesakes: Singer Gloria Estefan; singer Gloria Gaynor; activist Gloria Steinem

Glory

(Latin) a form of Gloria.

Image: With this name's image, the phrase "going for the glory" doesn't sound like a good idea. Glory is thought to be a ruthless backstabber who's constantly gossiping, sticking her nose in other people's business, and plotting her next conniving move. As for her appearance, she's said to be pretty, short, and stocky.

Famous Namesakes: Character Glory (*Buffy the Vampire Slayer*)

Grace

(Latin) graceful.

Image: If your name is a virtue, you have a lot to live up to. Grace is imagined as a compassionate and angelic woman who's dedicated, Christian, and—naturally—graceful. Pictured as slender and pretty with a nice smile, she's also known to be smart, well-spoken, and happy.

Famous Namesakes: Character Grace Adler (*Will & Grace*); actress Grace Kelly; singer Grace Slick; model Grace Jones; author Grace Paley

Gracie

(English) a familiar form of Grace.

Image: Gracie wants to save the world. She's regarded as a caring, considerate, and immensely sweet girl with an even sweeter smile. People feel this petite blond is polite, bright, and ambitious in her goals to help others.

Famous Namesakes: Comedian Gracie Allen

Greer

(Scottish) vigilant.

Image: Greer belongs to the horsy set. People see Greer as a well-bred, attractive woman who comes from old money. Naturally athletic, she's most likely a great equestrian. People disagree whether she's friendly or snobby.

Famous Namesakes: Actress Greer Garson; star kid Grier Hammond Henchy

Greta

(German) a short form of Gretchen, Margaret.

Image: Greta has success on her mind. She's imagined to be determined, strong-minded, and goal oriented. This mindset seems to bring out her creative, unique talents, but it also brings out her stubborn, bossy side. She's described as a stocky and blond German.

Famous Namesakes: News anchor Greta van Susteren; actress Greta Garbo

Gretchen

(German) a form of Margaret.

Image: Gretchen feels more comfortable working with algorithms than with other people. She's seen as a smart and studious woman who's awkward, geeky, but still sweet. She may be German and have either blond or red hair.

Famous Namesakes: Actress Gretchen Mol; singer Gretchen Wilson; news anchor Gretchen Carlson

 **★ Star Kids**

Grier Hammond

Want some laughs at your party? Invite Grier Hammond. People consider her to be a bubbly schmoozer who's a funny and witty addition to any get-together. She may even be a comedian by profession. So maybe in about twenty years, can we expect to see Grier Hammond, daughter of actress Brooke Shields and TV writer Chris Henchy, doing stand-up?

Gretel

(German) a form of Margaret.

Image: Gretel is, of course, a young fairytale heroine, which is why this name has a childlike image. People consider Gretel to be a naïve young girl with blond braids and rosy, chubby cheeks. She's most likely gentle, shy, polite, and quietly sweet.

Famous Namesakes: Character Gretel (*Hansel & Gretel*)

Guadalupe

(Arabic) river of black stones.

Image: Guadalupe has a kind and happy heart. This name calls to mind a caring, generous, and soft-spoken Latina who's short and plump. She's considered to be quite cheerful, and she has an ever-present smile to prove it.

Famous Namesakes: Religious icon Our Lady of Guadalupe; president Guadalupe Victoria

Guinevere

(French, Welsh) white wave; white phantom.

Image: In the King Arthur legend, Guinevere's love affair with Lancelot caused a great deal of strife. For this reason, most people think of Guinevere as a vulnerable and fragile woman who has come undone. She's described as a slender, ethereal beauty with long hair. People believe that under the sorrow, she's a gentle and smart woman.

Famous Namesakes: Legendary figure Guinevere

Gwen

(Welsh) a short form of Guinevere, Gwendolyn.

Image: This name rocks steady because of pop icon and fashion designer Gwen Stefani. Gwen reminds most people of a bold and strong-willed blond musician. Some folks, however, say Gwen is rude, snobby, and greedy.

Famous Namesakes: Singer Gwen Stefani; character Gwen Stacy (*Spider-Man*)

Gwendolyn

(Welsh) white wave; white browed; new moon.

Image: Gwendolyn hides a unique personality behind her bashfulness. She's thought to be a quiet and delicate girl whose shyness may make her a loner. Those who get to know her say she's smart, sweet, and strong-minded. She may be weirdly creative as well. Blond and feminine, she's described as a pixie with a button nose.

Famous Namesakes: Poet Gwendolyn Brooks

Gwyneth

(Welsh) a form of Gwendolyn.

Image: Gwyneth seems to have her pretty nose in the air. Many people believe she's rude and full of herself, although they also admit she's quite sophisticated and smart. Other people imagine she's quiet, prudish, and boring. Not surprisingly, she's pictured much like actress Gwyneth Paltrow: blond, tall, and beautiful.

Famous Namesakes: Actress Gwyneth Paltrow

Haley

(Scandinavian) heroine.

Image: Haley's high spirits are endearing—to most. She's pictured as a bouncy, perky, and happy-go-lucky cutie with blond hair and blue eyes. Many people find her to be lovable, but others say her loud, high-strung demeanor is annoying, especially because she can be temperamental and gossipy.

Famous Namesakes: Actress Hayley Mills; swimmer Hayley Lewis; actress Hayley Duff

Hallie

(Scandinavian) a form of Haley.

Image: Hallie is a merry gal. People see her as a heartfelt and helpful girl brimming with cheer and wit. She's said to be really cute with blond hair, green eyes, and a glowing smile.

Famous Namesakes: Actress Hallie Kate Eisenberg; character Hallie Parker (*The Parent Trap*); actress Halle Berry

Hanna

(Hebrew) a form of Hannah.

Image: Hanna is a high-powered dynamo. Most people imagine Hanna as a determined and successful business executive with smarts, grace, and charm. She's also thought to be beautiful and sophisticated, which no doubt is a plus. Some, however, say she's meek and too agreeable.

Famous Namesakes: Biblical figure Hannah; actress Daryl Hannah; television character Hannah Montana

Hannah

(Hebrew) gracious.

Image: Hannah has the skills and the heart to make a difference. She's imagined as a sweet, earnest, and compassionate girl with a longing to make the world a better place. People say she's wise beyond her years, full of personality, and ready to work hard. In addition, she's described as pretty and delicate with golden brown hair.

Famous Namesakes: Biblical figure Hannah; actress Daryl Hannah; television character Hannah Montana

Harmony

(Latin) harmonious.

Image: People see the literal meaning with this name's image. They imagine Harmony as a beautiful, soft-spoken, and emotionally sensitive woman who seeks harmony in her life. She's probably happy, polite, easygoing, and religious. She's also known to seek harmony through music. People suspect she has a lovely singing voice.

Famous Namesakes: Character Harmony Kendall (*Buffy the Vampire Slayer*)

Girls

Harriet

(French) ruler of the household. (English) a form of Henrietta.

Image: Harriet Nelson will always be one of America's favorite TV mothers, thanks to *The Adventures of Ozzie and Harriet*. So it's no surprise people picture Harriet as a caring and thoughtful mom with a quick wit, happy outlook, and old-fashioned style. A few people think she's pushy, as any mom must be from time to time.

Famous Namesakes: Actress Harriet Nelson; abolitionist Harriet Tubman; author Harriet Beecher Stowe; charcter Harriet Oleson (*Little House on the Prairie*);

Hasana

(Swahili) she arrived first.

Image: People can agree on only Hasana's ethnicity—and even that agreement is shaky. People imagine Hasana comes from an exotic ethnic background—whether Asian, Arabic, Latin, or African—and she has dark skin and hair. Beyond her heritage, people can't make up their minds: Some say she's loud, big-headed, and sleazy; others sense she's quiet, shy, and kind.

Famous Namesakes: None

Hayley

(English) hay meadow.

Image: Hayley is full of life, surprises, and energy. She's said to be fun-loving, spontaneous, and spunky, and she may be the first to admit she's also hyper. People say this petite young girl is very popular and cute, which makes her a natural trendsetter.

Famous Namesakes: Actress Hayley Mills; swimmer Hayley Lewis; actress Hayley Duff

 **★ Star Kids**

Hazel Patricia

Hazel Patricia doesn't even take joy in a juicy scoop. When people hear this name, they imagine a gruff and stern woman who works as a reporter for a local newspaper. She's said to be quiet, which may make her seem sneaky. Does this image mean there's a future in journalism for Hazel Patricia, daughter of actress Julia Roberts and cinematographer Danny Moder?

Hazel

(English) hazelnut tree; commanding authority.

Image: Hazel is a modest woman with modest traits. People think she's a small brunette, but they can't decide if she's sociable or shy. Either way, she's kind, gentle, and down-to-earth. People also imagine she's a middle-aged woman with ordinary looks.

Famous Namesakes: Star kid Hazel Patricia Moder

Heather

(English) flowering heather.

Image: Heather is your typical snob in the popular crowd. People think she's stuck-up, arrogant, spiteful, and jealous. She may be a cheerleader with her energy, smiles, and fit figure, but many people find her to be annoying and self-centered

Famous Namesakes: Activist Heather Mills; actress Heather Locklear; actress Heather Graham

Hedda

(German) battler.

Image: In many ways, Hedda is like a brick wall. She's described as a big-boned, tall, and muscular woman who's stern, overbearing, and stubborn. People also believe she's intelligent, loudly opinionated, and strong-willed.

Famous Namesakes: Gossip columnist Hedda Hopper; fiction character Hedda Gabler

Hedwig

(German) warrior.

Image: Hedwig aptly means "warrior." She's pictured as a stout, broad woman and a wise and protective mother. Of German descent, she's most likely happy and confident in her ability to look after her family.

Famous Namesakes: Character Hedwig (*Hedwig and the Angry Inch*); character Hedwig (*Harry Potter* series)

Heidi

(German) a short form of Adelaide.

Image: Heidi evokes a wide range of images. She may be a generous and sweet friend, a snobby and self-absorbed daddy's girl, or a sarcastic and rebellious dropout. As for her looks, people closely match her to supermodel Heidi Klum: She's thought to be a spindly and pretty blond with a lovely smile. She may even have a German accent.

Famous Namesakes: Model Heidi Klum; madam Heidi Fleiss; fiction character Heidi

Helen

(Greek) light.

Image: If only Helen's old schoolmates could see her now. In her younger years, Helen was most likely quiet and studious, which made her seem dorky. But now in her mature years, she's known to be a self-assured and successful leader who's witty, charming, loving, and helpful. Attractive even with wrinkles, she seems to be a confident woman.

Famous Namesakes: Actress Helen Hunt; mythological figure Helen of Troy; advocate Helen Keller; actress Helen Hayes; singer Helen Reddy; actress Helen Mirren

Helene

(French) a form of Helen.

Image: Helene may be refined, but she's also aloof. She's said to be an elegant, sophisticated, and perhaps even queenly French beauty with dark hair and a dark complexion. Unfortunately, she's also thought to be cold and snobby—even though aloofness may be how she hides her shyness.

Famous Namesakes: Poet Helene Johnson; mythological figure Helene

Helga

(German) pious. (Scandinavian) a form of Olga.

Image: Certain names carry some *heft*, and Helga is one of them. Everyone says Helga is a brutish, stern, huge, and imposing mountain of a woman who hails from *Deutschland*. She's very likely loud, overbearing, manly, and scary.

Famous Namesakes: Character Helga Hufflepuff (*Harry Potter* series)

Heloise

(French) a form of Louise.

Image: Heloise is hard to get along with. She's thought to be an old, dowdy woman who's unsocial, bookish, and grouchy. To make matters worse, she's also said to be stubborn and prudish, not to mention mean.

Famous Namesakes: Historical figure Heloise; advice columnist Heloise Evans

Henrietta

(English) ruler of the household.

Image: Henrietta has two distinctly different images. Most people see Henrietta as an introverted, awkward, and much-teased student teacher. Others, however, see her as a bossy, witchy, and snobby sophisticate. In either case, she's pictured as a heavyset fiftysomething with dark hair.

Famous Namesakes: Gymnast Henrietta Ónodi

Hermosa

(Spanish) beautiful.

Image: When help is needed, Hermosa will either pitch in or slink away. Many people regard her as a kind, ambitious, and smart woman who's always willing to lend a hand. In some situations, she may even be brave in her desire to assist others. But some suspect Hermosa isn't ambitious at all. Instead, they say she's lazy, complacent, sloppy, and downright obnoxious.

Famous Namesakes: None

Hilary

(Greek) cheerful, merry.

Image: The general public holds differing opinions about former First Lady and current Senator Hillary Rodham Clinton. Although the name is spelled differently, Hilary is thought to be an opinionated and ambitious woman who some people find bossy and annoying. She's well dressed with short blond hair.

Famous Namesakes: Politician Hillary Rodham Clinton; actress Hilary Duff; actress Hilary Burton; actress Hilary Swank

Holly

(English) holly tree.

Image: Most people think Holly is an overly sweet, optimistic, and open-minded girl, despite her poor upbringing. It's hard to tell if she's smart or flighty, but she's certainly thought to be salt of the earth. People picture her looking a lot like actress Holly Hunter, with red hair and a thin figure.

Famous Namesakes: Actress Holly Hunter; actress Holly Robinson-Peete

Honora

(Latin) honorable.

Image: People picture Honora in many complex ways: Some believe she's a caring and good-natured woman who tends to be a little weird. A few say she's a witchy and selfish snob who talks way too loudly and way too much. Still others contend she's shy and quiet, either because she's polite or because she's cowardly. At least people agree Honora is a homely fashion disaster with pale skin and dark hair.

Famous Namesakes: None

Hope

(English) hope.

Image: Hope is as gentle a creature as you will find. She's thought of as a goodhearted and soft-spoken lady who wouldn't hurt a fly. With a delicate frame, she's said to be a peaceful, faithful churchgoer. Some people, however, may think all that tranquility and overwhelming kindness makes her dull.

Famous Namesakes: Comedian Bob Hope; actress Hope Davis; actress Hope Lange

Hortense

(Latin) gardener.

Image: Hortense is so joyless, she's scary to be near. People consider Hortense to be bitter, angry, rude, and downright intimidating. Overweight and unattractive, she comes across as a sour and prudish outcast no one dares to be around.

Famous Namesakes: Author Hortense Calisher

Huberta

(German) bright mind; bright spirit.

Image: Huberta's enthusiasm sometimes comes across a little strong. She's imagined as a homely, rotund, and frumpy woman who's strong and sensible. She's typically joyous, but as a traditional, family-centered mother, she may be overbearing and even rude at times.

Famous Namesakes: None

Ida

(German) hardworking. (English) prosperous.

Image: You can picture Ida sitting in her rocking chair with a cup of Postum in hand, a cat in her lap, and a frown on her face. People say Ida is a wrinkly, hunchbacked granny who may have been a librarian in her younger years but who now lives alone with her cats. She's said to be insecure, prudish, and stern, which may explain why she's a loner.

Famous Namesakes: Activist Ida B. Wells; journalist Ida Tarbell

Ilene

(Irish) a form of Helen.

Image: Ilene's intelligence overwhelms her personality. She's thought to be a studious and hardworking problem solver who's well read, inquisitive, witty, focused, and perhaps a tad bit nerdy. People do say this brainiac is loving and kind, too. She likely has brown hair and brown eyes to match.

Famous Namesakes: Television producer Ilene Chaiken; actress Ilene Graff

Iman

(Arabic) believer.

Image: Somalian-born supermodel Iman is one of the world's most beautiful women, and this name's image clearly evokes her. People say Iman is a determined, confident, and successful African model. She's very likely gorgeous, tall, and skinny, and many people find her to have a regal quality. Then again, other people find her to be arrogant.

Famous Namesakes: Princess Iman bint al-Abdullah; model Iman Abdulmajid

Imogene

(Latin) image, likeness.

Image: Imogene may have a straight-laced profession, but that doesn't mean she can't dish with the best of them. Imogene is imagined as a warm and friendly older woman who may be a schoolmarm or a scientist. People suspect she's a busybody, and at times, her nosy gossip can be funny and animated.

Famous Namesakes: Actress Imogene Coco; singer Imogen Heap

India

(Sanskrit) river.

Image: India lifts her strong brand of leadership to celebrity status. She calls to mind a reserved yet emotionally strong woman. She's viewed as a brave, peacemaking leader with a starlike quality. People believe she has perfect beauty and dark skin.

Famous Namesakes: Singer India Arie

Inga

(Scandinavian) a short form of Ingrid.

Image: Inga has a soft side, but she can be hardnosed when she needs to be. She's said to be a Scandinavian woman who's tall and, of course, blond and blue-eyed. People say she's sensitive, sweet, and scholarly, but she may also be surprisingly stubborn.

Famous Namesakes: Actress Inga Swenson; speed skater Inga Artamonova

Ingrid

(Scandinavian) hero's daughter; beautiful daughter.

Image: Ingrid is a cold character. She's said to be a determined, willful, and intelligent woman. Some, however, feel she's domineering, humorless, and aloof. Her physical description links to silver-screen star Ingrid Bergman: People picture her as an elegant and statuesque Scandinavian blond with blue eyes.

Famous Namesakes: Actress Ingrid Bergman

Iolanthe

(English) a form of Yolanda.

Image: Folks know little about shy Iolanthe, so they unfortunately make things up about her. She's depicted as a gentle, sensitive, and bashful loner who many say is strange or weird. Although she's most likely a sweet and thoughtful woman, people gossip that she may be into witchcraft (perhaps a warped allusion to Iolanthe, the eponymous fairy from Gilbert and Sullivan's opera).

Famous Namesakes: Opera character Iolanthe

Irene

(Greek) peaceful.

Image: You won't catch Irene taking part in any wild, immature behavior. Most people think of Irene as kind, practical, and ladylike, but her conservative demeanor makes her a wee bit boring. She's thought to be generally unattractive, but she does have a nice, toothy smile. Taking a different view, some people think of Irene as a crude and mean liar.

Famous Namesakes: Singer Irene Cara; actress Irene Dunn

Iris

(Greek) rainbow.

Image: Iris has a bright, creative mind. She's described as a brilliant woman who's either reserved and timid or sassy and charming. Like novelist Iris Murdoch, she's thought to be a creative artist with something great to offer the world. People imagine she's a delicate and pale black-haired beauty, and they also find her to be kind, elegant, and wealthy.

Famous Namesakes: Mythological figure Iris; writer Iris Murdoch

Irma

(Latin) a form of Erma. (German) a short form of Irmgaard.

Image: Irma is mousy in both demeanor and appearance. Most people think she's an old woman with varicose veins, glasses, and gray hair pulled tightly in a bun. She's considered to be boring and nerdy, and she usually keeps to herself. Some people suspect she's kind, but she's also somewhat nervous and clumsy in social situations. It doesn't help that she's overweight and unattractive.

Famous Namesakes: Singer Irma Thomas; actress Irma P. Hall

Isabel

(Spanish) consecrated to God.

Image: Isabel has inner and outer beauty. Most people see Isabel as an angelic and radiant woman who's happy, sensitive, and whimsical. People also believe she's quite beautiful with piercing blue eyes and either black or blond hair. She's said to be talented, intelligent, and refined, and she can take charge when it comes to achieving her goals.

Famous Namesakes: Author Isabel Allende; character Isabel Archer (*The Portrait of a Lady*); actress Isabel Sanford; queen Isabel of Spain

Isabella

(Italian) a form of Isabel.

Image: With Isabella of Castile as a namesake, this name's image has queenly grace and class. People use words like *prim*, *proper*, *stylish*, *elegant*, and *regal* to describe Isabella, and she's pictured as a model-like glamour queen. Some even call her a prima donna, but others say she can be charming and fun when she lets her hair down.

Famous Namesakes: Actress Isabella Rossellini; queen Isabella of Castile; model Izabella Miko

Isi

(Spanish) a short form of Isabel.

Image: Isi is a little out there. She's thought to be an eccentric with odd clothes and weird creativity. Some people find her to be friendly, but she still gets teased for being a dork. She's most likely short and pretty.

Famous Namesakes: Character Dr. Izzie Stevens (*Grey's Anatomy*)

Italia

(Italian) from Italy.

Image: It's too bad Italia's beauty is only skin-deep. Italia is primarily regarded as a snobby and condescending model who's sexy, olive-skinned, and incredibly rich. A few people imagine she's kind and smart, but others say she's naïve yet rude.

Famous Namesakes: None

Ivory

(Latin) made of ivory.

Image: Ivory is a real sweetheart whose looks live up to her name. She's considered to be loving and giving as well as soft-spoken, gentle, and polite. It's understandable that people picture her as an extremely pale blond who's dainty and pretty.

Famous Namesakes: Film director James Ivory; professional wrestler Ivory; basketball player Ivory Latta

Ivy

(English) ivy tree.

Image: Ivy is a sassy, unique spirit that everyone loves. She strikes people as a kind and fun-loving girl who's popular, spunky, alternative, and cool. A feminine beauty, she's said to be resourceful and committed. And thanks to the plant of the same name, she may be a gardener.

Famous Namesakes: Character Poison Ivy (*Batman*)

Jackie

(American) a familiar form of Jacqueline.

Image: Jackie is outgoing—that is, she's usually *out going* to many hotspots. She strikes people as a popular and cool young woman who finds herself at many parties and clubs. Although some say she's personable and easygoing, others find her to be arrogant, snobby, and a little too strong at times. She's described as curvy with dark eyes and a big smile.

Famous Namesakes: Film character Jackie Brown; character Jackie Harris (*Roseanne*)

Jaclyn

(American) a short form of Jacqueline.

Image: Jaclyn swings between being forceful and being graceful. She's most likely determined and opinionated to the point of being overbearing. Thankfully, people say she also has a dignified, refined side that balances her bossy tendencies. She's portrayed as a brunette with a sporty figure.

Famous Namesakes: First lady Jacqueline Kennedy Onassis; actress Jacqueline Bisset; actress Jaclyn Smith

Jacqueline

(French) supplanter, substitute; little Jacqui.

Image: Jacqueline Kennedy Onassis is one of the most iconic women of the twentieth century, so it's only fitting that this name evokes her image. Jacqueline is imagined as a poised and elegant woman with a warm heart, a charming personality, a quiet intelligence, and a timeless beauty.

Famous Namesakes: First lady Jacqueline Kennedy Onassis; actress Jacqueline Bisset; actress Jaclyn Smith

Jada

(Hebrew) wise. (Spanish) a form of Jade.

Image: Most people see Jada as a hardworking and confident woman, although she may be blunt and unrefined at times. Her spunk and spirit seem to make her popular with others. She's most likely a pretty and petite African American woman, like actress Jada Pinkett Smith.

Famous Namesakes: Actress Jada Pinkett Smith

Jade

(Spanish) jade.

Image: Jade is as exquisite as the jewel she's named after. People imagine her as a carefree, fun, and sometimes wild woman with exotic features and olive skin. She may be an artist, she's most likely worldly, and there's a chance she's someone's trophy wife.

Famous Namesakes: Jewelry designer Jade Jagger

Jaime

(French) I love.

Image: Jaime is perky and brave, but that doesn't mean she walks on the wild side. People say Jaime is a friendly and vibrant girl who's funny, smart, and adventurous. That said, she's also known to be well-rounded and normal, so she never gets herself into too much trouble.

Famous Namesakes: Actress Jaime Pressley; actress Jaime King

Jana

(Hebrew) gracious, merciful. (Slavic) a form of Jane.

Image: Jana is a combination of brains and fun. People picture her as a pretty and petite brunette who may be slim or full-figured. She's said to be fun, witty, smart, and no doubt popular.

Famous Namesakes: Tennis player Jana Novotná; model Jana Svenson

Janae

(American) a form of Jane. (Hebrew) a form of Jana.

Image: Janae will strike up a conversation with anyone—no matter what language is spoken. People imagine this African American woman is sweet, goodhearted, and highly sociable. They believe Janae is full of smiles and jokes, and she's spunky and hip to boot. Always eager to interact with as many people as she can, this smart cookie is multilingual as well.

Famous Namesakes: None

Jane

(Hebrew) God is gracious.

Image: "Plain Jane" is right. People describe Jane with the following words: *reserved, modest, sensible, steady, pleasant, lonely,* and, of course, *plain.* She's most likely thin and tall, but with no other distinguishing features. Some people think she may yearn for love or excitement.

Famous Namesakes: Journalist Jane Pauley; actress Jayne Mansfield; actress Jane Seymour; actress Jane Fonda; author Jane Austen; fiction character Jane Eyre; actress Jane Russell

Janelle

(French) a form of Jane.

Image: Janelle is flamboyant, and she doesn't care what others think. Most people imagine Janelle as an upbeat extrovert who's cool, sassy, and self-secure. Perhaps a writer or artist, she's said to be hardworking and determined, but she always has her wild side. She's pictured as cute with a big smile and black hair.

Famous Namesakes: Model Janelle Perry

Janet

(English) a form of Jane.

Image: Janet is a natural choice for parents who need a babysitter. She's described as a helpful and caring girl who's pretty, trustworthy, and funny. Quite simply, people say she's the all-American girl next door.

Famous Namesakes: Singer Janet Jackson; actress Janet Leigh; attorney general Janet Reno; author Janet Evanovich

Janie

(English) a familiar form of Jane.

Image: Janie is either very *good* or very *bad*. She may be an innocent, jovial, and loving sweetheart. But she also may be a heartless, spoiled, and troubled homewrecker. Either way, she's most likely a petite brunette with big, sparkling green eyes.

Famous Namesakes: Character Janie Crawford (*Their Eyes Were Watching God*); theatre actress Janie Sell

Janine

(French) a form of Jane.

Image: Although the spelling of her name is different, actress Janeane Garofalo is whom many people think of when they hear the name Janine. They say Janine is hilarious, snarky, smart, high-strung, and perhaps bossy. She's likely a brunette who's cute in a plain way. But others think she's a sexy, busty, and naughty porn star like Janine Lindemulder.

Famous Namesakes: Actress Janine Turner; comedian Janeane Garofalo

Janis

(Hebrew, English) a form of Janice.

Image: Where's Bobby McGee when you need him? People can't hear the name Janis and not think of Janis Joplin: They say Janis is a wild, crazy, and cool singer with a hippie lifestyle and, unfortunately, a drug and alcohol problem. To complete the image, she's imagined with long, brown hair and a rather unattractive face.

Famous Namesakes: Singer Janis Joplin; model Janice Dickinson; singer Janis Ian

Janna

(Arabic) harvest of fruit. (Hebrew) a short form of Johana.

Image: Janna is fun to be around. People say she's kind, cheerful, and humorous—a very social gal. She's likely smart and intelligent as well as attractive and tall.

Famous Namesakes: Model Jana Svenson; tennis player Jana Novotná

Jasmine

(Persian) jasmine flower.

Image: Jasmine's personality is most likely as sweet as the scent of her namesake flower. Many people think Jasmine is a friendly and smiley woman who's playful, caring, and observant. But others contend she's a narcissistic and prissy snob or a shy and fragile wallflower. In any case, she's probably a dainty brunette with sexy looks. Of course, a few say she's a princess, like the heroine from Disney's *Aladdin*.

Famous Namesakes: Actress Jasmine Guy; character Princess Jasmine (*Aladdin*)

Jayne

(Hindi) victorious. (English) a form of Jane.

Image: Jayne is a total type A. She's organized, dependable, intelligent, and so tough that she sometimes intimidates others. People believe her appearance is just as well put together: She's thought to be attractive with beautiful black hair.

Famous Namesakes: Journalist Jane Pauley; actress Jayne Mansfield; actress Jane Seymour; actress Jane Fonda; author Jane Austen; fiction character Jane Eyre; actress Jane Russell

Jean

(Scottish) God is gracious.

Image: Jean is usually a good person—she just can't resist scuttlebutt. Most people think Jean is an intelligent, goodhearted, and religious woman. She's likely older with curly but mousy hair and a plump figure. Then again, some people suspect she can be bossy and gossipy from time to time.

Famous Namesakes: Novelist Jean Rhys; actress Jean Simmons; actress Gene Tierney; actress Jean Stapleton; actress Jean Harlow

Girls

Jeanette

(French) a form of Jean.

Image: Jeanette's life isn't always easy, and neither is her personality. When people hear the name Jeanette, they think of a moody and blunt blue-collar mother. With her strong personality, she can come across as stubborn and even mean, but more often than not, she can discipline with love and see silver linings.

Famous Namesakes: Actress Jeanette MacDonald; novelist Jeanette Winterson

Jelena

(Russian) a form of Helen.

Image: Jelena lives a life that everyone can learn from. The first thing people notice about Jelena is how smiley and friendly she is—she seems to get along with everyone. The next thing they notice is how gorgeous she is with her dark hair. She's also said to be a strong-willed, take-charge woman, but her spiritual faith gives her a centered, balanced outlook on life.

Famous Namesakes: Tennis player Jelena Jankovi; tennis player Jelena Doki

Jena

(Arabic) a form of Jenna.

Image: Jena is a precocious young lady. She's regarded as a dainty and cute honor-roll student who's both smart and sweet. She seems to be fun-loving and eager to laugh. An only child, she's spoiled by her loving parents, but she's not bratty.

Famous Namesakes: Actress Jena Malone; actress Jenna Elfman; actress Jenna Fisher

Jenay

(American, Hebrew) a form of Janae.

Image: Jenay was born to perform. She's most often viewed as a creative, artistic woman—perhaps a dancer or singer—with a toned, tall figure and pretty looks. People imagine she's personable and popular as well as quite intelligent.

Famous Namesakes: None

Jenna

(Arabic) small bird. (Welsh) a short form of Jennifer.

Image: Jenna Elfman played a carefree child of hippies on TV's *Dharma & Greg*. Perhaps this is why Jenna is thought to be a spirited and humorous party girl with a kind heart. She's also most likely attractive, intelligent, and environmentally conscious.

Famous Namesakes: Actress Jena Malone; actress Jenna Elfman; actress Jenna Fisher

Jennifer

(Welsh) white wave; white phantom.

Image: Jennifer is ready to take on any challenge. Most people imagine Jennifer as intelligent, successful, and eager to tackle risks with a good attitude and high spirits. Socially, some sense she's friendly and caring, but others imagine she's a preppy snob from the "in" crowd.

Famous Namesakes: Actress Jennifer Aniston; actress Jennifer Lopez; actress Jennifer Garner; actress Jennifer Connelly; actress Jennifer Tilly; actress Jennifer Jason Leigh; actress Jennifer Love Hewitt; actress Jennifer Hudson; author Jennifer Weiner

Jenny

(Welsh) a familiar form of Jennifer.

Image: Jenny is filled with good spirits. She's overwhelmingly described as sunny, fun-loving, perky, and happy to go with the flow. In addition, she's thought to have sandy blond hair, a petite figure, and a beautiful, easy smile. No wonder she's said to be liked by everyone.

Famous Namesakes: Talk show host Jenny Jones; actress Jennie Garth; actress Jenny McCarthy

Jeri

(American) a short form of Jeraldine.

Image: Jeri leaves people guessing. They aren't sure if she's a vivacious and fun party girl, an angry and vengeful schemer, or a boring and lame nerd. People tend to imagine Jeri as curvy and short with red hair.

Famous Namesakes: Actress Jeri Ryan; singer Geri Halliwell

Jessamine

(French) a form of Jasmine.

Image: Jessamine lives in the lap of luxury. She's envisioned as a snobby and self-centered rich woman who wears diamonds and fashionable clothes. She's said to be beautiful with dark hair and a tall, slender physique. Some may say she can be romantic and spirited, but others can't look past her spoiled self-absorption.

Famous Namesakes: None

Jessica

(Hebrew) wealthy.

Image: Jessica bubbles with personality, but she's far from perfect. People think Jessica is flirty, energetic, and smart, but they fear she's a bit untrustworthy because she's a gossip. She may also be conceited and materialistic. Other people have an entirely different view, thinking of Jessica as a fearless and powerful leader.

Famous Namesakes: Singer Jessica Simpson; actress Jessica Lange; character Jessica Rabbit (*Who Framed Roger Rabbit?*); actress Jessica Biel; actress Jessica Alba; model Jessica Stam

Jessie

(Hebrew) a short form of Jessica. (Scottish) a form of Janet.

Image: Thanks to Jessie the Yodeling Cowgirl of *Toy Story 2*, this name's image has a rugged sense of adventure. Jessie is pictured as a happy-go-lucky and cheerful country tomboy. She's also thought to be smart, bold, spunky, and mischievous. As for her looks, she's a cute red-head or brunette with a lanky, athletic body.

Famous Namesakes: Singer Jessie Daniels

Jezebel

(Hebrew) unexalted; impure.

Image: Because of Jezebel, the infamous biblical figure, this name connotes any wicked woman. Therefore, Jezebel is thought to be a heartless, conniving, and evil woman who's trashy, spoiled, selfish, and stupid. She's pictured as exotically beautiful with dark features.

Famous Namesakes: Biblical figure Jezebel

Jill

(English) a short form of Jillian.

Image: Jill's smiles say a lot about her personality. She's imagined as a sweet and caring brunette with a curious mind and cheerful outlook. People believe she's always smiling, although that may mean she's a bit flighty.

Famous Namesakes: Actress Jill Hennessy; actress Jill Clayburgh; singer Jill Scott

Jillian

(Latin) youthful.

Image: Jillian is a triple threat: She's described as attractive, intelligent, and lovable. She's also considered to be friendly, soft-spoken, and funny. Some people imagine she's an independent woman who marries late in life—if ever.

Famous Namesakes: Actress Jillian Barberie; actress Gillian Anderson; singer Gillian Welch

Jo

(American) a short form of Joana, Jolene, Josephine.

Image: Jo has a rugged appeal perhaps because her name sounds masculine. People see Jo as a rough 'n' tough tomboy or country gal. She's likely temperamental, loud, and independent, but many see a loving softness to her as well—much like Jo March of *Little Women*.

Famous Namesakes: Character Jo March (*Little Women*); character Jo Polniaczek (*The Facts of Life*)

Joan

(Hebrew) God is gracious.

Image: The exposé *Mommie Dearest* put actress Joan Crawford in an unfavorable light. This name evokes the same image of a brassy, demanding, and perhaps intimidating older woman. Joan is thought to be prudish, bad tempered, and self-centered—definitely not mother material. Those not thinking of Joan Crawford imagine a caring, smart, but gossipy woman.

Famous Namesakes: Actress Joan Allen; actress Joan Crawford; saint Joan of Arc; musician Joan Jett; comedian Joan Rivers; singer Joan Baez; actress Joan Collins

Joanna

(English) a form of Joan.

Image: Joanna will either stab you in the back, regale you with her knowledge, or buy you a beer at the honky-tonk. Some people regard Joanna as quick-tempered, two-faced, and mean spirited. Others say she's highly educated and dry. Then there are those who imagine her to be a loud country girl without any common sense. She may have dark hair, a stocky build, and glasses.

Famous Namesakes: Biblical figure Joanna; singer Joanna Newsom; actress Joanna Lumley; model Joanna Krupa

Jocelyn

(Latin) joyous.

Image: Jocelyn's good looks may or may not be matched with a good personality. Most people say Jocelyn is a stunning dark-haired beauty with olive skin. She's thought to be charming, well liked, and caring. Some people, however, think of her as an uppity snob.

Famous Namesakes: Singer Jocelyn Brown; surgeon general Jocelyn Elders; socialite Jocelyn Wildenstein

Jodi

(American) a familiar form of Judith.

Image: Jodi is one tomboy who likes to be in charge. People agree Jodi is a sporty gal with auburn hair and mostly boys for friends. At times, she can be self-centered and bossy, not to mention sarcastic. It's unclear whether she's thin or stocky, but she's probably short.

Famous Namesakes: Writer Jodi Picoult; actress Jodie Foster; singer Jody Watley

Jody

(American) a familiar form of Judith.

Image: Jody has people split into two camps: On one side, people say she's quiet, boring, and sensitive. On the other side, people insist she's loud, crazy, and outspoken. Both camps seem to agree she's a gangly, athletic blond.

Famous Namesakes: Singer Jody Watley; actress Jodie Foster; writer Jodi Picoult

Jolene

(Hebrew) God will add, God will increase. (English) a form of Josephine.

Image: Jolene works hard all day, but she knows how to kick up her heels when the whistle blows. She strikes people as a boisterous, cheerful, and friendly working-class gal. She most likely has Southern country charm and a strong, honest work ethic.

Famous Namesakes: Actress Jolene Blalock

Jolie

(French) pretty.

Image: True to her name's meaning, Jolie is "pretty" on the inside and out. She's thought to be a beautiful girl who brings out the best in others and has a great curiosity about life. People believe she's sweet and adventurous, and she's perhaps a talented artist. She always seems to have a smile on her face.

Famous Namesakes: Actress Angelina Jolie; singer Jolie Holland

Joni

(American) a familiar form of Joan.

Image: Joni is imagined as a hardworking and determined woman. Because of her strong focus, she's probably slow to warm up to people, but she's friendly, caring, and fun-loving once you get to know her. She may be short and a little plump.

Famous Namesakes: Singer Joni Mitchell; character Joanie Cunningham (*Happy Days*)

Jordan

(Hebrew) descending.

Image: When people hear this name, they can't help but think of a female version of sports legend Michael Jordan. They say Jordan is a talented basketball player with dark hair and a tall, fit physique. She's likely to be friendly, smart, hip, humorous—but also egotistical.

Famous Namesakes: Actress Jordan Ladd; model Jordan

Josephine

(French) a form of Joseph.

Image: Josephine's inner strength is rivaled only by her beauty. Josephine is viewed as a determined, willful, and independent woman who knows how to take care of herself and who stands up for what's right. Dark and beautiful, many people find her to be sexy. It's unclear whether she's quiet or outgoing.

Famous Namesakes: Historical figure Josephine de Beauharnais; singer Josephine Baker

Josie

(Hebrew) a familiar form of Josephine.

Image: It's hard to separate this name from the lead character of *Josie and the Pussycats*, comic book or film. People picture Josie as a spunky, cool, and wild redhead with a big smile. She's said to be kind and caring, which, coupled with her perkiness, makes her quite popular.

Famous Namesakes: Character Josie (*Josie and the Pussycats*); model Josie Maran; actress Josie Bissett

Journey

(English) journey.

Image: Is it any wonder that Journey has wanderlust? People imagine she's a free-spirited hippie who loves to take adventures around the world. This tall brunette is known to be energetic and silly, but also wise and graceful. Then again, some people suspect her "journey" merely led her to live on the beach, where she's unemployed and careless.

Famous Namesakes: None

Joy

(Latin) joyous.

Image: Joy embraces her name. She's described as a joyful, content, and smiling young girl. She's also said to be fun-loving, caring, and sweet—most likely because she's so well loved by her overjoyed parents.

Famous Namesakes: Actress Joy Bryant; comedian Joy Behar

Joyce

(Latin) joyous.

Image: Joyce does the best she can to provide for her kids. She's considered to be a good-natured and kindhearted divorced mom living an ordinary life in the suburbs. She's probably smart, hardworking, and organized, making her a perfect bookkeeper. People picture her as overweight and middle-aged.

Famous Namesakes: Actress Joyce Dewitt; advice columnist Joyce Brothers; author Joyce Carol Oates

Juanita

(Spanish) a form of Jane, Joan.

Image: Juanita is a total diva. People imagine she has a bad attitude, a huge ego, and a nasty streak. A Latina with dark hair and dark skin, she's thought to be ambitious and smart, but she also has a flair for melodrama.

Famous Namesakes: Actress Juanita Moore; activist Juanita Craft

Judith

(Hebrew) praised.

Image: Opinions about Judith diverge. Some people think she's self-confident and strong, but others call her bossy and opinionated. Some say she's dignified, but others feel she's aloof. Some believe she's a dependable friend, while others suspect she's manipulative and sneaky. And some claim she's smart, but others argue she's a know-it-all.

Famous Namesakes: Actress Judith Light; author Judith Krantz; poet Judith Viorst

Judy

(Hebrew) a familiar form of Judith.

Image: Judy's mouth rarely gets a rest. She's described as a bubbly and talkative woman with old-fashioned values. On the bright side, she's said to be a social butterfly. On the not-so-bright side, some say she's an overbearing and verbose busybody. A few people perhaps think of Judy Garland and say she's a singing and acting star.

Famous Namesakes: Actress Judy Garland; author Judy Blume; singer Judy Collins; actress Judy Davis; actress Judi Dench; actress Judy Holliday; actress Judy Greer, character Judy Jetson (*The Jetsons*)

Julia

(Latin) youthful.

Image: Julia may be sweet, or she may be a little spicy. Some people find Julia to be sensitive, graceful, and perhaps even naïve. Others, however, imagine that she's sassy, funny, and stubborn. In either case, she's probably a "pretty woman" who's tall with brown hair and a nice smile just like actress Julia Roberts'.

Famous Namesakes: Actress Julia Stiles; actress Julia Ormond; actress Julia Roberts; chef Julia Child; actress Julia Louis-Dreyfuss; activist Julia Butterfly Hill

Juliana

(Czech, Spanish) a form of Julia.

Image: Juliana is a genial soul. People see her as a kind, graceful, and pleasant woman with a lot of confidence and social savoir-faire. This pretty, small brunette is said to be fun-loving and happy.

Famous Namesakes: Queen Juliana of the Netherlands; actress Juliana Marguiles

Julianne

(English) a form of Julia.

Image: Julianne may just be another snobby rich girl. She comes across as an elegant sophisticate who's stuck-up, spoiled, and standoffish. Some, however, believe she's kind and outgoing. It's fairly certain that she's beautiful, feminine, and slim.

Famous Namesakes: Actress Julianne Moore; actress Julianne Phillips

Julie

(English) a form of Julia.

Image: Julie is everyone's best friend. She's considered to be approachable, empathetic, and loyal. Her nonjudgmental, logical thinking often makes her a peacemaker. Some say she has a fun, mischievous side, but others find her to be proper. People agree she's a cutie with light-blue eyes.

Famous Namesakes: Actress Julie Andrews; actress Julie Newmar; actress Julie Christie

Juliet

(French) a form of Julia.

Image: Juliet, Juliet, wherefore art thou Juliet? Like the tragic heroine of Shakespeare's *Romeo and Juliet*, this Juliet is imagined as a pure-hearted and thoughtful young woman with beautiful, flowing dark hair. Born into a rich, noble family, she's said to be proper and regal.

Famous Namesakes: Character Juliet (*Romeo and Juliet*); actress Juliette Lewis; actress Juliette Binoche

June

(Latin) born in the sixth month.

Image: June Cleaver from TV's *Leave It to Beaver* epitomized the cheery side of motherhood in the '50s. To this day, many people think of June as a light, sparkling, and sweet mom with old-fashioned ideals. They picture her with blond wavy hair and a lovely smile. (Interestingly, a few people imagine her as very tired-looking with no makeup and scraggly hair, which is probably a more realistic depiction of motherhood.)

Famous Namesakes: Actress June Allyson; singer June Carter Cash; character June Cleaver (*Leave It to Beaver*)

Justine

(Latin) a form of Justin.

Image: Justine is the right woman for the job. She's thought to be an intelligent, assertive, and goal-oriented woman who's as sophisticated as she is well spoken. Some people say she amiable and funny, but others believe she's spoiled and distant.

Famous Namesakes: Actress Justine Bateman; musician Justine Frischmann

Kacey

(Irish) brave. (American) a form of Casey.

Image: Kacey has a heart of gold, and that's all that matters. She's described as an incredibly kind girl who's generous, helpful, and easy to get along with. People also find this blond to be lighthearted and down-to-earth. That said, she's most likely ditzy, but people don't seem to mind.

Famous Namesakes: Singer Kasey Chambers; actor Casey Affleck; radio personality Casey Kasem

Kala

(Arabic) a short form of Kalila.

Image: Kala is calm, quiet, and creative. She's perceived as a limber and slender brunette with pale skin. People regard her as smart, sweet, and down-to-earth, although they also say she's rather shy. Some see Kala as arty and individualistic.

Famous Namesakes: None

Kalare

(Latin, Basque) bright; clear.

Image: Kalare wouldn't get stepped on if she'd just stand up for herself. People think Kalare is a shy and reserved introvert who's quite caring. Because she lacks confidence, she's known to be something of a doormat. She's pictured as a redhead or blond who's short and thin.

Famous Namesakes: None

Kali

(Hindi) the black one. (Hawaiian) hesitating.

Image: All the girls want to be friends with Kali. People say this attractive young woman is warmhearted and understanding as well as perky and outgoing. Her energetic, bold personality seems perfectly suited to cheerleading, but she's also a smart student with good grades.

Famous Namesakes: Screenwriter Callie Khouri; character Dr. Callie Torres (*Grey's Anatomy*)

Kalinda

(Hindi) sun.

Image: Kalinda has high energy but low self-esteem. She's imagined as an annoyingly talkative cheerleader whose insecurity makes her worry about what other students think of her. People say Kalinda wants to be popular so badly, she often comes across as superficial instead of kind. She's pictured as pretty but a little overweight, which may also add to her self-esteem problem.

Famous Namesakes: None

Kaliska

(Moquelumnan) coyote chasing deer.

Image: Perhaps Kaliska grew up too fast. People say she's a talkative and flirty young woman who's hypersexual and often inappropriate. Not surprisingly, she comes across as pushy, obnoxious, and rude at times. Some people say this tall, fit blond is ditzy, but others sense she's quite smart and quick.

Famous Namesakes: None

Kameko

(Japanese) turtle child.

Image: Quiet in social situations, Kameko comes alive when she's exploring the great outdoors. People say this Asian girl is active, adventurous, and athletic. Although she has wild energy, she certainly doesn't have a wild personality. On the contrary, Kameko is known to be kind, lovable, gentle, and even shy.

Famous Namesakes: None

Kanika

(Mwera) black cloth.

Image: When people say Kanika has a great personality, they mean she's gregarious and kindhearted. She's imagined as a bubbly and bright-eyed people-person who loves having fun. In addition, people believe Kanika isn't only daring and outrageous, but also sweet and helpful. She's most often pictured as African American, beautiful, slender, and tall.

Famous Namesakes: Actress Kanika Subramanian

Karen

(Greek) pure.

Image: The other kids may not see Karen's positives, but her teacher does. Karen is described as a kindhearted yet mousy teacher's pet. People describe her as truthful and loyal, but also a little old-fashioned and nerdy. She may be skinny or chubby, and she's probably a pretty brunette.

Famous Namesakes: Actress Karen Black; singer Karen Carpenter; actress Karen Allen; character Karen Walker (*Will & Grace*)

Kari

(Greek) pure. (Danish) a form of Caroline, Katherine.

Image: Kari lives for excitement. People say she's a friendly brunette who's hyper, excitable, and fun-loving. A bit of a tomboy, she most likely loves Rollerblading and other active sports. She seems to approach life with a good sense of humor.

Famous Namesakes: Actress Kari Wührer; actress Keri Russell; character Carrie White (*Carrie*); character Carrie Bradshaw (*Sex and the City*); actress Carrie Fisher; actress Carrie-Anne Moss; actress Kerry Washington

Kass

(Greek) a short form of Kassandra.

Image: Kass is a go-getter on the road to success, but is it a *high road* or a *low road*? She's imagined as a smart, assertive, and overachieving preppy. What's unclear, though, is whether this brunette is insensitive and obnoxious or honest and moral.

Famous Namesakes: Singer Mama Cass

Katarina

(Czech) a form of Katherine.

Image: One Katarina has loads of fun, but the other Katarina has none. Some people picture Katarina as an elegant but cold woman who's conservative, quiet, and outright boring. But others imagine she's loving, funny, adventurous, and the life of the party. One thing is for certain: She's pictured as an Eastern European with a slim figure and a pretty face.

Famous Namesakes: Figure skater Katarina Witt

Kate

(Greek) pure. (English) a short form of Katherine.

Image: Kate's real talent is managing to be invincible and unassuming at the same time. Kate is thought to be lively and fearless with a can-do spirit. But all the while, she's imagined as down-to-earth, friendly, and intelligent. She's likely cute, tall, and slim.

Famous Namesakes: Actress Kate Hudson; singer Kate Bush; actress Kate Winslet; actress Kate Jackson; actress Kate Bosworth; model Kate Moss; designer Kate Spade; actress Kate Beckinsale; actress Cate Blanchett

Katelyn

(Irish) a form of Katelin.

Image: Apparently, Katelyn's parents don't set many limits or rules for their precious daughter. Katelyn is thought to be a cute girl who's bossy, stubborn, short-tempered, and altogether full of herself—likely because her affluent parents spoil her rotten.

Famous Namesakes: Figure skater Caitlin "Kitty" Carruthers; swimmer Katilin Sandeno; character Caitlin Cooper (*The O.C.*)

Katharine

(Greek) a form of Katherine.

Image: It's hard not to see Hollywood legend Katharine Hepburn in this name's image. Katharine calls to mind a type A, hardworking woman with proper manners, an old-money upbringing, and a lovely smile. She's considered to be attractive, tall, and well groomed. Some people picture her older with white hair and a matronly elegance.

Famous Namesakes: Publisher Katharine Graham; actress Katharine Hepburn; actress Catherine Zeta-Jones; actress Catherine O'Hara; singer Katherine McPhee; actress Catherine Bell; empress Catherine the Great; actress Catherine Deneuve; actress Katherine Heigl

Katherine

(Greek) pure.

Image: As Katherine knows, being strong means knowing when to use a light touch and when to use a heavy hand. People believe Katherine is a determined and bold woman who knows what she wants—and knows how to get it. Some say she's a born leader who's noble and trustworthy, but others find her to be temperamental and strict.

Famous Namesakes: Actress Katherine Heigl; actress Catherine Zeta-Jones; actress Catherine O'Hara; singer Katherine McPhee; actress Catherine Bell; empress Catherine the Great; actress Catherine Deneuve; publisher Katharine Graham

Kathleen

(Irish) a form of Katherine.

Image: Kathleen's Irish eyes are usually smiling. She's thought to be a kind and caring Irish Catholic woman. People find her to be cheerful and fun-loving, but she's also straightforward and smart. A natural beauty, she's pictured with fair skin, green eyes, and light-brown hair pulled back in a ponytail.

Famous Namesakes: Actress Kathleen Turner; actress Kathleen Robertson

Kathy

(English) a familiar form of Katherine, Kathleen.

Image: Kathy is a typical mom: She cares, but perhaps a little too much. Kathy is described as a softhearted and motherly woman who likes to please and is always concerned about others. At times, she can be gossipy and nosy, but that's mostly just her way of being sociable. Sometimes she can be domineering, but she's usually happy and smiling.

Famous Namesakes: Comic strip character Cathy; actress Kathy Bates; model Kathy Ireland; cartoonist Cathy Guisewite; television host Kathie Lee Gifford

Girls

Katie

(English) a familiar form of Kate.

Image: Katie's maturity level will someday catch up to her intellect. People describe Katie as perky and spontaneous, although she often seems silly and childish. With a vivid imagination and resourceful creativity, she's said to be gifted and talented. She's most likely a sweet and wholesome young woman.

Famous Namesakes: News anchor Katie Couric; actress Katie Holmes; model Katie Price

Katina

(English, Russian) a form of Katherine.

Image: People disagree about Katina's personality. She's often imagined as a friendly chatterbox who's happy, playful, and sometimes headstrong. Some may even say she's too loud and too talkative. Others suspect Katina is shy, quiet, and simple. Either way, she's pictured as a waiflike blond with a bright smile and delicate features.

Famous Namesakes: Actress Katina Paxinou

Katrina

(German) a form of Katherine.

Image: Katrina is a bit of a daredevil. She's imagined as a mischievous, carefree, and unordinary woman who speaks her mind and lives life on the edge. Many find this petite risk taker to be kindhearted and generous, not to mention smart.

Famous Namesakes: Singer Katrina Leskanich

Katy

(English) a familiar form of Kate.

Image: Katy has a personable combination of qualities. Above all, people think Katy is cute, but they also find her to be sweet, spunky, and active. She's considered hip and savvy, but she's down-to-earth at the same time.

Famous Namesakes: News anchor Katie Couric; actress Katie Holmes; model Katie Price

Kay

(Greek) rejoicer. (Teutonic) a fortified place. (Latin) merry.

Image: Kay's classmates knew what they were doing when they voted her most likely to succeed. People think Kay is an admirable and friendly woman who was a straight-A student in high school and is a bright, strong-willed businesswoman today. She's most likely refined and cultured, and everyone loves being around her.

Famous Namesakes: Senator Kay Bailey Hutchinson

Kaya

(Hopi) wise child. (Japanese) resting place.

Image: The sadder Kaya feels, the more money she spends. People say Kaya is polite and friendly on the surface, but depressed and lonely deep down. She may shop to feel better about herself, gravitating toward antiques. She's pictured as an Indian woman with long, dark hair and beautiful dark eyes.

Famous Namesakes: Singer Kaya Jones

Kayla

(Arabic, Hebrew) laurel; crown.

Image: Kayla has a certain innocence about her. She comes across as a pretty lass who's sweet, sincere, and soft-spoken. Most people believe she's childlike and naïve with that girl-next-door quality.

Famous Namesakes: Character Kayla Brady (*Days of Our Lives*)

Kaylee

(American) a form of Kayla.

Image: Kaylee usually does a good job of hiding her deep-seated insecurities. This name makes people think of a popular and peppy girl who's sweet but secretly insecure. Sometimes Kaylee expresses her low self-esteem with needy dependency, and other times she seems prissy and moody. Most people, however, find this dainty and pretty blond to be a lot of fun.

Famous Namesakes: None

Kelby

(German) farm by the spring.

Image: Kelby may be confident, but conceited may be a better way to describe her. She's regarded as a spoiled daddy's girl who's quite full of herself. Blond, pretty, and popular, she's famous for acting nice in order to get what she wants.

Famous Namesakes: None

Kelly

(Irish) brave warrior.

Image: Breaking down Kelly's image may lead to a recipe for making a cheerleader: Combine perky energy with snobby meanness. Blend in popularity, gossipy chatter, and blond cuteness. Top with a dollop of ditziness. Voilà!

Famous Namesakes: Talk show host Kelly Ripa; singer Kelly Clarkson; singer Kelly Osbourne; actress Kelly Preston; singer Kelly Rowland; actress Kelly Packard; actress Kelly Reilly

Kelsey

(Scandinavian, Scottish) ship island. (English) a form of Chelsea.

Image: Perhaps Kelsey Grammer, who played the prim title character on TV's *Frasier*, affects this name's image? Kelsey is mostly viewed as a fussy and snobby intellectual whose upper-middle-class family sent her to prep school. Other people, however, think she may be outgoing, nice, and even flirty. She's probably a blond girly girl with fair skin.

Famous Namesakes: Actor Kelsey Grammer

Kendra

(English) a form of Kenda.

Image: Kendra is a strong, straightforward woman. She's imagined as independent, outgoing, and intelligent with a healthy sense of self-esteem. A few people believe she can be sarcastic and rude at times, but more people find her to be considerate and pleasant. She's most likely African American, tall, and athletic.

Famous Namesakes: Model Kendra Wilkinson

Kenya

(Hebrew) animal horn.

Image: Kenya is stunning for many reasons. This place name evokes an image of an African American woman with determined confidence, a strong mind, and almost regal grace. Kenya is said to be tall and beautiful, like a supermodel. Some people suspect she's a daring wild child as well.

Famous Namesakes: Actress Kenya Moore

Kerry

(Irish) dark-haired.

Image: Kerry's effervescence is infectious. She's thought to be a happy-go-lucky and bubbly brunette who's approachable and cheerful. People also imagine her to be caring, smart, and sporty. A handful of people are suspicious of her, perhaps thinking she's an untrustworthy sneak who uses others, but the majority says she's friends with everyone.

Famous Namesakes: Actress Kerry Washington; actress Kari Wührer; actress Keri Russell; movie character Carrie; character Carrie Bradshaw (*Sex and the City*); actress Carrie Fisher; actress Carrie-Anne Moss

Kessie

(Ashanti) chubby baby.

Image: Kessie leaves everyone smiling and laughing. People describe Kessie as goodhearted, affectionate, and incredibly nice. She's also said to be a joker who loves to laugh and make others do the same. As for her looks, she's likely plump, dark-skinned, and pretty.

Famous Namesakes: Disney character Kessie

Kiara

(Irish) little and dark.

Image: Kiara may be self-reliant, but perhaps that's because no one wants to deal with her. Kiara strikes others as an independent and strong-willed woman who's quite confident. People can't agree on whether she's a sweet and funny charmer or a temperamental and vain princess. They do agree that she's most likely African American, tall, and exotically beautiful.

Famous Namesakes: Actress Kiara Hunger

Kim

(Vietnamese) needle. (English) a short form of Kimberly.

Image: Kim is spirited, for good or bad. She's seen as a vivacious and high-energy gal who likes to take charge. Some say she's hot-tempered and arrogant, but others say she's loving and loyal. Either way, it's safe to say she's a bit of an airhead.

Famous Namesakes: Actress Kim Basinger; actress Kim Delaney; actress Kim Fields; actress Kim Catrall; actress Kim Novak; singer Kim Gordon; rapper Lil' Kim

Kimberly

(English) chief, ruler.

Image: If these two Kimberlys crossed paths, one wouldn't give the other the time of day. To some people, Kimberly is a classy but pompous preppy who's intelligent, self-important, rude, and basically friendless. Others, however, sense she's a sweet and smiley cheerleader who's out-going and spunky. In either case, she's pictured as skinny and tall.

Famous Namesakes: News anchor Kimberly Guilfoyle; actress Kimberly Elise; actress Kimberly Williams; socialite Kimberly Stewart

Kimi

(Japanese) righteous.

Image: Kimi doesn't realize what some people think of her—or if she does, she doesn't let it slow her down. Kimi is known to be a petite girl who's friendly, peppy, and popular. Some people, however, find her to be loud and obnoxious, and they also think she's dimwit-ted. Others say she's a sensitive sissy.

Famous Namesakes: Character Kimmy Gibbler (*Full House*); figure skater Kimmie Meissner

Kimmy

(English) a familiar form of Kimberly.

Image: Kimmy shows up at all the parties, even though she's never invited to any of them. She's said to be a goofy and annoyingly loud ditz who's lanky and blond. People suspect she loves wild nights out on the town, but they see her as nothing more than a tagalong.

Famous Namesakes: Character Kimmy Gibbler (*Full House*); figure skater Kimmie Meissner

Kira

(Persian) sun. (Latin) light.

Image: Kira has the world in her grasp. She's said to be a warmhearted woman with a good future ahead of her because she's bright, skilled, and strong-minded. Beautiful and sexy, Kira is known to be sassy, outgoing, and perhaps aggressive. Taking the opposite view, a few people believe she's shy and naïve.

Famous Namesakes: Character Kira Nerys (*Star Trek: Deep Space Nine*); figure skater Kira Ivanova

Kirsten

(Greek) Christian; anointed. (Scandinavian) a form of Christine.

Image: Kirsten carries herself above others, which may make her a leader. The name Kirsten reminds people of an arrogant, snobby woman who thinks she's better than everyone else. She's most likely smart and sophisticated, and she may hold some kind of leadership position. People describe her as a blond Swede who's slender and naturally beautiful.

Famous Namesakes: Actress Kirsten Dunst; character Kirsten Cohen (*The O.C.*)

Kishi

(Japanese) long and happy life.

Image: People have quite different ideas about Kishi's upbringing. Most people assert she's an innocent and playful young Asian girl who loves Beanie Babies and often has her head in the clouds. Like any little lady, she's said to be energetic and bubbly. Other people, however, imagine she comes from a cruel family, and thus is depressed, vindictive, and in need of therapy.

Famous Namesakes: None

Kitra

(Hebrew) crowned.

Image: Kitra wants to have fun—so you better stay out of her way. She's envisioned as a loud and rebellious girl who's dyed her hair jet-black, purple, or some other exotic shade. People say Kitra is full of life and rarin' to have fun, but she's also a nasty, untrustworthy bully. It doesn't help her image that she's dim and ditzy, too.

Famous Namesakes: None

Kona

(Hawaiian) lady. (Hindi) angular.

Image: Kona has so many positive attributes. People think she's kind, graceful, witty, intelligent, and assertive. She's also described as a beauty with dark hair and coffee-colored skin. Just to prove that no one is perfect, a handful of people complain that Kona is a little too loud at times.

Famous Namesakes: None

Kora

(Greek) a form of Cora.

Image: Kora projects different images to different people. While many people think Kora is a pleasant and happy do-gooder, some think she's timid and bland. Others say she's jealous and bitter, but then again, a few people call her a rebel. At least they agree that she's an older woman who's tall and frumpy.

Famous Namesakes: Actress Cora Witherspoon

Koren

(Greek) a form of Karen, Kora, Korin.

Image: Koren isn't afraid to take on anything in life. This name creates the impression of a confident, bold, and can-do woman who doesn't give up easily. In addition, she's said to be intelligent, gracious, and sophisticated. People describe Koren as a small, exotic beauty who may be Greek.

Famous Namesakes: Writer Koren Zailckas

Krista

(Czech) a form of Christina.

Image: Krista places great importance on popularity. To many, she seems like an outgoing and popular young woman of good spirits. A few people disagree, saying she's shy and meek, and still others argue that she's spoiled and rude. In any case, Krista likely identifies herself as part of a crowd rather than as an individual.

Famous Namesakes: Actress Krista Allen; teacher Christa McAuliffe; actress Christa Miller

Kristen

(Greek) Christian; anointed. (Scandinavian) a form of Christine.

Image: Kristen won't—or can't—hide the fact that she's a spoiled snob. People most often imagine Kristen as a prissy, fussy daddy's girl with a big attitude, a fondness for buying clothes, and the inability to hide her emotions. A few people have a more neutral perspective, saying she's friendly but rather ordinary.

Famous Namesakes: Actress Kristen Bell; actress Kristen Stewart; actress Kristin Kreuk; actress Kristin Scott Thomas; actress Kristin Chenoweth

Girls

Kristi

(Scandinavian) a short form of Kristine.

Image: Kristi is chatty, but she's also catty. People describe Kristi as a talkative and perky blond who seems friendly at first; however, she's most likely conceited and manipulative. She's pictured as tall and thin, and she may be a cheerleader.

Famous Namesakes: Figure skater Kristi Yamaguchi; model Christie Brinkley; model Christy Turlington; actress Kristy McNichol; actress Kristy Swanson; singer Cristy Lane

Kristin

(Scandinavian) a form of Kristen.

Image: Kristin is so popular because she's so fun to be around. She's seen as a happy-go-lucky and easygoing social butterfly who loves to party and talk a mile a minute. Most people believe Kristin is sweet, but a few detractors say she's snobby. She's said to be quite pretty, and she likely gets her blond hair and blue eyes from a Scandinavian heritage.

Famous Namesakes: Actress Kristin Scott Thomas; actress Kristin Chenoweth; actress Kristen Bell; actress Kristen Stewart; actress Kristin Kreuk

Kristina

(Greek) Christian; anointed. (Scandinavian) a form of Christina.

Image: Kristina knows when to cut loose and when to buckle down. In social situations, she's seen as a flirtatious gal who's funny, talkative, and loud. But in work situations, she's calm, goal oriented, and cooperative. People depict Kristina as a cutie with dimples.

Famous Namesakes: Singer Christina Aguilera; actress Christina Applegate; actress Christina Ricci; singer Christina Milian; character Christina Yang (*Grey's Anatomy*)

Kristine

(Scandinavian) a form of Christine.

Image: Kristine may tell you that nice guys—or gals—finish last. She's most often described as a shallow, selfish snob who's unfriendly and rude. Nevertheless, she's said to be a smart, successful professional with a lot of money. A few people have a more positive view, imagining she's warm-hearted and sociable. Either way, she's probably an attractive, blue-eyed blond with a slender frame.

Famous Namesakes: Speed skater Kristine Holzer; actress Christine Taylor; actress Christine Lahti; actress Christine Baranski

Krystal

(American) clear, brilliant glass.

Image: Krystal's reputation is good...and bad. On the plus side, she's pictured as a loud and social gal who's the life of the party and quick to make friends. On the minus side, people say she's a little too quick to "befriend" men. Some people even believe she's snobby and conceited. Everyone imagines Krystal as a skinny blond with big hair.

Famous Namesakes: Actress Krystal Bernard; singer Crystal Gayle; gospel singer Crystal Lewis

Kyla

(Irish) lovely. (Yiddish) crown; laurel.

Image: Kyla is known for her tender heart. People overwhelmingly believe Kyla is sweet, loving, giving, friendly, and sensitive. She's also imagined to be adorable with dark hair and brown eyes. Energetic, smart, and responsible, she seems to be happy do-gooder.

Famous Namesakes: Actress Kyla Pratt

Kylie

(West Australian Aboriginal) curled stick; boomerang. (Irish) a familiar form of Kyle.

Image: Kylie is 100 percent adorable. She's said to be a carefree, lighthearted, and sweet little girl who's irresistibly huggable. People imagine she's pretty, dainty, and blond, as well as clever and sprightly.

Famous Namesakes: Singer Kylie Minogue; model Kylie Bax

Kyra

(Greek) noble.

Image: Most folks say Kyra is a good person to know, but some say she's a good person to avoid. Kyra is primarily imagined as a sweet and lovable friend—the type who holds secrets in utmost confidence. She's likely demure, soft-spoken, and perhaps artistic. But a few people see her quite differently, calling her snobby and downright mean.

Famous Namesakes: Actress Kyra Sedgwick

Lacey

(Latin) cheerful. (Greek) a familiar form of Larissa.

Image: Lacey is dedicated to her friends and values. She's regarded as an understanding, compassionate girl who's eager to get along with everyone. People say Lacey is also eager to stand up for her beliefs, and being bright and hardworking helps her do just that. She's most likely beautiful with dark hair.

Famous Namesakes: Actress Lacey Chabert; country singer Lacy J. Dalton

Lacy

(Latin) cheerful. (Greek) a familiar form of Larissa.

Image: Lacy knows how to play the part of the likable girl. She's described as a delicate and pretty girl who seems charming, giggly, and even ditzy to many people. Those traits have likely made her popular, but deep down, she's said to be conceited, snobby, and selfish.

Famous Namesakes: Country singer Lacy J. Dalton; actress Lacey Chabert

Laila

(Arabic) a form of Leila.

Image: Laila seems nice, but it's hard to tell. She's said to be a mysterious and elegant woman who doesn't say much. Although she's shy, people suspect she's sweet and kind. Some describe her as a dark-haired and sexy athlete, like boxer Laila Ali.

Famous Namesakes: Boxer Laila Ali

Lainey

(French) a familiar form of Elaine.

Image: Lainey's crazy tales always keep her friends and family in stitches. She's described as a hilarious storyteller. She's popular not just for her stories, but also for her easygoing attitude. People picture Lainey as pretty with dark hair, dark eyes, and an athletic build.

Famous Namesakes: Actress Lainie Kazan

Lakeisha

(American) a combination of the prefix La + Keisha.

Image: Lakeisha is sassy but sweet. People picture her as an outgoing, feisty, and smart African American woman. She's also known to have a sweet side that makes her quite popular, but some think she can be moody at times. As for her looks, she's said to be very attractive with flawless skin.

Famous Namesakes: None

Lana

(Latin) woolly. (Irish) attractive, peaceful. (Hawaiian) floating; buoyant.

Image: Lana is pictured as a sexy and slender beauty who's smart, successful, and talented in either art or music. Many people believe she's carefree, popular, kind, and witty. But a few people imagine she's a spoiled, snobby rich girl.

Famous Namesakes: Actress Lana Turner; character Lana Lang (*Smallville*)

Lane

(English) narrow road.

Image: Lane has far more important goals than throwing herself into the dating scene. She's thought to be a helpful and kind woman who's interesting, smart, and hardworking. People imagine Lane is happily independent, forgoing dating for traveling and advancing her career.

Famous Namesakes: Actress Diane Lane; character Lane Kim (*Gilmore Girls*); character Lois Lane (*Superman*)

Lara

(Greek) cheerful. (Latin) shining; famous.

Image: Either there are three separate images of Lara, or she's a decidedly complicated woman. Lara comes across as a responsible and nice bookworm, a self-important and rude know-it-all, or an eccentric and high-strung neurotic. In any case, she's probably a pretty blond waif.

Famous Namesakes: Character Lara Croft (*Tomb Raider*); actress Lara Flynn Boyle

Larissa

(Greek) cheerful.

Image: Be on your toes when Larissa gets that smile on her face—you may be the victim of her next mischievous prank. People say Larissa is a bright young woman with an impish smile and love of practical jokes. A pretty brunette, she's famous for being bold, outgoing, and cheerful. She may also be from a wealthy family.

Famous Namesakes: Gymnast Larissa Latynina

Latonya

(American) a combination of the prefix La + Tonya. (Latin) a form of Latona.

Image: Latonya is headstrong but kindhearted. She's pictured as an African American woman who's fun-loving, loud, and friendly. People sometimes say she's silly, but they always say she's opinionated. Latonya is pictured with a voluptuous figure, and she perhaps had an underprivileged upbringing.

Famous Namesakes: Author Latonya Williams

Latoya

(American) a combination of the prefix La + Toya.

Image: Latoya is often unlikable, but she does redeem herself now and then. She's said to be an African American woman who's sometimes bossy, egocentric, whiny, and generally unpleasant. Other times, however, Latoya is known to be friendly and energetic. Either way, people believe she's a hard worker with a strong will.

Famous Namesakes: Singer LaToya Jackson

Laura

(Latin) crowned with laurel.

Image: People hold contrary views about Laura. They initially agree that she's a bone-thin brunette with a big brain. From there, some people claim she's meek, boring, and unable to form her own opinions, despite being rather intelligent. But others say Laura is feisty, fun, and strong-willed.

Famous Namesakes: Author Laura Ingalls Wilder; first lady Laura Bush; actress Laura Linney; actress Laura Innes; actress Laura San Giacomo; radio personality Dr. Laura Schlessinger; character Laura Spencer (*General Hospital*)

Laurel

(Latin) laurel tree.

Image: Laurel has dreamy charm. This name makes people think of a quiet, gentle woman who's as intelligent as she is caring. She's most likely a hopeless romantic who's always lost in thought, and she has a certain grace about her. People picture Laurel as an attractive and willowy blond with ivory skin and blue-green eyes.

Famous Namesakes: Actress Laurel Holloman

Lauren

(English) a form of Laura.

Image: Which is Lauren's best quality: her beauty, brains, or heart? Lauren is described as a friendly woman with very feminine features. She's sophisticated, hardworking, and confident in her intelligence. Some may even call her a showoff—if she weren't so sweet.

Famous Namesakes: Actress Lauren Bacall; actress Lauren Holly; actress Lauren Graham; singer Lauryn Hill; reality television star Lauren Conrad

Laurie

(English) a familiar form of Laura.

Image: Everyone wants Laurie as a best friend. Most people say she's a fun, bubbly girl with lots of energy and smiles. She's said to be a good pal— she's sweet, helpful, and dependable. Then again, a few people see her as a shy, insecure wallflower.

Famous Namesakes: Actress Laurie Metcalf; singer Lorrie Morgan; actress Lori Singer; actress Lori Laughlin

Laveda

(Latin) cleansed, purified.

Image: A few images of Laveda surface. Most people say she's an overweight and homely dullard. Others insist she's a kind woman whom many look to for leadership. A few people suspect she's loud and trashy. In any case, Laveda may be an African American with dark hair and long legs.

Famous Namesakes: None

Laverne

(Latin) springtime. (French) grove of alder trees.

Image: Every Sunday, Laverne's fellow worshippers carefully avoid sitting next to her in the pew. She's described as a matronly church lady with pursed lips, outdated clothes, a grumpy disposition, and a nose in everyone's business. A few people have a different view of Laverne, calling her silly and wild, perhaps like Penny Marshall's character in TV's *Laverne & Shirley*.

Famous Namesakes: Character Laverne De Fazio (*Laverne & Shirley*)

Lawanda

(American) a combination of the prefix La + Wanda.

Image: Lawanda's personality is as bold as her fashion sense. She strikes people as a talkative extrovert with a bit of an attitude. Some people say she's pushy, but others say she's just loud. She's thought to be African American, tall, and full figured, and she most likely has a flair for fashion.

Famous Namesakes: Actress LaWanda Page

Lea

(Hawaiian) the goddess of canoe makers. (Hebrew) a form of Leah.

Image: There's little concurrence about Lea. She probably has chestnut hair and a cute smile, but no one agrees on her personality: She may be a bright artist, a stuck-up whiner, a caring helper, or a spunky charmer.

Famous Namesakes: Actress Lea Thompson; singer Lea Salonga

Leah

(Hebrew) weary.

Image: Leah's intentions are good, but her delivery needs some work. She's described as a warm and loving woman with natural beauty and good intentions. But people say Leah has a knack for sticking her foot in her mouth, and her blunt honesty can be insensitive and even obnoxious. Because she's smart, funny, and generally kind, people understand that her opinions are always well-meaning.

Famous Namesakes: Actress Leah Remini; biblical figure Leah; model Liya Kebede

Leandra

(Latin) like a lioness.

Image: Leandra certainly has style, but she has substance, too. She's considered to be a sweet and stylish trendsetter who's bright and self-sufficient. Although she's known to love friends, kids, and even animals, sometimes this hipster needs some alone time. People picture Leandra as very pretty, tall, and lean with dark blond hair.

Famous Namesakes: None

Leigh

(English) a form of Lee.

Image: Leigh may come from a well-to-do family, but she doesn't lead a coddled life. Leigh strikes people as a wealthy and beautiful sophisticate who's nonetheless a successful, hardworking, and intelligent professional. She's envisioned as polite, confident, caring, and diplomatic. Outside of work, she's said to be an athletic and playful free spirit.

Famous Namesakes: Actress Vivien Leigh

Leila

(Hebrew) dark beauty; night. (Arabic) born at night.

Image: All kids claim their mothers are the most beautiful women in the world, but everyone agrees with Leila's children. People say Leila is a stunning woman with enchanting eyes and a glowing complexion. She's thought to be sweet and affectionate—traits she calls upon as a mother. She's also known to have quiet confidence and intelligence.

Famous Namesakes: Actress Leila Shenna

Leilani

(Hawaiian) heavenly flower; heavenly child.

Image: It's simple to see why Leilani is so beloved. This name makes people think of a lovely, dark-skinned Hawaiian who's caring, good-natured, and irresistibly lovable. Adding to her charm, she's also said to be considerably smart, easygoing, and honest. With her island heritage, Leilani may be a hula dancer.

Famous Namesakes: Model Leilani Dowding

Lenora

(Greek, Russian) a form of Eleanor.

Image: Lenora is as skittish as she is bookish This name makes people think of a librarian who's helpful and friendly with children, but quite shy with adults. She's pictured as lanky and bespectacled.

Famous Namesakes: None

Leona

(German) brave as a lioness.

Image: Infamous real-estate mogul Leona Helmsley lends her "queen of mean" reputation to this name's image. Leona is thought to be a spiteful, self-centered, and vicious woman with lots of wealth. People admit she's strong-willed and independent, but she's also greedy and shallow.

Famous Namesakes: Hotel magnate Leona Helmsley; singer Leona Naess

Letitia

(Latin) a form of Leticia.

Image: Is Letitia a holy woman or a sex symbol? People say she may be either. Some find Letitia to be honest, helpful, proper, and religious. They say she may even be a nun. Others believe she's a sexy and seductive model, like Victoria's Secret starlet Laetitia Casta.

Famous Namesakes: Model Laetitia Casta

Lia

(Greek) bringer of good news. (Hebrew, Dutch, Italian) dependent.

Image: Lia is making her way. She's said to be creative, talented, and intriguing. Although people also say Lia is soft-spoken and introverted, her talent—coupled with her perfectionism, strong will, and intelligence—just may make her famous someday. It probably doesn't hurt that she's willowy with curly hair and exotic beauty.

Famous Namesakes: Model Liya Kebede; actress Leah Remini; biblical figure Leah

Libby

(Hebrew) a familiar form of Elizabeth.

Image: You'll find Libby either in the center of a crowd or in a corner by herself. Everyone imagines Libby as plump, short, and pretty. Beyond her looks, some people imagine she has a big personality—she's funny, original, and loud. But others say the opposite, picturing her as a sad and lonely girl without friends. In either case, she's sweet and kind.

Famous Namesakes: Character Libby (*Lost*)

Liberty

(Latin) free.

Image: The word *liberty* evokes visions of self-determination, as proved in this name's image. Some think Liberty is a free-spirited thrill seeker with sassy independence. She's a personable, beautiful extrovert who just may be a model, actress, or Miss USA. Intelligent and strong, she's famous for standing up for what she believes in.

Famous Namesakes: None

Lila

(Arabic) night. (Hindi) free will of God. (Persian) lilac.

Image: Lila is successful in social circles as well as business circles. People believe she's always happy and always flocked by friends. In her career, Lila is noted for being self-assured, ambitious, analytical, and hardworking. Physically, she's thought to be dainty, pale, and beautiful, like a porcelain doll.

Famous Namesakes: Actress Lila Kedrova; country singer Lyla McCann

Lilac

(Sanskrit) lilac; blue purple.

Image: Lilacs are such delicate, pretty flowers. For this reason, people see Lilac as a petite and gentle bookworm who's a little shy but very smart. She's most likely slender, fair, and curly-haired. All in all, Lilac is said to be as sweet, lovely, and earthy as the flower of the same name.

Famous Namesakes: None

Lilah

(Arabic, Hindi, Persian) a form of Lila.

Image: Lilah has culture and character. People get the impression she's attractive, kind, and sophisticated to the point of being fancy. Quiet and loving, she most likely has strong morals and religious beliefs.

Famous Namesakes: Actress Lila Kedrova; country singer Lyla McCann

Lilith

(Arabic) of the night; night demon.

Image: Here's the secret to getting along with Lilith: Just smile and say, "You're right." People say Lilith is strong and independent, which means she likes to be in control, likes to debate, and (naturally) likes to be right. At times, this creates the impression that she's stuck-up and snobby. But when she isn't debating, she comes across as caring, friendly, and down-to-earth. People picture her as fragile and pale.

Famous Namesakes: Character Lilith Sternin (*Cheers*); biblical figure Lilith

Lillian

(Latin) lily flower.

Image: Everything about Lillian is gentle. She's imagined as a soft-spoken and soft-mannered woman who's sweet, graceful, and wise. Easygoing and mousy, she seems to be the last person who'd ever rock the boat. People believe Lillian is physically gentle as well, describing her as a dainty older woman with classic beauty.

Famous Namesakes: Actress Lillian Gish; author Lillian Hellman

Lily

(Latin, Arabic) a form of Lilly.

Image: Lily has a hard time holding back her love for life. People imagine Lily is typically polite and gentle, but she can sometimes be a bundle of joy and energy. She's also known to be loving and happily content with herself. People picture her as pretty with a small build and a fair complexion, much like a white lily.

Famous Namesakes: Actress Lily Tomlin character Lily Potter (*Harry Potter* series); model Lily Cole

Lina

(Greek) light. (Arabic) tender. (Latin) a form of Lena.

Image: Lina seems to be a good, upstanding person. Many people state she's an intelligent, creative, and hardworking woman. She's also known to be kind, helpful, and funny. Overall, most people say she's pretty cool. But others believe Lina is a dishonest and distasteful girl who leeches off others. Either way, she's described as pretty, tan, and thin.

Famous Namesakes: Director Lina Wertmüller

Linda

(Spanish) pretty.

Image: No matter what life brings, Linda is determined to keep smiling. She's envisioned as an easygoing, caring woman who's full of smiles and wit. She's said to be talkative and popular, but she also has an independent, hardworking attitude that's seen her through some tough moments. As for her looks, Linda is pictured as a pleasantly plump brunette.

Famous Namesakes: Musician Linda McCartney; actress Linda Hamilton; actress Linda Cardellini; singer Linda Ronstadt; actress Linda Blair

Lindsay

(English) a form of Lindsey.

Image: This image possibly describes former teen queen Lindsay Lohan; but then again, it may describe just about any teen. Lindsay is imagined to be a loud, lively, and popular girl. Most people think she's also self-absorbed and bratty, but a few say she's friendly and sweet. She's often pictured as a skinny blond.

Famous Namesakes: Actress Lindsay Lohan; actress Lindsay Wagner; actress Lindsay McKeon; tennis player Lindsey Davenport

Lindsey

(English) linden-tree island; camp near the stream.

Image: Lindsey is envisioned as a popular, flirty, and attractive party girl. Some say she's friendly, sweet, and talented, but others say she's a spoiled, cliquish backstabber who's skilled at spreading rumors (perhaps better describing former teen queen Lindsay Lohan).

Famous Namesakes: Actress Lindsay Lohan; actress Lindsay Wagner; actress Lindsay McKeon; tennis player Lindsey Davenport

Linnea

(Scandinavian) lime tree.

Image: If you're looking for straight talk and matter-of-fact thinking, Linnea is your woman. Some may describe her as practical and down-to-earth, but others come right out and call her no-nonsense and tough as nails. Tall and imposing, this European blond seems physically tough as well. But underneath her bluntness, she's also known to be friendly.

Famous Namesakes: Actress Linnea Quigley

Lisa

(Hebrew) consecrated to God. (English) a short form of Elizabeth.

Image: Is Lisa wild or mild? Many people see Lisa as an attention seeker who's reckless and wild but also sweet. Some see her differently, imagining her as quiet, serious, and careful. Everyone, however, depicts her as good-looking and rail thin.

Famous Namesakes: Singer Lisa Marie Presley; character Lisa Simpson (*The Simpsons*); actress Lisa Bonet, actress Lisa Kudrow, actress Lisa Edelstein; actress Lisa Rinna

Liz

(English) a short form of Elizabeth.

Image: Liz knows exactly how to work the system. Deep down, she's said to be a brash and headstrong woman who knows all and wants all. But people believe she hides those bossy tendencies under a perky and giddy façade—likely an intelligent move on her part, because she's envisioned as a glamorous and pampered trophy wife.

Famous Namesakes: Actress Liz Taylor; designer Liz Claiborne; singer Liz Phair

Liza

(American) a short form of Elizabeth.

Image: Liza Minnelli has a legendary talent as well as a legendary personality. Therefore, people say Liza is a wild free spirit who's confident, happy, and fun to be with. But sometimes her spirit makes her seem arrogant, rude, obnoxious, and big-mouthed. Nevertheless, people still say this slim brunette is talented and successful.

Famous Namesakes: Singer Liza Minnelli; actress Liza Huber

Lizina

(Latvian) a familiar form of Elizabeth.

Image: An uncommon name like Lizina will raise some questions—and eyebrows. People describe her as a shy, withdrawn loner who has trouble making friends. This "dizzy lizzy" may not be very smart, and she's probably weird. She's pictured as pretty, pale, and much too thin.

Famous Namesakes: None

Lois

(German) famous warrior.

Image: Lois's IQ is phenomenal, but her sociability skills are disgraceful. This name makes people think of an eccentric nerd who's insecure, old-fashioned, and decked out in hiked-up pants, a pocket protector, and glasses. She's no doubt a hardworking genius, but people call her a dork nonetheless.

Famous Namesakes: Character Lois Lane (*Superman*); character Lois Griffin (*Family Guy*); actress Lois Chiles; character Lois (*Hi & Lois*)

Lola

(Spanish) a familiar form of Carlotta, Dolores, Louise.

Image: Lola is quite a cheeky gal. She's described as a flamboyant flirt who's loud, spontaneous, and assertive. Some people find her to be fun and playful, but others just say she's obnoxious. She's portrayed as dark and exotic-looking—perhaps Spanish.

Famous Namesakes: Character Lola (*Run Lola Run*)

Lolly

(English) sweet; candy.

Image: With such a jaunty name, you have to imagine Lolly is fun. She's seen as a playful and gregarious blond cutie who laughs a lot. Some people call her quirky and eccentric, but others say she's ditzy and childish. Nevertheless, Lolly is most likely a kind gal, and she has a lot of fun. A few people picture her as a waitress in a café.

Famous Namesakes: Pop singer Lolly

Lonna

(Latin, German, English) a form of Lona.

Image: It seems Lonna leads a double life. For example, her social acquaintances describe her as a confident woman with a strong will and strong desires. She's most likely flirtatious and amorous, attracting men with her blond hair and statuesque figure. But her coworkers see a totally different Lonna: They say she's efficient, organized, quiet, and smiley.

Famous Namesakes: None

Lorena

(English) a form of Lauren.

Image: Lorena Bobbitt became a tabloid celebrity when she dis*membered* her husband in 1993, and this name's image has never been the same. People picture Lorena as a tough and stubborn woman who won't get pushed around and won't stop until she gets what she wants. This dark-haired Latina is known to be fiery, quick to anger, and sometimes cruel.

Famous Namesakes: Singer Lorena McKennitt; angry wife Lorena Bobbitt

Girls

Loretta

(English) a familiar form of Laura.

Image: Folks are always surprised that such vulgar behavior can come from such a sweet thing like Loretta. Perhaps inspired by rowdy country legend Loretta Lynn, this name creates the image of a wild gal who loves drinkin', swearin', jokin' around, and hangin' with men. As brassy as she may seem, she's said to be a kind and caring soul.

Famous Namesakes: Singer Loretta Lynn; actress Loretta Young

Lori

(Latin) crowned with laurel. (French) a short form of Lorraine. (American) a familiar form of Laura.

Image: Lori has the zest and gumption to open her own salon someday. Lori is thought of as a fun-loving, flirtatious, and well-liked woman who loves life and is young at heart. She's also said to be warm and caring. People imagine her as a sandy-haired beautician who wears too much makeup on her pretty face, but she's quite determined and ambitious.

Famous Namesakes: Actress Laurie Metcalf; singer Lorrie Morgan; actress Lori Singer; actress Lori Laughlin

Lorna

(Latin) crowned with laurel.

Image: There's a lot to say about Lorna, but very little of it is good. People think Lorna is a mean woman who's snobby, two-faced, sneaky, and hot-tempered. In general, she's said to be weird and unable to relate to others. She's most likely plump, short, and dowdy. As a lone positive note, people acknowledge that she's smart.

Famous Namesakes: Fiction character Lorna Doone; actress Lorna Luft

 **★ Star Kids**

Lourdes Maria Ciccone

Lourdes Maria Ciccone has mixed feelings about her family—you would, too, if you were part of the Mafia. When people hear this name, they think of a gangster's wife. She seems to enjoy being a pampered socialite, but she's also emotional and feels guilt for her family's crimes. She may be Latino or Italian; either way, she has dark hair, olive skin, and a voluptuous figure. Coincidentally, megastar Madonna's daughter, Lourdes Maria Ciccone, does come from an Italian family, but it's unlikely she feels guilty for any of their crimes.

Lorraine

(Latin) sorrowful.

Image: Lorraine is an everyday, real woman. She's thought to be likable and honest, smart and thorough, happy and down-to-earth. People imagine she's a good friend. This raspy-voiced blond may be middle-aged, but she's still as leggy as she was in her heyday.

Famous Namesakes: Playwright Lorraine Hansberry; actress Lorraine Bracco

Louisa

(English) a familiar form of Louise.

Image: Louisa is known for her kindness and happiness. She's pictured as a sweet and considerate extrovert who's jolly and feisty. She can even be quite loud at times. As for her looks, people say she's a dark-haired and petite beauty with light skin and a broad smile.

Famous Namesakes: Author Louisa May Alcott

Louise

(German) famous warrior.

Image: Louise is as quick with the sarcasm as she is with a smile. She's most likely an over-the-hill waitress who can be cranky and sarcastic one minute and boisterous and lovable the next. To complete the image, people suspect Louise smells of cigarette smoke.

Famous Namesakes: Actress Louise Brooks; actress Louise Fletcher; actress Louise Lombard

Lucia

(Italian, Spanish) a form of Lucy.

Image: Lucia has clear morals but ambiguous ethnicity. When people hear this name, they think of a warm and dutiful woman. Lucia is thought to be reserved and conservative, and perhaps she's even saintly (although that may be a reference to Saint Lucia, the Caribbean island nation). With dark hair, she may be Italian, Spanish, Mexican, Indian, or Native American.

Famous Namesakes: Actress Lucia Mendez

Lucie

(French) a form of Lucy.

Image: People imagine that Lucie's personality is unique. She's described as a free-spirited and unconventional young girl who's friendly, talkative, and carefree. Lucie is said to be childlike and innocent—perhaps even naïve—but that's what makes her so special. Physically, she's imagined as a cutie in pigtails.

Famous Namesakes: Actress Lucie Arnaz; actress Lucy Liu; character Lucy (*Peanuts*); actress Lucy Lawless; activist Lucy Stone

Lucille

(English) a familiar form of Lucy.

Image: Lucille Ball is considered to be the Queen of Comedy. It's not surprising, then, that this name calls to mind a witty, fun-loving comic. People imagine Lucille is caring and goodhearted as well as old-fashioned and intelligent. Of course, she probably has red hair and blue eyes.

Famous Namesakes: Comedian Lucille Ball

Lucinda

(Latin) a form of Lucy.

Image: Lucinda demands to know everything about everyone. She's thought to be a bossy know-it-all with too much self-esteem. People find her to be loud, nosy, and controlling. A few kind souls, however, say she's caring and perhaps a little sassy.

Famous Namesakes: Musician Lucinda Williams

Lucy

(Latin) light; bringer of light.

Image: Just like the name Lucille, this name's image links to comic queen Lucille Ball. Lucy strikes people as a playful and wacky comedian who's outgoing, affectionate, peppy, and smart. She's depicted as a pretty redhead.

Famous Namesakes: Actress Lucie Arnaz; actress Lucy Liu; character Lucy (*Peanuts*); actress Lucy Lawless; activist Lucy Stone

Lulu

(Arabic) pearl. (English) soothing, comforting.

Image: It's hard to say "Lulu" without smiling, just as it's hard to *be* Lulu without smiling. People envision Lulu as a cheerful, silly, and mischievous girl who's loads of fun to be around. Like Little Lulu, the comic strip character, she's pictured as short with a cute, round face and curly hair.

Famous Namesakes: Comic strip character Little Lulu; singer Lulu

Luna

(Latin) moon.

Image: Luna's art is captivating, but as a person she's even more so. Luna is thought to be a unique and open-minded artist, an independent spirit, and an enchanting personality. Even her appearance seems creative: She's described as a sexy brunette who wears fashionable garb and wild headscarves.

Famous Namesakes: Character Luna Lovegood (*Harry Potter* series)

Lupita

(Latin) a form of Lupe.

Image: Lupita's disposition is as full of life as is her dancing. Lupita is described as a lively and talented salsa dancer who hails from Spain or a Latin American country. She's most likely social and happy, but she's probably absent-minded as well. Nevertheless, she's seen as a kind and generous woman who loves her family.

Famous Namesakes: Actress Lupita Ferrer; actress Lupita Tovar

Lydia

(Greek) from Lydia, an ancient land in Asia.

Image: People don't know much about Lydia, so they're left to speculate. She's primarily pictured as a mysterious and withdrawn loner who's thought to be intelligent. Her solitary lifestyle leads some to assume she's an arrogant elitist, but others guess that she's simply independent. Lydia is most likely short and thin.

Famous Namesakes: Socialite Lydia Hearst

Lyla

(French) island.

Image: Sweet and outgoing, Lyla's charm shines through her music. This name conjures up the image of a caring and kind girl who likes to smile and lives to please. She's most likely confident and energetic as well. Lyla is thought to be a talented country singer, perhaps a nod to Lila McCann.

Famous Namesakes: Actress Lila Kedrova; country singer Lila McCann

Lynette

(Welsh) idol. (English) a form of Linette.

Image: Lynette has a peaceful, easy spirit. She's seen as a gentle woman who's sweet, sincere, and easygoing. Sometimes her soft-spoken nature makes her seem shy, but people generally find her to be approachable and talkative. To a few, she's so chatty, she comes across as a crabby busybody. Whatever her demeanor, she's a diminutive blond with freckles.

Famous Namesakes: Character Lynette Scavo (*Desperate Housewives*); designer Lynette Jennings

Lynn

(English) waterfall; pool below a waterfall.

Image: Lynn has just the right personality to look after others. She's thought to be a friendly, warm, and quiet woman. People claim her easygoing, conciliatory disposition makes her a perfect caregiver. Lynn is envisioned as matronly with perfectly styled hair.

Famous Namesakes: Actress Lynn Redgrave; singer Loretta Lynn; actress Lynn Whitfield; second lady Lynne Cheney

Mabel

(Latin) lovable.

Image: Mabel is crotchety, but there may be more to her than you think. People say Mabel is an elderly lady with orthopedic shoes and a miserable attitude. She's considered to be mean and cranky—she doesn't seem to like people, and people don't seem to like her. But then again, some suspect her grumpiness may be a cover for her shyness. They focus on the positive, pointing out that she's fond of baking cookies, just like any other grandma.

Famous Namesakes: Actress Mabel King

Mackenzie

(Irish) child of the wise leader.

Image: Mackenzie is a caring and pleasant girl who has a tomboyish, sporty streak that makes her hyper at times. Physically, she's depicted as a Black Irish beauty with dark hair and pale skin, but she may be a red-haired, green-eyed lass. Although she's most likely smart and strong-willed, she has her gullible moments from time to time.

Famous Namesakes: Actress Mackenzie Phillips

Maddie

(English) a familiar form of Madeline.

Image: Life is a bit more lively when Maddie is around. This name creates an image of a pretty girl with a great smile and a perky swing to life. Sometimes she's sweet and sincere, but others say she's spoiled and selfish. Everyone agrees she's lots of fun.

Famous Namesakes: Character Maddie Hayes (*Moonlighting*); actress Maddie Corman

Madeline

(Greek) high tower.

Image: There's a lot to Madeline. She strikes people as a wealthy, sophisticated brunette with a petite figure, pretty face, and big blue eyes. She's considered to be nice, but she's also demure to the point of appearing aloof. Under the reserved demeanor, she's said to be confident, smart, and generally complex.

Famous Namesakes: Secretary of state Madeleine Albright; actress Madeline Stowe; actress Madeline Kahn; author Madeline l'Engle; singer Madeline Peyroux; fiction character Madeline

Madison

(English) good; child of Maud.

Image: Madison puts on quite a performance. Above all, people think she's immensely entertaining: They imagine her to be funny, bold, and theatrical. Showmanship aside, she's also said to be loving, devoted, and open-minded. She's pictured as a brown-haired, brown-eyed girl.

Famous Namesakes: First lady Dolly Madison; novelist Madison Smartt Bell; singer Madison Cross; character Madison (*Splash*)

Mae

(English) a form of May.

Image: One of Mae's many talents is to break into tears when she doesn't get what she wants. People believe she's harsh and mean as well as shamefully manipulative. When she's not being so nasty, she comes across as loud and daring, and she may be a talented musician.

Famous Namesakes: Actress Mae West; character Aunt May (*Spider-Man*); character May Welland (*The Age of Innocence*); model May Anderson

Magdalen

(Greek) high tower.

Image: With the biblical Mary Magdalene as a namesake, it's no surprise that this name has a religious image. People say Magdalen is a devout, caring, graceful, and intelligent woman with dark hair. They believe she either lives a nunlike lifestyle or *is* a nun.

Famous Namesakes: Biblical figure Mary Magdalene

Girls

Maggie

(Greek) pearl. (English) a familiar form of Magdalen, Margaret.

Image: People conjure up two visions of Maggie. Many imagine she's a meek, bland, and perhaps even sad woman who's stuck in her sad, dull ways. But others envision Maggie as a sharp-tongued and sarcastic working-class waitress who's joyful and full of energy. People also can't decide if she's a redhead or blond, but she's most likely older.

Famous Namesakes: Actress Maggie Gyllenhaal; character Maggie the Cat (*Cat on a Hot Tin Roof*); actress Maggie Smith; character Maggie Simpson (*The Simpsons*)

Maira

(Irish) a form of Mary.

Image: People can't agree whether Maira is personable, so it may be best to approach her carefully. Although some people think she's snippy, impatient, and humorless, others see her as caring, sweet, and social. In either case, Maira is imagined to be a smart preppy with a plump figure and dark hair, and she may be a photographer.

Famous Namesakes: None

Maire

(Irish) a form of Mary.

Image: Is Maire a follower or a leader? Many describe her as a compassionate and nice woman who's shy, a little short on confidence, and comfortable following others. But just as many people say the opposite, saying Maire is strong-willed, smart, responsible, and eager to lead. In either case, she's depicted as a tall, thin brunette who's middle-aged.

Famous Namesakes: Folk singer Maire Brennan

Maisie

(Scottish) a familiar form of Margaret.

Image: Maisie is a barrel of fun. She gives the impression of a friendly and gentle girl who's funny, lots of fun, and full of contagious smiles. With wild curls, dark hair, and big blue eyes, she's said to be individualistic, creative, and open-minded.

Famous Namesakes: Fiction character Maisie Dobbs

Malana

(Hawaiian) bouyant, light.

Image: Malana has boundless beauty but a humble personality. She's regarded as an olive-skinned woman with gorgeous, dark features. Beyond her looks, people imagine she's quiet—perhaps because she's polite and conservative, but perhaps because she's shy. Malana is also said to be smart, sweet, and loving to her friends and family.

Famous Namesakes: Character Malena Scordia (*Malena*)

Mallory

(German) army counselor. (French) unlucky.

Image: Mallory is ready to lead the revolution. She may have the classic beauty of a model, but she's said to be a smart-mouthed rebel with a lot to say. Some people find her determination and outspokenness overpowering or rude, but others say she's quite intelligent. This revolutionary spitfire most likely comes from a wealthy family.

Famous Namesakes: Character Mallory Keaton (*Family Ties*); model Mallory Snyder

Mandy

(Latin) lovable.

Image: Mandy is the most popular girl in school, but popularity can cut both ways. She's pictured as confident, perky, sweet, and sporty. These traits, along with her blond hair and cute looks, have likely earned Mandy a prized place among the "in" crowd. But anyone outside that crowd thinks she's snobby, controlling, and even cruel.

Famous Namesakes: Actress and singer Mandy Moore

Mansi

(Hopi) plucked flower.

Image: Mansi's clients look forward to her personality even more than they do her styling. She comes across as a free-spirited, strong-willed, and happy-go-lucky African American woman. Some may even say she's a wild child. Although Mansi tends to be outspoken, she's also known to be a good listener who's intuitive and easy to talk to—traits that are perfect for her profession as a hairstylist.

Famous Namesakes: None

Mara

(Hebrew) melody. (Greek) a short form of Amara. (Slavic) a form of Mary.

Image: Mara sees high school as more than just a popularity contest. People think she's an insightful, diligent, and intelligent bookworm who's probably on the speech team. Although she's said to be kind and confident, she's not overly popular, having only a few friends. She's most likely pretty with brown hair and big brown eyes.

Famous Namesakes: Actress Mara Wilson; character Marah Lewis (*Guiding Light*)

Marcella

(Latin) martial, warlike.

Image: Emotionally and physically, Marcella is always composed. She's described as a level-headed and rational woman with poise and grace. People envision Marcella as tall and feminine, and they believe she's quite compassionate. She may have a creative side as well.

Famous Namesakes: Chef Marcella Hazan

Marcia

(Latin) martial, warlike.

Image: Like her or not, Marcia is often a wild and crazy gal. Most people think of her as a loud and bold party girl. Some find her outgoing ways lovable, comical, and friendly. But others say she's obnoxious and goofy. A few people have a completely different view, saying Marcia is a stuck-up priss.

Famous Namesakes: Actress Marsha Mason; character Marcia Brady (*The Brady Bunch*); actress Marcia Cross; actress Marcia Gay Harden

Marcy

(English) a familiar form of Marcella, Marcia.

Image: Marcy knows all the scuttlebutt in her suburban neighborhood. This name reminds people of a friendly but gossipy soccer mom. People say she's caring and funny, but her outspokenness and rumor mongering have given this brunette a reputation as a big mouth.

Famous Namesakes: Character Marcy (*Peanuts*); actress Marcy Walker

Margaret

(Greek) pearl.

Image: Margaret has a kind soul, but opinion is split about her spirit. She's clearly seen as a caring and understanding woman. From there, some say Margaret is timid, shy, and very unlikely to fight back. But others—perhaps remembering former British Prime Minister Margaret Thatcher—imagine she's bossy, in control, and guaranteed to get her way.

Famous Namesakes: Prime minister Margaret Thatcher; author Margaret Mitchell; anthropologist Margaret Mead; writer Margaret Atwood; activist Margaret Sanger; comedian Margaret Cho

Margarita

(Italian, Spanish) a form of Margaret.

Image: It's pretty easy to see how people come up with this name's image. Folks can't help but think of Margarita as a wild and fun-loving Latina who likes to drink and party. With her curly dark hair and stocky build, she's known to be funny and sweet as well.

Famous Namesakes: Designer Margarita Missoni

Margaux

(French) a form of Margaret.

Image: The glamorous but tragic life of Margaux Hemingway likely affects this name's image. People get the impression that Margaux is a cold, uptight, but beautiful French model. Although she's said to be elegant and impeccably dressed, she's rather melancholy and perhaps even suicidal.

Famous Namesakes: Model Margaux Hemingway; actress Margot Kidder; ballerina Margot Fonteyn

Margot

(French) a form of Margaret.

Image: When it comes to her job, Margot likes books much more than she likes people. This name gives the impression of a snooty, selfish, and rude woman who's pudgy and short with brown hair. On the more positive side, people imagine she's well read and inquisitive, and some think she may be a teacher or librarian—albeit a snobby, snippy one.

Famous Namesakes: Actress Margot Kidder; ballerina Margot Fonteyn; model Margaux Hemingway

Marguerite

(French) a form of Margaret.

Image: Marguerite is still a class act. She's regarded as a well-educated and stylish older woman. Classy and beautiful, she's considered to be kind, gentle, and honest. People say she's quite lively, especially when it comes to dancing.

Famous Namesakes: Writer Marguerite Duras; physicist Marguerite Perey; actress Marguerite Moreau

Maria

(Hebrew) bitter; sea of bitterness. (Italian, Spanish) a form of Mary.

Image: Maria is as tough as she is tender. People describe her as a Latina who's strong-willed and headstrong; however, she's known to also have a soft side as a sweet and caring mother. Sometime Maria seems shy and quiet, but other times she can be personable and loud.

Famous Namesakes: Opera singer Maria Callas; character Maria (*West Side Story*); character Maria (*The Sound of Music*); journalist Maria Shriver; tennis player Maria Sharapova; actress Maria Bello; television host Maria Menounos

Mariah

(Hebrew) a form of Mary.

Image: A megastar like Mariah Carey can make a big impression on a name's image. People imagine Mariah as an arrogant and sometimes mean diva with a sexy appearance and dynamic singing talent. She's believed to be confident and outgoing, and she's well respected and popular.

Famous Namesakes: Singer Mariah Carey

Marie

(French) a form of Mary.

Image: Marie laments how much life has changed since she was a girl. She's said to be a loving and kind middle-aged Latina who finds herself clinging to old-fashioned morals. Marie is described as witty and intelligent, and people say she feels strongly about her beliefs.

Famous Namesakes: Queen Marie Antoinette; physicist Marie Curie; singer Marie Osmond

Mariel

(German, Dutch) a form of Mary.

Image: Don't let Mariel's meek demeanor fool you—she's quite sharp. She's regarded as bashful and mousy but good at her job. That's because this pretty brunette is said to be smart, organized, and professional. People also consider Mariel to be sweet when she loosens up.

Famous Namesakes: Actress Mariel Hemingway

Marietta

(Italian) a familiar form of Marie.

Image: Marietta is a lighthearted lady. She's imagined as a kind, supportive woman with an optimistic demeanor and a cheerful sense of humor. She may not be very smart, but that doesn't dampen her sweet, jovial mood. People picture Marietta as a dark-haired, matronly Italian woman.

Famous Namesakes: Opera singer Marietta Alboni; humorist Marietta Holley

Marilyn

(Hebrew) Mary's line or descendants.

Image: Marilyn Monroe was one of the most beautiful—and tragic—figures of the twentieth century. Is it any wonder that people think of a bubbly and buxom blond when they hear this name? They say Marilyn is sweet, ditzy, and spontaneous, but unfortunately also troubled with mental problems and drug addiction.

Famous Namesakes: Actress Marilyn Monroe; musician Marilyn Manson; columnist Marilyn vos Savant

Marissa

(Latin) a form of Maris, Marisa.

Image: Marissa knows just how to brighten someone's day. She's said to be a happy-go-lucky and caring brown-eyed brunette who likes to cheer up others with her smile. She's also imagined to be bright and curious.

Famous Namesakes: Actress Marisa Tomei; character Marissa Cooper (*The O.C.*); actress Marissa Jaret Winokur; model Marissa Miller

Marit

(Aramaic) lady.

Image: Folks can listen—and laugh—to Marit's stories all night. People picture Marit as an intelligent and well-read woman who's the life of any party, thanks to her hilarious and charming wit, jolly demeanor, and endless assortment of interesting tales.

Famous Namesakes: Singer Marit Larsen

Marjorie

(Greek) a familiar form of Margaret. (Scottish) a form of Mary.

Image: Marjorie is either quick to chat or quick to cave. Most people think Marjorie is a joyful and giggly gossip with enthusiasm and cheer to spare. But a few people imagine she's a passive and mousy "yes" woman who's too easily intimidated. Physically, she may be pale, tall, and freckled.

Famous Namesakes: Novelist Marjorie Kinnan Rawlings

Girls

Marlene

(Greek) high tower. (Slavic) a form of Magdalen.

Image: There are two options when it comes to Marlene: On one hand, she may be reserved and dull with an unpleasant, stubborn demeanor. On the other hand, she may be playful and kind with a happy, carefree attitude. Either way, people say Marlene is matronly, big-boned, and light-haired.

Famous Namesakes: Actress Marlene Dietrich; painter Marlene Dumas

Marley

(English) a form of Marlene.

Image: Late, great reggae legend Bob Marley is inextricably tied to this name's image. Marley is imagined as a gifted and artistic musician who's spiritual, independent, fearless, and definitely not conservative. She's said to be a hip hippie. People picture her as dark-skinned with long dreadlocks.

Famous Namesakes: Actress Marley Shelton; actress Marlee Matlin

Marlo

(English) a form of Mary.

Image: Marlo has a kind heart to go with her big mouth. People say Marlo is usually caring and sensitive, but she can seem like a spirited busybody at the same time. She's said to be talkative and opinionated, smart and strong-willed. She's pictured with dark hair and an olive complexion.

Famous Namesakes: Actress Marlo Thomas

Marnie

(Hebrew) a short form of Marnina.

Image: Apparently, Marnie views herself in a light no one else sees. People say Marnie is whiny and immature as well as selfish and full of herself. The odd part is, people don't understand why she's so narcissistic. Frankly, they find her to be nothing special at all, with her thick glasses and short, plump build.

Famous Namesakes: Film character Marnie; singer Marni Nixon

Marsha

(English) a form of Marcia.

Image: Marsha is either prissy or popular. Most people think Marsha is a prudish and dull blond who has a big mouth and an even bigger ego. Although she comes across as a snob, she may be dorky as well. Other people, however, believe she's a funny, goofy extrovert who's very well liked.

Famous Namesakes: Actress Marsha Mason; character Marcia Brady (*The Brady Bunch*); actress Marcia Cross; actress Marcia Gay Harden

Marta

(English) a short form of Martha, Martina.

Image: Marta doesn't realize what a good person she is. She comes across as a shy woman who's educated and gentle with children, but still insecure. Her low self-esteem may stem from her homely, frumpy appearance. People imagine she's European and middle-aged.

Famous Namesakes: Singer Marta Sanchez

Martha

(Aramaic) lady; sorrowful.

Image: Pop icon Martha Stewart has a contradicting image: charming homemaker *and* hardnosed businesswoman. This name's image is also contradictory: People imagine Martha as a motherly and loving housewife who likes to decorate and cook, but is also two-faced, stern, and ruthless. Interestingly, people picture her as a round, homely, and old woman with glasses—not at all like Martha Stewart.

Famous Namesakes: First lady Martha Washington; entrepreneur Martha Stewart; choreographer Martha Graham; biblical figure Martha; character Martha Kent (*Superman*); singer Martha Reeves

Martina

(Latin) martial, warlike.

Image: This name has a sporty edge, thanks to tennis stars Martina Hingis and Martina Navratilova. People think Martina is an athlete who's friendly yet serious and committed to her sport. Some say she's shy, others say she's quiet, but everyone imagines she's tall, thin, and Eastern European. She probably wears her hair in a bob.

Famous Namesakes: Tennis player Martina Hingis; singer Martina McBride; tennis player Martina Navratilova

Mary

(Hebrew) bitter; sea of bitterness.

Image: The mother of Jesus, biblical Mary is *the* namesake of one of the most popular names. People picture Mary as a nurturing and gentle mother who's religious, traditional, and simple. She most likely has a conservative, mousy appearance.

Famous Namesakes: Biblical figure Mary; Mary Queen of Scots; fiction character Mary Poppins; biblical figure Mary Magdalene; singer Mary J. Blige; reporter Mary Hart; character Mary Jane Watson (*Spider-Man*); entrepreneur Mary Kay Ash; artist Mary Cassatt

Mary Beth

(American) a combination of Mary + Beth.

Image: Mary Beth is a bookish lady. This name calls to mind a sensitive and sweet woman who's old-fashioned, quiet, and intelligent. Some people imagine Mary Beth is prudish and dull, but others see she's full of life underneath her timid demeanor. She's typically pictured as a plain brunette with a medium build.

Famous Namesakes: Political figure Mary Beth Cahill; actress Mary Beth Evans; actress Mary Beth Hurt; actress Mary Beth McDonough

Mary Ellen

(American) a combination of Mary + Ellen.

Image: Mary Ellen is a pleasant young woman who happens to like staying home on Saturday nights. She's pictured as a talkative, down-to-earth, and well-liked Catholic schoolgirl. Mary Ellen is said to be smart and hardworking, but she may be a bit of a homebody.

Famous Namesakes: Photographer Mary Ellen Mark

Matilda

(German) powerful battler.

Image: Matilda is a curious, lively girl. People say Matilda is a likable and outgoing tomboy with red hair, green eyes, and freckles. She's known to have a witty sense of humor and a love for the outdoors. She's most likely good at school and well read, but she still looks at the world with wide-eyed wonder.

Famous Namesakes: Character Matilda Wormwood (*Matilda*)

Maud

(English) a short form of Madeline, Matilda.

Image: It's hard to get a break if your name sounds like *mad*. People describe Maud as a homely, masculine-looking grouch. She probably has no humor, no imagination, and no fun. A few people remember Bea Arthur's character on the TV sitcom *Maude* and say she's a funny and frank woman.

Famous Namesakes: Actress Maud Adams; character Maude Findlay (*Maude*)

Maura

(Irish) dark. A form of Mary, Maureen.

Image: Maura usually gets her way. Some people call her self-assured and determined, but others label her as bratty, full of herself, and short-tempered if she doesn't get her way. She's most likely a smart, successful woman, but she can also be crafty when she feels the need. When Maura isn't being so difficult, she comes across as good-natured and close to her family.

Famous Namesakes: Author Maura Murphy; actress Maura Tierney; actress Maura West

Maureen

(French) dark. (Irish) a form of Mary.

Image: These two images of Maureen seem several decades apart. Some people say Maureen is an older churchgoer who plays bingo and lives alone with her cats. Others say she's a young beauty who's cool, fashionable, popular, and funny. Either way, people consider her to be sweet and sensible.

Famous Namesakes: Tennis player Maureen Connolly; actress Maureen O'Hara; Maureen O'Sullivan; actress Maureen McCormick

Mauve

(French) violet colored.

Image: No middle ground for Mauve—her personality is one extreme or the other. Nobody is sure whether Mauve is a shy and studious recluse or a wild and crazy party animal. But people say she's definitely a small and pale brunette.

Famous Namesakes: None

Maxine

(Latin) greatest.

Image: Maxine has a heart of gold—and a lot of "gold" from her divorce settlement. She's pictured as a compassionate softie who's outspoken, impulsive, and cheerfully outgoing. Middle-aged and beautiful, Maxine is most likely a rich and spoiled divorcée, but deep down, she wants the best for everyone.

Famous Namesakes: Poet Maxine Kumin; singer Maxine Nightingale

May

(Latin) great. (Arabic) discerning. (English) flower; month of May.

Image: May pours herself into her homemaking. May strikes people as a pleasant, demure, but simple-minded housewife. She's described as a frail brunette with pretty, porcelain skin that's beginning to wrinkle. Although she's typically gentle and sweet, she seems to run a tight ship at home.

Famous Namesakes: Character Aunt May (*Spider-Man*); character May Welland (*The Age of Innocence*); actress Mae West; model May Anderson

Maya

(Hindi) God's creative power. (Greek) mother; grandmother. (Latin) great.

Image: Maya knows how to have fun while getting things done. People describe Maya as a caring, personable, and book-smart woman. She's said to be fun-loving, but she's also goal oriented. She's portrayed as a slim petite with very dark hair and a beautiful caramel-colored complexion.

Famous Namesakes: Poet Maya Angelou; comedian Maya Rudolph

McKayla

(American) a form of Michaela.

Image: McKayla is a charming little lady. She's envisioned as a young, outgoing girl who's full of life, giggles, and smiles. People believe she's lovely with blond pigtails. She's also said to be lovable, smart, and well behaved, even if she can be strong-willed at times. Taking a different view, a few people see McKayla as a grown-up model or actress.

Famous Namesakes: None

Mead

(Greek) honey wine.

Image: Mead is a social misfit. This name makes people think of a shy and nerdy outcast who's smart but sad, nervous, and misunderstood. Her appearance doesn't help her image: She's pictured as short and unattractive with red hair, pale skin, and thick glasses. It's no wonder that people describe Mead as vulnerable.

Famous Namesakes: Anthropologist Margaret Mead

Megan

(Greek) pearl; great. (Irish) a form of Margaret.

Image: Megan is delightful. She's imagined as a kind and caring woman with a pretty smile and pretty complexion. She's thought to be outgoing, peppy, witty, and no doubt well liked. People suspect she has Irish heritage.

Famous Namesakes: Actress Megan Mullally; actress Megan Ward; author Megan McCafferty

Meka

(Hebrew) a familiar form of Michaela.

Image: When you name sounds like *meek*, people may be inclined to view you a certain way. Meka is considered to be a soft-spoken and passive introvert who's small, skinny, and cute. While she may be shy, she's also intelligent and creative. People also suspect she's quite happy with her life.

Famous Namesakes: Journalist Meka Nichols

Melanie

(Greek) dark-skinned.

Image: Melanie is a cool mom. This name calls to mind a loving and sweet mother who's fun, confident, and free-spirited. Melanie is no doubt popular with kids and adults alike. She's also said to be a pretty and slim blond.

Famous Namesakes: Actress Melanie Griffith; character Melanie Wilkes (*Gone with the Wind*); singer Melanie Brown; singer Melanie Chisholm

Melinda

(Greek) honey.

Image: For Melinda, every day is filled with anxiety. People describe Melinda as a nervous, jumpy hypochondriac. She's said to be timid as a mouse, smart in a geeky way, and, not surprisingly, self-conscious and insecure. Perhaps these unhealthy traits stem from the fact that her overprotective parents babied her for far too long.

Famous Namesakes: Philanthropist Melinda Gates

Melissa

(Greek) honey bee.

Image: Melissa is high energy and high-class. She's considered to be energetic and outgoing, although it may be more accurate to say she's hyper and wild. She's probably rich, spoiled, and snobby at times, but she's also smart and talented in many areas. People describe Melissa as a short blond.

Famous Namesakes: TV commentator Melissa Rivers; musician Melissa Manchester; actress Melissa Joan Hart; singer Melissa Etheridge; actress Melissa George

Melody

(Greek) melody.

Image: Melody is as sweet as a song. She's overwhelmingly viewed as a caring, lovable, and generous young woman. She's typically full of life and joyous, but she can seem a bit shy in certain situations. Melody is pictured as a petite, long-haired brunette.

Famous Namesakes: Actress Melody Scott Thomas

Mercedes

(Latin) reward, payment. (Spanish) merciful.

Image: *Fast and furious* describe Mercedes's approach to life. Most people think Mercedes is a loud, wild, and high-maintenance woman who may be a stripper. She's likely tall and exotically beautiful. A few positive thinkers imagine she's sweet, sensitive, and shy.

Famous Namesakes: Actress Mercedes Ruehl

Meredith

(Welsh) protector of the sea.

Image: Meredith doesn't win many people over. She's thought to be snobby, mean, prissy, bossy, and moody. On a more positive note, she may be organized and smart. Meredith may also be social, although some people simply call her a loud, obnoxious gossip. Dark-haired and tall, she may be beautiful or she may be homely.

Famous Namesakes: Character Meredith Grey (*Grey's Anatomy*); actress Meredith Baxter; journalist Meredith Vieria; singer Meredith Brooks

Meryl

(German) famous. (Irish) shining sea.

Image: Meryl is not a pleasant woman, to say the least. People imagine Meryl to be an incredibly mean and arrogant bully. Although some say this tall and skinny woman is classy and elegant, others imagine she's a schoolmarm or an old maid with an unkempt appearance.

Famous Namesakes: Actress Meryl Streep

Girls

Mia

(Italian) mine.

Image: Mia is a fascinating original. People think of her as an arty, unique woman who's beautiful, confident, and wise. They say she's quite mysterious—she can be energetic and outgoing one minute, but thoughtful and quiet the next. Mia is most likely short with olive skin and dark hair.

Famous Namesakes: Actress Mia Farrow; soccer player Mia Hamm; model Mia Tyler

Michaela

(Hebrew) a form of Michael.

Image: A feminine version of the name Michael, this name's image has girlish and boyish traits. People describe Michaela as an attractive brunette who's feminine but physically strong. She's considered to be warmhearted and sociable, but she's also brazen and tomboyish.

Famous Namesakes: Character Michaela Quinn (*Dr. Quinn, Medicine Woman*)

Michelle

(French) who is like God?

Image: Michelle is headstrong but possibly offensive. She's often pictured as a confident and brainy leader with a fun sense of humor. But sometimes her strong, independent attitude makes her come across as standoffish, rude, and even mean. Physically, Michelle is pictured as pretty and petite.

Famous Namesakes: Actress Michelle Pfieffer; singer Michelle Branch; actress Michelle Phillips; actress Michelle Lee; figure skater Michelle Kwan; actress Michelle Williams; actress Michelle Trachtenberg

Mickie

(American) a familiar form of Michaela.

Image: Expect fun, not depth, from someone with this bubbly name. Mickie is pictured as a silly and youthful prankster who's friendly to everyone. People don't expect her to be a deep thinker—they say she's quite ditzy—but she's still a lot of fun. As for her looks, she's most likely dark-haired, short, and cute.

Famous Namesakes: Professional wrestler Mickie James

Mildred

(English) gentle counselor.

Image: Mildred is a grandma on the go. She's thought to be a white-haired lady who enjoys spaghetti dinners at church, baking cookies for her grandkids, and tending her prized roses. She's most likely good-natured and loved by all, even if she can be a bit absent-minded at times.

Famous Namesakes: Film character Mildred Pierce; author Mildred Taylor

Millicent

(English) industrious. (Greek) a form of Melissa.

Image: Unfortunately, Millicent is either evil or nerdy. Most people believe she's a malicious and scary witch—a nod perhaps to the similar-sounding Maleficent, villain of Disney's *Sleeping Beauty*. Those not thinking of witches imagine Millicent as a dorky yet prissy girl who's big, dowdy, and acne-prone.

Famous Namesakes: Activist Millicent Garrett Fawcett

Millie

(English) a familiar form of Amelia, Emily, Mildred, Millicent.

Image: Millie just fell off the turnip truck. When people think of this name, they imagine an innocent and sweetly naïve woman who's easy to take advantage of. Millie is most likely a country hick from down on the farm, and she's helpful, vivacious, but not too smart. She's envisioned as a plump, older brunette.

Famous Namesakes: Actress Millie Perkins; singer Millie Jackson; character Millie Dillmount (*Thoroughly Modern Millie*)

Milly

(English) a familiar form of Amelia, Emily, Mildred, Millicent.

Image: Milly is a regular at the coffee klatch. She's said to be a warmhearted, intelligent, and old-fashioned woman who's chubby, dowdy, and short. Some say Milly is a bit of a busybody, but others just call her friendly.

Famous Namesakes: Actress Millie Perkins; singer Millie Jackson; character Millie Dillmount (*Thoroughly Modern Millie*)

Mimi

(French) a familiar form of Miriam.

Image: Mimi is either a sweet old lady or a boorish character. Some see her as a kind and affectionate grandmother who'd do anything for others. Those who remember Mimi the flamboyant secretary of TV's *The Drew Carey Show* say she's loud, obnoxious, and rude, not to mention gaudily dressed and made-up.

Famous Namesakes: Actress Mimi Rogers

Mindy

(Greek) a familiar form of Melinda.

Image: Mindy's bouncy personality can go two ways. To most people, Mindy is a cute, friendly, and fun flirt with dark hair and a button nose. To some, though, she's a snobby ditz who thinks she's better than everyone. In either case, she may be a cheerleader.

Famous Namesakes: Character Mindy McConnell (*Mork & Mindy*); actress Mindy Cohn; singer Mindy McCready

Minka

(Polish) a short form of Wilhelmina.

Image: Minka is a bit of a minx. This name evokes the image of a playful and bubbly flirt who's always laughing. She's said to be easygoing as well as free spirited and outspoken. People picture her with black hair, milky skin, and dark blue eyes.

Famous Namesakes: Actress Minka Kelly

Minnie

(American) a familiar form of Mina, Minerva, Minna, Wilhelmina.

Image: Minnie ranges from bashful to ditzy. People think Minnie is a petite and thin woman who's sometimes friendly and sometimes shy. When she's feeling outgoing, she can be quite peppy, which unfortunately makes her seem like a flighty airhead.

Famous Namesakes: Disney character Minnie Mouse; actress Minnie Driver; comedian Minnie Pearl; singer Minnie Ripperton

Girls

Miranda

(Latin) strange; wonderful; admirable.

Image: Miranda displays several sides of her complex personality. People say Miranda can be sociable and understanding—at times. In other instances, she appears shy and sensitive or even bossy and mean. She's most likely smart, and she's also thought to be athletic with her tall, slim physique.

Famous Namesakes: Character Miranda Hobbes (*Sex and the City*) actress Miranda Richardson; character Miranda Bailey (*Grey's Anatomy*); singer Miranda Lambert; model Miranda Kerr; actress Miranda Otto

Mireille

(Hebrew) God spoke. (Latin) wonderful.

Image: Mireille has good behavior to go with her good grades. This name reminds people of a studious and bookish young woman. Shy, soft-spoken, and perhaps even fragile, this wallflower rarely expresses her wild side. Mireille is pictured as tall, lithe, and beautiful, and she may be French.

Famous Namesakes: Singer Mireille Mathieu

Miriam

(Hebrew) bitter; sea of bitterness.

Image: Miriam lives a simple, moral life. This name calls to mind a kindly grandmother who's gentle and patient. She's said to be a conservative and pious woman, which sometimes makes her prudish and judgmental—some will say that also means she leads a boring life, but she seems comfortable with her quiet existence.

Famous Namesakes: Biblical figure Miriam; actress Miriam Margoyles

Missy

(English) a familiar form of Melissa, Millicent.

Image: Missy causes a commotion. She's thought to be a short woman who's annoyingly loud and energetic. People also believe she's rude, conceited, and full of attitude. A few people, however, argue that Missy has a big heart and is eager to help others. Although pictured with a husky figure, she's likely to be sporty and competitive.

Famous Namesakes: Singer Missy Higgins; rapper Missy Elliot; model Missy Rayder

Misty

(English) shrouded by mist.

Image: Misty isn't sophisticated, and that's a bit of an understatement. When people hear this name, they think of a trampy and trashy Las Vegas stripper who has stringy, bleached-blond hair with dark roots. She's most likely self-centered, pushy, obnoxious, and daft. People suspect Misty may have grown up in a poor, country family.

Famous Namesakes: Singer Misty Edwards

Mitzi

(German) a form of Mary, Miriam.

Image: This poor girl may get stuck with the nickname "Ditzy Mitzi." She's described as a dumb but sweet blond who's thin, short, and blue-eyed. Mitzi is said to be bouncy and hyper, if not wild, in a scatterbrained way.

Famous Namesakes: Actress Mitzi Kapture; actress Mitzi Gaynor

Modesta

(Italian, Spanish) a form of Modesty.

Image: Modesta proves that modesty and confidence aren't mutually exclusive qualities. People describe this olive-skinned Latina as, of course, modest and good-natured. But they also say she's a confident, independent, and determined go-getter.

Famous Namesakes: Saint Modesta

Modesty

(Latin) modest.

Image: If you ask Modesty to describe her best traits, she'll probably blush and giggle. It's no surprise people think Modesty is coy, sweet, innocent, and, of course, modest. She's said to be either young or young-at-heart, and she probably enjoys writing poetry and music. As for her appearance, she's likely skinny and pale with a nice smile.

Famous Namesakes: Comic strip character Modesty Blaise

Moira

(Irish) great. A form of Mary.

Image: Moira isn't like the other students. She's imagined as a dorky math wiz loaded with book smarts and logic. She's considered to be kind, but her practical, traditional behavior makes her seem very unusual to her classmates. She may be foreign.

Famous Namesakes: Actress Moira Shearer; actress Moira Kelly

Molly

(Irish) a familiar form of Mary.

Image: Molly is delightfully demure. She's described as an adorable, innocent, and quiet girl. She's pictured with brown hair and cute freckles. She's most likely smart and sensitive, and a few people believe she loves a day out on the water.

Famous Namesakes: Actress Molly Ringwald; comedian Molly Shannon

Mona

(Irish) noble. (Greek) a short form of Monica, Ramona, Rimona.

Image: Forget her age—Mona is alive and kickin'. She's thought to be a playful, fun, and even flirty old lady with a stout figure and jet-black hair. Smart and confident, people say Mona is active, joyful, and always friendly.

Famous Namesakes: Character Mona Robinson (*Who's the Boss?*)

★ Star Kids

Moon Unit

Moon Unit's quirkiness is just the tip of the iceberg. She's described as an odd and carefree hippie who may be a musician or a performance artist. Then again, she may be too unfocused and loony to work at all, even though she's quite smart. She's pictured as thin and pale with long, black hair. All in all, Moon Unit seems to be a fitting name for the daughter of eccentric musician Frank Zappa.

Monica

(Greek) solitary. (Latin) advisor.

Image: Monica can be as naughty or nice as she wants to be. She primarily comes across as a vain, selfish, and manipulative princess. While she's quite rude in certain situations, Monica can be fun, popular, and even sweet. In any situation, this dark-haired, petite lady is usually assertive, smart, and strong.

Famous Namesakes: Character Monica Gellar (*Friends*); R&B singer Monica; infamous White House intern Monica Lewinsky; actress Monica Potter; actress Monica Bellucci

Monique

(French) a form of Monica.

Image: Take Monique as she comes—the good, the bad, and the ugly. She's described as a rich and high-maintenance African American woman with an attitude. She may be spoiled and snobby as well as cranky and bossy. At the same time, she's said to be a confident and outspoken go-getter with a great sense of humor. People imagine Monique loves to party and have a wild time, especially when it comes to seducing men with her curvy body and exotic looks.

Famous Namesakes: Comedian Mo'Nique; designer Monique Lhuiller

Girls

Montana

(Spanish) mountain.

Image: Montana doesn't like to be cooped up indoors. This name makes people think of a joyful and loud extrovert who's rugged and outdoorsy, whether she's a tree-hugger or a cowgirl. Montana is said to be sassy, independent, and strong—and pretty to boot.

Famous Namesakes: Television character Hannah Montana

Morgan

(Welsh) seashore.

Image: Morgan can be a bit difficult at times. She strikes people as a beautiful, wealthy woman who's strong to the point of being bossy and snobby to the point of being rude. She does seem to be smart, however, and at least a few people imagine Morgan can be sweet in certain situations.

Famous Namesakes: Actress Morgan Fairchild; mythological figure Morgan le Fay

Muriel

(Arabic) myrrh. (Irish) shining sea.

Image: Perhaps this name is shaped by the title character of *Muriel's Wedding*. She's pictured as a fun-loving and charming woman whom everyone loves to be around—despite the fact that she's nerdy and unattractive with a big nose and buckteeth.

Famous Namesakes: Character Muriel Heslop (*Muriel's Wedding*)

Mya

(Burmese) emerald. (Italian) a form of Mia.

Image: Everyone sees Mya in a unique way. To many, she's an attentive, sensitive, and wise woman. Then again, others describe her as perky and bouncy. A few think she's loud, aggressive, and bossy, and some claim she's quiet and industrious. All in all, Mya is most likely a cute Latina.

Famous Namesakes: Singer Mya; poet Maya Angelou; comedian Maya Rudolph

 **Star Kids**

Moxie CrimeFighter

Pow! *Biff*! *Zang*! Moxie CrimeFighter to the rescue! People think she's a fearless and invincible superhero who's spunky and spirited, yet always honorable. She's probably muscular enough to take down bad guys. Setting aside superpowers, other people imagine she's a unique and attention-craving performance artist. This last image is probably close to the truth, considering Moxie CrimeFighter is the daughter of illusionist Penn Jillette.

Myra

(Latin) fragrant ointment.

Image: Myra proves that old brainiacs never die, they just get dorkier. This name evokes the image of a shy but smart woman. Even in old age, Myra's glasses, gangly figure, and know-it-all demeanor still make her seem like a nerd. People believe she mostly keeps quiet but sighs whenever she's annoyed.

Famous Namesakes: Fiction character Myra Breckenridge

Myrna

(Irish) beloved.

Image: Myrna is friendless—no surprise there. People perceive her to be a cranky and rude woman with no qualms about bossing others around. Unhappy, sarcastic, and uncaring, Myrna is most likely lonely and without friends. To complete the image, she's described as overweight, old, and sloppy.

Famous Namesakes: Actress Myrna Loy

Nadia

(French, Slavic) hopeful.

Image: Nadia is both sweet and strong. She's thought to be friendly and gentle but determined and focused. Like famed gymnast Nadia Comaneci, she's said to be feminine and pretty with dark hair, and she may be foreign. Some also picture her as agile, petite, and strong.

Famous Namesakes: Gymnast Nadia Comaneci; character Nadia Yassir (*24*); character Nadia Santos (*Alias*); actress Nadia Bjorlin

Nadine

(French, Slavic) a form of Nadia.

Image: Nadine wishes there were someone else in her life. She's regarded as a shy and aloof homebody who's not only single but also friendless. She's said to be bookish and polite, but her lonely existence leaves her deeply unhappy. Physically, Nadine is said to be tall, heavyset, and brunette.

Famous Namesakes: Novelist Nadine Gordimer; singer Nadine Coyle; actress Nadine Velazquez

Nailah

(Arabic) a form of Naila.

Image: Nailah isn't just a fashion model—she's a role model. She's pictured as a pretty, dark-haired model who's friendly, energetic, and determined to succeed. Because of her confidence and talent, many people think of Nailah as a winner, and her family and friends are quite proud of her accomplishments.

Famous Namesakes: None

Nancy

(English) gracious. A familiar form of Nan.

Image: Fictional teen sleuth Nancy Drew is skilled at solving mysteries, and those same skills are present in this name's image. Nancy is thought to be smart, curious, and hardworking. She can be prim, proper, and somewhat preppy, but people also believe she's quick-witted, chatty, and easy to befriend. This tall brunette is said to have good intentions and lots of energy.

Famous Namesakes: Speaker of the house Nancy Pelosi; fiction character Nancy Drew; first lady Nancy Reagan; figure skater Nancy Kerrigan; musician Nancy Wilson; talk show host Nancy Grace

Nanette

(French) a form of Nancy.

Image: Nanette may be polite and moral, but she won't get pushed around. She's described as a generous, sweet, and respectful hometown girl. Some may call her and her values old-fashioned and conservative, but Nanette can also be sassy and quick to stand up for herself. People depict her as a skinny, short, and buxom blond.

Famous Namesakes: Designer Nanette Lepore

Naomi

(Hebrew) pleasant, beautiful.

Image: This name's image bears a physical resemblance to supermodel Naomi Campbell. She's described as a flawless bombshell who's tall, dark-skinned, and exotic. Beyond her looks, Naomi is said to be charming, articulate, and self-assured. People find her to be flirty and fun.

Famous Namesakes: Actress Naomi Watts; model Naomi Campbell; singer Naomi Judd; writer Naomi Wolf

Narcissa

(Greek) daffodil.

Image: Narcissa may fit her name perfectly. Most people think she's, of course, a narcissistic, snooty, and rich foreigner. As for her looks, she's imagined to be gawky, pale, and pretty—although not as pretty as she may think. A few people argue on her behalf, claiming Narcissa is misunderstood and actually quite nice.

Famous Namesakes: Character Narcissa Malfoy (*Harry Potter* series)

Natalia

(Russian) a form of Natalie.

Image: Natalia is a bit of an enigma. She's described as a sweet and happy woman who's dark, slender, and beautiful. Intelligent as well as artistic, she may be a doctor, a dancer, or a writer. She may even be a model. Some people say Natalia tends to be quiet, which gives her an air of mystery.

Famous Namesakes: Ballerina Natalia Romanovna Makarova; model Natalia Vodianova

Natalie

(Latin) born on Christmas day.

Image: Natalie has brains behind her beauty. She's pictured as a fair-haired and classically beautiful woman who's smart, confident, and well spoken. People also imagine she's funny, talkative, and independent.

Famous Namesakes: Actress Natalie Wood; actress Natalie Portman; singer Natalie Imbruglia; singer Natalie Merchant

Natasha

(Russian) a form of Natalie.

Image: This name is used stereotypically for Russian femme fatales, like Natasha of TV's *The Rocky and Bullwinkle Show*. This Natasha is thought to be a cruel, ruthless woman who's self-centered and spoiled. With her black hair, willowy figure, and beauty, she's also said to be a sensual and mysterious Russian.

Famous Namesakes: Actress Natassja Kinski; actress Natasha Richardson; actress Natasha Henstridge; singer Natasha Bedingfield

Neena

(Spanish) a form of Nina.

Image: These two personalities of Neena couldn't be more different. This name makes people think of a willowy, leggy redhead who's either a well-meaning, well-read sweetheart or a wild and money-loving gold digger.

Famous Namesakes: Actress Neena Gupta; designer Nina Ricci; singer Nina Persson; singer Nina Gordon; singer Nina Simone

Nellie

(English) a familiar form of Cornelia, Eleanor, Helen, Prunella.

Image: Nellie Oleson was the bratty rich girl on TV's *Little House on the Prairie*, and some of her personality spills over into this name's image. Nellie is described as a bossy, snotty, and selfish blond with ringlets. Although she's known to be of only average intelligence, she comes across as a know-it-all. She also seems to be a prissy goody-goody.

Famous Namesakes: Character Nellie Oleson (*Little House on the Prairie*); journalist Nellie Bly; singer Nellie McKay; singer Nelly Furtado

Nerissa

(Greek) sea nymph.

Image: Nerissa may have a light touch or a heavy hand. She's most often described as a dainty, sexy woman with dark hair and dark skin. From there, some depict her as kind, graceful, well spoken, and loving. Others find her to be bold, daring, and weird—she may even be an outcast.

Famous Namesakes: Character Nerissa (*The Merchant of Venice*)

Nessa

(Scandinavian) promontory. (Greek) a short form of Agnes.

Image: Opinions are split about Nessa. Some people say she's caring, intelligent, and peaceful. Others believe she's meek, melancholy, and pessimistic. Still others claim she's jovial, spunky, and popular. As for her looks, everyone agrees Nessa is pretty and petite with brown hair and green eyes.

Famous Namesakes: Singer Nessa Morgan

Nevaeh

(American) the word *heaven* spelled backward.

Image: People seem to be at odds about Nevaeh. Some say she's smart; others say she's not a great thinker. Some say she's hardworking; others say she's lazy and spoiled. Some say she's charming; others say she's awkward. As for her looks, some say she's African American; others say she's Latino. Lastly, some say she's beautiful; others say she's homely.

Famous Namesakes: None

Nia

(Irish) a familiar form of Neila.

Image: Nia does more than just hit the books. She's thought to be a shy and soft-spoken college student who's as pretty as a model. People say she's hardworking, studious, and independent, but in her free time, Nia seems to enjoy reading romance novels and watching soap operas.

Famous Namesakes: Actress Nia Long; actress Nia Peeples

Nicole

(French) a form of Nicholas.

Image: Is Nicole a snob, or is she just misunderstood? She's described as a stuck-up, rude, and intolerable woman who doesn't have many friends. Some people, however, say she seems snobby only because she's intelligent, strong-willed, and stubborn—and because she can be a bit of a showoff.

Famous Namesakes: Actress Nicole Kidman; socialite Nicole Richie; singer Nicole Scherzinger; designer Nicole Miller

Nicolette

(French) a form of Nicole.

Image: Nicolette inspires myriad images. People see her as a breathtaking blond who may be any of the following: a ditzy and shallow shopaholic, a spontaneous and strong-willed independent, a snooty and popular priss, or an eccentric and wild theatre major.

Famous Namesakes: Actress Nicolette Sheridan

Nidia

(Latin) nest.

Image: No matter how unpleasant she may be, people can't get enough of Nidia. She's primarily considered to be a loud party girl with a superthin figure and olive skin. Even though she's bossy, rude, and totally stuck-up, people still find Nidia to be interesting and popular.

Famous Namesakes: Professional wrestler Nidia

Nike

(Greek) victorious.

Image: It may seem like stating the obvious, but people imagine Nike is a sports nut who's cocky, bullheaded, and competitive. She's most likely built for sports with her tall, toned body. Unfortunately, some people find her jock act to be rude and unimaginative, although a few find it to be funny.

Famous Namesakes: Mythological figure Nike

Nikita

(Russian) victorious people.

Image: Nikita is self-possessed and cool. She strikes people as a tall, gorgeous, and blond Russian woman with a warm smile and lots of friends. She's said to be a confident and successful go-getter, but some people believe Nikita has an independent, self-centered streak at times.

Famous Namesakes: Premier Nikita Khrushchev

Nikki

(American) a familiar form of Nicole.

Image: Nikki is the picture-perfect mean girl. She's imagined as an enthusiastic and talkative cheerleader who's cute, blond, and thin. She's also said to be an honor-roll student. But positives aside, people suspect Nikki can be mean, moody, and snobby. She seems to care more about her expensive wardrobe than she does about other people.

Famous Namesakes: Model Niki Taylor; actress Nikki Cox; poet Nikki Giovanni; actress Nikki Reed

Nina

(Spanish) girl. (Native American) mighty. (Hebrew) a familiar form of Hannah.

Image: Here's a real firecracker. The name Nina calls to mind a petite woman who's spirited, fun, loud, and confident. She's most likely a dark-haired and dark-complexioned Latina. People imagine she's loving and lively as well as witty and smart.

Famous Namesakes: Singer Nina Simone; actress Neena Gupta; designer Nina Ricci; singer Nina Persson; singer Nina Gordon

Noel

(Latin) Christmas.

Image: Noel uses her talents and gifts for her faith. She's imagined as a conscientious, sensitive, and affable Christian singer. Noel is pictured to be beautiful with crystal-clear blue eyes and blond hair. She's most likely talented, gentle, graceful, and a little naïve.

Famous Namesakes: Musician Noel Gallagher; composer Noel Coward

Nola

(Latin) small bell. (Irish) famous; noble.

Image: Nola is paralyzed by anxiety. She's described as an introverted brunette who's nervous and eccentric. Although she's said to be smart and sweet, Nola doesn't like big crowds, doesn't speak up, and doesn't go out unless she hides her plain figure under several layers of clothing.

Famous Namesakes: Actress Nola Fairbanks

Nora

(Greek) light.

Image: Writers Nora Roberts and Nora Ephron lend a literary spin to this name's image. People imagine Nora is shy, private, and so consistently serious, she's a bit boring. Then again, other people believe she's simply dry. Social skills aside, she's said to be a smart writer. As for her appearance, she likely has dark hair, a big nose, and snappy attire.

Famous Namesakes: Author Nora Roberts; writer Nora Ephron; singer Norah Jones

Noreen

(Irish) a form of Eleanor, Nora. (Latin) a familiar form of Norma.

Image: Noreen is a dweeb. People think she's a lonely wallflower who's nerdy and frumpy with a nasally voice. Although she's typically quiet, Noreen can be a bossy and annoying goody-goody at times. Being tall, skinny, and big-nosed doesn't seem to help her image much, either.

Famous Namesakes: Author Noreen Ayres

Norell

(Scandinavian) from the north.

Image: Norell may be sporty or dorky. Most people describe her as a friendly, studious, and naturally athletic African American woman who may have grown up on the wrong side of the tracks. Other people, however, claim she's a bland, boring, and bullied geek.

Famous Namesakes: None

Norma

(Latin) rule, precept.

Image: It may be hard to see Norma as anything but a pill. Most people think Norma is a prudish and boring wallflower who keeps to herself and has little self-esteem. She's said to be intelligent and kind, although others believe she's rude and petty. Her appearance seems to match her personality: She's a plain-looking brunette with bad hair and an average build.

Famous Namesakes: Actress Norma Jean Baker (Marilyn Monroe); designer Norma Kamali; movie character Norma Rae

Nyssa

(Greek) beginning.

Image: Nyssa makes an impression at work, at home, and on the street. She's said to be an intelligent and strong-willed professional with an interest in liberal politics. Outside of work, she's known to be a sweet family woman. Nyssa seems to have a very memorable appearance: She's described as having Amazonian height and dark, curly hair.

Famous Namesakes: Character Nyssa of Traken (*Dr. Who*)

Nyx

(Greek) night.

Image: Nyx is a dark mystery. She's imagined to be an observant and deep thinker who's quiet, shy, mysterious, or strange, depending on whom you ask. Short and pale with dark hair, she's said to be more negative than positive, although that's putting it mildly. Some people label her as depressed and lonely—themes that play out in her poetry and art.

Famous Namesakes: Mythological figure Nyx

Oceana

(Greek) ocean.

Image: Oceana is quiet and a little mysterious, which leads people to wonder about her life. People imagine she's an earthy hippie who's eccentric and strange. They assume she lives at the beach and loves to swim—and a few people even hypothesize she's a mermaid with long brown hair. Then again, others say there's no great mystery: Oceana is simply serene, calm, and nice.

Famous Namesakes: None

Octavia

(Latin) eighth.

Image: The word *sharp* describes Octavia in several ways. She's perceived as an ambitious and smart go-getter who's fearless and outspoken. People believe she's wealthy, dignified, but also snobbish, and she seems to be surly and easily annoyed as well. Some imagine Octavia as a talented singer with black hair, a lean figure, and beautiful eyes.

Famous Namesakes: Historical figure Octavia Minor; social reformer Octavia Hill

Odele

(Greek) melody, song.

Image: People don't know what to make of this little old lady. Some say Odele is an elderly bookworm who's shy, sensitive, and emotional. But others say she's a jolly old-timer who's outgoing, goofy, and loud, despite her age. Either way, she's most likely skinny and African American.

Famous Namesakes: None

Odera

(Hebrew) plough.

Image: Odera's current lifestyle may be much different than it was when she was growing up. This name evokes an image of a creative— if not bizarre—woman with lots of ideas and an open mind. She's said to be warmhearted, well liked, and never without a boyfriend. Oddly, some believe this pretty blond was brought up in a poor, trashy family.

Famous Namesakes: None

Oletha

(Scandinavian) nimble.

Image: Oletha is probably the oldest child in a large family. This name evokes the image of a family-oriented woman who's loving but often too critical and old-fashioned. In her better moments, she's said to be resourceful and humorous. Oletha is likely big-boned with black hair, green eyes, and an olive complexion.

Famous Namesakes: None

Olga

(Scandinavian) holy.

Image: Don't even think of messing with Olga. People say she's a big, burly, and homely foreigner who's personality matches her appearance. She's described as stern, unforgiving, abrasive, domineering, and loud. With her manly, muscular build, Olga may easily be a shot-putter.

Famous Namesakes: Gymnast Olga Korbut

Olive

(Latin) olive tree.

Image: Olive is cheery and maybe a little cheeky. She's seen as a jolly, flirty talker with a silly, funny flair. She's more than just laughs, though: She's also said to be courageous, caring, and smart. Like Popeye's sweetie, Olive Oyl, she's likely skinny with black hair.

Famous Namesakes: Character Olive Oyl (*Popeye*); character Olive (*Little Miss Sunshine*)

Olivia

(Latin) a form of Olive. (English) a form of Olga.

Image: What's not to like about Olivia? She's pictured as a happy, likable, and sincere woman. Most people envision this pretty blond as sophisticated and sensible as well. A few people have an opposite view, however, imagining Olivia as self-centered and disrespectful.

Famous Namesakes: Singer Olivia Newton-John; R&B singer Olivia; actress Olivia de Havilland; actress Olivia Hussey; actress Olivia Wilde

Olympia

(Greek) heavenly.

Image: The first Olympic Games were held in the ancient city of Olympia, Greece, which means this name's image carries an athletic spirit. Olympia is imagined as a leanly muscular and tall athlete who's determined, competitive, and aggressive. Some may believe that her prowess makes her a diva.

Famous Namesakes: Actress Olympia Dukakis; social reformer Olympia de Gouges; senator Olympia Snowe

Onella

(Hungarian) a form of Helen.

Image: Onella is a groovy "granola" gal. People picture her as a peace-loving environmentalist who's sweet and helpful. Her hippie, tree-hugging ways most likely secure her a spot in the cool crowd, as do her creativity and love of music. Onella is described as pale, wispy, and short with blue eyes.

Famous Namesakes: None

Opal

(Hindi) precious stone.

Image: You'll find one Opal sitting on a park bench and one sitting in a boardroom. Opal is often perceived as a loving and warm older woman who's a little mousy and conservative. Others imagine she's a sarcastic, opinionated, and high-strung career woman.

Famous Namesakes: Character Opal Gardner (*All My Children*)

Ophelia

(Greek) helper.

Image: Few literary characters are as memorable as Ophelia of Shakespeare's *Hamlet*. With that character in mind, people imagine Ophelia as a vulnerable, tragic yet loyal introvert plagued by mental problems. She's pictured as a classic beauty with high cheekbones.

Famous Namesakes: Character Ophelia (*Hamlet*)

Oprah

(Hebrew) a form of Orpah.

Image: There's no doubt people think of talk show queen Oprah Winfrey when they hear this name. Oprah is described as a caring, giving, and strong African American woman. She's said to be a successful and individualistic go-getter who inspires and motivates others to reach for their goals.

Famous Namesakes: Talk show host Oprah Winfrey

Orella

(Latin) announcement from the gods; oracle.

Image: Orella is a rags-to-riches story—solely because of whom she married. People say Orella is a dumb country girl who grew up on a farm but found herself a rich husband. (Thanks to her sexy, thin figure.) Now she's said to be a trophy wife with nouveau riche elegance, sophistication, and snobbery.

Famous Namesakes: None

Othelia

(Spanish) rich.

Image: The images of Othelia are polarized. A few people believe she's a shy, tender loner. But others think she's an outspoken, domineering, and arrogant drama teacher. Othelia most likely has long hair and dark or olive skin.

Famous Namesakes: None

Paige

(English) young child.

Image: For being so young, Paige is quite poised. This name makes people think of a polite, kind, and bright young lady who's small and cute. People tend to think she's the outgoing and likable girl next door, and she always remains unruffled and serene.

Famous Namesakes: TV host Paige Davis; actress Paige Moss; actress Paige Turco

Pamela

(Greek) honey.

Image: There are *big* reasons why this image resembles sex symbol Pamela Anderson. People immediately imagine Pamela as dense and dumb, but also sweet and funny in a perky way. That said, this top-heavy blond has a reputation as a loose floozy who can be quite selfish.

Famous Namesakes: Actress Pamela Anderson; actress Pamela Reed; author Pamela Des Barres; actress Pamela Sue Martin

Pandita

(Hindi) scholar.

Image: Perhaps people think of *bandida* when they hear the name Pandita. Why else do they imagine Pandita as a cunning and sneaky Mexican thief? She's pictured as husky and swarthy, and she's thought to be nearly silent. When she does speak, she's usually very polite.

Famous Namesakes: Social reformer Pandita Ramabai

Pansy

(Greek) flower; fragrant. (French) thoughtful.

Image: Pansy lives up—or perhaps *down*—to her name. She's believed to be a pansy; that is, a timid, stuttering wimp who lacks normal social graces. People also think Pansy is ugly, with yellow teeth, greasy hair, and acne.

Famous Namesakes: Character Pansy Parkinson (*Harry Potter* series)

Paris

(French) the capital of France.

Image: Socialite Paris Hilton is famous simply for being famous, and it's hard to separate this name's image from hers. People say Paris is fun-loving, wild, and carefree, but also snobby, spoiled, and selfish. A beautiful blond with cosmopolitan fashion sense, she comes across as ditzy to some and deceivingly smart to others.

Famous Namesakes: Socialite Paris Hilton; character Paris (*Romeo and Juliet*); mythological figure Paris

Pat

(Latin) a short form of Patricia, Patsy.

Image: This image bears some resemblance to Pat, the androgynous sketch character played by comedian Julia Sweeney on *Saturday Night Live*. People say Pat is a dull, friendless woman who's unintelligent and no fun to be around. Not helping her image, she's pictured as homely, frumpy, lumpy, and manly.

Famous Namesakes: First lady Pat Nixon

Patience

(English) patient.

Image: Patience hides away in the periodicals, but she's a gentle soul when you get to know her. She's imagined as a shy, reclusive, old-fashioned, and unstylish librarian. Those who have the chance to converse with Patience say she's soft-spoken, tenderhearted, and, of course, patient. She's said to be pretty in a plain way as well as lanky.

Famous Namesakes: Character Patience Phillips (*Catwoman*)

Patrice

(French) a form of Patricia.

Image: Patrice has quiet kindness. She's imagined to be gentle, sweet, and always caring for others. Although people describe Patrice as serious and not very talkative, they believe this healthy, blue-eyed blond is self-assured and independent.

Famous Namesakes: Prime minister Patrice Lumumba

Patricia

(Latin) noblewoman.

Image: Patricia is a sea of tranquility. She strikes people as a calm, comforting woman with green eyes, blond hair, and a short, stocky build. She's said to be quiet, shy, well mannered, and serene. Some people imagine she'd be a wonderful friend.

Famous Namesakes: Actress Patricia Heaton; actress Patricia Arquette; singer Patricia Kaas; designer Patricia Field; model Patricia Velasquez

Patti

(English) a familiar form of Patricia.

Image: No one can make a decision about Patti. To some, she's an energetic, loud, and funny gal. To others, she's a mean, lying, and fake backstabber. To still others, she's a serious, even-tempered, and withdrawn wallflower. People also can't decide about her looks, saying she's chubby or thin, old or girlish, blond or brunette.

Famous Namesakes: Actress Patty Duke; heiress Patty Hearst; singer Patti LaBelle; singer Patti Griffin; musician Patti Smith

Paula

(Latin) small.

Image: Paula has nice qualities, but she takes them a little too far. People believe Paula is smart and quiet, but to the point of being nerdy. She's also said to be polite, but to the point of being rigid and uptight. She may have an average build and a homely appearance.

Famous Namesakes: Singer Paula Abdul; news anchor Paula Zahn; cook Paula Deen; actress Paula Patton; singer Paula Cole

Paulette

(Latin) a familiar form of Paula.

Image: Paulette may be a smart but withdrawn geek who hangs out at the library, a caring and friendly kindergarten teacher who has a soft spot for kids and stray animals, or a snooty and posh Parisian who's a vain clotheshorse. In each of these cases, Paulette is described as pretty, cute, and sexy, respectively.

Famous Namesakes: Actress Paulette Goddard; country singer Paulette Carlson

Pauline

(French) a form of Paula.

Image: Hospital patients look forward to a visit from Pauline. This name gives the impression of an affectionate, caring, and jolly woman who's most likely a nurse. She's perceived to be outgoing, funny, and smart—all perfect traits for someone in her line of work. People also depict Pauline as brunette and rotund.

Famous Namesakes: Critic Pauline Kael; poet Pauline Johnson; actress Pauline Collins

Pavla

(Czech, Russian) a form of Paula.

Image: Pavla is the last person to put her foot in her mouth. She's perceived as a strong, practical Russian woman with self-control. This brunette is known to be quiet, intelligent, and a little shy, preferring to observe before speaking. Pavla is also said to be lovable and kind.

Famous Namesakes: Filmmaker Pavla Fleischer

Paz

(Spanish) peace.

Image: Paz gives peace a chance. People think she's good-humored and jolly, but she's also as passive and peaceful as her name suggests. She's said to be a caring activist who wants to make a difference. As for her looks, Paz is most likely a dark-haired and olive-skinned Latino beauty.

Famous Namesakes: Actress Paz Vega; poet Octavio Paz

Pearl

(Latin) jewel.

Image: Pearl will either invite you for tea or top off your coffee mug. Most people think Pearl is a caring and elegant little old lady with traditional values and a sweet nature. But others see her as a street-smart and outspoken waitress who works at an all-night diner. She's most likely dainty, pretty, and blue-eyed.

Famous Namesakes: Author Pearl S. Buck; singer Pearl Bailey

⭐ Star Kids

Peaches Honeyblossom

There seem to be three different career paths for Peaches Honeyblossom. Some people perceive her to be a sweet, upper-class Southern homemaker. Others say she's a comedian with a sarcastic sense of humor. A few say she's an adult-film actress. As it turns out, Peaches Honeyblossom Michelle Charlotte Angel Vanessa—daughter of late British TV personality Paula Yates and political activist Bob Geldof—is enjoying a career as a fashionable celebutante and aspiring college student.

Peggy

(Greek) a familiar form of Margaret.

Image: Peggy may rub you the wrong way, but she's harmless. She's regarded as a curly-haired and chubby woman who's naïve but happy—as evidenced by her big smile. Many people find Peggy to be annoyingly loud and obnoxious, but that's just her style of humor.

Famous Namesakes: Columnist Peggy Noonan; actress Peggy Lipton; singer Peggy Lee

Penelope

(Greek) weaver.

Image: For Penelope, there's nothing better than an escapade in some new land. This name calls to mind an adventurous, intelligent woman with childlike energy and a love for exploring. She's perceived to be happy, polite, and generous as well. People envision Penelope as short, slender, and very pretty.

Famous Namesakes: Actress Penelope Cruz; actress Penelope Ann Miller; character Penelope (*The Odyssey*)

Pennie

(Greek) a familiar form of Penelope, Peninah.

Image: Some may say this Pennie is from heaven. She comes across as a loving, kindhearted, and friendly girl who's full of fun spirit. People find her to be playful and outgoing, and sometimes she can even be silly. Like a true penny, Pennie is a coppery redhead with freckles and a cute smile.

Famous Namesakes: Director Penny Marshall; photographer Pennie Smith; character Penny Lane (*Almost Famous*)

Petula

(Latin) seeker.

Image: For every step forward, Petula takes a step back. People say she's sweet and kind, yet also meek and nervous. She's considered to be wholesome, straight-laced, and book smart, yet she's also gullible. Petula may have a few extra pounds, curly brown hair, and a love for flowers.

Famous Namesakes: Singer Petula Clark

Phaedra

(Greek) bright.

Image: Phaedra disguises her true self. Deep down, she's most likely a resilient and passionate go-getter with a lot of courage and brains. But people say she comes across as a shy, reserved introvert. Those who realize her reticence isn't authentic may even say Phaedra is mysterious and sneaky. Physically, she's imagined as gaunt and olive-skinned.

Famous Namesakes: Mythological figure Phaedra

Phoebe

(Greek) shining.

Image: Of all the characters on TV's *Friends*, Phoebe Buffay was perhaps the most unique. Not surprisingly, this Phoebe is thought to be an unusual and fun-loving woman who's weird in an interesting way. She's described as bohemian and scatterbrained, yet funny. To complete the image, she's pretty, slender, and blond.

Famous Namesakes: Character Phoebe Buffay (*Friends*); actress Phoebe Cates

Phylicia

(Latin) fortunate; happy. (Greek) a form of Felicia.

Image: Phylicia uses her focus and kindness in a career that will make a difference in others' lives. People imagine Phylicia to be a dark-haired and attractive African American woman who's ambitious, professional, and always in charge. She most likely has a job helping others. She's said to be from a wealthy family, so she's sophisticated, neatly stylish, and perhaps haughty in some situations.

Famous Namesakes: Actress Phylicia Rashád; character Felicia Forrester (*The Bold and the Beautiful*)

Phyllis

(Greek) green bough.

Image: Phyllis may get meaner with age. Most people think she's an arrogant, uncaring, and rude elderly woman. She's most likely dull, old-fashioned, frumpy, and unattractive. Some people see Phyllis differently, saying she's either sweet and goodhearted or wise and witty (like comedian Phyllis Diller).

Famous Namesakes: Comedian Phyllis Diller; activist Phyllis Schlafly; character Phyllis Lindstrom (*The Mary Tyler Moore Show*)

Piper

(English) pipe player.

Image: Unlike some perky people, Piper has more to offer than just energy. This name creates the impression of a vivacious, energetic, and fun extrovert. She's said to be spunky, but also smart, warmhearted, hardworking, and responsible. She may be a leader. As for her appearance, Piper is pictured as a dark-haired beauty with freckles and a lithe physique.

Famous Namesakes: Actress Piper Laurie; actress Piper Perabo

Polly

(Latin) a familiar form of Paula, Pauline.

Image: Polly takes her giggly pep to the extreme. She's imagined to be peppy, perky, cheery, and smiley—maybe too much so. People describe Polly as blond, adorable, and a little roly-poly. She's very likely an airhead, but she's also quite sweet.

Famous Namesakes: Entertainer Polly Bergen; actress Polly Holliday; actress Polly Walker

Poria

(Hebrew) fruitful.

Image: Perhaps it's because the name Poria sounds a bit like *portly*.... People primarily imagine Poria as a heavyset girl with strong features like big eyes, full lips, and olive skin. They also believe she's friendly or even motherly and is always a good listener. She seems to be content with her life, although she may be a little shy and a bit slow.

Famous Namesakes: None

Portia

(Latin) offering.

Image: If you feel the temperature fluctuate, leave the thermostat alone—it's just Portia. She comes across as primarily a cold, aloof ice princess who's pampered and snooty. But she's also hotly passionate, strong-willed, intelligent, and ambitious. People agree she's a too-thin and pretty blond, perhaps like actress Portia de Rossi.

Famous Namesakes: Character Portia (*The Merchant of Venice*); actress Portia de Rossi

Posy

(English) flower, small bunch of flowers.

Image: A posy is a small bouquet of sweet-smelling flowers, so it's only fitting that Posy inspires a delightful image. She's thought to be a flighty free spirit who's bubbly, goofy, optimistic, and lovable. She most likely has red hair and a skinny, short frame. A few people wonder if Posy is a writer.

Famous Namesakes: Actress Parker Posey; cartoonist Posy Simmonds

 **Star Kids**

Poppy Honey

Poppy Honey is a people pleaser, although it's unclear to what extent she'll go to please them. Most people imagine she's a giggly and bubbly girl with honey-blond hair. She's known to be friendly in her job, which may or may not mean a career as a stripper, porn star, or prostitute. In any case, she's probably not very smart. So although Jamie Oliver is known as TV's Naked Chef, perhaps he hopes daughter Poppy Honey won't make "naked" a major part of her job description.

Priscilla

(Latin) ancient.

Image: It's no wonder most people say Priscilla is obnoxious. She's thought to be a loud, hyper, and scatterbrained gossip. She also comes across as petty, spoiled, and above it all. A few people, however, believe Priscilla is a better-than-average person, calling her a beautiful spirit loved by all. Physically, she's pictured to be slender, pretty, and brunette—perhaps like actress Priscilla Presley.

Famous Namesakes: Actress Priscilla Presley

Prudence

(Latin) cautious; discreet.

Image: Here's an obvious image: Prudence is a prude. She's described as a cranky and unfriendly old woman who's guarded, self-conscious, and old-fashioned. She tends to be mild and soft-spoken, which means she's dull and boring. People admit Prudence is loyal and honest with her Christian values, but she's just too stuck-up.

Famous Namesakes: Activist Prudence Crandall; singer Prudence Johnson

Pythia

(Greek) prophet.

Image: If Pythia's life weren't so bleak, she probably wouldn't be such a good musician. People imagine Pythia is pessimistic, cold, depressed, and even pitiful. Perhaps she leads an empty existence, but she's known to draw upon it for her gifted singing and songwriting. As for her appearance, she's likely Greek with long, curly black hair.

Famous Namesakes: Mythological figure Pythia

Qadira

(Arabic) powerful.

Image: Qadira would rather observe than join in. She's viewed as a shy and gentle Middle Eastern woman who gets flustered at times. For this reason, she tends to stay in the background as an alert observer—and her distance perhaps makes her seem aloof to some people. Physically, she's thought to be attractive, and she likely wears a hijab.

Famous Namesakes: None

Rachael

(Hebrew) a form of Rachel.

Image: Whatever company employs Rachael as its receptionist should reexamine how she presents herself to others. Rachael is imagined as a loud and talkative secretary with an obnoxious, tacky laugh. This big-nosed brunette also comes across as unfriendly, mean, and witchy.

Famous Namesakes: Actress Rachael Leigh Cook; talk show host Rachael Ray; actress Rachael Harris; character Rachel Green (*Friends*); actress Rachel McAdams; actress Rachel Weisz; actress Rachel Bilson

Rachel

(Hebrew) female sheep.

Image: While Rachel may be self-reliant, that doesn't mean she's self-centered. She's imagined as a strong-minded, assertive, and independent woman, but she's also caring and nurturing. People find Rachel to be sincere and unpretentious, and she's famous for kidding around. Perhaps a reference to *Friends* character Rachel Green, she's pictured with light-brown hair and a sexy, slender figure.

Famous Namesakes: Character Rachel Green (*Friends*); actress Rachel McAdams; actress Rachel Weisz; actress Rachel Bilson; actress Rachael Leigh Cook; talk show host Rachael Ray; actress Rachael Harris

Racquel

(French) a form of Rachel.

Image: Racquel has sex appeal, but there's little appeal to her personality. She's pictured much like sex symbol Raquel Welch—an attractive model-actress with brown hair and buxom curves. Beyond her looks, Racquel is said to be shallow, brazen, and arrogant, although some label her vivacious and sophisticated.

Famous Namesakes: Actress Raquel Welch

Rae

(English) doe. (Hebrew) a short form of Rachel.

Image: If you need help with the PTA fundraiser, Rae is your gal. People say she's a small-town mom who's outgoing, active, and adventurous. She's also said to be strong, confident, and determined, although people can't decide if she's smart or uneducated. Either way, they picture Rae with red hair and freckles.

Famous Namesakes: Movie character Norma Rae; actress Rae Dawn Chong; actress Charlotte Rae

Ramona

(Spanish) mighty; wise protector.

Image: Ramona Quimby, the pesky character from a series of children's books by Beverly Cleary, may color this name's image. Ramona is imagined as a mischievous and silly brunette who some may call an annoying, immature pest. She can be temperamental and overly sensitive at times. Some people—perhaps those who don't know the Cleary series—say Ramona is an old, frail lady.

Famous Namesakes: Fiction character Ramona Quimby

Randi

(English) a familiar form of Miranda, Randall.

Image: Randi may smoke, even though she has asthma. People imagine she's a cynical and jaded introvert with a rebellious edge. She may be smart, but her intelligence is buried under her sad and antisocial demeanor. Physically, Randi is thought to be a pretty brunette with pale skin and weak lungs.

Famous Namesakes: Radio personality Randi Rhodes

Raven

(English) blackbird.

Image: Raven's personality and appearance are as dark as her name suggests. She's described as a mysterious and sullen loner. Some people feel she's ill-tempered, difficult, and most definitely out of control. This strong-willed wild child most likely has black hair and olive skin as well as tattoos and piercings.

Famous Namesakes: Actress Raven Symone

Reagan

(Irish) little ruler.

Image: Reagan is quite comfortable with speaking, but she may speak colloquially or eloquently. This name makes most people think of a likable and cheerful chatterbox who's sweet and helpful. Others imagine she's an educated, articulate, and independent woman. Either way, Reagan is envisioned as light-haired and beautiful.

Famous Namesakes: President Ronald Reagan

Reanna

(German, English) a form of Raina. (American) a form of Raeann.

Image: When Reanna's friends need help, she's the first one they call. She comes across as a stand-up gal who's sweet, talkative, and always there for her friends. People consider her to be smart and resourceful as well as sophisticated and elegant. With her black hair, Reanna may be of Italian heritage.

Famous Namesakes: Model Reanna Taylor

Reba

(Hebrew) fourth-born child.

Image: This name's image perfectly matches that of country star Reba McEntire. People think Reba is a red-haired country singer who's assertive and outspoken, sweet and lovable, and outgoing and funny. Last but not least, she most likely has a charming Southern accent.

Famous Namesakes: Singer Reba McEntire

Rebecca

(Hebrew) tied, bound.

Image: There's so much good to say about Rebecca. She's described as a spunky, happy, and adventurous woman. She's also said to be generous, intelligent, hardworking, and sophisticated. People picture her appearance just as positively: They believe Rebecca is pretty with long, curly, dark hair; freckles; and green eyes.

Famous Namesakes: Fiction character Rebecca; actress Rebecca De Mornay; fiction character Rebecca of Sunnybrook Farm; actress Rebecca Romijn; actress Rebecca Gayheart; biblical figure Rebecca

Reese

(Welsh) a form of Reece.

Image: Actress Reese Witherspoon has become America's sweetheart, and she's made an impact on this name's image. People think Reese is confident, spunky, and energetic as well as friendly, fun, and good-humored. A few people suspect she's devious and sneaky for some reason, although most believe she's responsible and positive. Physically, she's pictured as a sexy, slim blond.

Famous Namesakes: Actress Reese Witherspoon

Regan

(Irish) a form of Reagan.

Image: Regan approaches life with great sincerity. This name conjures up an image of a wide-eyed, earnest, and trusting girl. She's imagined to be jovial and friendly, not to mention honest and eager. In addition, people picture Regan with beautiful red hair and a sweet smile.

Famous Namesakes: Character Regan MacNeil (*The Exorcist*)

Regina

(Latin) queen. (English) king's advisor.

Image: This queenly name carries some majesty. Regina is envisioned as confident and strong royalty. She's likely outspoken to the point of being blunt. And, of course, she's rich. People picture her as a dark-skinned, tall woman.

Famous Namesakes: Actress Regina King; actress Regina Hall; musician Regina Spektor; singer Regina Belle

Reilly

(Irish) a form of Riley.

Image: People aren't sure if Reilly is a name for a girl or a boy, and they also aren't sure what image this name inspires. Most people imagine Reilly as a polite and sensitive person with a kind face. Others say Reilly is smart, outgoing, and popular—a regular boy or girl next door. Still others picture a cocky cowboy or cowgirl out on the rodeo circuit. In any case, Reilly is most likely tall, skinny, and attractive.

Famous Namesakes: Actress Kelly Reilly

Renee

(French) a form of Renée.

Image: Renee is a crowd favorite, and not just because she's so funny. She's said to be a droll and clever brown-haired beauty. People imagine she's as sweet as she is fun, but she's also levelheaded. These rave reviews make it clear to see why Renee is so popular.

Famous Namesakes: Actress Renee Zellweger; actress Renee Russo; opera singer Renee Fleming

Rhea

(Greek) brook, stream.

Image: Rhea Perlman was a household name when she played feisty waitress Carla on TV's *Cheers*. Her image may explain why people consider this Rhea to be a grumpy yet funny smart aleck who's well loved for being so bold. With curly hair, she's also thought to be chubby and tall.

Famous Namesakes: Actress Rhea Perlman; model Rhea Durham

Rhiannon

(Welsh) witch; nymph; goddess.

Image: Rhiannon is an expressive spirit with some mystery to her. People say she's a compassionate, artistic woman who may be a poet or musician—an idea perhaps inspired by the Fleetwood Mac song "Rhiannon." With finely chiseled features and piercing green eyes, she's thought to be a beauty. Many people claim she's brave and strong, but others suspect she's quiet, mousy, and friendless.

Famous Namesakes: None

Rhoda

(Greek) from Rhodes, Greece.

Image: Rhoda is secure in her solitary lifestyle. People see her as a quiet and independent woman who has a caring and lovely personality but still prefers being alone. She's known to be smart and well read, and she's detail oriented—perhaps to the point of being uptight. People describe Rhoda physically as a stocky brunette with a round face.

Famous Namesakes: Character Rhoda Morgenstern (*Rhoda*)

Rhonda

(Welsh) grand.

Image: Rhonda speaks her mind, for good or bad. This name makes people think of an opinionated, sassy, and loud woman. She's most likely heavyset and African American. Viewed in a positive light, Rhonda is sharp-witted and tough. Viewed in a not-so-positive light, she's disgruntled, nasty, and pushy.

Famous Namesakes: TV host Rhonda Shear; actress Rhonda Fleming

Ricki

(American) a familiar form of Erica, Frederica, Ricarda.

Image: Ricki has a soft side and a rugged side. She comes across as a caring and bright young woman who's easygoing at school and at home. Although it seems contradictory, people believe she's a romantic dreamer and a tomboy at the same time.

Famous Namesakes: Talk show host Ricki Lake

Riona

(Irish) saint.

Image: Life is smooth for Riona. She's considered to be a quiet introvert who's calm, peaceful, and blissfully laid-back. Perhaps she's even shy. People most often picture her with dark hair, dark eyes, and dark skin. They also imagine she's too skinny for her build.

Famous Namesakes: None

Rita

(Sanskrit) brave; honest. (Greek) a short form of Margarita.

Image: Be prepared—Rita is a bit forward. She's said to be friendly, fun, and flirty, although she may come on too strong at times. Many people find her to be pushy, even if she's kind and generous overall. Along with her strong personality is a strong physical presence: She's said to be a dark-featured Spanish beauty with a tall, domineering stature.

Famous Namesakes: Actress Rita Wilson; actress Rita Hayworth; actress Rita Moreno; news anchor Rita Cosby

Roberta

(English) a form of Robert.

Image: Because the name Roberta is a version of the name Robert, this image is a bit masculine. Roberta is considered to be an outspoken, opinionated, and strong-willed woman in a leadership position. People imagine she's chunky, manly, and tall with auburn hair. She seems to have warm, caring side, though.

Famous Namesakes: Singer Roberta Flack

Robyn

(English) a form of Robin.

Image: Robyn's finer traits balance out her rougher ones. She comes across as a self-sufficient and strong woman who always get her way through bossy, stubborn tactics. But Robyn is also considered to be big-hearted, honest, and cheerful. She may be short and a bit overweight.

Famous Namesakes: Actress Robin Givens; radio personality Robin Quivers; choreographer Robin Antin

Rochelle

(French) large stone. (Hebrew) a form of Rachel.

Image: Rochelle's kindness is admirable, but it makes her somewhat vulnerable, too. She's thought to be a caring, thoughtful woman who loves friends, family, and children. She's said to be always happy, talkative, and perhaps a little flirty. Unfortunately, though, some people think Rochelle is a bit naïve and easily convinced—not to mention easily hurt.

Famous Namesakes: None

★ Star Kids

Rowan Francis

Rowan Francis sounds like quite a fella. Many people describe him as a cool and confident man's man who enjoys his career as a teacher. Others see him as a shy, goofy, and unconventional guy. Either way, he's said to be tall and pencil thin. With this image in mind, it seems likely Rowan Francis, *daughter* of actress Brooke Shields and TV writer Chris Henchy, will experience some mix-ups about her gender during her lifetime.

Roma

(Latin) from Rome.

Image: Roma's focus is entirely on work. She's imagined as an ambitious, intelligent, and self-confident businesswoman who'd rather have a career than a family. She's typically caring and friendly, but sometimes Roma can be private and quiet, and other times she can be outgoing and loud. People say her dark features give her a sexy, exotic look.

Famous Namesakes: Actress Roma Downey

Romola

(Latin) a form of Roma.

Image: Romola's multifaceted personality makes her hard to read. Some people say she's a quiet, shy introvert, but perhaps that's because she's a foreigner who's learning a new language. Others find her to be snobby, but that may be because she's independent—or even because she's so shy. At any rate, Romola is depicted as a chubby woman with dark hair and dark skin.

Famous Namesakes: Actress Romola Garai

Rori

(Irish) famous brilliance; famous ruler.

Image: Rori can be quite stubborn, but she's a good person. She's thought to be a headstrong, bossy, yet lovable go-getter. People believe she's a talkative attention-seeker, but she can also be tender, sincere, and open. Rori most likely has an average build and fine features, and she may be of Irish descent.

Famous Namesakes: Character Rory Gilmore (*Gilmore Girls*); film maker Rory Kennedy

Rosa

(Italian, Spanish) a form of Rose.

Image: Either people have different opinions about Rosa or she has a multifaceted personality. People see Rosa as kind and caring, hardworking and determined, serene and laid-back, happy and spirited, and shy and mysterious. There's clear consensus about her appearance: She's said to be a dark-haired Latina with olive skin and feminine beauty.

Famous Namesakes: Civil rights icon Rosa Parks

Rosalie

(English) a form of Rosalind.

Image: Rosalie keeps an even keel, even when she's having fun. She's described as a social, happy-go-lucky woman who's talkative, inviting, and bubbly. That said, she's also thought to be kind and gentle, always conducting herself in even-tempered, mild-mannered ways. She's pictured with a curvy body, a beautiful smile, brown eyes, and rosy cheeks.

Famous Namesakes: Sculptor Rosalie Gascoigne

Rosalyn

(Spanish) a form of Rosalind.

Image: It's easy to imagine Rosalyn visiting with grandchildren in her parlor. This name makes people think of a gentle and caring grandmother who's classy, sophisticated, and rich. Some people, however, argue Rosalyn's sweetness and refinery make her a bore. Even in her advanced age, she's still considered beautiful with her fair skin.

Famous Namesakes: First lady Rosalyn Carter; actress Roselyn Sanchez

Rose

(Latin) rose.

Image: Rose is the picture of poise and grace. She's imagined as a proper, elegant, yet perhaps old-fashioned grandmother. She's said to be kind, helpful, and inspiring. In her spare time, Rose seems to enjoy a good read. Still stylish and beautiful, she's envisioned with red hair and pale skin with a rosy hue.

Famous Namesakes: Character Rose Nylund (*The Golden Girls*); actress Rose McGowan; matriarch Rose Kennedy

Roseanna

(English) a combination of Rose + Anna.

Image: Perhaps Roseanne Barr affects this name's image? Roseanna is imagined by many people as a sassy and sarcastic comedian who borders on being rude and annoying. She's most likely plump and brunette. Others, however, imagine Roseanna to be a meek and gentle housewife and mother.

Famous Namesakes: Actress Roseanna Arquette

Roseanne

(English) a combination of Rose + Ann.

Image: Comedian Roseanne Barr changed American television with her true-to-life sitcom—and this name's image shares her spunk. People overwhelmingly picture Roseanne with a chubby stature and round cheeks. They also believe she's an outspoken and sometimes abrasive loud mouth. But no one can deny her sense of humor, even if it can be vulgar every now and then.

Famous Namesakes: Comedian Roseanne Barr

Rosemary

(English) a combination of Rose + Mary.

Image: You probably won't hear Rosemary say much. She comes across as caring and kind-hearted, but she's also very quiet. Some believe that's because she's calm and patient, but others say she's actually shy. Rosemary is also thought to be old-fashioned and traditional, especially when it comes to religion. In addition, this fit and pretty redhead is most likely well read, neat, and organized.

Famous Namesakes: Character Rosemary Woodhouse (*Rosemary's Baby*); singer Rosemary Clooney

Roxanna

(Persian) a form of Roxann.

Image: Roxanna is a bit desperate. When people hear this name, they think of an insecure, codependent hairdresser or cocktail waitress who's gossipy, loud, and looking for true love. Unfortunately, she's famous for trying too hard to be liked. Roxanna is most likely thin and attractive (although not as attractive as she thinks) with long hair and clothing that's inappropriate for her advanced age.

Famous Namesakes: None

Girls

 **Star Kids**

Rumer Glenn

People can't decide if Rumer Glenn avoids attention or seeks it out. Some claim she's shy, quiet, and eager to avoid the limelight. But just as many others believe she's a loud, funny extrovert who lives for attention—almost to the point of being annoying. Either way, she's pictured to be good-looking and trim. Rumer Glenn, daughter of actors Demi Moore and Bruce Willis, seems to love attention, especially since she's known to often hang out with wild starlet Lindsay Lohan.

Rue

(German) famous. (French) street. (English) regretful; strong-scented herbs.

Image: Rue is a small woman with a big attitude. Perhaps thanks to Rue McClanahan, who played saucy Blanche Devereaux on TV's *The Golden Girls*, people say Rue is brash, outspoken, and spunky with a sharp wit. More likely than not, she's cunning and strong-willed. Physically, she's lithe, pale, and plain-looking.

Famous Namesakes: Actress Rue McClanahan

Ruth

(Hebrew) friendship.

Image: Ruth's personality may be just about anything. Many people think Ruth is helpful, gentle, faithful, and honorable. Others say she's confident, bold, boisterous, and larger than life. And then there are a few who believe she's merely average and generic. As for her appearance, she may be tall or squat, but she's thought to be homely.

Famous Namesakes: Biblical figure Ruth; judge Ruth Bader Ginsburg; actress Ruth Gordon; actress Ruth Hussey

Sabina

(Latin) a form of Sabine.

Image: Sabina is friendly, but she also needs some time alone with her thoughts. She's seen as a sweet and kind foreigner who gets along with everyone. Sabina is most likely smart and articulate, but she can also be quiet and wistful at times. People believe she's a tall, lithe, and naturally pretty blond.

Famous Namesakes: Character Sabina (*The Unbearable Lightness of Being*); singer Sabina Sciubba

Sable

(English) sable; sleek.

Image: A sable is a luxurious fur, which may explain why this name's image has a posh, fashionable flair. People suspect Sable is a wealthy, refined woman with great fashion sense. Energetic, highly creative, and Ivy League–educated, she may even run her own design company. She's said to be attractive with sable-black hair, and she's also known to be witty and sweet.

Famous Namesakes: Professional wrestler Sable

Sabra

(Hebrew) thorny cactus fruit. (Arabic) resting.

Image: Sabra has a spirited personality, for better or worse. People think Sabra is a feisty, strong-willed woman who's tall, dark, and exotic. While some see her as confident, proud, and happy, others say she's stuck-up, spoiled, and witchy. People agree that she's most likely a sly, quick thinker.

Famous Namesakes: Mythological figure Princess Sabra

Sabrina

(Latin) boundary line. (English) princess. (Hebrew) a familiar form of Sabra.

Image: No one ever accuses Sabrina of running at the mouth. Most people see her as a tall, thin, and dark-haired beauty who's rather quiet. Her lack of verbosity may stem from shyness, although some people believe she's secretive or perhaps even frightened in social situations. Although Sabrina doesn't say much, she's still said to be sweet, kind, and creative.

Famous Namesakes: Character Sabrina Spellman (*Sabrina the Teenage Witch*); character Sabrina Fairchild (*Sabrina*); actress Sabrina Lloyd

Sagara

(Hindi) ocean.

Image: Sagara has an allure that's all her own. She's said to be a proud, strong, and perhaps even regal Indian woman with dark eyes, skin, and hair. People imagine she's earthy and calm as well as poetic and insightful. All in all, there seems to be a mysterious, exotic air to Sagara.

Famous Namesakes: Anime character Sanosuke Sagara

Sage

(English) wise.

Image: Few people can see Sage's true personality through her irresponsible behavior. People say she's a wild and carefree spirit with a sexy appearance and sly smile, but at times she borders on being reckless and crazy. Apart from her antics, however, Sage is thought to be a sensitive, kind, and intelligent woman.

Famous Namesakes: Musician Sage Francis

Sally

(English) princess.

Image: Every afternoon, Sally has the neighborhood gals over for coffee and gossip. This name reminds people of a sociable and very chatty housewife. Although she's happy and funny, Sally is considered to be a loud mouth, and she most likely can't keep a secret. People imagine she's slightly chubby.

Famous Namesakes: Actress Sally Struthers; talk show host Sally Jessy Raphael; actress Sally Field; runner Sally Gunnell; astronaut Sally Ride

Samantha

(Aramaic) listener. (Hebrew) told by God.

Image: By night, Samantha is said to be a sociable, vivacious woman who loves to party and loves life in general. But by day, she's known as a brilliant, successful businesswoman who's hardworking, aggressive, and outspoken. People suspect Samantha came from a well-bred, wealthy background, which makes her a bit of a princess. She's also thought to be beautiful and physically fit with brown hair and eyes.

Famous Namesakes: Character Samantha Jones (*Sex and the City*); character Samantha Stephens (*Bewitched*); singer Samantha Mumba; actress Samantha Morton; TV host Samantha Harris

Samara

(Latin) elm-tree seed.

Image: There's so much to like about Samara. She's described as a Middle Eastern woman who's bubbly, fun-loving, and always wearing a big smile. People picture Samara as beautiful and petite with dark hair and dark eyes. Bright, kind, and funny—it's easy to see why she's so popular.

Famous Namesakes: Character Samara Morgan (*The Ring*)

Sandra

(Greek) defender of mankind.

Image: If Sandra wants for anything, it's not confidence. Sandra strikes people as a quick-thinking and tough-minded woman. She's said to be independent, dynamic, assertive, and quite confident. She may be a lawyer. Outside of work, this tall blond comes across as a flirty people-person—another role that showcases her self-assurance.

Famous Namesakes: Actress Sandra Dee; actress Sandra Bullock; judge Sandra Day O'Connor; author Sandra Cisneros; actress Sandra Oh; comedian Sandra Bernhard

Sandy

(Greek) a familiar form of Cassandra, Sandra.

Image: We should all strive to be like Sandy. People say Sandy is a generous and kind woman who loves unconditionally, is quick to forgive, and treats everyone equally. She's known to be funny, witty, easygoing, and charismatic as well. This fair blond is just as beautiful on the outside, too.

Famous Namesakes: Actress Sandy Duncan; character Sandy Olsson (*Grease*); actress Sandy Dennis

Sapphire

(Greek) blue gemstone.

Image: Sapphire sure has sex appeal, but not many other positive qualities. People imagine Sapphire is a spoiled, shallow, and self-centered stripper or aspiring model who's beautiful, sexy, and statuesque. She's most likely outgoing and popular, but she's also quite flighty.

Famous Namesakes: None

Sara

(Hebrew) a form of Sarah.

Image: Sara is a wonderful person to know. She's thought to be a loving, caring woman with a great personality—that is, she's known to be happy, honest, and funny. A few people, however, say this pretty brunette is quiet and shy.

Famous Namesakes: Actress Sara Gilbert; actress Sarah Michelle Gellar; actress Sara Ramirez; biblical figure Sara; duchess Sarah Ferguson; singer Sarah McLachlan; actress Sarah Jessica Parker; actress Sarah Bernhardt; singer Sara Evans; actress Sarah Chalke

Sarah

(Hebrew) princess.

Image: Every little thing about Sarah is gentle. She's thought to be wholesome and sweet natured, shy and soft-spoken, and peaceful and patient. Appropriately, people even picture her with a petite frame, gentle face, kind eyes, and a warm smile.

Famous Namesakes: Actress Sara Gilbert; actress Sarah Michelle Gellar; actress Sara Ramirez; biblical figure Sara; duchess Sarah Ferguson; singer Sarah McLachlan; actress Sarah Jessica Parker; actress Sarah Bernhardt; singer Sara Evans; actress Sarah Chalke

Sarina

(Hebrew) a familiar form of Sarah.

Image: People aren't sure if Sarina has a fine character to match her fine leadership skills. Sarina is said to be a determined, goal-oriented leader with lots of confidence and a sharp mind. But that determination may make her a conniving and snobby backstabber or a kind and graceful class act. In any case, she's pictured with dark hair, a beautiful face, and olive skin.

Famous Namesakes: Singer Sarina Paris; tennis player Serena Williams; character Serena (*Bewitched*)

Sasha

(Russian) defender of mankind.

Image: For Sasha, art is born of suffering. Sasha is pictured as a gloomy, eccentric, and tortured artist. Many people call her unique (when being polite) or kooky (when being honest). Adding to her gloom, she's also said to be self-centered, aloof, rude, and high maintenance. People describe her as thin and blessed with dark physical features that match her dark mood.

Famous Namesakes: Actress Sasha Alexander; comedian Sasha Baron Choen; figure skater Sasha Cohen

Savanna

(Spanish) a form of Savannah.

Image: Savanna is a gentle spirit with a fiery passion for saving the earth. People say Savanna is a friendly and sweet woman with a bright smile. She's generally serene, quiet, and mild-mannered, but she can be quite a go-getter when it comes to conservation. She's said to be an environmental activist and an animal lover.

Famous Namesakes: Character Savannah Jackson (*Waiting to Exhale*)

Savannah

(Spanish) treeless plain.

Image: Savannah is not afraid to tell it like it is. She's described as a fearless and strong-willed gal who's also friendly, happy, and sweet. Her sassiness tends to come out as blunt sincerity, but people take her words seriously because she's as intelligent as she is dependable. This pretty Southern girl is said to have a small build and long, blond hair.

Famous Namesakes: Character Savannah Jackson (*Waiting to Exhale*)

★ Star Kids

Scout LaRue

Scout LaRue is a plucky gal whom everyone loves. When they hear this name, people imagine a spunky, energetic, and cool woman who's quite popular. With such a fun personality and a tall, lean figure, she may be a model, an athlete, or an artist. If she's anything like her parents, popularity comes easily to Scout LaRue, daughter of actors Demi Moore and Bruce Willis.

Scarlett

(English) bright red.

Image: Frankly, my dear, this name's image is a perfect match to *Gone with the Wind* heroine Scarlett O'Hara. Like her namesake, this Scarlett is thought to be a conceited and snappy vixen who's wealthy, headstrong, and precocious. Her sexy, slender figure and dark, curly hair most definitely add to her allure. Some people, however, find her to be polite, soft-spoken, and engaged in a secret, private life no one knows about.

Famous Namesakes: Actress Scarlett Johansson; character Scarlett O'Hara (*Gone with the Wind*)

Selena

(Greek) a form of Selene.

Image: Sadly, this name's image overwhelmingly recalls Selena Quintanilla-Pérez, the late Tejano singer who was murdered at the height of her stardom. People describe Selena as a beautiful and kindhearted Latina singing sensation. She's well-spoken, charming, and feminine with her dark hair, skin, and eyes.

Famous Namesakes: Singer Selena Quintanilla-Pérez; character Selina Kyle (*Batman*)

Selina

(Greek) a form of Celina, Selena.

Image: Selina's rough life forced her to develop hardnosed traits. She's imagined as a manipulative woman with a bad attitude, a low IQ, and a hunger for attention. Slender and exotic-looking, Selina is said to be independent, two-faced, and hardworking—traits she had to acquire in order to fend for herself.

Famous Namesakes: Character Selina Kyle (*Batman*); singer Selena Quintanilla-Pérez

Serena

(Latin) peaceful.

Image: Aptly, Serena is a gentle, easy soul. People imagine she's as calm, content, and serene as her name implies. She's likely quiet and soft-spoken, which some may say makes her a little mysterious. Although Serena is easygoing, she's also regarded as a confident, strong, and smart woman. As for her looks, she's pictured as a slender brunette who's somewhat tall and very attractive.

Famous Namesakes: Tennis player Serena Williams; character Serena (*Bewitched*); singer Sarina Paris

Serenity

(Latin) peaceful.

Image: Fittingly, Serenity brings quietude and calm to those around her. People envision her as a kindhearted and understanding woman with caring eyes. She's very likely gentle, patient, quiet, and—of course—serene. This beautiful blond may even be a hippie, although some suspect she's more elegant than earthy.

Famous Namesakes: None

Shakila

(Arabic) pretty.

Image: Shakila's warm heart gives her a special place in the eyes of her friends and family. People think she's a caring, compassionate African American woman who's always ready to listen. She's described as popular, classy, and cool, and people may look to her for leadership. Adding even more to her charm, Shakila is said to be attractive with high cheekbones and curly hair.

Famous Namesakes: Singer Shakila

Shakira

(Arabic) thankful.

Image: Colombian singer Shakira is an international sensation, largely thanks to her seductive belly-dancing. For this reason, Shakira comes across as a warm, exuberant, and adventurous singer and dancer. People find her beautiful and sexy, especially because of her well-toned body.

Famous Namesakes: Singer Shakira Ripoll

Shanna

(Irish) a form of Shana, Shannon.

Image: Shanna can pencil you in for dinner at 7:15. She strikes people as a popular, outgoing woman who intricately and diligently plans every part of her week. Because she's so fun-loving, most of the plans seem to involve activities like dancing and sports. Shanna is pictured to be tall, pretty, and perhaps of Jewish heritage.

Famous Namesakes: Actress Shanna Moakler

Shannon

(Irish) small and wise.

Image: Perhaps like actress Shannen Doherty, this Shannon has many appealing qualities that unfortunately also come with many unappealing ones. People say Shannon is wild, confident, and fearless. She's thought to have an intoxicating laugh and a witty comeback for any remark. In addition, people describe her as tall, dark, and beautiful. Alas, she's also considered to be self-absorbed, impatient, conniving, and mean spirited.

Famous Namesakes: Gymnast Shannon Miller; actress Shannon Elizabeth; actress Shannen Doherty; actress Shannon Tweed; actress Shannyn Sossamon

Shari

(French) beloved, dearest. (Hungarian) a form of Sarah.

Image: If you stop at that greasy spoon just off the interstate, you'll find Shari pullin' a double shift. She's said to be an energetic and witty waitress who works hard and has a hard life. She's most likely weary and worn, but she nevertheless manages to be sweet, charming, and slow to anger. People imagine she's a striking brunette who's middle-aged and rough voiced from smoking too many smokes.

Famous Namesakes: Puppeteer Shari Lewis; actress Sherry Stringfield; actress Shari Belafonte; comedian Cheri Oteri

Sharlene

(French) little and strong.

Image: When it comes to meddling, Sharlene can't take what she dishes out. Sharlene comes across as an untrusting, watchful, and cautious woman. People say she's quite determined to guard her independence. But at the same time, she's also known to be a nosy, loud gabber who can't help but meddle in other people's lives.

Famous Namesakes: Actress Charlene Tilton; fitness guru Charlene Prickett; singer Sharlene Spiteri

Sharon

(Hebrew) desert plain.

Image: It's hard to put your finger on Sharon's personality. People aren't sure if she's a crabby and arrogant perfectionist, a fun-loving and outgoing adventurer, or a sweet and soft-spoken introvert. People tend to agree, however, that Sharon is a middle-aged woman who's busty, homely, and dowdy.

Famous Namesakes: Actress Sharon Stone; actress Sharon Tate; personality Sharon Osbourne; actress Sharon Case

Shauna

(Hebrew, Irish) a form of Shana, Shaun.

Image: Shauna can be a little unruly. This name calls to mind an independent and outgoing woman who's self-assured and, at times, aggressive. People imagine she may like to drink beer, have a wild time, and be loud and annoying. She's most likely athletic and pretty.

Famous Namesakes: Model Shauna Sand; actress Shauna Kain

Sheba

(Hebrew) a short form of Bathsheba.

Image: People picture Sheba as "the Queen of Sheba"—that is, she's a powerful, assertive, and willful woman. She's said to be exotically beautiful with dark hair and an ever-present smile. Some describe Sheba as happy and benevolent; others say she's close-minded and unforgiving. Most people agree, however, that she lives a spoiled lifestyle with a great deal of spending.

Famous Namesakes: Biblical figure the Queen of Sheba

Girls

Sheena

(Hebrew) God is gracious. (Irish) a form of Jane.

Image: Sheena knows just how to bat her eyelashes. She comes across as a popular and outgoing cheerleader. She's suspected to be a flirty tease, but in a sweet way. In addition, people picture Sheena as attractive, thin, and dark complexioned.

Famous Namesakes: Singer Sheena Easton; comic book character Sheena, Queen of the Jungle

Sheila

(Latin) blind. (Irish) a form of Cecelia.

Image: Sheila divides opinions. On one side, people imagine her as an arrogant, rude, and high-maintenance blond with a pretty face and a polished wardrobe. On the other side, people claim Sheila is a reserved, boring, and studious nerd who's skinny with big glasses.

Famous Namesakes: Musician Sheila E; activist Sheila Wellstone

Shelby

(English) ledge estate.

Image: Shelby shoots the breeze with every person she passes on the street. She's described as a sweet, social, and smart Southerner. People say this small-town gal knows just about everyone and can chat with them all. She's envisioned as chubby and short with curly, blond hair; freckles; and blue eyes.

Famous Namesakes: Character Shelby Eatenton Latcherie (*Steel Magnolias*); singer Shelby Lynne

Shelly

(English) meadow on the ledge. (French) a familiar form of Michelle.

Image: Shelly *probably* has a great personality. She's most often described as a kind, loving, and outgoing woman. Some people say she's likable, but every now and then she can be a little overbearing. Others have a completely different view, saying Shelly is quiet, timid, and bland. Outgoing or shy, she's pictured as a big blond with glasses.

Famous Namesakes: Author Mary Wollstonecraft Shelley; actress Shelly Long

 **Star Kids**

Shiloh Nouvel

Shiloh Nouvel is completely bohemian. She's described as a devotee of classical literature, music, and art, and she may even be a writer herself. People also find her to be spiritual, passionate, and confident. She's most likely beautiful with long, black hair. As the daughter of actors Angelina Jolie and Brad Pitt, Shiloh Nouvel may easily grow up to be boho-chic. At the very least, there's no doubt she'll live up to the beautiful part.

Sherry

(French) beloved, dearest.

Image: Sherry may be heard a mile away, or she may not be heard even if you were standing right next to her. Most people believe Sherry is silly, loud, and fun, but perhaps selfish and insecure as well. A few people claim, however, that she's insecure, shy, and quiet. In either case, she's seen as a short and round brunette.

Famous Namesakes: Actress Sherry Stringfield; actress Shari Belafonte; comedian Cheri Oteri; puppeteer Shari Lewis

Shirley

(English) bright meadow.

Image: Shirley still spreads cheer to all those around her. People think she's a happy, cheerful, and helpful woman. Always a social butterfly, she can be scatterbrained and goofy sometimes, but people say that just adds to her sweetness. She's most likely older than sixty-five, but she's not ready to retire from her job as a waitress. She's still known for that Shirley Temple look with curly, blond hair and rosy cheeks.

Famous Namesakes: Actress Shirley MacLaine; actress Shirley Jones; singer Shirley Manson; actress Shirley Temple; author Shirley Jackson; singer Shirley Bassey

Shonda

(Irish) a form of Shona.

Image: This image bears close resemblance to Shonda Rhimes, creator of TV's *Grey's Anatomy*. People say Shonda is a highly motivated and hardworking African American woman. She's probably outspoken, outgoing, and hilarious. Some call her honest and straightforward, but others label her bossy and obnoxious. A few people even envision her working in health-care, either as a nurse or a doctor.

Famous Namesakes: Writer Shonda Rimes

Shoshana

(Hebrew) a form of Susan.

Image: Shoshana has all the right stuff for success. She's thought to be a well-liked and lovable woman who's never short on energy, eagerness, and confidence. Perhaps recalling fashion designer Shoshanna Lonstein Gruss, people say Shoshana is a stylish and successful designer who's beautiful, dark-haired, and Jewish.

Famous Namesakes: Actress Shoshannah Stern; designer Shoshanna Lonstein Gruss

Sierra

(Irish) black. (Spanish) saw toothed.

Image: Sierra pushes herself to achieve amazing goals. Most people think Sierra is a brilliant overachiever who excels in both academics and athletics. While she's said to be serious and intense in her activities, she's caring and loving with her friends and family. She's most likely pretty with a fit physique and blue-green eyes. (Perhaps she's *very* pretty and fit, because some take a whole new approach, thinking she may be an exotic dancer.)

Famous Namesakes: None

Simone

(Hebrew) she heard.

Image: Simone seems to have inner and outer beauty, but looks can be deceiving. She's thought to be a sexy and lithe woman who's as kind and considerate as she is beautiful. Some people believe she's intelligent, laid-back, and soft-spoken as well. But others disagree, saying Simone is two-faced, cunning, bossy, and snobby.

Famous Namesakes: Writer Simone de Beauvoir; actress Simone Simon; character Simone Deveaux (*Heroes*)

Siobhan

(Irish) a form of Joan.

Image: Siobhan inspires many images. Most people see her as kind, generous, and eager to stand up for others. Some believe she's elegant, ladylike, and aristocratic—not to mention snobbish. A few people claim she's a dependent and careless follower who never takes responsibility. And then there are those who state she's intelligent, well spoken, and artistic. At least everyone agrees that this Irish lass is tall with red hair and green eyes.

Famous Namesakes: Actress Siobhán McKenna; actress Siobhan Fallon; singer Siobhan Donaghy

Sissy

(American) a familiar form of Cecelia.

Image: It doesn't take a genius to see that Sissy is, well, a sissy. This name gives the impression of a whiny, prissy wimp who's shy, timid, and quick to submit. She's most likely someone's little sister and is short and scrawny.

Famous Namesakes: Actress Sissy Spacek

Skye

(Arabic) water giver. (Dutch) a short form of Skyler.

Image: Skye's good will is a big as the sky. She's described as a tall and pretty girl who's good-natured, kind, and always thinking of others. She may be earthy and outdoorsy, which people find quite refreshing. She's said to be spirited but somewhat shy at the same time.

Famous Namesakes: Singer Skye Sweetnam; character Skye Chandler Quartermaine (*General Hospital*); actress Ione Skye

Sofia

(Greek) a form of Sophia.

Image: Sofia may be bashful, but she's no wallflower. She's described as a soft-spoken and shy Italian beauty. Don't be fooled by her quiet nature, though: She's also said to be worldly, sophisticated, and intelligent, not to mention warmhearted and sweet.

Famous Namesakes: Director Sofia Coppola; actress Sophia Loren; actress Sophia Bush; actress Sofia Vergara; actress Sophia Myles; character Sophia Petrillo (*The Golden Girls*)

Sondra

(Greek) defender of mankind.

Image: It may take some tough tactics, but Sondra gets things done. People say she's an arrogant and bossy know-it-all. At work, she most likely uses her strong will, high energy, and loud mouth to organize her team and meet her goals. In addition, this African American woman is also said to be eloquent and sophisticated. Outside of work, she's happy, sentimental, and fond of watching old movies.

Famous Namesakes: Character Sondra Huxtable Tibideaux (*The Cosby Show*)

Sonya

(Greek) wise. (Russian, Slavic) a form of Sophia.

Image: It's hard to say what personality Sonya displays is true. This brunette is most often described as a popular and talkative people-person who's quick to stick up for others. Tall and slender, Sonya may be a ballerina. But others say she's snobby, arrogant, ill-tempered, and overly dramatic.

Famous Namesakes: Figure skater Sonja Henie; actress Sonya Smith

Sophia

(Greek) wise.

Image: Sophia is sweet natured, kindhearted, and well mannered. People claim she's friendly and pleasant in an elegant, graceful, and almost regal way. The prim-and-proper routine can make this dark-featured beauty seem prissy at times, but when she lets her hair down, Sophia can be giggly and fun.

Famous Namesakes: Director Sofia Coppola; actress Sophia Loren; actress Sophia Bush; actress Sofia Vergara; actress Sophia Myles; character Sophia Petrillo (*The Golden Girls*)

Sophie

(Greek) a familiar form of Sophia.

Image: One of Sophie's favorite pastimes is going to the opera. She's described as a cultured, well-mannered, and refined woman. Although some may call her a snob, this tiny, pretty brunette is usually known to be sweet and charming in a soft-spoken way.

Famous Namesakes: Actress Sophie Marceau; singer Sophie Ellis Bextor; activist Sophie Scholl; model Sophie Dahl; character Sophie Zawistowski (*Sophie's Choice*)

Girls

Stacey

(Greek) resurrection. (Irish) a short form of Anastasia, Eustacia, Natasha.

Image: Stacey has two images, and you can find both of them in a typical junior high school setting. Some people think Stacey is a brainy-but-nerdy girl who's introverted, klutzy, and gawky. Others imagine she's an egotistical and boy-crazy airhead who's always dressed in the coolest fashions and perfectly made-up. Either way, she's most likely pretty and slightly chunky.

Famous Namesakes: Actress Stacy Dash; actress Stacy Keibler; TV host Stacy London; singer Stacy "Fergie" Ferguson

Stacia

(English) a short form of Anastasia.

Image: Which way do you see Stacia? Do you think she's a wild and outlandish party girl who's loud, chatty, and as sassy as they come? Is she a prim and polite dancer with a delicate personality and figure? Perhaps she's both?

Famous Namesakes: None

Stacy

(Greek) resurrection. (Irish) a short form of Anastasia, Eustacia, Natasha.

Image: Stacy may have a good time, but she has not-so-good qualities. She's pictured as a tall and slender brunette who's always party-ing, talking, and smiling. As vivacious as she may be, she's probably also self-centered, attention starved, high maintenance, and ditzy.

Famous Namesakes: Actress Stacy Dash; actress Stacy Keibler; TV host Stacy London; singer Stacy "Fergie" Ferguson

Starr

(English) star.

Image: What will you get if you wish upon Starr? Some people suspect she's an obnoxious combination of cockiness, self-centeredness, loudness, and brattiness. Others beg to differ, believing she's arty, cool, fashionable, and unique. A few people even imagine Starr as a trashy stripper with fake nails and hair exten-sions. In any case, she's most likely beautiful.

Famous Namesakes: TV host Star Jones

Stella

(Latin) star. (French) a familiar form of Estelle.

Image: Stella is more than just a pretty face. She strikes people as a beautiful and sexy woman who's kindhearted, demure, and politely classy, especially when she first meets people. When she warms up, she comes across as confident and self-sufficient. In contrast, some people imagine Stella has low self-esteem and can be rather mean.

Famous Namesakes: Designer Stella McCartney; character Stella Kowalski (*A Streetcar Named Desire*); actress Stella Adler

Stephanie

(Greek) crowned.

Image: Stephanie can have just about any per-sonality, so take your pick: People describe her as perky and bubbly, snobby and witchy, sweet and loving, dumb and ditzy, boring and bland, or simply common and average. Her appear-ance garners a bit more consensus, with most picturing her as a blond with blue eyes and a slim build.

Famous Namesakes: Actress Stephanie Powers; model Stephanie Seymour; actress Stephanie Zimbalist; radio personality Stephanie Miller

Girls

Stevie

(Greek) a familiar form of Stephanie.

Image: Stevie would be better off if she acted like herself and not someone she'll never be. People say Stevie is a lanky nerd who tries so hard to act cool and fit in. In reality, this red-head is nice, funny, and smart, and sometimes she can even be loud and outspoken.

Famous Namesakes: Singer Stevie Nicks

Stockard

(English) stockyard.

Image: Stockard may be proper, but that doesn't mean she can't have a sense of humor—much like actress Stockard Channing has. Stockard is said to be a well-mannered, strong-willed brunette who comes from an upper-class family. Some people say she's wise, but others suspect she's wisecracking, making her as funny as she is smart.

Famous Namesakes: Actress Stockard Channing

Storm

(English) storm.

Image: Thanks to the *X-Men* comics and films, the image for Storm is wedded to that of the heroine of the same name. Many people believe Storm is a courageous superhero who's strong, powerful, and ready to help the less fortunate. She may also be mysterious, dark, and rebel-lious, especially because of her power to create chaos with a storm.

Famous Namesakes: Character Storm (*X-Men*)

Stormy

(English) impetuous by nature.

Image: Like a storm rising on an otherwise per-fect day, Stormy can quickly move from pleasant to unpleasant. She's described as a cheerful and energetic girl, although some call her high-strung. She's most likely a wild, loud partier, and her behavior can be a bit obnoxious. She can even be mean, grouchy, and conceited at times. People can't decide if Stormy is homely or cute.

Famous Namesakes: None

Sue

(Hebrew) a short form of Susan, Susana.

Image: Sue is likable, but she has her issues. She comes across as a friendly people-person, but she most likely spends far too much time shopping, gambling, and gossiping. She's also said to be messy and lazy, and her appearance is unkempt and unhealthy as well.

Famous Namesakes: Author Sue Taylor Grafton; author Sue Townsend; designer Sue Wong; talk show host Sue Johanson; character Sue Richards (*The Fantastic Four*)

Summer

(English) summertime.

Image: Summer is as warm and carefree as the season that shares her name. She's described as a cheerful and pleasant blond who's probably the child of hippies. Like her parents, she's said to be easygoing, free spirited, and earthy. She may also be flighty, fun-loving, and wild. People picture Summer with a lean, sporty figure; a fair complexion; and a beautiful smile.

Famous Namesakes: Character Summer Roberts (*The O.C.*); swimmer Summer Sanders

Sunny

(English) bright, cheerful.

Image: Fittingly enough, Sunny has a sunny disposition. She's envisioned as a happy, warm, and loving blond who wears a big smile. Although she's sweet, sensitive, and helpful, she's most likely not the most intelligent person in the room.

Famous Namesakes: Character Sunny Beaudelaire (*Lemony Snicket* series)

Sunshine

(English) sunshine.

Image: Can't you just hear the Beatles singing "Good Day Sunshine"? As her name suggests, Sunshine is a cheerful, optimistic, and peppy girl with lots of smiles and giggles. She's probably a cute, sunny blond with freckles. Some people see her as a flower child with a hippie, environmental outlook. And although she's known to be quite lovable, she's not known to be intelligent.

Famous Namesakes: R&B singer Sunshine Anderson

Susan

(Hebrew) lily.

Image: Susan's strong personality is sometimes misconstrued. She's thought to be a sincere and pleasant woman who's a great friend. She's most likely smart, strong-willed, and spirited, and sometimes that combination of traits can make her seem intimidating. In actuality, this big-boned brunette is often goofy. A few people imagine her differently, saying she's a quiet and sophisticated bookworm.

Famous Namesakes: Actress Susan Sarandon; activist Susan B. Anthony; actress Susan Lucci; actress Susan Dey; author Susan Cheever

Susannah

(Hebrew) a form of Susan.

Image: As silly as it may be, the folksong "Oh! Susanna" shapes the image for this name. Susannah is imagined as a friendly and fun free spirit who loves big gatherings and music. Some say this cute redhead is an old-fashioned Southern debutante who's strong-willed and perhaps a bit spoiled. Spoiled or not, she's most often heard whistling a tune.

Famous Namesakes: Actress Susannah York; character Susannah Polk (*Susannah*); screenwriter Susannah Grant; singer Susannah Hoffs

★ Star Kids

Suri

Suri doesn't say much, unless you get her talking about days gone by. People envision her as a petite Asian woman who's quiet, modest, and passive. Intelligent and inquisitive, she's most likely a historian who comes alive when she tells tales about the past. This image may mean that Suri, the daughter of actors Tom Cruise and Katie Holmes, will love to recount her parents' bizarre and much-publicized romance.

Suzanne

(English) a form of Susan.

Image: Suzanne walks into a conference room feeling self-assured and ready to succeed. People describe her as an ambitious, competitive, and strong-willed businesswoman. At times, she can be bossy and pushy, but more often, she seems to be energetic and upbeat. Suzanne is most likely beautiful and perfectly put together, as well as entertaining and funny.

Famous Namesakes: Actress Suzanne Somers; actress Suzanne Pleshette; singer Suzanne Vega

Suzette

(French) a form of Susan.

Image: Suzette is ditzy and childish, but she certainly has her share of fun. She's perceived as a bubbly, fun-loving flake. She usually seems sweet, but she can also be a flirt, if not a floozy. People imagine Suzette's silliness can sometimes slide into childish, immature behavior. She's most likely a blond.

Famous Namesakes: Beauty queen Suzette Charles

Suzie

(American) a familiar form of Susan, Susana.

Image: Suzie is sociable, or at least that's what most people say. She's thought to be a bubbly, chatty extrovert with a welcoming smile. A curly-haired blond, she's most likely sweet and generous, and people find her easy to talk to. A few people, however, hold a contrasting view, imagining Suzie as rude, stuck-up, and even mean.

Famous Namesakes: Musician Suzie Quatro

Svetlana

(Russian) bright light.

Image: Russian gymnast Svetlana Khorkina is as famous for her testy behavior as she is for her athletic prowess. Not surprisingly, this Svetlana gives the impression of a tall Russian blond who's self-centered, argumentative, and competitive. She's known to be studious when it comes to her craft, but she also has a mean, hateful streak.

Famous Namesakes: Gymnast Svetlana Khorkina

Sybil

(Greek) prophet.

Image: So much of this name's image stems from *Sybil*, the popular book and miniseries based on the life of a woman with multiple personalities. People imagine Sybil as a fragile, brittle woman with intensive mood and personality swings. At different times, she can seem rude and snobbish, clever and cunning, or guarded and mysterious. She's pictured as a skinny brunette who's pretty but pale with glasses.

Famous Namesakes: Patriot Sybil Ludington; actress Cybil Shepherd

Sydney

(French) from Saint-Denis, France.

Image: Sydney has some spunk—and so much more. Above all else, she's pictured as an attractive brunette with freckles. Beyond that, she's said to be a sporty tomboy who's spunky, feisty, and witty. Sydney tends to be the center of attention, but people believe she's also caring, smart, and sometimes rather serious.

Famous Namesakes: Character Sydney Bristow (*Alias*); actress Sydney Tamiia Poitier

Sylvana

(Latin) forest.

Image: Sylvana has a mystical quality. This name evokes an image of a quiet and exotic woman who speaks with an accent. She may be arty, and she may even be into witchcraft or other dark, mysterious activities. Physically, Sylvana is described as dark-haired and full figured.

Famous Namesakes: Actress Sylvana Simons

Sylvia

(Latin) forest.

Image: This name's image bears the sad, heavy weight of poet Sylvia Plath and her tragic life. People imagine Sylvia as a depressed, mentally unstable, and deeply intelligent writer. She's envisioned as beautiful, brunette, and thin with haunted eyes. At times she seems kind and graceful, but at other times, she's unapproachable and aloof.

Famous Namesakes: Author Sylvia Plath; author Sylvia Browne

★ Star Kids

Tallulah Belle

Tallulah Belle is truly a belle. People suspect she's a Southern sweetie who's bouncy, animated, and a great cook. She may even own a little diner. As for her looks, she's pictured with fair skin, blue eyes, curls, and nice legs. For this image to match the youngest daughter of actors Demi Moore and Bruce Willis, Tallulah Belle will have to start practicing her Southern drawl.

Tabitha

(Greek, Aramaic) gazelle.

Image: Tabitha may be fun-loving, but then again, she may be straight-laced. People agree she's well read and clever as well as pretty, brunette, and athletic. Beyond that, some people say she's a spirited, happy-go-lucky sweetheart, but others claim she's an ornery, prim priss. A few even call her a witch, although perhaps that's a reference to the character Tabitha of TV's *Bewitched*.

Famous Namesakes: Biblical figure Tabitha; character Tabitha (*Bewitched*)

Taffy

(Welsh) a familiar form of Taffline.

Image: As candy goes, taffy is sweet with little substance; as images go, Taffy is much the same. People describe her as bubbly, fun, and silly, not to mention sweet and lovable. Her silly, ditzy demeanor can make her seem off-the-wall, different, and perhaps even crazy. Physically, Taffy is thought to be a tall blond, but her clothes don't match and she's not very neat.

Famous Namesakes: None

Taka

(Japanese) honored.

Image: Taka may be strong, but she's not stern. This name evokes the image of a bold and fearless woman who's regal and in control. At the same time, she's known to be energetic, cheery, and playful. People describe Taka as beautiful and petite with brown eyes and olive skin.

Famous Namesakes: None

Tamara

(Hebrew) palm tree.

Image: Tamara has a sassy, fun side. Much like Tamera Mowry of TV's *Sister, Sister*, she's described as a olive-skinned looker with dark hair and a medium build. People imagine she's funny, bubbly, and a little wild, loving rock music and fashion. She's also thought to be friendly and smart.

Famous Namesakes: Actress Tamera Mowry; singer Tamyra Grey; actress Tamara Tunie

Tameka

(Aramaic) twin.

Image: Tameka can enliven anyone's day. She's said to be a spirited and vibrant African American woman. Always smiling and cheerful, she's known to have a sunny disposition and a great sense of humor. Tameka also seems to be a bit of a risk taker. People imagine she's skinny and tall.

Famous Namesakes: TV host Tamika Ray; stylist Tameka Foster

Tammy

(English) twin. (Hebrew) a familiar form of Tamara.

Image: Everyone needs a friend like Tammy. She's thought to be a nurturing, sensitive, and patient woman who loves to help others. She's also said to be intelligent, sophisticated, and confident. In addition to being kind and bright, she's described as jolly and fun-loving. People picture Tammy with enchanting blue eyes and a nice smile.

Famous Namesakes: Singer Tammy Wynette; personality Tammy Faye Bakker

Girls

Tanith

(Phoenician) goddess of love.

Image: Tanith goes a mile a minute. People see her as a fast-talking and loud extrovert. She's most often friendly, but sometimes she can be short-tempered and a little crazy. She may be more athletically gifted than mentally so, and she's pictured to have dramatic beauty.

Famous Namesakes: Ice dancer Tanith Belbin

Tanya

(Russian, Slavic) fairy queen.

Image: This name has a brassy shine to it, perhaps thanks to country music star Tanya Tucker. Tanya strikes people as a bossy and sometimes even nasty bleached-blond country gal. She's most likely very confident, although people say she's not very chaste and not very smart.

Famous Namesakes: Actress Tanya Roberts; singer Tanya Tucker

Tara

(Aramaic) throw; carry. (Irish) rocky hill. (Arabic) a measurement.

Image: Much of this name's image stems from that of Tara Reid, one of Hollywood's wildest party girls. Tara is said to be a fun, bold, and self-indulgent woman who's known for her crazy antics. She's as beautiful as a model with her brown hair and slim figure, and she's most likely a singer, dancer, or actress. But many people find her to be moody and conceited at times. Some people have an entirely different view, saying she's an outdoorsy, smart, and thoughtful tomboy.

Famous Namesakes: Actress Tara Reid; figure skater Tara Lipinski; beauty queen Tara Conner

Taryn

(Irish) a form of Tara.

Image: Taryn is a wacky but cool character. She comes across as a creative, intelligent, and ambitious eccentric. She may be a decorator, artist, or simply someone's cool, fun aunt. While she's usually vivacious and quick, sometimes this tall, thin brunette can be quiet.

Famous Namesakes: Actress Taryn Manning

Tasha

(Greek) born on Christmas day. (Russian) a short form of Natasha.

Image: Tasha seems to participate in *every* extracurricular. She's viewed as a perky, positive girl who's full of spirit and eager to please. This leggy, cute blond is talented in many areas—including cheerleading, sports, and drama—and many people say she's funny as well. That said, a few people find Tasha to be a bit snobbish.

Famous Namesakes: Actress Tasha Smith; character Tasha Yar (*Star Trek: The Next Generation*)

Tatiana

(Slavic) fairy queen.

Image: Tatiana demonstrates that bookworms can be outgoing, too. Many people envision her as an intelligent and literary woman, perhaps even a professor. She's no recluse, though: She's known to be talkative, spirited, and feisty. As for her appearance, Tatiana is pictured as a tall and husky African American who men find quite attractive.

Famous Namesakes: Grand duchess Tatiana Nikolaievna of Russia

Tatum

(English) cheerful.

Image: Tatum either exudes confidence or exudes insecurity. To most people, this name conjures up the image of a self-assured, happy extrovert who loves to lead the pack. But other people find Tatum to be a prudish drama queen who lives off inherited money yet still has an unstable life.

Famous Namesakes: Actress Tatum O'Neal

Tawny

(Gypsy) little one. (English) brownish yellow, tan.

Image: Actress-model Tawny Kitaen first strutted onto the scene in a heavy metal music video, and her saucy reputation affects this name's image. People say Tawny is a sassy, rebellious, and flirty stripper with fake breasts, fake blond hair, and a fake tan. Not surprisingly, she's also considered to be shallow and self-absorbed.

Famous Namesakes: Actress-model Tawny Kitaen

Taylor

(English) tailor.

Image: Fun likely follows Taylor wherever she goes. People describe her as cheerful, playful, flirty, and fun-loving. She's said to be popular because of her carefree disposition, but being a perfect-looking blond helps as well. Some people, however, see Taylor as a feisty and outspoken politician (no doubt a nod to American president Zachary Taylor); a snobby and sneaky bully; or a calm and down-to-earth sweetie.

Famous Namesakes: Singer Taylor Swift; singer Taylor Hicks; singer Taylor Dane

Tegan

(Welsh) a form of Teagan.

Image: Tegan may have a geeky career, but she's no social misfit. Most people view her as a skinny, small computer engineer whose book smarts make her borderline nerdy, but she's still charismatic and outgoing. Tegan likely has black hair that's contrasted by pale skin. A few people, however, see her as a bratty, spoiled Irish golfer.

Famous Namesakes: Singer Tegan Quin; character Tegan Jovanka (*Dr. Who*)

Terri

(Greek) a familiar form of Theresa.

Image: It's almost as if Terri physically *can't* stop talking, even when she wants to. She's considered to be a cheerful, perky, and fun-loving gal who chatters nonstop. People assume she has a cell phone permanently attached to her ear. With her bouncy and chatty energy, she probably works as a dance instructor or personal trainer. Surprisingly, Terri can be quite competitive.

Famous Namesakes: Actress Teri Garr; actress Teri Hatcher; actress Teri Polo

Tess

(Greek) a short form of Quintessa, Theresa.

Image: Tess is a well-rounded mom. She's described as a fun and outgoing woman with an infectious laugh and a hippie-like, carefree spirit. Complementing her happy-go-lucky side is her motherly, caring side. Physically, she's pictured as a pretty and plump brunette.

Famous Namesakes: Character Tess Durbeyfield (*Tess of the d'Urbervilles*); actress Tess Harper

Tessa

(Greek) reaper.

Image: Once you know Tessa's story, it's easy to see why she's so happy. People imagine she's a fun-loving, cheerful, and spunky woman. She may not be the brightest bulb, but she married into an upscale lifestyle. Of course, people say that's because she's a selfish gold digger who happens to have long legs, a feminine face, and long, blond locks.

Famous Namesakes: None

Thea

(Greek) goddess.

Image: Clients find it easy to share with Thea. She's thought to be a compassionate, loyal, and intelligent woman. Encouraging and inspirational, she may work as a counselor, which is a perfect fit for her funny, easygoing, yet always diplomatic disposition. Physically, she's pictured to be beautiful, lithe, and dark-haired.

Famous Namesakes: Comedian Thea Vidale; jazz singer Thea Gill; mythological figure Thea

Girls

Thema

(African) queen.

Image: As Thema demonstrates, leadership and sociability don't always go hand in hand. She's depicted as a strong, successful leader—perhaps even a warrior. But despite her ability to command others, Thema is said to be cold and detached, preferring isolation. As for her appearance, she's pictured as a beauty with brown hair and brown eyes.

Famous Namesakes: None

Theone

(Greek) gift of God.

Image: Theone has men tripping over themselves. She's said to be a modern-day Greek goddess who's lovely, tall, sweet, and congenial. Clearly, people believe she's a man-crazy heartbreaker. At the same time, she's also said to be hardworking, highly educated, and driven to succeed.

Famous Namesakes: None

Theresa

(Greek) reaper.

Image: Theresa either pushes others around or gets pushed around herself. Most people picture Theresa as a dumb, heartless, and ruthless meanie. Others see her as the exact opposite: They think she's a friendly yet timid pushover. Either way, she's probably tall, big-boned, and sexy with olive skin. Of course, a few people say she's religious and pious, like saintly Mother Teresa.

Famous Namesakes: Nun Mother Teresa; actress Theresa Russell; actress Theresa Randle

Therese

(Greek) a form of Theresa.

Image: Therese has a prestigious career and a prestigious upbringing. People believe she's an intelligent, articulate woman who may be a writer, doctor, scientist, or researcher. With her dignified, quiet demeanor, she's sometimes misunderstood as aloof or snooty. Her upper-class roots most likely adds to the misunderstanding. But deep down, this beautiful brunette is said to be nice, loving, and trusting.

Famous Namesakes: Saint Therese of Lisieux

Thomasina

(Hebrew) twin.

Image: To put it mildly, Thomasina is uninteresting. She's perceived as a self-centered, prissy, and uptight bookworm. She's also known to be quiet, serious, and rather dull. At times, she can seem pleasant, but she usually comes across as selfish. People can't decide if she's pretty and petite or ugly and hairy.

Famous Namesakes: Cook Thomasina Miers

Tia

(Greek) princess. (Spanish) aunt.

Image: In high school and in politics, Tia knows what it takes to get the votes. She's said to be an outgoing, charming, and popular woman who's a good communicator. As a teenager, Tia was voted homecoming queen; as an adult, she was voted to office as a civic leader. People seem to like her compassion and hopeful attitude as well as her strong will. Physically, she's pictured as an attractive Asian, like actress Tia Carrere.

Famous Namesakes: Actress Tia Carrere

Tierney

(Irish) noble.

Image: Sometimes Tierney lets her emotions run away. She's regarded as bubbly and cheerful, although often ditzy. She's said to be quite sensitive and compassionate, although she cries a lot. Finally, she's described as a rich socialite, although she's spoiled and bossy at times. As for her looks, she's pictured as tall and a bit chubby with long, blond hair.

Famous Namesakes: Actress Gene Tierney; actress Maura Tierney; jazz singer Tierney Sutton

Tiffany

(Latin) trinity. (Greek) a short form of Theophania.

Image: *Fer shur*, Tiffany is, like, totally a Valley girl. She's overwhelmingly seen as a dimwitted and flighty blond airhead. Some go as far as to call her a bimbo. Intelligence aside, people are divided as to whether she's supersweet or supersnobby.

Famous Namesakes: Singer Tiffany; actress Tiffani Thiessen

Tina

(Spanish, American) a short form of Augustine, Martina, Christina, Valentina.

Image: If you're waiting for a pause in Tina's conversation, make yourself comfortable—it'll be a while. People describe Tina as a bubbly, talkative gal who never stops yapping. Although she's known to be opinionated, she's not very bright. Despite all this, some say she's sweet and kind, but others find her to be trashy. She's most likely short, attractive, and brunette.

Famous Namesakes: Actress Tina Louise; singer Tina Turner; actress Tina Yothers; comedian Tina Fey

Tisha

(Latin) joy.

Image: Tisha's friends think she's the greatest, no matter if she's loud or quiet. She's said to be a kind and caring African American cutie with a lot of friends. Everyone finds Tisha to be fun, happy, and humorous, but people disagree whether she's loud or soft-spoken. She's most likely skinny, tall, and sultry with a lot of dark hair.

Famous Namesakes: Actress Tisha Campell

Toni

(Greek) flourishing. (Latin) praiseworthy.

Image: More likely than not, Toni is the bright spot in someone's day. This name evokes the image of a sunny, friendly, and confident woman. She always seems to have a smile to share and a joke to tell. She's most likely African American or perhaps Italian. That said, a few people believe she's pushy, high-strung, and maybe even crooked.

Famous Namesakes: Author Toni Morrison; singer Toni Braxton; actress Toni Collette; singer Toni Basil

Tonya

(Slavic) fairy queen.

Image: Figure skater Tonya Harding is one of history's most infamous Olympians, on and off the ice. Because of her, this Tonya is seen as a jealous, selfish woman with poor self-esteem. Even though she's competitive and pushy, she's also known to be easily swayed—perhaps because she's not very bright.

Famous Namesakes: Figure skater Tonya Harding; actress Tonya Pinkins

Torie

(English) a form of Tori, Tory.

Image: Torie is antiestablishment, but don't think that means she's not a good person. This name reminds people of a self-assured, wild, and fun punk who's quite a go-getter. Although she's brazen, Torie is also known to be kind and happy. People suspect she communicates her attitude through the tattoos and piercings all over her small body.

Famous Namesakes: Actress Tori Spelling

Torrance

(Irish) a form of Torrence.

Image: Torrance comes at people with a torrent of willpower. She's imagined as a fearless, stubborn, and bossy leader. She's also said to be rude, snobby, and arrogant—perhaps because she's wealthy. People envision her as tall, athletic, and attractive, and she may very well be the captain of the cheer squad.

Famous Namesakes: Character Torrance Shipman (*Bring It On*)

Tova

(Hebrew) a form of Tovah.

Image: There's something a little uncommon about Tova. People suspect she's strange—maybe because she's a free-spirited hippie, maybe because she's open-minded in a weird way, maybe because she seems a little slow. Underneath the strangeness, though, Tova is most likely a responsible and reliable Jewish woman with dark features.

Famous Namesakes: Actress Tovah Feldshuh

Tracy

(Latin) warrior. (Greek) a familiar form of Theresa.

Image: Tracy will never be called a girly girl. People depict her as a battler—they say she's courageous, brave, and hardworking. Physically, she's a bit masculine as well. Nevertheless, people find Tracy to be kind, clever, and fun.

Famous Namesakes: Actress Tracy Gold; actress Tracy Ellis Ross; actress Tracy Ullman; designer Tracy Reese; singer Tracy Chapman

Tricia

(Latin) a form of Trisha.

Image: Tricia's perky image has a seedy side that only a few see. She comes across as a popular yet ditzy cheerleader with lots of pep, athletic ability, and determination. She's most likely thin, tall, and attractive. Some people, however, imagine she's also a bit trashy, living in a trailer park and smoking behind her parents' backs.

Famous Namesakes: First daughter Tricia Nixon; model Tricia Helfer

Trina

(Greek) pure.

Image: Rap artist Trina gives this name some hardnosed street cred. People say Trina is a small girl with a big foul mouth, a penchant for starting fights, and a wild sense of style. Some find her to be funny and popular, but others think she's trashy and cheap.

Famous Namesakes: Rapper Trina

Trinity

(Latin) triad.

Image: Trinity either just passed the bar or she works at the Bar-T Ranch. She's imagined most often as a smart and sophisticated attorney from a wealthy family. Others view her completely differently, saying Trinity may be a cowgirl who never has time for books. In either case, she's said to be thin, strong, and pretty with sandy hair.

Famous Namesakes: Character Trinity (*The Matrix*)

Trish

(Latin) a short form of Beatrice, Trisha.

Image: Once you get to know her, you'll find that Trish has many layers. She seems to be a bubbly, happy extrovert who's sexy, blond, and busty. But take another look, and you'll see she's also honest, respectful, and kind. Look even more closely and see that Trish is a strong-willed and intelligent woman who strives for perfection and success.

Famous Namesakes: Professional wrestler Trish Stratus

Trista

(Latin) a short form of Tristan.

Image: Reality-TV star Trista Rehn-Sutter lends her perky character to this name's image. People imagine Trista as a vibrant cheerleader who's fun, flirty, and almost too sweet. That said, she doesn't seem to be a pushover: People say she's an athletic overachiever who fights for what she wants. To complete the image, she's depicted as a petite and attractive blond with blue eyes.

Famous Namesakes: Reality-TV star Trista Rehn-Sutter

Trudy

(German) a familiar form of Gertrude.

Image: Trudy is like any other little girl. She's seen as a young schoolgirl who's innocent to the point of being gullible. Overall, though, she's said to be playful, giggly, hyper, and fun. People picture her as African American.

Famous Namesakes: Actress Trudie Styler

Tyne

(English) river.

Image: This name's image most likely gets its verve from feisty actress Tyne Daly of TV's *Cagney & Lacey* and *Judging Amy*. Tyne is said to be an assertive, strong-willed woman who sometimes seems overbearing, stubborn, and even mean. But people believe this plump, middle-aged brunette is tough because she cares. In some situations, she can seem carefree and fun.

Famous Namesakes: Actress Tyne Daly

Tyra

(Scandinavian) battler.

Image: It's nearly impossible to separate this name from supermodel and talk show host Tyra Banks. For this reason, people say Tyra is a gorgeous and leggy African American model who's successful and confident. Perhaps a little too confident, however, because she sometimes seems snobby, smug, and full of herself in a cheap way. Still, many people find her to be smart and caring.

Famous Namesakes: Model Tyra Banks

Urania

(Greek) heavenly.

Image: It's hard to believe Urania is happy with her life. After all, she's thought to be an antisocial and depressed loner who's boring, defensive, and easily irritated. Her only positive quality seems to be her intelligence. It certainly isn't her looks, because Urania is described as gaunt, homely, and pale.

Famous Namesakes: Mythological figure Urania

Uriana

(Greek) heaven; the unknown.

Image: Uriana is funny, although perhaps in a laughing-*at*-her, not laughing-*with*-her, way. She's said to be a brainy, dorky, and uptight brownnoser. People claim she's a big-talking know-it-all, and she tends to be funny and sarcastic. As for her looks, she's described as tall and frumpy with pimples, glasses, and long, brown hair.

Famous Namesakes: None

Ursula

(Greek) little bear.

Image: Anyone who's seen Disney's *The Little Mermaid* knows that Ursula the Sea Witch is a formidable foe. For this reason, people over-whelmingly think Ursula is a horrible, evil, and witchlike woman who's power hungry and quick to trample anyone in her path. Her appearance is just as unpleasant: She's said to be ugly, plump, and masculine. Those not thinking of animated villains believe Ursula is a weird and withdrawn tomboy.

Famous Namesakes: Actress Ursula Andress; character Ursula the Sea Witch (*The Little Mermaid*)

Valarie

(Latin) a form of Valerie.

Image: A few options come to mind for the name Valarie. For starters, many people imagine she's a stuck-up, conceited snot. But just as many others get the impression she's a meek and nervous librarian who's inexplicably ashamed of herself. Lastly, a handful of people regard her as a compassionate sweetheart.

Famous Namesakes: Actress Valarie Rae Miller; actress Valerie Bertinelli; actress Valerie Harper

Vanessa

(Greek) butterfly.

Image: Vanessa has a healthy self-esteem, and for good reason: She's perceived as an ambitious, smart, and sophisticated woman. She's most likely caring, sensitive, and happy as well. In addition to being a gorgeous brunette, she's also known to be a talented and versatile actress (perhaps like Vanessa Redgrave).

Famous Namesakes: Actress Vanessa Williams; TV host Vanessa Minnello; actress Vanessa Redgrave; singer Vanessa Carlton

Vanna

(Cambodian) golden. (Greek) a short form of Vanessa.

Image: Vanna White gave game show *Wheel of Fortune* some glamour, but perhaps she doesn't boost this name's image. This Vanna strikes people as a spoiled yet glamorous blond aristocrat who's snooty and full of herself. She's believed to be ditzy, but she does look good in designer dresses, thanks to her too-thin figure and model-like beauty. A few dissenters state that she's funny, clever, and sincere.

Famous Namesakes: Game show host Vanna White

Veda

(Sanskrit) sacred lore; knowledge.

Image: Look out, corporate America, because Veda is blazing her trail. She's described as a creative and worldly ad exec who's as sophisticated as she is intelligent. Adding to her appeal, she's also said to be strikingly attractive, friendly, and well mannered.

Famous Namesakes: Character Veda Sultenfuss (*My Girl*)

Velma

(German) a familiar form of Vilhelmina.

Image: Who can forget Velma, the bespectacled nerd of *Scooby-Doo* fame? Most people imagine Velma is a dull, humorless, and bookish geek in raggedy clothes. She's probably dependable and hardworking, and she perhaps can be strong at times, but she's usually quite nervous.

Famous Namesakes: Character Velma Dinkley (*Scooby-Doo*); character Velma Kelly (*Chicago*)

Vera

(Latin) true. (Slavic) faith.

Image: Designer Vera Wang creates enchanting bridal gowns, and she leaves her style on this name's image, too. People think Vera is a sophisticated and graceful professional with creative vision, strong confidence, and powerful determination. She's also said to be friendly, caring, and never without a smile. She's likely a dark-haired and beautiful Asian.

Famous Namesakes: Designer Vera Wang; actress Vera Farmiga; film character Vera Drake

Verena

(Latin) truthful.

Image: Verena is well known for her ladylike disposition and style. This name gives the impression of an elegant and proper woman with regal sophistication. She's most likely soft-spoken and a bit shy out of politeness. A dark-haired vision, Verena is commonly found in stylish dresses that capture her feminine charm.

Famous Namesakes: Saint Verena

Verna

(Latin) springtime. (French) a familiar form of Laverne.

Image: Verna has a logical mind but a laid-back vibe. People claim she's a practical, systematic, and factual thinker. At the same time, she's also said to be funny, fun-loving, and easygoing. Perhaps because this name is a feminine variation of the name Vern or Vernon, people describe Verna as a somewhat masculine and unattractive woman.

Famous Namesakes: Actress Verna Bloom

Veronica

(Latin) true image.

Image: Veronica isn't *entirely* bad. She is, however, primarily thought of as a rude, witchy, selfish, and bossy brat with brown hair, brown eyes, and lots of money. People say she wants everything done her way and done perfectly. That said, Veronica seems to redeem herself a bit by being clever and funny.

Famous Namesakes: Reporter Veronica Guerin; TV character Veronica Mars; character Veronica Lodge (*Archie* comic book series)

Vicki

(Latin) a familiar form of Victoria.

Image: Vicki may have a few foibles. Some people say she's a considerate and helpful people-person who's spirited and fun. They suspect, however, that she's a little short on common sense and she's too fond of gossip. Other people see Vicki altogether differently, saying she's a boring, old-fashioned introvert. In either case, she's pictured as a stocky woman with a perm and fake nails.

Famous Namesakes: Comedian Vicki Lawrence; actress Vicki Lewis

 **★ Star Kids**

Violet Anne

Violet Anne is a flower—a *wallflower*, that is. She's imagined as a quiet and shy librarian or homemaker. She's considered to be sweet and helpful, and she can be quite fun once she warms up. People imagine her as a brunette with a lovely smile. As Violet Anne—daughter of actors Ben Affleck and Jennifer Garner—grows up in the spotlight, will she bloom in its glow or stick to the shadows?

Victoria

(Latin) victorious.

Image: With such a regal name, Victoria is bound to be a strong woman. Inevitably, she's considered to be an uppity, strong-willed snob who conducts herself in a superior, powerful, and bold manner. She's no doubt rich, aristocratic, and beautiful, which means she's no doubt vain and arrogant as well. Nevertheless, a few people imagine Victoria as good-natured and caring.

Famous Namesakes: Queen Victoria; singer Victoria Beckham; actress Victoria Principal; actress Victoria Rowell; model Victoria Silvstedt

Violet

(French) a plant with purplish blue flowers.

Image: Everything about this name calls to mind a delicate violet in a sunny field. People say Violet is demure, modest, and very feminine. She most likely has a petite frame, dark hair, and—of course—violet eyes. She's thought to be sweet and polite, and she seems to enjoy a good read. Overall, she comes across as a lighthearted romantic.

Famous Namesakes: Star kid Violet Anne Affleck; character Violet Beauregarde (*Charlie and the Chocolate Factory*)

Girls

Virginia

(Latin) pure, virginal.

Image: You'll probably find Virginia with a cup of tea, a far-off look, and a smile on her face. Most people imagine Virginia as compassionate, respectful, and inviting. She may be quiet and demure, and she's often lost in her idealistic daydreams. Physically, she's envisioned with dark hair and a fragile figure. A few people, however, say Virginia may be a chain-smoking barfly with a raspy voice and a need for attention.

Famous Namesakes: Writer Virginia Woolf; actress Virginia Madsen; actress Virginia McKenna

Vivian

(Latin) full of life.

Image: People have contrasting opinions about Vivian. Some say she's a vivacious, bold, and fun woman with an independent zest for life. But others say the contrary—she's a shy, nerdy spinster and wallflower. With especially this latter view in mind, Vivian is viewed as an old woman without style or flair.

Famous Namesakes: Actress Vivian Leigh; actress Vivian Vance; designer Vivienne Westwood

Wanda

(German) wanderer.

Image: Saying Wanda is rough around the edges is an understatement. She seems to be a loud and silly party girl with a hearty—and most likely obnoxious—laugh. For each person who says she's strong-willed and adventurous, another claims she's foul mouthed, trashy, and even immoral. Physically, Wanda doesn't win anyone over, with her bad teeth and coarse skin.

Famous Namesakes: Comedian Wanda Sykes; singer Wanda Jackson

Wendy

(Welsh) white; light-skinned.

Image: Wendy simply wants to help out. She's known as a caring and kind woman who's eager to lend a hand wherever and however she can. She's likely a hippie with a penchant for rebellion, which perhaps means she assists the disenfranchised. People envision Wendy as a tall brunette, but they can't decide if she's flighty or intelligent.

Famous Namesakes: Character Wendy Darling (*Peter Pan*); playwright Wendy Wasserstein; radio personality Wendy Williams

Whitney

(English) white island.

Image: People just don't see eye to eye about Whitney. One side finds her to be a fun, perky, and smiley preppy. The other side disagrees strongly, saying she's a spiteful, selfish, and obnoxious diva. Opinions clash even about her appearance: Some claim Whitney is perfectly beautiful, like a model. But others insist she's emaciated and sickly. Perhaps the only agreement is that she's a sharp, talented woman.

Famous Namesakes: Singer Whitney Houston

Wilhelmina

(German) a form of Wilhelm

Image: As someone in charge of others' welfare, Wilhelmina draws upon her compassion and dedication. She's depicted as a large and plump woman who's caring, sweet, and eager to listen. She may be a caretaker, which is a good fit for her hardworking and loyal character.

Famous Namesakes: Character Wilhelmina Slater (*Ugly Betty*); model Wilhelmina Cooper

Willow

(English) willow tree.

Image: A name like Willow creates such a lovely picture. Like a young willow tree, she's imagined as waiflike, pretty, and demure. She's known to be kind and helpful, and with her open-minded, calm manner, she often acts as a peacemaker. It's a safe bet to assume that people believe Willow is an earthy, hippie-like nature lover.

Famous Namesakes: Character Willow Rosenberg (*Buffy the Vampire Slayer*); TV host Willow Bay

Winda

(Swahili) hunter.

Image: People resoundingly agree Winda is unlikable, although they disagree about the specifics. They describe her as any of the following: slow and dumb, nasty and short-tempered, annoying and whiny, loud and goofy, boring and dull, or weird and different. Winda's appearance doesn't help her image: She's pictured as homely and chubby.

Famous Namesakes: Writer Winda Benedetti

Winifred

(German) peaceful friend. (Welsh) a form of Guinevere.

Image: Winifred winds down most of her days in her musty library. She's seen as an old bookworm with old money and old-fashioned ideals. At times, she can seem warm and affectionate, but she's usually serious, boring, and antisocial. Although Winifred may have been pretty in her youth, people admit she's unattractive now.

Famous Namesakes: TV producer Winifred Hervey

Winona

(Lakota) oldest daughter.

Image: This name's image is an amalgamation of the images of two famous namesakes: actress Winona Ryder and country singer Wynonna Judd. Some people describe Winona as a popular and cool girl with a great personality and an ability to get along with everyone. She's pictured as a dark-haired and small cutie, and she's said to be funny and smart—and perhaps a little unstable. Then again, others suspect she's a trashy, backwoods partier with a wild streak and a plain face.

Famous Namesakes: Actress Winona Ryder; singer Wynonna Judd

Winter

(English) winter.

Image: There are three shades to Winter's image: 1) Some people think she's a cold and detached recluse who spends her time reading. 2) Others imagine she's a boisterous and kind girl who's rather happy-go-lucky. 3) A few describe her as a unique and gentle soul with her own creative style. Whichever the case, people picture Winter as a pale blond with a thin physique and striking blue eyes.

Famous Namesakes: None

Yasmine

(Persian) jasmine flower.

Image: Yasmine's personality depends on her occupation. People think of her as an articulate lawyer, a flirty makeup-counter salesclerk, or a sassy aerobics instructor. Physically, she's described as a very attractive brunette with dark skin.

Famous Namesakes: Actress Yasmine Bleeth

Girls

Yoko

(Japanese) good girl.

Image: There's only one Yoko Ono, and there's only one image for this name. Yoko is imagined to be an eccentric Asian artist with black hair, a small stature, and plenty of quirks. Despite her weirdness, people admit she's serious, smart, and resourceful with her career and life.

Famous Namesakes: Artist Yoko Ono

Yolanda

(Greek) violet flower.

Image: Yolanda uses her humor to speak her mind. She's pictured as an African American woman who's svelte and attractive with dark hair. Beyond her looks, she's considered to be a funny and strong-willed joker who's always outspoken. She's also said to be hardworking and quite caring.

Famous Namesakes: Gospel singer Yolanda Adams; singer Yolanda Perez

Yvette

(French) a familiar form of Yvonne.

Image: Yvette lives the lifestyle of the haute couture. She comes across as a fashionable and cultured French sophisticate who's rail thin and model perfect. Not surprisingly, she's also known to be snobby, rude, rich, and self-centered. When she can set her snobbery aside, she's said to be a smart social butterfly.

Famous Namesakes: Model Yvette Nelson

Yvonne

(French) young archer. (Scandinavian) yew wood; bow wood.

Image: Who's the boss? The answer is Yvonne, and you better not forget it. Yvonne is primarily perceived as a bossy, pushy woman who's always in charge. Sometimes her techniques may seem mean, but overall, people admit she's a hard worker. She's most likely a Spanish looker with long, black hair.

Famous Namesakes: Actress Yvonne De Carlo

Zahara

(Swahili) a form of Zahra.

Image: Zahara proves that you don't need to be loud to be heard. She's said to be an African model who's often quiet, shy, and reserved. That said, she can be quite confident and even aggressive when she goes after something she wants. Nonetheless, Zahara never seems to lose her sweetness and politeness.

Famous Namesakes: Star kid Zahara Jolie-Pitt

Zaida

(Arabic) a form of Zada.

Image: Zaida amazes all with her wisdom, vitality, and attractiveness. She's seen as a feisty, opinionated, and powerful intellectual. People say she's more than just brains, though: She's also known to have a dazzling, vivacious personality and exotic beauty.

Famous Namesakes: None

Zaza

(Hebrew) golden.

Image: Zaza has pizzazz. This name makes people think of a generous, sassy, and witty woman. Although she's saucy, people also point out how kind she is. Like similarly named Zsa Zsa Gabor, Zaza is depicted as a blond with long legs, beautiful eyes, and a large chest.

Famous Namesakes: None

Zelia

(Spanish) sunshine.

Image: Zelia has a zeal for work and life. This name reminds people of a strong, capable go-getter. She may be eager to take risks, yet she's responsible and smart enough to know when to be conservative. Sexy and strong, Zelia also seems determined to have a lot of fun and take the right risks in her personal life.

Famous Namesakes: Author Zélia Gattai; anthropologist Zelia Nuttall

Zena

(Ethiopian) news. (Persian) woman. (Greek) a form of Xenia.

Image: It doesn't matter that the spelling is off—Zena reminds people of Xena of TV's *Xena: Warrior Princess*. Zena is envisioned as a buff and brave battler with mystical, strange powers. She's most likely intelligent, stubborn, and a born leader. Tall and raven-haired, she's said to be attractive, although in a masculine way.

Famous Namesakes: TV character Xena

Zephyr

(Greek) west wind.

Image: A zephyr is a pleasant wind, and this name's image fits quite nicely—whether it be for a girl or boy. Zephyr is imagined as an outgoing and energetic free spirit. He or she is most likely a caring, gentle friend who likes to have fun. People describe Zephyr as a striking blond.

Famous Namesakes: None

Zizi

(Hungarian) a familiar form of Elizabeth.

Image: How can you take Zizi seriously? This name makes people think of a silly, happy, and adorable young woman. She's said to be a hopeless romantic who loves to be in love. Alas, she's not known to be very intelligent, and people suspect she's not very useful in the professional world. In fact, some people think Zizi is over the top.

Famous Namesakes: Ballerina Zizi Jeanmarie

Zoe

(Greek) life.

Image: Zoe is downright nutty. People overwhelmingly describe her as silly, spontaneous, playful, and even crazy. They also say she's talented and creative, although maybe in a nerdy, goofy way. Naturally pretty, Zoe seems to be a kind and happy character.

Famous Namesakes: Radio personality Zoe Ball; actress Zoe Saldana

Zola

(Italian) piece of earth.

Image: This unique name must belong to an equally unique woman. Zola is envisioned as creative and independent in the most interesting way. She seems cool, collected, and calm, and her sometimes quiet nature gives her an air of mystery. Aptly, Zola is pictured to be an exotic stunner with dark hair and an attractive smile.

Famous Namesakes: Olympian Zola Budd

Images
of Boys'
Names

Aaron

(Hebrew) enlightened. (Arabic) messenger.

Image: You'll find Aaron's nose in a book. He's thought to be a smart but sweet bookworm who's tall and wears glasses. People imagine he's very outgoing, and he always finishes what he starts.

Famous Namesakes: Biblical figure Aaron; actor Aaron Eckhart; singer Aaron Carter; politician Aaron Burr

Abel

(Hebrew) breath. (Assyrian) meadow. (German) a short form of Abelard.

Image: If you're mankind's first murder victim, your name carries some baggage. People tend to associate this name with Abel from the Bible. They say Abel is moral and wise, but he's also a sad pushover.

Famous Namesakes: Biblical figure Abel

Abraham

(Hebrew) father of many nations.

Image: Honest Abe is a worthy namesake. People associate the name Abraham with Abraham Lincoln and imagine a highly intelligent and trustworthy leader who's tall, dark, and bearded.

Famous Namesakes: Biblical figure Abraham; president Abraham Lincoln; psychologist Abraham Maslow

Abram

(Hebrew) a short form of Abraham.

Image: Abram is a pillar of wisdom and leadership. For many people, the name Abram conjures up an image of a self-assured, assertive, and wise man. He's also pictured as an older fellow.

Famous Namesakes: Another name for biblical figure Abraham

Ace

(Latin) unity.

Image: Ace is number one—and that's both good and bad. People seem to think of Ace as a sweet, nice guy who loves to be the center of attention. But he can sometimes find himself in lapses of mean outspokenness.

Famous Namesakes: Movie character Ace Ventura; musician Ace Frehley

Adam

(Phoenician) man; mankind. (Hebrew) earth; man of the red earth.

Image: What a good friend—or husband— Adam would make. Adam is pictured as a physically fit and handsome man who's shy, kind, and intelligent. He's thought to be as sensitive as he is sincere.

Famous Namesakes: Biblical figure Adam; actor Adam Sandler; singer Adam Ant; actor Adam West

Addison

(English) son of Adam.

Image: Addison may be a preppy, but deep down, he's a good person. People think Addison is genuine, caring, and successful. He may not be boastful, but he can't help but enjoy the lavish home and goods his money buys.

Famous Namesakes: Poet Joseph Addison

Adler

(German) eagle.

Image: Adler is a force of nature. People imagine he's a woodsy naturalist who's strong and tall and who carries himself with respectable authority. He's considered to be fiery and passionate, yet sensitive enough to be careful with his words.

Famous Namesakes: Psychologist Alfred Adler

★ Star Kids

Ahmet Emuukha Rodan

Ahmet Emuukha Rodan is both a geek and a gentleman. People believe he's a physicist, engineer, or computer programmer. He may even build microchips. While his career may classify him as a geek, he seems to be a polite, proper, and well-composed gentleman outside of work. In reality, Ahmet Emuukha Rodan, son of eccentric musician Frank Zappa, seems to be a gentleman, too—but his career as a musician/actor/author is far from the Silicon Valley scene.

Adolf

(German) noble wolf.

Image: It's impossible to separate this name's image from that of Adolf Hitler. For this reason, people describe Adolf as a cruel and socially awkward control freak with Hitler's trademark moustache and lank dark hair.

Famous Namesakes: Nazi dictator Adolf Hitler

Adon

(Hebrew) Lord.

Image: Adon is a bit of a contradiction: Although people feel he's kind, chivalrous, and handsome, he doesn't have many friends. Perhaps it's because he's too strong-willed and serious.

Famous Namesakes: Phoenician mythological figure Adon

Adrian

(Greek) rich. (Latin) dark.

Image: People think of Adrian as the boy next door: He's described as caring, wholesome, cheerful, and open. You probably wouldn't mind if he dated your daughter. (Or at least you wouldn't mind it *much*.)

Famous Namesakes: Several popes named Adrian; baseball player Adrián Beltré; actor Adrien Brody; character Adrian Monk (*Monk*)

Adriel

(Hebrew) member of God's flock.

Image: Here's someone you can count on. People think Adriel is friendly and caring with the right amount of determination and will to get things done.

Famous Namesakes: Biblical figure Adriel

Ahmad

(Arabic) most highly praised.

Image: Ahmad may be the center of attention, but that may be because he pushed his way there. Ahmad is described as a young Middle Easterner who's bossy and loud yet socially outgoing.

Famous Namesakes: Football player Ahmad Rashad

Aidan

(Irish) fiery.

Image: *Sex and the City*'s Aidan Shaw has made an impression on this name's image. Aidan is described as a sensitive, caring guy who's always a good listener. People think his laid-back manner and outgoing ways make him fun to be around. Physically, he's pictured as handsome and strong.

Famous Namesakes: Actor Aidan Quinn; character Aidan Lynch (*Harry Potter* series)

Ajay

(Punjabi) victorious; undefeatable.

Image: Keep your friends close, and Ajay even closer. People see a nasty, bratty side to Ajay, but he'll likely charm you with his wit and sophistication. He's also thought to have a strong physique.

Famous Namesakes: Actor Ajay Devgan

Boys

Akeem

(Hebrew) a short form of Joachim.

Image: Akeem may be quiet, but he always stands up for himself. People say Akeem is an aloof but determined Arab. He's pictured as tall and dark-haired.

Famous Namesakes: Character Prince Akeem (*Coming to America*); original name of basketball player Hakeem Olajuwon

Aladdin

(Arabic) height of faith.

Image: The name Aladdin is famous from *Arabian Nights*, but Disney's *Aladdin* cartoon has taken the name to new heights. People imagine Aladdin as a sly, quick-thinking young man of Middle Eastern descent. He's thought to be sweet and adventurous, and there's clearly something magical about him.

Famous Namesakes: Character Aladdin (*Arabian Nights*)

Albert

(German, French) noble and bright.

Image: You don't have to be a genius to picture Albert. Most people think Albert is geeky and smart, probably because of the most famous namesake: Albert Einstein. Most people also believe Albert is funny, outgoing, and helpful, but a few imagine he's a shy outcast who keeps his big brains to himself.

Famous Namesakes: Scientist Albert Einstein; humanitarian Albert Schweitzer; actor Albert Brooks; TV and movie character Fat Albert; baseball player Albert Pujols

Alberto

(Italian) a form of Albert.

Image: Alberto is the life of the party. People see him as a Latino who's fun-loving, large, and confident. They believe he loves to socialize, eat, and tell jokes.

Famous Namesakes: Skier Alberto Tomba; attorney general Alberto Gonzales

Alcott

(English) old cottage.

Image: Would you care to join Alcott for tea? People envision Alcott as a snooty aristocrat who's ever so prim and proper. This Brit is most likely blond and lanky.

Famous Namesakes: None

Alden

(English) old; wise protector.

Image: Alden is always the gentleman. This name evokes an image of an elegant, well-mannered intellectual. People also imagine Alden is physically strong.

Famous Namesakes: Mayflower Pilgrim John Alden

Alec

(Greek) a short form of Alexander.

Image: Actor Alec Baldwin brings a lot to this name's image. People say Alec is a funny and cool charmer. His tall, strong build and handsome looks seem to add to his appeal.

Famous Namesakes: Actor Alec Baldwin; actor Alec Guinness

Alejandro

(Spanish) a form of Alexander.

Image: Alejandro is a colorful and kind character. He's imagined as a good-looking and muscular Spanish man who's loving, fun, and faithful.

Famous Namesakes: Director Alejandro Amenábar; musician Alejandro Fernádez

Alex

(Greek) a short form of Alexander.

Image: Class clowns get the laughs, but sometimes they also get detention. People think Alex is a class clown who's charming and smart, but he has the tendency to be too immature and cocky for his own good.

Famous Namesakes: Game show host Alex Trebeck; baseball player Alex Rodriguez; character Alex P. Keaton (*Family Ties*); author Alex Haley

Alexander

(Greek) defender of mankind.

Image: Like the great conqueror who bears his name, Alexander is a natural-born leader. He's pictured as a caring protector and provider who's well liked as well as wise. Being tall, strong, and handsome, people also imagine he's sought by women and may be something of a heartbreaker.

Famous Namesakes: King Alexander the Great; inventor Alexander Graham Bell; poet Alexander Pope; Founding Father Alexander Hamilton

Alfonso

(Italian, Spanish) a form of Alphonse.

Image: Don't pick a fight with Alfonso—he'll be ready to rumble. Alfonso strikes people as a name for a macho Italian man who's arrogant and insecure, but at times funny and energetic. He just may ride into town on his chopper.

Famous Namesakes: Actor Alfonso Ribeiro; baseball player Alfonso Soriano

Alfred

(English) elf counselor; wise counselor.

Image: Alfred prefers to keep to himself. People say he's an awkward loner who's reserved and uptight, but smart and polite when he comes out of his shell. His homely, big-nosed looks may attract bullies.

Famous Namesakes: Director Alfred Hitchcock; character Alfred E. Neuman (*MAD*); character Alfred Pennyworth (*Batman*)

Alfredo

(Italian, Spanish) a form of Alfred.

Image: Like a poet, Alfredo experiences an array of emotions. He's pictured as a respectful and clever poet who can quickly change from charming and flirtatious to jealous and sullen. He's thought to be heavy and perhaps European.

Famous Namesakes: Baseball player Alfredo Amézaga; singer Alfredo Kraus

Ali

(Arabic) greatest. (Swahili) exalted.

Image: The name Ali is full of Muhammad Ali's spirit and swagger. Ali is envisioned as a strong-willed, spontaneous, and handsome dark-haired man. People believe his determination has made him wealthy and famous.

Famous Namesakes: Boxer Muhammad Ali; Sacha Baron Cohen character Ali G

Alistair

(English) a form of Alexander.

Image: Soap opera character Alistair Crane from *Passions* has given this name a villainous air. Alistair is pictured as a pompous aristocrat fond of playing evil pranks. Offstage, however, Alistair is imagined as a caring and self-confident man.

Famous Namesakes: *Masterpiece Theatre* host Alistair Cooke; character Alistair "Mad Eye" Moody (*Harry Potter* series)

Allen

(Irish) a form of Alan.

Image: Allen may be a tad on the dorky side, but he probably has more money than you. People think Allen is a rich computer nerd who's smart but boring. Despite his skinny build and thick glasses, he (or his bankroll) is known to attract beautiful women.

Famous Namesakes: Poet Allen Ginsberg; basketball player Allen Iverson

Alphonse

(German) noble and eager.

Image: There's little appeal to Alphonse. He's imagined as an unattractive but intelligent smarty-pants. Some say he's quiet and shy, but others say he's petulant and grumpy. He's most likely overweight and hairy. A few people have a different view, seeing Alphonse as a snappy hairdresser.

Famous Namesakes: Mobster Alphonse "Al" Capone; artist Alphonse Mucha

Alvin

(Latin) white; light-skinned. (German) friend of elves.

Image: Is it any surprise Alvin still lives in his parents' basement? Most people think of Alvin as a computer geek who's as socially awkward as he is brainy. The image is complete with his thick-rimmed glasses and skinny, boyish build.

Famous Namesakes: Cartoon character Alvin the Chipmunk; choreographer Alvin Ailey

Amir

(Hebrew) proclaimed. (Punjabi) wealthy; king's minister. (Arabic) prince.

Image: Amir doesn't care about making friends. Tall and dark, he's imagined as an unsympathetic individual driven by ambition and intelligence.

Famous Namesakes: Islamic title Amir al-Mu'minin; poker player Amir Vahedi

Amos

(Hebrew) burdened, troubled.

Image: Say hello to Amos, and he'll reply with a shy smile. People imagine him as polite, quiet, and kind. He may be small, but he's cute with green eyes and red hair.

Famous Namesakes: Cookie maker Wally "Famous" Amos; biblical figure Amos

Anders

(Swedish) a form of Andrew.

Image: On the outside, Anders is a smooth operator; on the inside, he has some issues. He's regarded as a suave and serious metrosexual who's secretly self-conscious and lonely. People think he overcompensates for his insecurity with a stuck-up, stubborn attitude.

Famous Namesakes: Scientist Anders Celsius

Andre

(French) a form of Andrew.

Image: You'll find Andre with a bevy of beauties. People think Andre is popular with the ladies because he's witty, cultured, and sure of himself. Others think it's because he's tall and olive-skinned.

Famous Namesakes: Tennis player Andre Agassi; wrestler André the Giant; rapper André 3000; actor Andre Braugher

Andrew

(Greek) strong; manly; courageous.

Image: Andrew is everyone's pal. He's polite, goodhearted, and friendly. He may even have a sneaky, clever streak in him. Physically, he's described as tall and lanky.

Famous Namesakes: Presidents Andrew Jackson and Andrew Johnson; composer Andrew Lloyd Webber; biblical figure Andrew

Andy

(Greek) a short form of Andrew.

Image: Andy is the kind of guy you just want to look after. People may think Andy is a wimpy and puny guy with freckles and red hair, but he has all the qualities of a good friend: He's trustworthy, sweet, and amiable.

Famous Namesakes: Artist Andy Warhol; actor Andy Griffith; comedian Andy Ritcher; actor Andy Garcia; comedian Andy Kaufman

Angel

(Greek) angel. (Latin) messenger.

Image: Whenever you need someone to talk to, Angel is there. He's described as a selfless, insightful, and meek man with a slight build and dark, good looks. People think of him as a good listener as well as a wise counselor.

Famous Namesakes: Character Angel (*Buffy the Vampire Slayer* and *Angel*); character Angel Dumott Schunard (*RENT*); jockey Angel Cordero, Jr.

Angelo

(Italian) a form of Angel.

Image: Angelo will make you an offer you can't refuse. People think Angelo is a tough, bad-tempered, and bossy Italian. Watch him carefully—he's known to be smooth but sleazy.

Famous Namesakes: Character Angelo (*Measure for Measure*); composer Angelo Badalamenti

Angus

(Scottish) exceptional; outstanding.

Image: Angus is Scottish to the core. Most people imagine Angus as a hefty Scot who's stoic and respectful. He may be dimwitted, but he's hardworking nonetheless. At times, he can be a little gruff, if not hotheaded.

Famous Namesakes: Musician Angus Young; Celtic mythological figure Angus the Young; actor Angus T. Jones

Ansel

(French) follower of a nobleman.

Image: Photographer Ansel Adams gives this name's image a worldly appeal. People see Ansel as a well-traveled and well-read photographer. He most likely regales his friends with wonderful stories of his experiences.

Famous Namesakes: Photographer Ansel Adams

Anthony

(Latin) praiseworthy. (Greek) flourishing.

Image: Anthony has a passion for life. People see him as an exuberant romantic with handsome, dark looks from his Italian or Mediterranean heritage.

Famous Namesakes: Actor Anthony Hopkins; actor Anthony Perkins; actor Anthony Edwards; singer Anthony Kiedis

Antoine

(French) a form of Anthony.

Image: Antoine makes a great soap opera character. People say he's a handsome Frenchman who's confident, loyal, and charming. But people also say he's a bit conceited.

Famous Namesakes: Author Antoine de Saint-Exupéry; basketball player Antoine Walker

Antonio

(Italian) a form of Anthony.

Image: It's no wonder women swoon for Antonio. Like famous namesake Antonio Banderas, he's described as a heroic, charming, and sweet Lothario with dark eyes, skin, and hair.

Famous Namesakes: Actor Antonio Banderas; composer Antonio Vivaldi; character Antonio (*The Merchant of Venice*)

Archie

(German, English) a familiar form of Archer, Archibald.

Image: Which Archie do you prefer? People think of Archie as either a goofy and freckled redhead, like the eponymous character of *Archie* comics, or a balding husband who's narrow-minded but loyal, like Archie Bunker of *All in the Family*.

Famous Namesakes: Character Archie Bunker (*All in the Family*); character Archie Andrews (*Archie*); football player Archie Manning

Argus

(Danish) watchful, vigilant.

Image: Of all the voices clamoring at the pub, Argus's is the loudest. People say Argus is a burly and boisterous Scot with a big laugh and a bigger yell when he's feeling surly.

Famous Namesakes: Character Argus Filch (*Harry Potter* series); Greek mythological figure Argus

Arlen

(Irish) pledge.

Image: You can almost picture Arlen sitting hunched over in a rocking chair in his antebellum mansion. Arlen is said to be a frail, aging Southerner who's timid and insecure despite his vast wealth.

Famous Namesakes: Senator Arlen Specter; football player Arlen Harris

Armand

(Latin, German) a form of Herman.

Image: Armand's personality is as slick as his hair. People say Armand is an unattractive yet conceited slickster who talks too fast and wears designer suits.

Famous Namesakes: Actor Armand Assante; designer Armand Diradourian; character Armand (*The Vampire Chronicles*)

Armando

(Spanish) a form of Armand.

Image: Armando could be on the cover of a romance novel. He's seen as a passionate and dashing bodice ripper with suave Latin looks. People think his creativity and stubborn streak make him only more attractive.

Famous Namesakes: Baseball player Armando Benítez

Armen

(Hebrew) a form of Armon.

Image: After a long day crunching numbers at the office, Armen is happy to come home to a loving family. People think Armen is highly intelligent and good with numbers. Outside of work, he's seen as a handsome and caring family man.

Famous Namesakes: TV personality Armen Keteyian

Arnie

(German) a familiar form of Arnold.

Image: There are two types of Arnies, and neither one gets along with the other. People view Arnie as either a nerd with a pocket protector and thick glasses who can't get a girlfriend, or a loud, beer-swillin', tobacco-chewin' country boy.

Famous Namesakes: Nickname for Arnold Palmer and Arnold Schwarzenegger

Arnold

(German) eagle ruler.

Image: Don't be surprised if Arnold gives you a sales pitch that's too good to be true. People imagine him as a bespectacled, clumsy geek who's a dubious used-car salesman. Outside of work, he probably doesn't have many friends.

Famous Namesakes: Actor and California governor Arnold Schwarzenegger; golfer Arnold Palmer; character Arnold Jackson (*Diff'rent Strokes*)

Aron

(Hebrew) a form of Aaron.

Image: If you hang around Aron, you'll find yourself feeling as relaxed as he is. People regard Aron as a warm, approachable, self-assured guy with a strong build and sparkling eyes.

Famous Namesakes: Another name for biblical figure Aaron

Arsen

(Greek) a short form of Arsenio.

Image: It's tough when your name is pronounced the same as a felony. When people hear Arsen, they imagine an arsonist who's slow, lazy, and sneaky. He's most likely ugly and sweaty to boot.

Famous Namesakes: None

Arthur

(Irish) noble; lofty hill. (Scottish) bear.
(English) rock. (Icelandic) follower of Thor.

Image: Arthur is a noble scholar. People picture him as a studious and scientifically minded intellectual. They say he's a tall, middle-aged gent with thick glasses. He's likely to be helpful and generous as well as respected and reliable. Adding to his charm, Arthur is also known to have a lovable wit.

Famous Namesakes: Legendary figure King Arthur; character Arthur Bach (*Arthur*); tennis player Arthur Ashe; playwright Arthur Miller

Arturo

(Italian) a form of Arthur.

Image: If you like jazz, you'll love this name's image, which is most likely inspired by trumpeter and pianist Arturo Sandoval. Arturo is said to be a dark-haired and handsome character who's smooth and suave. People also believe this Latino jazz artist has romantic, poetic sensibility, not to mention a lot of charm.

Famous Namesakes: Boxer Aturo Gatti; character Maximillian Arturo (*Sliders*)

Asher

(Hebrew) happy; blessed.

Image: That Asher—he sure is a charmer. Asher is thought to be funny, sweet, and well liked. He probably has a smile on his face, and he'll put one on yours, too.

Famous Namesakes: Biblical figure Asher

Ashton

(English) ash-tree settlement.

Image: One image of Ashton is snobby, and the other is cool. To most people, Ashton is a condescending, conceited, cocky, and competitive preppy from an old-money family. He likely has pale skin and a bony frame. A few people—perhaps thinking of actor Ashton Kutcher—imagine he's outgoing, happy, and funny.

Famous Namesakes: Actor Ashton Kutcher

★ Star Kids

Audio Science

People think Audio Science is a top-to-bottom geek. Taking the name quite literally, they imagine he's a sound technician who's goofy and awkward. They imagine this introvert has wacky hair and clothes as well as thick glasses. In real life, actress Shannyn Sossamon may not have expected the geeky undertones when she named her son Audio Science, but she most likely chose that unique name for its literal reference. (She's also a music-mixing DJ.)

Aubrey

(German) noble; bearlike.

Image: Aubrey is full of Southern hospitality and charm. People describe him as a sweet-natured, smart, and proper Southern gentleman. He's pictured with a thin frame, blue eyes, and a ready smile.

Famous Namesakes: Writer John Aubrey

Auden

(English) old friend.

Image: Auden's head is always in the clouds. He's seen as a dainty poet and dreamer—perhaps because of English-born poet W. H. Auden. People feel Auden is kindhearted and quiet, but too easily distracted to be reliable.

Famous Namesakes: Poet W. H. Auden

August

(Latin) a short form of Augustine, Augustus.

Image: August is as laid-back as the summer month of the same name. People see August as the creative type—perhaps an actor or writer—who's gentle, compassionate, and handsome.

Famous Namesakes: Playwright August Wilson

Augustus

(Latin) majestic; venerable.

Image: If the name Augustus is fit for an emperor, you know it carries some weight. People consider Augustus a wise, powerful man who commands respect. Physically, his large carriage is most likely powerful, too.

Famous Namesakes: Emperor Augustus; character Augustus Gloop (*Charlie and the Chocolate Factory*)

Aurek

(Polish) golden-haired.

Image: Aurek is a kingly name. People imagine Aurek as a royal leader who's mysterious and odd. With a strong chin, he's probably stern, brooding, and quick-tempered.

Famous Namesakes: None

Austin

(Latin) a short form of Augustine.

Image: Austin is a kind soul. People imagine he's gentle, caring, and loyal, and he also has a great sense of humor. Perhaps inspired by Austin, Texas, several people think Austin has a traditional cowboy or country style.

Famous Namesakes: Film character Austin Powers

Avery

(English) a form of Aubrey.

Image: Avery was voted most likely to succeed, and for good reason. Avery comes across as very intelligent, self-assured, and popular. In his youth, he may have been class president. As a man, he may be a doctor.

Famous Namesakes: Actor Avery Brooks; basketball coach Avery Johnson

Axel

(Latin) axe. (German) small oak tree; source of life. (Scandinavian) a form of Absalom.

Image: Welcome to the jungle—Guns N' Roses frontman Axl Rose has left his hard-rock mark on any version of this name. People say Axel is a tough, raunchy, and self-centered rock star with long, greasy hair and a slender face.

Famous Namesakes: Character Axel Foley (*Beverly Hills Cop*); singer Axl Rose

Bailey

(French) bailiff, steward.

Image: A unisex name like this leaves people guessing, so this image works for a girl or a boy. People imagine Bailey as lively, playful, charming, happy, and loving. This youngster most likely has a small build, brown hair, and an adorable smile. Still, a few people imagine Bailey may be a cranky and stubborn dullard without any creativity or intelligence.

Famous Namesakes: Comic strip character Beetle Bailey; character Bailey Salinger (*Party of Five*); football player Champ Bailey

Ballard

(German) brave; strong.

Image: Money can't buy Ballard happiness. Ballard comes across as a snobby, tall, and incredibly rich sophisticate. Despite his wealth, people believe he's lonely and sad.

Famous Namesakes: Singer Hank Ballard

Bane

(Hawaiian) a form of Bartholomew.

Image: Like any bane, this Bane is the cause of his own undoing. People describe him as a needy, arrogant man who aches to be the center of attention. He's seen as gangly with big facial features.

Famous Namesakes: Character Bane (*Batman*)

Barak

(Hebrew) lightning bolt.

Image: Barack Obama became an instant political star at the 2004 Democratic National Convention, and his popularity has grown ever since. For this reason, people imagine Barak as an intelligent, confident, and charismatic African American politician. He's said to be ambitious, strong, and handsome. And like any politician, he's often described as a smooth talker.

Famous Namesakes: Biblical figure Barak; senator Barack Hussein Obama

Baron

(German, English) nobleman, baron.

Image: Baron is a menacing figure. People imagine he's a mean, humorless man with a large build and an overbearing demeanor. At times, he can be downright crazy.

Famous Namesakes: Basketball player Baron Davis; WWI pilot Manfred "The Red Baron" von Richthofen

Barrett

(German) strong as a bear.

Image: Barrett wouldn't be so stuck-up if his trust fund suddenly ran out. People say Barrett is a snobby, know-it-all pansy spoiled by his posh upbringing.

Famous Namesakes: Singer Barrett Strong; football player Barrett Brooks

Barry

(Welsh) son of Harry. (Irish) spear, marksman. (French) gate, fence.

Image: Here's a warm and fuzzy name. Barry sounds like *bear*, which maybe why people think of him as a big, cuddly teddy bear who's sweet, witty, and talented.

Famous Namesakes: Baseball player Barry Bonds; singer Barry Manilow; director Barry Levinson; baseball player Barry Zito

Bart

(Hebrew) a short form of Bartholomew, Barton.

Image: You'll find one Bart reading Henry Miller, and another Bart chugging Miller Lite. People say Bart is either a nerdy, awkward bookworm with big glasses and pimples, or a lazy and rude tough guy with a beer belly and bald spot.

Famous Namesakes: Character Bart Simpson (*The Simpsons*); football player Bart Starr; pirate Bartholomew "Black Bart" Roberts; gymnast Bart Conner

Bartholomew

(Hebrew) son of Talmaí.

Image: Bartholomew is proof that beauty and success don't necessarily go hand in hand. People feel Bartholomew is rich and successful, but he's a bit of a weird introvert who's heavy and unattractive.

Famous Namesakes: Biblical figure Bartholomew; character Bartholomew "Bart" Simpson (*The Simpsons*)

Barton

(English) barley town; Bart's town.

Image: You'll find Barton behind the wheel of a rusty, old pickup truck. Barton seems to be a name for a smart and good-humored country boy with rugged good looks. People believe he has a sweet side, but he's also strong-willed.

Famous Namesakes: Film character Barton Fink

Basil

(Greek, Latin) royal, kingly.

Image: Basil may just look down his nose at you. People imagine Basil as a snooty and stuffy upper-class Brit who's well educated but dull. Physically, he's described as thin and pasty.

Famous Namesakes: Eastern Orthodox saint Basil of Caesarea; cartoonist Basil Wolverton

Baul

(Gypsy) snail.

Image: Baul doesn't know his own strength. People picture Baul as a forthright and courageous man with Herculean strength that makes him clumsy. Sometimes he may be full of laughs and fun, and other times he may be methodical and bland.

Famous Namesakes: None

Beaman

(English) beekeeper.

Image: Your secret is safe with Beaman. To many people, Beaman seems like rich man who's trustworthy and discreet when it comes to confidential information. His fancy English ways make him seem snobby, though.

Famous Namesakes: None

Beau

(French) handsome.

Image: Beau may look tough, but his sensitivity just may surprise you. People imagine Beau as a masculine, muscular guy who has a shy, quiet, and even timid side deep down.

Famous Namesakes: Actor Beau Bridges; fashion icon Beau Brummel

Ben

(Hebrew) a short form of Benjamin.

Image: There are two different Bens—or perhaps just two sides to his personality. People agree that Ben is a sweet, dark-haired boy. From there, opinions split as to whether he's fun-loving and silly or shy and quiet.

Famous Namesakes: Actor Ben Affleck; actor Ben Stiller; actor Ben Kingsley; actor Ben Stein; singer Ben Folds

Benett

(Latin)

Image: It's easy to picture Benett's photo on the back of a bestselling novel. Benett evokes the image of a hardworking and successful writer. People say he's handsome and sophisticated with a warm, friendly smile.

Famous Namesakes: Singer Tony Bennett

Benjamin

(Hebrew) son of my right hand.

Image: Good times seem to follow Benjamin. People say he's a considerate, smart, and charismatic athlete who likes to have a good time. Physically, he's envisioned as tall and good-looking with dark hair and eyes.

Famous Namesakes: Founding Father Benjamin Franklin; actor Benjamin Bratt

Bennett

(Latin) little blessed one.

Image: Bennett is already planning to attend MIT. People imagine him as a studious, mathematically brilliant prep schooler who's arrogant and serious. He's most likely tall and fit with brown eyes and hair.

Famous Namesakes: Singer Tony Bennett

Benny

(Hebrew) a familiar form of Benjamin.

Image: The fun-loving ways of British comic legend Benny Hill have rubbed off on this name's image. Benny is pictured as a carefree, good-natured partier who may strike some as immature and overindulged. He's also seen as short and dough-faced.

Famous Namesakes: Musician Benny Goodman; comedian Benny Hill

Benson

(Hebrew) son of Ben.

Image: People tend to associate the name Benson with the popular '80s TV character played by Robert Guillaume. They say he's a refined and smart—if not snooty—African American butler.

Famous Namesakes: Character Benson DuBois (*Benson*)

Bentley

(English) moor; coarse grass meadow.

Image: Bentley has a lot in common with the luxury car that shares his name. People say Bentley is a tall, stuffy snob who's well mannered and proper but often morose.

Famous Namesakes: Singer Dierks Bentley; auto entrepreneur Walter Owen Bentley

Berk

(Turkish) solid; rugged.

Image: Berk gets himself into trouble, but at least he can find his way out of it. Berk gives the impression of a weird outcast who's always picked on because of his obnoxious, know-it-all ways. Luckily for him, people also think he has a knack for talking his way out of predicaments.

Famous Namesakes: None

Bern

(German) a short form of Bernard.

Image: What mood will Bern be in today? People imagine Bern is quiet and smart, and depending on how his day is going, he can be either grouchy or kind.

Famous Namesakes: Character Lord Bern (*The Voyage of the Dawn Treader*)

Bernard

(German) brave as a bear.

Image: Bernard marches to the beat of his own drum—when he can find it. People think Bernard is a one-of-a-kind character who's bookish but messy. He's also known to be a little lazy. People see him as a husky and tall fellow who likes to eat.

Famous Namesakes: Several saints named Bernard; playwright George Bernard Shaw

Bert

(German, English) bright, shining.

Image: Like the *Sesame Street* Muppet of the same name, Bert is uptight and argumentative with a nerdy persona. Unlike the Muppet, however, this Bert is described as a little overweight and unkempt. (That's actually more like Ernie.)

Famous Namesakes: Character Bert (*Sesame Street*); baseball player Bert Blyleven; actor Burt Reynolds

Bilal

(Arabic) chosen.

Image: Bilal simply won't take no for an answer, if you can get a word in edgewise. People say Bilal is a stubborn and odd Middle Easterner who's irritatingly talkative.

Famous Namesakes: Singer Bilal

Bill

(German) a short form of William.

Image: Bill is an all-around good guy. People feel he's generous, neighborly, dependable, and smart.

Famous Namesakes: President Bill Clinton; comedian Bill Cosby; actor Bill Murray; Microsoft founder Bill Gates; showman William "Buffalo Bill" Cody

Boys

Billy

(German) a familiar form of Bill, William.

Image: Billy is a bumpkin with a heart of gold. Most people think Billy is a hick who's quick to help others and quick to tell mischievous jokes. Although he's not much of a thinker and is slow to react, he can be opinionated.

Famous Namesakes: Outlaw Billy the Kid; actor Billy Bob Thorton; singer Billy Joel; actor Billy Crystal; actor Billy Baldwin

Bjorn

(Scandinavian) a form of Bernard.

Image: You've probably seen Bjorn on the cover of a magazine. People tend to picture Bjorn as a model or movie star with stunning, exotic features. It's no surprise, however, that people also say he's selfish, conceited, and hungry for attention.

Famous Namesakes: Tennis player Björn Borg; musician Björn Ulvaeus

Blade

(English) knife, sword.

Image: Watch out—Blade can cut you. People think Blade is a rough and violent punk who's physically imposing. He's imagined as cocky, flashy, and always looking for a good time.

Famous Namesakes: Movie and comic book character Blade

Blaine

(Irish) thin, lean. (English) river source.

Image: Blaine has his life in perfect balance. People say he's an all-around good person with a tender heart. They picture him as a smart and successful businessman who loves to unwind in the comfort of his family.

Famous Namesakes: Magician David Blaine; golfer Blaine McCallister

Blake

(English) attractive; dark.

Image: The name Blake seems straight out of upper-class society, perhaps because of Blake Carrington from TV's *Dynasty*. People think Blake is a spoiled rich kid living on daddy's money. He's portrayed as nicely groomed and athletic, yet he's rude and narcissistic.

Famous Namesakes: Poet William Blake; comedian Blake Clark; character Blake Carrington (*Dynasty*)

Bo

(English) a form of Beau, Beauregard. (German) a form of Bogart.

Image: Fire up the General Lee—Bo Duke from *The Dukes of Hazzard* just may be the role model for this name's image. People think Bo is an easygoing, uncomplicated country boy who works with his hands. They also say he's outgoing and fearless. His tall, muscular, and masculine looks seem to make him a popular flirt.

Famous Namesakes: Athlete Bo Jackson; singer Bo Didley; character Bo Duke (*The Dukes of Hazzard*); singer Bo Bice

Bob

(English) a short form of Robert.

Image: Bob is the middle-class everyman. People think Bob is an average, ordinary guy with average intelligence, average looks, and average friendliness. He's known to be likable, although easily overlooked.

Famous Namesakes: Senator Bob Dole; entertainer Bob Hope; singer Bob Dylan; game show host Bob Barker; singer Bob Marley

Bobby

(English) a familiar form of Bob, Robert.

Image: Bobby is a lot of fun, but he'll probably wear you out. People view Bobby as a jolly, goofy, and friendly brown-haired boy. All that goofiness can turn into hyperactivity, though.

Famous Namesakes: Singer Bobby Brown; basketball coach Bobby Knight; politician Bobby Kennedy; chess master Bobby Fischer; hockey player Bobby Orr

Bond

(English) tiller of the soil.

Image: Bond. Just Bond. People say Bond is a cocky and charming flirt who's tan and buff.

Famous Namesakes: Movie and book character James Bond

Boris

(Slavic) battler, warrior.

Image: Boris isn't the sharpest knife in the drawer. People perceive him as a burly, Russian brute who isn't very smart and isn't very attractive. He's likely to follow others.

Famous Namesakes: Russian politician Boris Yeltsin; tennis player Boris Becker; actor Boris Karloff

Brad

(English) a short form of Bradford, Bradley.

Image: People imagine Hollywood hunk Brad Pitt when they hear this name—and who can blame them? Brad is described as a sexy, muscular guy who's kind, outgoing, and smart.

Famous Namesakes: Actor Brad Pitt; football player Brad Johnson

Braden

(English) broad valley.

Image: Braden has his good side and his bad side. People think he's an attractive and physically imposing man who can be quite caring, although he sometimes lies and causes trouble.

Famous Namesakes: Baseball player Braden Looper

Bradford

(English) broad river crossing.

Image: Bradford thinks about two things: himself and having a good time. People imagine he's a tall and muscular athlete who's cocky and snobby. That said, people also believe his party-boy ways make him quite popular.

Famous Namesakes: Colonist William Bradford

Bradley

(English) broad meadow.

Image: Can there be such a thing as a hunky geek? People see Bradley as an unpopular math geek with allergies and a nasally voice, yet they also think he has a muscular build and a gorgeous face. Either way, he's probably goal oriented and strong-willed.

Famous Namesakes: Actor Bradley Cooper; actor Bradley Whitford; senator Bill Bradley

Brady

(Irish) spirited. (English) broad island.

Image: Brady is all about the money. People think Brady is an intelligent, take-charge guy who tends to be arrogant and cold, but he's made a fortune in finance.

Famous Namesakes: Baseball player Brady Anderson; TV's *The Brady Bunch*; football player Brady Quinn

Bram

(Scottish) bramble, brushwood. (Hebrew) a short form of Abraham, Abram.

Image: A little confidence could go a long way for Bram. People believe he's a reserved and bookish pushover who's better at helping others than helping himself.

Famous Namesakes: Author Bram Stoker

Brandon

(English) beacon hill.

Image: You'll find the Brandons of the world in the well-to-do suburbs. For most people, Brandon conjures up the image of a snobbish yuppie who carries on like a spoiled only child. He's thought to be strong and handsome, and he tends to be a conformist.

Famous Namesakes: Actor Brandon Routh; actor Brandon Lee; character Brandon Walsh (*Beverly Hills, 90210*)

Brant

(English) proud.

Image: Everybody loves a clown. Brant is said to be a friendly, fun-loving class clown with a lanky body and a big smile.

Famous Namesakes: Satirist Sebastian Brant

Brayden

(English) a form of Braden.

Image: Brayden could come from many different walks of life. He's regarded by most as a preppy brainiac from an upper-class family. But others see Brayden as an athlete who wants to make it to the pros, and some imagine him as a farm-hand who loves the outdoors. In any case, he's also described as muscular and attractive.

Famous Namesakes: Actor Eric Braeden

Breck

(Irish) freckled.

Image: Breck is a lot of fun, but don't sell him short. The name Breck makes people picture a kind and friendly free spirit. Physically, Breck is described as tall and handsome, but he's a lot smarter than he looks.

Famous Namesakes: Director Breck Eisner

Brendan

(Irish) little raven. (English) sword.

Image: Brendan is a stand-up guy. People imagine he's warmhearted, dependable, honest, and fun. He's also considered to be slim with a nice smile.

Famous Namesakes: Actor Brendan Fraser; saint Brendan of Clonfert; hockey player Brendan Shanahan

Brent

(English) a short form of Brenton.

Image: Brent is a likable guy, but he loathes big crowds. People imagine he's bulky and strong, and he enjoys hunting and fishing much more than shopping at busy malls. People also say he has a goofy side.

Famous Namesakes: Actor Brent Spiner; sportscaster Brent Musburger

Brett

(Scottish) from Great Britain.

Image: Brett is a great friend for playing sports or just hanging out. People imagine he's considerate, attractive, charming, and a good listener. Perhaps because of Green Bay Packers quarterback Brett Favre, people also imagine he loves sports, which keep him fit and strong.

Famous Namesakes: Singer Brett Michaels; football player Brett Favre; hockey player Brett Hull; wrestler Brett Hart

Brian

(Irish, Scottish) strong; virtuous; honorable.

Image: What's not to like about Brian? Brian strikes people as polite, caring, and intelligent. Add handsome looks with brown hair, and it's easy to see how he can be so charismatic and likable.

Famous Namesakes: Skater Brian Boitano; football player Brian Urlacher; singer Brian Wilson; singer Brian McKnight; singer Brian Setzer

Brock

(English) badger.

Image: If anything, Brock is confident—maybe too much so. He's imagined as a smarmy, self-centered jerk who's big-boned, muscular, and attractive with dark hair.

Famous Namesakes: Wrestler Brock Lesnar; actor Brock Peters; football player Brock Edwards

Brooklyn

(English) a combination of Brook + Lynn.

Image: Try to stay on Brooklyn's good side. Brooklyn makes people think of a energetic and fun guy who's small with dark hair. He may, however, swing from being sweet and helpful to rough and intimidating.

Famous Namesakes: Star kid Brooklyn Beckham

Bruce

(French) brushwood thicket; woods.

Image: This name's image may be a strange case of Dr. Jekyll and Mr. Hyde. Some people think Bruce is sweet and caring but not too bright. Other people, however, think he's a tough, obnoxious brute.

Famous Namesakes: Singer Bruce Springsteen; actor Bruce Willis; martial artist Bruce Lee; football player Bruce Smith

Bryan

(Irish) a form of Brian.

Image: Bryan has a take-charge attitude that's usually on display. He's seen as a lanky, strong-willed go-getter who loves to be the center of attention. Because of all his antics, he tends to be a bit untrustworthy.

Famous Namesakes: Singer Bryan Adams; statesman William Jennings Bryan; director Bryan Singer

Bryce

(Welsh) a form of Brice.

Image: Bryce certainly knows what he wants. People believe he's a determined leader who's smart and energetic, but perhaps too demanding. With his tall, healthy build, Bryce may channel some of his drive into sports.

Famous Namesakes: Football player Bryce Fisher

Bryson

(Welsh) son of Brice.

Image: Bryson is a great combination of personality and looks. People perceive he's compassionate, friendly, and bright—qualities fitting for a leader. He's probably tall, dark, and handsome with a strong physique.

Famous Namesakes: Singer Peabo Bryson; author Bill Bryson

Bud

(English) herald, messenger.

Image: Look past Bud's low IQ, and you'll find a true friend. People see Bud as a dumb hick, but he makes up for it with his soft heart and friendly ways.

Famous Namesakes: Baseball commissioner Bud Selig; comedian Bud Abbott; character Bud Bundy (*Married...with Children*)

Buddy

(American) a familiar form of Bud.

Image: What do you expect from a guy named Buddy? Naturally, people believe Buddy is sweet, friendly, and happy. They picture him as big-boned and dark-haired. Then again, some people think Buddy is a dimwitted redneck with freckles and buckteeth.

Famous Namesakes: Singer Buddy Holly; actor Buddy Epson; singer Buddy Guy; actor Buddy Hackett

Butch

(American) a short form of Butcher.

Image: Don't mess with someone named Butch. Everyone says Butch is a big, burly bully who's none too bright.

Famous Namesakes: Robber Butch Cassidy

Byron

(French) cottage. (English) barn.

Image: Deep beneath Byron's awkwardness is a heart of a poet. Most people say Byron is a lonely, bullied misfit. Perhaps because of *Don Juan* poet Lord Byron's influence, some also see a noble and poetic side to Byron.

Famous Namesakes: Poet Lord Byron; golfer Byron Nelson

Caden

(American) a form of Kadin.

Image: Caden is either a workaholic or a beach bum. Most people say he's a successful, motivated, and smart businessman—perhaps a real estate agent or a banker. But then again, some people can't help but picture him as a goofy, fun-loving guy out on a beach, either playing sports or surfing all day long. He may have a part-time job at the surf shop. Either way, people picture Caden as a lanky strawberry blond.

Famous Namesakes: None

Caesar

(Latin) long-haired.

Image: Caesar is strong both physically and mentally. People see him as a muscular, broad-shouldered Greek or Latino who's tough, passionate, and fearless. Of course, Julius Caesar also influences this name's image: Some people see Caesar as a deceitful ruler.

Famous Namesakes: Emperor Julius Caesar; "Dog Whisperer" Cesar Millan; activist César Chávez; comedian Sid Caesar

Cain

(Hebrew) spear; gatherer.

Image: People will probably remember your name if you killed your brother. Many people associate this name with the biblical Cain and thus say he's a spiteful murderer who's muscular. The few who don't think of the Bible say Cain is hardworking and smart.

Famous Namesakes: Biblical figure Cain

Caleb

(Hebrew) dog; faithful. (Arabic) bold, brave.

Image: One image of Caleb is of a stand-up guy; the other image is of a guy who probably can't stand up. Most people describe Caleb as an extremely dedicated and hardworking man who's caring as well as charismatic. A few people, however, see him as a seedy, hard-living alcoholic. Either way, he's most likely handsome and a little on the chubby side.

Famous Namesakes: Biblical figure Caleb; character Caleb (*East of Eden*)

Calvin

(Latin) bald.

Image: Calvin is an upstanding individual. People think of Calvin as a tall man who's thoughtful and trustworthy, and his sense of humor makes him popular with others. He's also known to have a cautious, skeptical side.

Famous Namesakes: Designer Calvin Klein; comic strip *Calvin and Hobbs*; president Calvin Coolidge; theologian John Calvin

Cameron

(Scottish) crooked nose.

Image: Cameron has flair. He's thought to be a tall, blond actor with an active, outdoorsy lifestyle. People imagine he's spunky, sweet, and worldly.

Famous Namesakes: Director Cameron Crowe

Campbell

(Latin, French) beautiful field. (Scottish) crooked mouth.

Image: In corporate America or in the Wild West, Campbell is a great guy. People can't decide if he's a sophisticated professional who's well dressed and well spoken or if he's a rugged rancher in cowboy hat and boots. Either way, everyone agrees Campbell is outgoing, spunky, and smart. He's also said to be a good listener, especially when it comes to conversations with his mom.

Famous Namesakes: Actor Bruce Campbell; football player Earl Campbell; singer Glen Campbell; actor Campbell Scott

Carey

(Greek) pure. (Welsh) castle; rocky island.

Image: Carey's unisex name leaves a lot of folks wondering. First, people aren't sure if Carey is a girl or a boy. They're also unsure whether to describe Carey as a meek and smart bookworm or an outgoing and upbeat joker. Whatever the case, Carey most likely has pale skin and blue eyes.

Famous Namesakes: Tattoo artist Carey Hart; actor Drew Carey; sportscaster Harry Carey; actor Jim Carrey; actor Cary Grant

Carl

(German, English) a short form of Carlton. A form of Charles.

Image: Carl is a sociable guy, even though he's a bit of a geek. People say Carl is goofy, sweet, and smart to the point of being nerdy. His friends are known to enjoy his funny stories.

Famous Namesakes: Astronomer Carl Sagan; athlete Carl Lewis; psychiatrist Carl Jung; racecar driver Carl Edwards

Carlo

(Italian) a form of Carl, Charles.

Image: Ladies hope they get a chance to chat with Carlo. People think Carlo is gregarious, self-assured, and ambitious—qualities that make him a natural flirt. Of either Italian or Mexican heritage, he most likely has dark features and olive skin.

Famous Namesakes: Director Carlo Ponti

Carlos

(Spanish) a form of Carl, Charles.

Image: Carlos loves to talk. People view him as a chatty, outgoing, and energetic man of Latino descent. His accented speech may be loud, but it's always friendly.

Famous Namesakes: Comedian Carlos Mencia; musician Carlos Santana; baseball player Carlos Delgado

Carlton

(English) Carl's town.

Image: Carlton can act like a real baby sometimes. For many people, the name Carlton evokes the image of a well-educated and well-dressed snob who's spoiled, whiny, and pompous.

Famous Namesakes: Baseball player Steve Carlton; baseball player Carlton Fisk; character Carlton Banks (*The Fresh Prince of Bel Air*)

Carmel

(Hebrew) vineyard, garden.

Image: Carmel doesn't need to bother with knowledge. People think he's a kind, warm-hearted, and religious man who's probably less informed than he should be. He's described as short and chubby with brown hair and golden skin.

Famous Namesakes: None

Carrick

(Irish) rock.

Image: Here's someone who excels in athletics and studies. Carrick is regarded as a sporty smarty who's outgoing and witty with freckles and red hair.

Famous Namesakes: None

Carson

(English) son of Carr.

Image: Carson has a good head on his shoulders. People picture him as a confident, fit guy. He may have a well-to-do background, but he's practical and cool.

Famous Namesakes: Talk show host Johnny Carson; talk show host Carson Daly; football player Carson Palmer

Carter

(English) cart driver.

Image: Perhaps the name Carter is influenced by *ER* character John Carter. People say Carter is intelligent, charismatic, and warm. Being described as tall and handsome only adds to his charm.

Famous Namesakes: President Jimmy Carter; character Dr. John Carter (*ER*); Declaration of Independence signer Carter Braxton

Boys

Casey

(Irish) brave.

Image: Casey is determined to have fun. He's imagined as strong-willed, playful, and energetic. People say he's cute with rosy cheeks and a button nose, and he tends to gossip.

Famous Namesakes: Baseball player Casey Stengel; golfer Casey Martin; actor Casey Affleck; poem "Casey at the Bat"

Casper

(Persian) treasurer. (German) imperial.

Image: Everyone knows Casper the Friendly Ghost, and that image seems to follow this name. Casper is described as a friendly, kindhearted boy who's pale, shy, and somewhat strange.

Famous Namesakes: Character Casper the Friendly Ghost; actor Casper Van Dien

Cecil

(Latin) blind.

Image: It's probably a good thing Cecil is holed up in his library. People say he's a name for a skinny, wimpy British aristocrat. He's considered to be a meek bookworm who's so snooty, he's close-minded.

Famous Namesakes: Director Cecil B. Demille; baseball player Cecil Fielder

Cedric

(English) battle chieftain.

Image: Cedric has a sharp wit—sometimes too sharp. The name Cedric makes people think of a witty, clever, and distinguished preppy. He's usually polite, but sometimes his sarcasm can seem rude.

Famous Namesakes: Comedian Cedric the Entertainer

Chad

(English) warrior. A short form of Chadwick.

Image: You'll probably find Chad doing just one more lap around the track. He's seen as an athletic, good-looking blond who's independent and persistent.

Famous Namesakes: Actor Chad Allen; actor Chad Lowe

Chance

(English) a short form of Chancellor, Chauncey.

Image: Chance's personality lives up to his name. People picture him as a rowdy risk taker who's cocky and clever. They also say his handsome good looks are as rugged as his character.

Famous Namesakes: None

Chandler

(English) candle maker.

Image: As Chandler Bing might say, could the inspiration for this name *be* any more obvious? People can't seem to separate this name from the *Friends* character. They say he's goofy, very sarcastic, yet sweet with brown hair.

Famous Namesakes: Character Chandler Bing (*Friends*)

Charles

(German) farmer. (English) strong and manly.

Image: While there are glimpses of British heir Prince Charles in this name's image, there are also flashes of a more dashing man. Charles conjures up the image of a brilliant but stodgy man who gained wealth and power with his strong, decisive will. He's pictured as tall, sturdy, and dark.

Famous Namesakes: British prince Charles; author Charles Dickens; basketball player Charles Barkley; pilot Charles Lindbergh; broker Charles Schwab

Charlie

(German, English) a familiar form of Charles.

Image: Charlie is happiness wrapped in a big, cuddly package. People see Charlie as kind, cheerful, and smart. He's imagined as a big teddy bear with a cute smile.

Famous Namesakes: Actor Charlie Sheen; actor Charlie Chaplin; character Charlie Brown (*Peanuts*); singer Charlie Daniels

Charlton

(English) a form of Carlton.

Image: Charlton is a strong yet complicated figure. This robust, husky man comes across as proper, dignified, and stoic to some, but egotistical and inflexible to others. People suspect he's a bit of a womanizer, and he may be a politician.

Famous Namesakes: Actor Charlton Heston

Chase

(French) hunter.

Image: As his name suggests, Chase runs with a zest for life. People describe him as an energized, playful, and outgoing athlete who's passionate about living life to the fullest.

Famous Namesakes: Actor Chevy Chase; baseball player Chase Utley

Chester

(English) a short form of Rochester.

Image: It doesn't take long to realize why Chester is a loner. People see him as a meek geek who quietly keeps to his books and studies. Making matters worse, he's pictured as skinny and clumsy. When he does come out of his mopey shell, however, he's probably a jester.

Famous Namesakes: President Chester A. Arthur; singer Chester Bennington

Chet

(English) a short form of Chester.

Image: Chet probably never imagined his life would turn out this way. People think Chet is arrogant, rude, and not very bright. They suspect he's a down-home country boy who peaked as a high-school jock, but he's now resigned to selling cars with sleazy sales tactics.

Famous Namesakes: Singer Chet Atkins; musician Chet Baker

Chris

(Greek) a short form of Christian, Christopher.

Image: Chris is your average, up-the-middle nice guy. People see him as kind and trusting as well as funny and smart. He's most likely well mannered.

Famous Namesakes: Comedian Chris Rock; singer Chris Isaak; basketball player Chris Webber; singer Chris Cornell

Christian

(Greek) follower of Christ; anointed.

Image: Christian is a catch. People imagine he has a big, generous heart and handsome, alluring looks. He's even known to open doors for ladies.

Famous Namesakes: Actor Christian Bale; actor Christian Slater; designer Christian Dior; basketball player Christian Laettner

Christopher

(Greek) Christ-bearer.

Image: Christopher has book smarts *and* people smarts. People say he's an educated man who's superfriendly and quick to help others. He's pictured as tall with a pleasant, outgoing smile.

Famous Namesakes: Actor Christopher Reeve; character Christopher Robin (*Winnie-the-Pooh*); actor Christopher Walken; actor Christopher Atkins

Chuck

(American) a familiar form of Charles.

Image: Chuck may be mousy, but he's nice as can be. People see Chuck as a shy, sensitive, and slightly chubby guy. When he can overcome his bashfulness, people say he's kind and helpful to everyone.

Famous Namesakes: Singer Chuck Berry; actor Chuck Norris; rapper Chuck D; pilot Chuck Yeager

Clarence

(Latin) clear; victorious.

Image: There's nothing worse than a know-it-all who knows nothing. Clarence is described as a doofy and mousy mama's boy. He seems to think he knows everything. He also seems to think his weird sense of humor is hilarious—but no one agrees.

Famous Namesakes: Supreme Court justice Clarence Thomas; singer Clarence Carter; lawyer Clarence Darrow

Clark

(French) cleric; scholar.

Image: Two legendary Clarks cast their shadows on this name's image. Some people describe Clark as a caring, trustworthy square who seems to lack common sense, like Superman's alter ego, Clark Kent. Others describe him as a dashing, distinguished, and romantic charmer, like silver-screen star Clark Gable.

Famous Namesakes: Character Clark Kent (*Superman*); actor Clark Gable; TV personality Dick Clark; explorer William Clark

Claude

(Latin, French) lame.

Image: Here's one overachiever who won't let anything get in his way. Claude is regarded as a standoffish and overly ambitious Frenchman. With his upper-class business background, he's known to dress his stocky build in stylish suits.

Famous Namesakes: Composer Claude Debussy; artist Claude Monet; actor Jean-Claude Van Damme

Clay

(English) clay pit.

Image: Clay Aiken may not have been an *American Idol* winner, but he has made an impression on this name's image. People say Clay is a talented musician who's confident, calm, kind, and cute.

Famous Namesakes: Boxer Cassius Clay, birth name of Muhammad Ali; singer Clay Aiken; statesman Henry Clay

Clayton

(English) town built on clay.

Image: Clayton does everything by the book. People say he's an intellectual who's straight-laced and businesslike. He's believed to be confident and quiet, but he's kind once you get to know him.

Famous Namesakes: Character Clayton (Disney's *Tarzan*); actor Clayton Moore; bassist Adam Clayton

Cletus

(Greek) illustrious.

Image: If you're making a movie about a dimwitted, gap-toothed, freckle-faced hillbilly, Cletus is what you should call him. People imagine Cletus is the epitome of a country-fried hick.

Famous Namesakes: Character Cletus the Slack-Jawed Yokel (*The Simpsons*); character Cletus Hogg (*The Dukes of Hazzard*)

Cliff

(English) a short form of Clifford, Clifton.

Image: Everybody likes Dr. Cliff. People think of Cliff as a popular physician—perhaps because of Dr. Cliff Huxtable of TV's *The Cosby Show*. Cliff is imagined as smart, confident, and observant, which means he makes great decisions for his patients.

Famous Namesakes: Actor Cliff Robertson; character Cliff Huxtable (*The Cosby Show*); character Cliff Clavin (*Cheers*)

Clifford

(English) cliff at the river crossing.

Image: Clifford is misunderstood: He comes across as annoying and loud, but he really means to be sweet, silly, and playful. Perhaps remembering *Clifford the Big Red Dog*, people picture Clifford as a tall redhead.

Famous Namesakes: Book and cartoon character Clifford the Big Red Dog

Clint

(English) a short form of Clinton.

Image: Clint Eastwood may have played the Man with No Name, but his persona sure does influence this name's image. People imagine Clint as a rugged, stone-faced, and confident gunslinger, not unlike many of the Western characters Clint Eastwood has portrayed.

Famous Namesakes: Actor Clint Eastwood; singer Clint Black; actor Clint Howard

Clinton

(English) hill town.

Image: Former American president Bill Clinton was one of the most memorable personalities of the twentieth century, so it's no wonder that this name's image is tied to him. Clinton is described a slick and powerful man whom people like in spite of his lying and womanizing ways.

Famous Namesakes: President Bill Clinton; singer George Clinton

Clyde

(Welsh) warm.

Image: You'll find Clyde out in the barn, throwing hay bales. People say he's a lumbering, bulky oaf. Gruff and tough in his old age, he probably does manual labor as a farmhand, getting his coveralls sweaty every day.

Famous Namesakes: Robber Clyde Barrow; basketball player Clyde Drexler

Cody

(English) cushion.

Image: Maybe all those stories Kathie Lee Gifford told about her son, Cody, while cohosting *Live with Regis and Kathie Lee* had a negative effect. People describe Cody as a manipulative, spoiled, and bratty blond. This mama's boy may be a handful when he gets stubborn and ornery.

Famous Namesakes: Showman William "Buffalo Bill" Cody; star kid Cody Gifford

Colby

(English) dark; dark-haired.

Image: People seem to agree that Colby is a cute sandy blond with a button nose. From there, some picture him as a stuffy snob from whom his mother expects great success. Yet others have a much more "cheesy" view of the name, seeing him as a kindhearted dairy farmer.

Famous Namesakes: CIA director William E. Colby; hockey player Colby Armstrong

Cole

(Latin) cabbage farmer. (English) a short form of Colbert, Coleman. (Greek) a short form of Nicholas.

Image: Cole is a complex character. People see him as a wild and rugged man who can be moody and withdrawn at times. He's most likely smart and mischievous, as well as sensitive and intense. Overall, he's seen as a caring man with handsome, strong looks.

Famous Namesakes: Composer Cole Porter; singer Nat "King" Cole; designer Kenneth Cole

Colin

(Irish) young cub. (Greek) a short form of Nicholas.

Image: See traces of Colin Farrell and his playboy ways in this name's image? Colin is said to be intelligent, dryly funny, and confident to the point of being cocky. People say he's tall, dark, and handsome, and he has a hard time committing to anything or anyone.

Famous Namesakes: Actor Colin Farrell; comedian Colin Quinn; actor Colin Firth; secretary of state Colin Powell

Collin

(Scottish) a form of Colin, Collins.

Image: Collin should be thankful that not everyone agrees about him. Some people think Collin is handsome yet dumb, pigheaded, and boring. A few people see a more positive side to him, saying he's cheerful and gregarious.

Famous Namesakes: Singer Collin Raye; actor Collin Chou

Connor

(Scottish) wise. (Irish) a form of Conan.

Image: Connor is never at a loss for words—or jokes. He's imagined as an articulate and friendly joker who's sly and quick on his feet. Perhaps an only child, he's spoiled by his rich parents, but he's still a caring person.

Famous Namesakes: Character Connor MacLeod (*Highlander*)

Conrad

(German) brave counselor.

Image: Conrad is his own worst enemy. People say Conrad is a conniving, manipulative sleaze with dark hair and pale skin. His insecure and self-indulgent ways may have led him down a path to depression.

Famous Namesakes: Author Joseph Conrad; hotel founder Conrad Hilton; actor Conrad Bain

Constantine

(Latin) firm, constant.

Image: Constantine is determined to do what's right. People describe him as an intelligent and trustworthy man with stubborn—almost arrogant—determination. Physically, he's imagined with olive skin and dark hair.

Famous Namesakes: Emperor Constantine the Great; character John Constantine (*Constantine* and *Hellblazer*)

Cooper

(English) barrel maker.

Image: Cooper lives life in the fast lane. He's pictured as a wild and rambunctious risk taker who drives fast and lives for stressful situations. A people pleaser, this handsome guy probably likes to show off.

Famous Namesakes: Actor Gary Cooper; reporter Anderson Cooper

Corbin

(Latin) raven.

Image: Corbin's personality is as exciting as oatmeal. People feel Corbin is so wholesome and nice, he's boring. He may be either a computer geek or the nerdy guy on the football team who's a quiet loner.

Famous Namesakes: Actor Corbin Bernsen; actor Corbin Bleu

Corey

(Irish) hollow.

Image: Corey may not be the leader of the pack, but he's the one getting the laughs. People see him as a goofy, silly, and entertaining guy who's fun to be around. He most likely developed his class clown ways to compensate for his petite, weak build.

Famous Namesakes: Actor Corey Haim; actor Corey Feldman

Cornelius

(Greek) cornel tree. (Latin) horn colored.

Image: Cornelius is most likely somewhere in a lab, dreaming up wacky inventions. People think of Cornelius as a nerdy and inventive brainiac who wears suspenders to hold up his pants on his skinny build. Some describe him as quiet and shy, but others see him as outgoing and friendly.

Famous Namesakes: Entrepreneur Cornelius Vanderbilt; character Cornelius Fudge (*Harry Potter* series)

Cory

(Latin) a form of Corey. (French) a familiar form of Cornell. (Greek) a short form of Corydon.

Image: Cory is a worrywart. People imagine him as a cute, fair-haired guy who's sweet and kind when he's not filled with anxiety.

Famous Namesakes: Baseball player Cory Lidle; character Cory Matthews (*Boy Meets World*); character Cory Baxter (*Cory in the House*)

Coty

(French) slope, hillside.

Image: Coty is the type of person you don't want to know. Coty gives the impression of a dirty, greasy jerk who isn't very bright. He's a bit of a slimeball.

Famous Namesakes: French President René Coty

Craig

(Irish, Scottish) crag; steep rock.

Image: Craig is an all-American. People imagine Craig as fast paced and hardworking—traits he developed during his military service. Now a civilian, he's seen as a friendly salesman who's still an organized go-getter. Physically, he's pictured as tall, toned, and ruggedly handsome.

Famous Namesakes: Talk show host Craig Kilborn; actor Craig T. Nelson; actor Daniel Craig

Curt

(Latin) a short form of Courtney, Curtis.

Image: Curt thinks; therefore, he is. People say Curt is a philosophical, deep thinker. This tall, handsome blond is thought to be warmhearted yet assertive and masculine.

Famous Namesakes: Baseball player Curt Schilling

Curtis

(Latin) enclosure. (French) courteous.

Image: If you were Curtis, you'd have low self-esteem, too. People think Curtis is an annoying and insecure guy. He probably tries to be kind, but he has no manners and not a lot of brain power. His lanky looks may not be anything to feel good about, either.

Famous Namesakes: Singer Curtis Mayfield; football player Curtis Martin; rapper Curtis "50 Cent" Jackson

Cyrus

(Persian) sun.

Image: Cyrus is always polite, even though he's headstrong. He's pictured as a good-tempered gentleman with a creative and intellectual flair, but his talents make him a bit egocentric. Perhaps of Greek descent, he's physically fit and tall.

Famous Namesakes: Singer Billy Ray Cyrus; inventor Cyrus McCormick

Dakota

(Dakota) friend; partner; tribal name.

Image: Dakota is a people-person, but he's also a nature lover. People say Dakota is an inviting, caring, and outgoing guy who's very well liked. Perhaps reflecting the rugged states that share his name, he's thought to be outdoorsy and eager to have some fun. He's probably tall, dark, and handsome.

Famous Namesakes: None

Dale

(English) dale, valley.

Image: Dale loves to work the room. People say Dale's a popular and fun-loving guy with a great sense of humor. Add suave blond looks, and people can see why he's always chatting with women.

Famous Namesakes: Racecar drivers Dale Earnhardt, Sr. and Dale Earnhardt, Jr.; racecar driver Dale Jarrett; character Dale (*Chip 'n' Dale*)

Dalton

(English) town in the valley.

Image: Dalton is proof that you don't have to be nice to be successful. Most people regard Dalton as an opinionated and rude Southern rancher whose shrewd business sense has made him rich and powerful. He's pictured as lanky and handsome, but he tends to be self-centered.

Famous Namesakes: Chemist John Dalton; actor Timothy Dalton

Damian

(Greek) tamer; soother.

Image: In the horror film *The Omen*, Damien is the spawn of Satan, and his persona forever blighted the image of any version of his name. With the movie character firmly in mind, people say Damian is a demonic and cunning devil who wears black and gets away with evil.

Famous Namesakes: Singer Damian Marley; character Father Damien Karras (*The Exorcist*); singer Damian Rice; character Damien Thorn (*The Omen*)

Dan

(Vietnamese) yes. (Hebrew) a short form of Daniel.

Image: Anchorman Dan Rather leaves a mark on this name's image. Most people think of Dan as an old newsman who's smart, trustworthy, and humorous—but perhaps a little dull. Then again, maybe Dan Conner of TV's *Roseanne* has left a mark, too. A few people see Dan as an average-looking mechanic or blue-collar guy.

Famous Namesakes: News anchor Dan Rather; vice president Dan Quayle; actor Dan Ackroyd; football player Dan Marino

Daniel

(Hebrew) God is my judge.

Image: Family and friends rely on Daniel's ability to resolve disputes. He's envisioned as a tall, athletic man with a handsome smile. He's probably kind, generous, and a bit shy—that is, he's more apt to listen than to talk. Intelligent, dependable, and easygoing, many people imagine Daniel is a peacemaker who's slow to anger and is well respected.

Famous Namesakes: Biblical figure Daniel; actor Daniel Day-Lewis; frontiersman Daniel Boone; actor Daniel Radcliffe; actor Daniel Craig

Danny

(Hebrew) a familiar form of Daniel.

Image: Danny sure is a happy-go-lucky guy. He's pictured as a cheeky, red-haired, Irish joker. People say he's youthful and energetic.

Famous Namesakes: Actor Danny Glover; actor Danny DeVito; actor Danny Bonaduce; actor Danny Masterson

Dante

(Latin) lasting, enduring.

Image: Dante is as suave as his name sounds. People think of Dante as a cultured and dashing flirt with alluring, Italian looks. He's considered to be empathetic yet assertive.

Famous Namesakes: Poet Dante Alighieri; football player Daunte Culpepper; football player Dante Hall

Darby

(Irish) free. (English) deer park.

Image: There are two Darbys, and they're polar opposites. Some people view Darby as an übergeek who looks like a gangly horse. Others imagine he's a confident party animal with many friends and hunky features.

Famous Namesakes: Character Darby O'Gill (*Darby O'Gill and the Little People*); musician Darby Crash; cartoonist Darby Conley

Darius

(Greek) wealthy.

Image: Darius is a joy to be around. He strikes people as a polite, respectful, and handsome African American who's daring and strong. Always an extrovert, he's most likely outgoing and joyful.

Famous Namesakes: Basketball player Darius Miles; singer Darius Rucker

Darren

(Irish) great. (English) small; rocky hill.

Image: It's hard to put a finger on Darren's character. People aren't sure whether Darren is goofy and fun-loving, bold and daring, arrogant and cocky, outgoing and popular, or even spiritual and priestly. Most people, however, think Darren is tall, lean, and dark.

Famous Namesakes: Actor Darren McGavin; football player Darren Sharper; director Darren Aronofsky

Darrion

(Irish, English) a form of Darren.

Image: Look out for Darrion—people envision him as a strong, muscular mountain of a man. In addition to being physically imposing, some people also find Darrion to be a jock with a tough mean streak.

Famous Namesakes: Football player Darrion Scott

Darrius

(Greek) a form of Darius.

Image: Darrius's flirty and playful personality is hard to miss. People see Darrius as a footloose, happy charmer who's tall, strong, and most likely African American. He's thought to be intelligent as well as handsome.

Famous Namesakes: Singer Darrius Willrich

Darryl

(French) a form of Darrell.

Image: Darryl may be an airhead, but that doesn't stop him. He's imagined as a dumb oddball who remains overly confident and outgoing despite his shortcomings. Tall and lean, Darryl probably also has a goofy side.

Famous Namesakes: Baseball player Darryl Strawberry; comedian Darryl Hammond; hockey player Darryl Sutter

Daryl

(French) a form of Darrell.

Image: A country boy, Daryl is low maintenance. He's thought of as a kindhearted and laid-back hick with a toothpick in his mouth. People describe him as tall, dark-haired, and thick-bodied.

Famous Namesakes: Singer Daryl Hall

Dave

(Hebrew) a short form of David, Davis.

Image: Dave is an everyday nice guy. People imagine him as a caring, lovable, and dependable person who makes a great friend. He may have average looks, but he's neat and clean.

Famous Namesakes: Writer Dave Barry; singer Dave Matthews; comedian Dave Chappelle; actor Dave Foley

David

(Hebrew) beloved.

Image: People happily look to David for leadership. He's pictured with a tall, athletic build, and he's known to be caring and thoughtful with a quiet confidence that makes him a good leader. Hardworking and responsible, David may also have a lighter, outgoing side.

Famous Namesakes: Talk show host David Letterman; actor David Schwimmer; actor David Spade; singer David Bowie; biblical figure David

Deangelo

(Italian) a combination of the prefix De + Angelo.

Image: Although the spelling of his name is different, R&B singer D'Angelo influences this name's image. Deangelo is said to be an intelligent, approachable, and fun-loving African American. People say he's sexy with a muscular body and a gorgeous smile.

Famous Namesakes: Singer D'Angelo; football player DeAngelo Williams

Deman

(Dutch) man.

Image: The name Deman looks an awful lot like *demon*, which must be why people imagine Deman as an evil and selfish troublemaker with devilish features. At best, people think he's meek and shy.

Famous Namesakes: Military intelligence pioneer Ralph Van Deman

Dennis

(Greek) a follower of Dionysus, the god of wine.

Image: Dennis can use a little humility to go with his intelligence. People think Dennis is a geeky and bespectacled know-it-all who tends to be conceited. Surprisingly, they also say he has a strong, agile build.

Famous Namesakes: Comedian Dennis Leary; basketball player Dennis Rodman; character Dennis Mitchell (*Dennis the Menace*); actor Dennis Quaid

Denny

(Greek) a familiar form of Dennis.

Image: How Denny got to be such a popular guy is a mystery. People say Denny always has friends around, despite the fact that he's immature and a little grungy. Maybe his friends understand that deep down, he's sweet and means well.

Famous Namesakes: Singer Denny Doherty; Speaker of the House Denny Hastert; football coach Denny Green

Denver

(English) green valley.

Image: With the mountainous beauty of the capital of Colorado as inspiration, Denver is a free-spirited and rugged name. People see Denver as a hippie with an affinity for the outdoors. They say he has a peaceful, cool attitude and an arty uniqueness. Physically, he's pictured with Nordic features like blond hair and blue eyes.

Famous Namesakes: Singer John Denver; actor Bob Denver; actor Denver Pyle

Derek

(German) a short form of Theodoric.

Image: Derek Jeter, the star shortstop of the New York Yankees, may affect this name's image. People think Derek is congenial, fun, and very handsome. They say he's so sure of himself, especially when it comes to sports, that he may come across as cocky.

Famous Namesakes: Character Dr. Derek Shepherd (*Grey's Anatomy*); baseball player Derek Jeter; character Derek Zoolander (*Zoolander*)

Desmond

(Irish) from south Munster.

Image: The name Desmond makes people think of a good-natured charmer who's intelligent and confident. His tall, dark looks most likely make him popular with girls, and some may even call him a player.

Famous Namesakes: Football player Desmond Clark; humanitarian Desmond Tutu; character Desmond Hume (*Lost*)

Devin

(Irish) poet.

Image: Looks can be deceiving, and so can Devin's character. People say Devin has dark, good looks that mask his proud and deceitful personality. He's considered to be intelligent and daring, making him a sly, slimy character.

Famous Namesakes: Football player Devin Hester; basketball player Devin Harris

Devlin

(Irish) brave, fierce.

Image: Devlin certainly doesn't mean "little devil," but that's how some people see him. Devlin is regarded as an untrustworthy and devilish trickster of Irish ancestry. He can be snide, sneering, and sneaky.

Famous Namesakes: Poet Denis Devlin

Dexter

(Latin) dexterous, adroit. (English) fabric dyer.

Image: Dexter—or formally, Poindexter—has long been a synonym for *geek*, and here's proof: Dexter is viewed almost universally as an introverted science wiz with glasses and a squeaky voice. Some people think he's sweet, but others find him to be an annoying brownnoser.

Famous Namesakes: Singer Dexter Holland; character Dexter (*Dexter's Laboratory*)

Dick

(German) a short form of Frederick, Richard.

Image: It's not easy when your name has a pejorative connotation. Not surprisingly, some people see Dick as a mean, snooty jerk who's stingy. When people can see beyond Dick's negative qualities, they imagine him as a high-spirited, successful man who's well known in town—especially in the bars where he loves to drink with friends.

Famous Namesakes: TV personality Dick Clark; vice president Dick Cheney; actor Dick Van Dyke; sportscaster Dick Vitale

Diego

(Spanish) a form of Jacob, James.

Image: Diego is a deep thinker. He's described as a serious and thoughtful man with dark features and a Spanish or Latino heritage. People say he's intuitive, and at times, his thoughts can make him friendly and kind or moody and abrupt.

Famous Namesakes: Artist Diego Rivera; soccer player Diego Maradona; actor Diego Luna

Dimitri

(Russian) a short form of Demetrius.

Image: Women shouldn't expect commitment from Dimitri. This name calls to mind a magnetic ladies' man who isn't ready to settle down. People think he's bright and successful, but with his handsome looks and Russian or Greek accent, he can be vain.

Famous Namesakes: Chemist Dmitri Mendeleev

Dirk

(German) a short form of Derek, Theodoric.

Image: Geek or jock—either way, you won't forget Dirk. People picture Dirk as a studious science geek with snooty arrogance or a dimwitted jock with a sweet disposition. Physically, he's described as handsome with Scandinavian looks.

Famous Namesakes: Basketball player Dirk Nowitzki; character Dirk Diggler (*Boogie Nights*)

Dominic

(Latin) belonging to the Lord.

Image: Dominic is the portrait of an artistic soul. People think he's an arty, smart, and determined man with very handsome Italian looks. Perhaps an art teacher, he's serious and polite but always good-natured.

Famous Namesakes: Saint Dominic; actor Dominic Monaghan

Don

(Scottish) a short form of Donald.

Image: Don is rough around the edges, but people love him anyway. He's imagined as a boorish, loud clod who's nonetheless personable and fun. He's probably short with plain dark features.

Famous Namesakes: Legendary figure Don Juan; actor Don Johnson; baseball player Don Mattingly; actor Don Knotts

Boys

Donald

(Scottish) world leader; proud ruler.

Image: There's Donald—hiding behind a book. People picture Donald as an intelligent, successful, and talented man. He's probably kind but shy, seeking the quiet comfort of a good book.

Famous Namesakes: Tycoon Donald Trump; actor Donald Sutherland; secretary of defense Donald Rumsfeld; cartoon character Donald Duck

Donovan

(Irish) dark warrior.

Image: This name can attribute its "Mellow Yellow" groove to '60s British pop star Donovan. People picture Donovan as a freewheeling, intelligent, and well-liked hippie. He's also said to be tall, dark-haired, and handsomely tan.

Famous Namesakes: Football player Donovan mcnabb; singer Donovan

Dorcas

(Hebrew) gazelle.

Image: Dorcas can use a real friend. Dorcas gives the impression of a strange man who tries too hard to fit in with people who treat him poorly. Unkempt and unattractive, he most likely has low self-esteem.

Famous Namesakes: Biblical figure Dorcas

Dorian

(Greek) from Doris, Greece.

Image: Oscar Wilde's novel painted *The Picture of Dorian Gray*, and here's another picture: Dorian is envisioned as a tall, dark, and handsome man who's so persistent, talkative, and overly dramatic that he can be aggravating.

Famous Namesakes: Dorian Gray (*The Picture of Dorian Gray*)

Douglas

(Scottish) dark river, dark stream.

Image: Douglas is goal oriented, but he's wound too tight. Nearly everyone says Douglas is a driven, smart, and assertive—if not aggressive—perfectionist. Physically, he's imagined with blond hair and glasses.

Famous Namesakes: Actor Douglas Fairbanks; general Douglas A. Macarthur; actors Kirk and Michael Douglas

Doyle

(Irish) a form of Dougal.

Image: Whether he's outgoing or shy, Doyle has some issues. People can't decide if Doyle is an adventurous class clown or an introverted nerd. Either way, they think he's bratty and mad at the world. Most people think he's short and stout.

Famous Namesakes: Musician Doyle Lawson; author Arthur Conan Doyle; author Roddy Doyle; poker player Doyle Brunson

Drake

(English) dragon; owner of the inn with the dragon trademark.

Image: Drake has had everything handed to him, but he wants more. People say Drake is a spoiled and cold man from a wealthy family—but he also has the determination, willfulness, and smarts to become powerful on his own. He's thought to be muscular and very tall with dark, pretty-boy features.

Famous Namesakes: Explorer Francis Drake; actor Drake Hogestyn

Drew

(Welsh) wise. (English) a short form of Andrew.

Image: Drew defines *nice guy*. Above all, people think Drew is sweet, caring, and friendly. He's said to be cool and popular with a sexy smile.

Famous Namesakes: Actor Drew Carey; football player Drew Brees; football player Drew Bledsoe

Dudley

(English) common field.

Image: You can't spell Dudley without *dud*. Most people say Dudley is a sensitive but boring nerd. Other people don't think he's smart at all—instead, they see him as a bumbling simpleton. Either way, he's described as an unattractive and pudgy dud.

Famous Namesakes: Actor Dudley Moore; cartoon character Dudley Do-Right

Duff

(Scottish) dark.

Image: The name Duff conjures up images of heavy metal bassist Duff McKagan and his thin, long-haired, leather-clad looks. In an interesting contrast, others believe the name Duff belongs to an intellectual.

Famous Namesakes: Duff beer from *The Simpsons*; rock musician Duff McKagan

Duncan

(Scottish) brown warrior.

Image: Duncan is chatty with his mates—unless there are girls nearby. Duncan is regarded as a friendly, jolly guy who's down to earth but bashful around the opposite sex. People say he's tall with brown hair and a baby face.

Famous Namesakes: Character Duncan MacLeod (*Highlander: The Series*); character Duncan (*Macbeth*); actor Michael Clarke Duncan; basketball player Tim Duncan

Dunn

(Scottish) a short form of Duncan.

Image: There's something a little strange about Dunn. He's imagined as an unusual and mysterious guy with broad shoulders and a tall frame. People think he often takes a relaxed, surfer attitude toward life, but at times he can turn possessive and creepy.

Famous Namesakes: Football player Warrick Dunn; musician Ronnie Dunn

Dustin

(German) valiant fighter. (English) brown rock quarry.

Image: Dustin has a smile on his face and his hair in his eyes. Most people describe Dustin as a happy, fun-loving guy who's easy to befriend. He's seen as athletic and hardworking, but he does have rare moments of whining. People picture him with a mop of dusty blond hair.

Famous Namesakes: Actor Dustin Hoffman

Dusty

(English) a familiar form of Dustin.

Image: Dusty lives up to his name. When people hear the name Dusty, they think of a dirty and dumb redneck who likes to ride ATVs, leaving a big cloud of dust behind him. He's said to be short and chubby, loud and tough, but he always goes to church on Sundays.

Famous Namesakes: Wrestler Dusty Rhodes

Dwayne

(Irish) dark.

Image: Dwayne is a good ol' boy who says he's nothin' special. He's imagined as a lanky, dark-skinned yokel with simple, backwoods ways. People feel he can be goofy at times, but he usually goes through life without much notice from other folks.

Famous Namesakes: Character Dwayne Wayne (*A Different World*); wrestler and actor Dwyane "The Rock" Johnson; basketball player Dwayne Wade

Dwight

(English) a form of DeWitt.

Image: Dwight is none too bright. People say he's a dimwitted hick who's lazy and dull. At times, this skinny fellow can be outgoing and outspoken in his own backward, uneducated way.

Famous Namesakes: President Dwight Eisenhower; singer Dwight Yoakam; baseball player Dwight Gooden

 **Star Kids**

Dweezil

It's simple: Dweezil is dweeby. He's said to be an awkward nerd who's smart, but not as smart as he thinks he is. Despite his inflated sense of self, he probably doesn't have the ability to get or keep a job. People imagine he spends most of his time playing guitar in his parents' garage. Dweezil Zappa, son of music legend Frank Zappa, *is* a guitarist, but he's been gainfully employed as a rock star and actor for many years.

Dylan

(Welsh) sea.

Image: Dylan is a rare breed who's fun yet dependable. People think of Dylan as a cheerful, playful guy, but he's also loyal and caring. They say this light-eyed looker is always smiling.

Famous Namesakes: Singer Bob Dylan; poet Dylan Thomas; actor Dylan McDermott

Earl

(Irish) pledge. (English) nobleman.

Image: People envision Earl as an older man who's a doting, sweet father. He may be chubby and a bit of a hick, but he's good-tempered and religious.

Famous Namesakes: Supreme Court justice Earl Warren; actor James Earl Jones; character Earl Hickey (*My Name Is Earl*)

Ed

(English) a short form of Edgar, Edsel, Edward.

Image: Ed doesn't do so well in social situations. He's thought to be an awkward and bashful blue-collar guy. People suspect he mumbles and keeps his head down, and at times his shyness turns into grumpiness.

Famous Namesakes: TV personality Ed Sullivan; talking horse Mr. Ed; talk show host Ed McMahon; actor Ed Harris; character Ed Stevens (*Ed*)

Eddie

(English) a familiar form of Edgar, Edsel, Edward.

Image: Several comedians share this name, including Eddie Murphy, so people definitely see Eddie as a funny guy. He's imagined as a goofy smart aleck and clown. He may not be overly attractive, but he's kind and well liked.

Famous Namesakes: Actor Eddie Murphy; singer Eddie Vedder; actor Eddie Arnold; musician Eddie Van Halen

Edgar

(English) successful spearman.

Image: Quoth Edgar, "Nevermore." People connect this name to poet Edgar Allan Poe and his macabre works like "The Raven." They imagine Edgar is melancholy, somber, intelligent, and mysterious.

Famous Namesakes: Poet Edgar Allan Poe; musician Edgar Winter; baseball player Edgar Martinez

Edmund

(English) prosperous protector.

Image: Edmund may not be the friendliest person, but he does have a great wardrobe. The name Edmund conjures up the image of a snooty and well-educated professional who's tall, dark, and impeccably dressed.

Famous Namesakes: Poet Edmund Spenser; explorer Edmund Hillary; politician Edmund Muskie; character Edmund Pevensie (*The Chronicles of Narnia*)

Eduardo

(Spanish) a form of Edward.

Image: Eduardo is a romantic and a gentleman—maybe. Most people say this Latino is kind, loving, and faithful as well as polite and gentlemanly. A few, however, see a not-so-pleasant side to Eduardo, imagining him as a bad guy or a fighter.

Famous Namesakes: Actor Eduardo Yanez; actor Eduardo Palomo; baseball player Eduardo Perez

Edward

(English) prosperous guardian.

Image: Edward is a stately figure. People describe him as a wealthy and well-bred man who's gentle yet determined. They believe his intelligence serves him well in either business or medicine.

Famous Namesakes: British prince Edward; actor Edward Norton; journalist Edward R. Murrow; film character Edward Scissorhands

Edwin

(English) prosperous friend.

Image: Edwin is a bit too stodgy and a bit too gentlemanly. He makes people think of a bookish Brit prone to stuffy gallantry. He's most likely smart and quiet to the point of being dull, so he mostly keeps to himself.

Famous Namesakes: Writer Edwin Muir; singer Edwin McCain

Eldon

(English) holy hill. A form of Elton.

Image: When nerdy kids grow up, they turn into Eldon. Eldon seems like a name for an old loner who's geeky but sweet and shy when you get to know him. People imagine his wrinkly body is skinny and tall.

Famous Namesakes: Actor Elden Henson

Eli

(Hebrew) uplifted. A short form of Elijah, Elisha.

Image: With Biblical roots, the name Eli has spiritual associations. People picture Eli as a caring and sensitive man faithful to God. Handsome and fit, he may be wise, confident, and hopeful.

Famous Namesakes: Director Eli Roth; inventor Eli Whitney; football player Eli Manning

Elias

(Greek) a form of Elijah.

Image: Elias has a dark side that can lead him down the wrong path. Elias is said to be a strange and dark troublemaker. People imagine he likes to be fun and carefree, but that lifestyle may lead him to drug use and jail time.

Famous Namesakes: Writer Elias Canetti; actor Elias Koteas; another name for biblical figure Elijah

Elijah

(Hebrew) a form of Eliyahu.

Image: It's no surprise that people associate this name with Elijah, the biblical prophet. Elijah is said to be a moral and faithful man. He's imagined to be sensitive, strong, and wise.

Famous Namesakes: Biblical figure Elijah; actor Elijah Wood

Elliot

(English) a form of Eli, Elijah.

Image: Elliot is picked last for sport teams, but first for lab partners. He's described as a book-smart and shy guy whose weak, skinny build isn't fit for athletics. In the comfort of his friends, he can be hilarious.

Famous Namesakes: Lawman Eliot Ness; writer T. S. Eliot; character Elliott (*E. T.*)

Ellis

(English) a form of Elias.

Image: Ellis practically lives in the library. He strikes people as a gracious and kind bookworm who's always in the middle of a good read. He's pictured as small and thin with brown hair and eyes.

Famous Namesakes: Designer Perry Ellis

Elmer

(English) noble; famous.

Image: After laughing at the goofy antics of Elmer Fudd for years, it's hard to separate the Looney Tune from this name. Elmer is pictured as a dimwitted, old farmer who's timid, quiet, and silly. People also say he's short and bald with a big head.

Famous Namesakes: Character Elmer Fudd (*Looney Tunes*); book character Elmer Gantry

Elmo

(Greek) lovable, friendly. (Italian) guardian. (Latin) a familiar form of Anselm. (English) a form of Elmer.

Image: People can't seem to think of anyone but the *Sesame Street* character Elmo when they hear this name. They say Elmo is a silly red Muppet who's happy all the time as well as cuddly.

Famous Namesakes: Character Elmo (*Sesame Street*); comedy singer Elmo Shropshire; Saint Elmo

Elton

(English) old town.

Image: While this name doesn't exactly mirror pop star Elton John, you can see traces of his image in it. Elton is imagined as a shy and nerdy man who prefers books to people. People believe he's proper and well groomed, but round and somewhat homely.

Famous Namesakes: Singer Elton John; basketball player Elton Brand

Elvin

(English) a form of Alvin.

Image: It's easy to see Elvin as an elfish fellow. People say Elvin is a nerdy genius who's tiny with elflike ears. Sometimes he can be sweet, but he's often devious and sneaky.

Famous Namesakes: Basketball player Elvin Hayes; musician Elvin Bishop

Elvis

(Scandinavian) wise.

Image: Elvis Presley is the king of rock 'n' roll, and he's the king of this name's image, too. People imagine Elvis as a talented entertainer who's cool, slick, and exciting. He's said to be a flirt with his sexy looks and black hair.

Famous Namesakes: Singer Elvis Presley; singer Elvis Costello; skater Elvis Stojko

Emerson

(German, English) son of Emery.

Image: Emerson is a class act. People imagine he's a well-read, kind, and classy man. Tall and thin, he can be timid in certain situations.

Famous Namesakes: Racecar driver Emerson Fittipaldi; writer Ralph Waldo Emerson

Emery

(German) industrious leader.

Image: Don't blame Emery for his sheltered life. He's viewed as a bright and studious bookworm who's likable yet shy. He was most likely born into a rich, country club family who instilled him with class and style but sheltered him by sending him to prep school. When Emery does warm up, people say he's witty and easygoing. He's depicted as a pretty boy with a lean build and dark hair.

Famous Namesakes: Hockey player Ray Emery

Emil

(Latin) flatterer. (German) industrious.

Image: Either at the library or on the links, Emil is a refined man. People think Emil is studious and bookish, but he also loves quiet, refined sports like golf. With dark hair and olive skin, he may be of Italian descent.

Famous Namesakes: Baseball player Emil Brown; artist Emil Nolde

Emilio

(Italian, Spanish) a form of Emil.

Image: There are two contrasting images of Emilio: People imagine him as a controlling, foul-mouthed man with a shady background. Or they imagine him as a thoughtful and suave gentleman who always smiles. Either way, he's seen as a short Mexican man with dark good looks.

Famous Namesakes: Actor Emilio Estevez; musician Emilio Estéfan

Emmanuel

(Hebrew) God is with us.

Image: With his biblical name, Emmanuel has a peaceful, spiritual side. People say Emmanuel is a serene and religious man with quiet strength. He's considered to be compassionate, wise, and endearing.

Famous Namesakes: Actor Emmanuel Lewis; birth name of biblical figure Jesus Christ

Emmett

(German) industrious; strong. (English) ant.

Image: So what if Emmett prefers biology to sports or girls? Emmett is seen as a young man who's polite, kind, and somewhat of a mama's boy. People believe he's stocky, and his glasses make him cute in a studious way.

Famous Namesakes: Character Emmett "Doc" Brown (*Back to the Future*); football player Emmitt Smith

Ennis

(Greek) mine. (Scottish) a form of Angus.

Image: Ennis keeps his mind mostly on school. He's envisioned as serious and studious, stoic and shy. But he can be friendly and even goofy from time to time when he wants to lightens up.

Famous Namesakes: Character Ennis Del Mar (*Brokeback Mountain*)

Enrique

(Spanish) a form of Henry.

Image: Thanks to Enrique Iglesias, people think of Enrique as a romantic Latino musician who has a flashy style. People also think he's endearing but a bit conceited.

Famous Namesakes: Singer Enrique Iglesias; actor Enrique Murciano

Ephraim

(Hebrew) fruitful.

Image: Ephraim is well rounded: He's thought to be a talented and curious man who's most likely patient and committed as well as religious. As for his looks, he's described as tall and dark.

Famous Namesakes: Biblical figure Ephraim

Eric

(Scandinavian) ruler of all. (English) brave ruler. (German) a short form of Frederick.

Image: Eric is a rock. People overwhelmingly see him as a kind and loving man who's emotionally supportive. People say his tall, muscular build makes him physically supportive as well. A popular guy, Eric is most likely funny and outgoing, but he does have a jealous side.

Famous Namesakes: Singer Eric Clapton; actor Eric Bana; explorer Erik the Red; hockey player Eric Landros; character Eric Foreman (*That 70s Show*)

Ernest

(English) earnest, sincere.

Image: Poor Ernest has thick glasses to help him spot bullies in the locker room. Ernest is primarily thought of as a goofy-looking dweeb who gets bullied by his peers. It doesn't help his image that people say he's the class brainiac.

Famous Namesakes: Author Ernest Hemingway; actor Ernest Borgnine; character Ernest P. Worrel (*Ernest Goes to Jail*)

Boys

Ernie

(English) a familiar form of Ernest.

Image: People imagine Ernie in one of two ways: He's either a lonely, depressed man who's a wimpy pushover, or he's a generous and caring guy with a down-to-earth sense of humor. In either case, people picture him as short and chubby.

Famous Namesakes: Character Ernie (*Sesame Street*); comedian Ernie Kovacs; golfer Ernie Els

Ervin

(English) sea friend. A form of Irving, Irwin.

Image: Close your eyes and picture a nerd—you'll probably see Ervin. People think he's a quirky, gangly dork with a funny walk, an obnoxious laugh, and glasses. He may be studious and shy, yet he always has a big, goofy grin.

Famous Namesakes: Basketball player Ervin Johnson; basketball player Earvin "Magic" Johnson

Ethan

(Hebrew) strong; firm.

Image: Ethan is more of a listener than a talker. People consider him to be reserved, compassionate, and down to earth. They say he's handsome, but he can be a little mousy at times.

Famous Namesakes: Actor Ethan Hawke; revolutionary Ethan Allen; director Ethan Coen; character Ethan Hunt (*Mission: Impossible*)

Eugene

(Greek) born to nobility.

Image: Eugene's acquaintances will probably describe him as...*different*. Eugene is said to be a dorky bookworm who's shy, if not stuck-up. People picture him as tall with buckteeth and big eyes.

Famous Namesakes: Playwright Eugene O'Neill; politician Eugene McCarthy; actor Eugene Levy

Evan

(Irish) young warrior. (English) a form of John.

Image: Evan can't keep himself out of trouble. He's regarded as a handsome man who's impulsive and self-indulgent. People suspect he's smart and sweet, but his spontaneity often leads him to make bad decisions.

Famous Namesakes: Reality-TV star Evan Marriott; skater Evan Lysacek; singer Evan Dando; character Evan Baxter (*Evan Almighty*)

Ewan

(Scottish) a form of Eugene, Evan.

Image: Perhaps because of film star Ewan McGregor, most people give this name's image a creative twist. They imagine Ewan as a novelist, poet, or actor. Yet people can't agree on whether he's charming and smart mouthed or shy and soft-spoken. In any case, he's most likely a pale and thin Scot.

Famous Namesakes: Actor Ewan McGregor

Ezekiel

(Hebrew) strength of God.

Image: Ezekiel's image is mostly inspired by the biblical prophet who shares his name. People describe Ezekiel as a deeply religious man who's quiet, wise, and studious. Breaking away from the biblical image, however, some people see him as a flirty joker.

Famous Namesakes: Biblical figure Ezekiel

Ezra

(Hebrew) helper; strong.

Image: Perhaps this name conjures up distant associations of controversial poet Ezra Pound. People say Ezra is a harsh and selfish man, and he probably doesn't have many friends. He's pictured as deep, serious, and sophisticated with dark features.

Famous Namesakes: Poet Ezra Pound; biblical figure Ezra

Fabian

(Latin) bean grower.

Image: Fabian likes to have a good time, no matter what it costs. People say Fabian is a gorgeous but conceited European who's popular and outgoing. Perhaps friends flock to him because he's indulgent and a big spender.

Famous Namesakes: Singer Fabian

Fabio

(Latin) a form of Fabian. (Italian) a short form of Fabiano.

Image: This Fabio may be a stud, like the ubiquitous romance cover model of the same name, but he has his downside. Everybody agrees Fabio is handsome but arrogant, passionate but cheesy, and buff but dumb.

Famous Namesakes: Model Fabio Lanzoni

Ferdinand

(German) daring, adventurous.

Image: Ferdinand is the picture of quiet elegance. The image of Ferdinand calls to mind an upper-class man who's elegant, introspective, and self-possessed. Physically, he most likely has olive skin and dark hair.

Famous Namesakes: Explorer Ferdinand Magellan; archduke Franz Ferdinand; Filipino president Ferdinand Marcos

Fergus

(Irish) strong; manly.

Image: Fergus will do anything to reach his goals. He's imagined as intellectual and ambitious, but that ambition makes him manipulative and sneaky. People describe him as a freckled redhead with a scrawny build.

Famous Namesakes: Comic character Fergus McDuck; legendary Scottish king Fergus Mór

Ferguson

(Irish) son of Fergus.

Image: Ferguson is a know-it-all showoff. He's viewed as a conceited snob who tries to impress people with his intelligence. When he doesn't succeed, Ferguson most likely whines to his mother.

Famous Namesakes: Talk show host Craig Ferguson; poker player Chris "Jesus" Ferguson

Fernando

(Spanish) a form of Ferdinand.

Image: People think of flamboyant actor Fernando Lamas when they hear this name—or perhaps they just think of Billy Crystal's *Saturday Night Live* send-up of him. Fernando is described as a macho and annoying braggart who's suave and strong-willed. People suspect he uses his Latino features to charm women, but he often comes across as sleazy.

Famous Namesakes: Baseball player Fernando Valenzuela; actor Fernando Lamas; character Fernando (*Saturday Night Live*)

Fidel

(Latin) faithful.

Image: It's nearly impossible to separate this name's image from Cuban leader Fidel Castro. Fidel is pictured as a heartless dictator who's strong-willed, smart, and masculine.

Famous Namesakes: Cuban president Fidel Castro

Finnegan

(Irish) light-skinned; white.

Image: There's never a dull—or quiet—moment when Finnegan is around. People find this name fit for a gregarious, cheerful Irishman who has a great sense of humor as well as a short temper. Whether he owns a pub or works at some blue-collar job, he's said to be loud and fun-loving. Not surprisingly, Finnegan is imagined with freckles and red hair.

Famous Namesakes: Character Finnegan (*Finnegan's Wake*)

Fletcher

(English) arrow featherer, arrow maker.

Image: Fletcher may seem shy at first, but give him some time. He's described as a quiet but friendly guy who opens up once you get to know him. People can't decide if he's brainy or if he's not so bright. Either way, he's pictured as tall and skinny with a nice smile.

Famous Namesakes: Character Irwin Fletcher (*Fletch*); *Bounty* mutineer Fletcher Christian

Floyd

(English) a form of Lloyd.

Image: Floyd is a little "out there." He's described as a slow, goofy, and strange man who's not very attractive. He may even be a hippie or druggie, perhaps an allusion to the psychedelic roots of the rock band Pink Floyd.

Famous Namesakes: Band Pink Floyd; boxer Floyd Patterson; cyclist Floyd Landis

Flynn

(Irish) son of the red-haired man.

Image: Anyone who voted Flynn for homecoming king was being facetious. This name calls to mind a nerdy young man who's quite smart but also quite weird. People imagine he's shy, spineless, and decidedly not popular. That said, he's probably sweet beneath the dweeby exterior. Appropriately, Flynn is envisioned as gawky, pale, and freckled.

Famous Namesakes: Actor Errol Flynn

Ford

(English) a short form of names ending in "ford."

Image: Sorry to say, but Ford isn't a nice guy. People perceive Ford as coldhearted, rough, and self-centered. He's thought to be unsociable and uncivilized, but strong as an ox.

Famous Namesakes: Industrialist Henry Ford; president Gerald Ford; character Ford Fairlane (*The Adventures of Ford Fairlane*)

Forrest

(French) forest; woodsman.

Image: Where else would you picture Forrest but in the great outdoors? Forrest is described as a gifted, caring, and sometimes goofy boy who loves the wilderness. He's also said to be tall, skinny, and dirty due to his outdoor adventures.

Famous Namesakes: Film and book character Forrest Gump; actor Forrest Whitaker

Francis

(Latin) free; from France.

Image: Francis is a gentle soul. The name Francis calls to mind a sweet, loving man. He's described as quiet, if not meek, but he's still easy to talk to. People also say he's slender and plain.

Famous Namesakes: Director Francis Ford Coppola; philosopher Francis Bacon; saint Francis of Assisi

Frank

(English) a short form of Francis, Franklin.

Image: People see Frank in two lights…and they're both negative. He's either a sloppy and grumpy old man or a socially inept techie with a strange sense of humor.

Famous Namesakes: Singer Frank Sinatra; singer Frank Zappa; architect Frank Lloyd Wright; football player Frank Gifford; baseball player Frank Thomas

Franklin

(English) free landowner.

Image: Franklin has good qualities, but he takes them too far. People think Franklin is smart to the point of being nerdy, and proud to the point of being arrogant. He's likely old with glasses—perhaps a connection to Benjamin Franklin.

Famous Namesakes: President Franklin Roosevelt; Founding Father Benjamin Franklin; president Franklin Pierce

Fred

(German) a short form of Alfred, Frederick, Manfred.

Image: Fred's image has a blue-collar feel. He's described as a kindhearted, dependable, and hardworking everyman. He may be a bit chubby from not being as physically active as he should be.

Famous Namesakes: Character Fred Flintstone (*The Flintstones*); actor Fred Astaire; singer Fred Durst; golfer Fred Couples

Freddie

(German) a familiar form of Frederick.

Image: Freddie proves you don't have to be cool to be fun. He's imagined as a dorky kid who's scrawny and unpopular with the cool crowd, but his true friends think he's great fun.

Famous Namesakes: Actors Freddie Prinze, Sr. and Freddie Prinze, Jr.; singer Freddie Mercury; singer Freddie Jackson; character Freddy Krueger (*Nightmare on Elm Street*)

Frederick

(German) peaceful ruler.

Image: Frederick is no-nonsense. People regard him as an authoritative and standoffish man who's refined but pompous. Whether they like him or not, people say his hard work and intelligence have made him quite successful.

Famous Namesakes: Abolitionist Frederick Douglass; several kings named Frederick

Frick

(English) bold.

Image: People have a lot to say about Frick. They describe him as all the following: selfish and mean, goofy and fun, unusual and weird, loving and nice, quiet and lonely, and stupid and slow. Those who realize *frick* is a PG version of the R-rated "F" word say he likes to swear. Overall, Frick is imagined to be unattractive with buckteeth and freckles.

Famous Namesakes: Art patron Henry Clay Frick

Fritz

(German) a familiar form of Frederick.

Image: People can't quite make up their minds about Fritz. Some say he's reserved and gentle, while others imagine he's egotistical and forceful. Either way, he's described as a lanky redhead with freckles.

Famous Namesakes: Vice president Walter "Fritz" Mondale; cartoon character Fritz the Cat; writer Fritz Leiber

Fynn

(Ghanaian) Geography: another name for the Offin River in Ghana.

Image: Spending time with Fynn is always pleasant. He's described as a soft-spoken and well-mannered man who's not without charm and humor. With his friendly disposition, knowledgeable mind, and attractive looks, he's clearly a lot of fun to be around.

Famous Namesakes: Author and character Fynn (*Mister God, This Is Anna*)

Gabe

(Hebrew) a short form of Gabriel.

Image: If you were Gabe, you'd be smiling, too. Gabe is said to be charismatic and sly with a dry sense of humor. People imagine he's carefree and happy, and he always has a winning smile. Then again, some people think Gabe can be a jerk.

Famous Namesakes: Actor Gabe Kaplan; baseball player Gabe Kapler

Gabriel

(Hebrew) devoted to God.

Image: The Bible names Gabriel as an archangel, and this name still carries that heavenly image. Gabriel is thought to be a helpful and watchful man who's serene, smart, and mysterious. People believe he's strong and handsome with an angelic face.

Famous Namesakes: Archangel Gabriel; actor Gabriel Bryne; writer Gabriel José García Márquez; singer Juan Gabriel; singer Peter Gabriel

Boys

Gage

(French) pledge.

Image: Something about this name makes people think of strength. Folks imagine that Gage has a strong, confident personality—he's outgoing, popular, witty, and also caring. In addition, they suspect he's physically strong with a tall, athletic physique and a strong, handsome face. He most likely even has strong focus when it comes to work or play.

Famous Namesakes: General Thomas Gage

Gareth

(Welsh) gentle. (Irish) a form of Garrett.

Image: The jury is still out on Gareth. He may be a soccer star or a chess-playing nerd; he may be quite witty or very dull. People agree, however, that he's strong and handsome with lots of wild hair.

Famous Namesakes: Arthurian figure Gareth

Garrett

(Irish) brave spearman.

Image: Garrett is type A, all the way. People think Garrett is an ambitious and strong-willed go-getter. An outgoing guy with lots of friends, he's said to be funny and smart with an athletic build and a cute face.

Famous Namesakes: Actor Brad Garrett; lawman Pat Garrett; actor Garrett Hedlund

Garrison

(English) Garry's son. (French) troops stationed at a fort; garrison.

Image: Garrison is a dynamic personality. He's said to be a combination of intelligence, fun, and gentlemanly politeness. People imagine he has a strong, athletic build and handsome features.

Famous Namesakes: Radio personality Garrison Keillor

Garth

(Scandinavian) garden, gardener. (Welsh) a short form of Gareth.

Image: People rope country singer Garth Brooks into this name's image. Garth is pictured as a country boy with old-fashioned values and a stocky build. He's most likely sincere, but he also has a fun sense of humor.

Famous Namesakes: Singer Garth Brooks; character Garth Algar (*Wayne's World*)

Gary

(German) mighty spearman. (English) a familiar form of Gerald.

Image: Gary has everything going for him—well, almost everything. People imagine Gary as a warm family man who's smart, friendly, and easygoing. His only problem may be his low self-esteem, because he's not particularly handsome.

Famous Namesakes: Actor Gary Cooper; comedian Garry Shandling; actor Gary Coleman; politician Gary Hart

Gavin

(Welsh) white hawk.

Image: Gavin's friends focus on his good qualities and overlook the not-so-good ones. People say Gavin is compassionate, popular, and fun. He's pictured as tall and cute with a dark complexion. At times, however, he may come across as pretentious.

Famous Namesakes: Actor Gavin MacLeod; singer Gavin DeGraw; singer Gavin Rossdale

Gaylord

(French) merry lord; jailer.

Image: Gaylord isn't one to break from tradition. People picture Gaylord as a wimpy but well-to-do British man who's thin and tall. He's described as overly conservative.

Famous Namesakes: Character Gaylord Focker (*Meet the Parents*); baseball player Gaylord Perry; gymnast Mitch Gaylord

Gene

(Greek) a short form of Eugene.

Image: Gene is complicated, but inspired. People think Gene is a moody man who's sometimes mean and hard to please, although sometimes he's jovial and kind. Either way, he's likely artistic and creative.

Famous Namesakes: Actor Gene Autrey; actor Gene Hackman; musician Gene Simmons; actor Gene Kelly; writer Gene Roddenberry

George

(Greek) farmer.

Image: Picture the chess club—now picture George as its champion. Get the idea? People see George as a gangly, acne-prone nerd who plays a mean game of chess. He's thought to be intelligent but close-minded.

Famous Namesakes: Presidents George H. W. Bush and George W. Bush; president George Washington; actor George Clooney; comedian George Burns; boxer George Foreman

Gerald

(German) mighty spearman.

Image: Here's a contrast: People say Gerald is either obnoxious and socially inept or smart and quietly authoritative. Either way, he's likely an older man, perhaps a grandfather.

Famous Namesakes: President Gerald Ford; actor Gerald McRainey; singer Gerald Levert

Geraldo

(Italian, Spanish) a form of Gerald.

Image: When most people hear the name Geraldo, they immediately think of TV journalist Geraldo Rivera. They say Geraldo is loud, opinionated, and sensationalistic with dark hair and a bushy moustache. Some even go so far as to say he's ridiculous.

Famous Namesakes: TV personality Gerlado Rivera; baseball player Geraldo Guzman

Gerard

(English) brave spearman.

Image: The two visions of Gerard are as different as night from day. Some people think of Gerard as a wild and crazy partier. Other people think he's a shy guy who's nervous and clumsy.

Famous Namesakes: Actor Gérard Depardieu; poet Gerard Hopkins; actor Gerard Butler

Gideon

(Hebrew) tree cutter.

Image: Gideon is gentle giant. People think of him as a geeky bookworm who's soft-spoken with a tall, slender frame. He's imagined to be trustworthy and kind.

Famous Namesakes: Biblical figure Gideon; character Dr. Ben Gideon (*Gideon's Crossing*)

Gilbert

(English) brilliant pledge; trustworthy.

Image: What could Gilbert possibly have to be cranky about? He's described as a rich and spoiled geek who, for some reason, is still greedy and grumpy. Perhaps thinking of comedian Gilbert Gottfried, people see him with beady eyes and messy hair.

Famous Namesakes: Comedian Gilbert Gottfried; dramatist W. S. Gilbert; character Gilbert Grape (*What's Eating Gilbert Grape*)

Gino

(Greek) a familiar form of Eugene. (Italian) a short form of names ending in "gene," "gino."

Image: Gino's mood swings will make you dizzy. People say Gino is a temperamental guy who can be suave and even amiable when he isn't being cocky and brash. He's pictured with a muscular frame and swarthy handsomeness.

Famous Namesakes: Football player Gino Toretta; singer Gino Vanelli

Boys

Giuseppe

(Italian) a form of Joseph.

Image: With his wandering spirit, Giuseppe never stays too long in one place. People think Giuseppe is a nomad of sorts, letting his wise, mystic ways lead him from place to place. He's pictured as an older Italian man with dark features.

Famous Namesakes: Composer Giuseppe Verdi; director Giuseppe Tornatore

Glen

(Irish) a short form of Glendon.

Image: Glen likes things a certain way—his. Most people imagine Glen as a hardworking businessman who needs to be in control and cares too much about appearances. He probably doesn't like to be wrong. Physically, he's pictured as blond and handsome, but round.

Famous Namesakes: Singer Glen Campbell; musician Glenn Miller; basketball player Glen Rice; movie *Glengarry Glen Ross*

Godfrey

(Irish) God's peace. (German) a form of Jeffrey.

Image: Godfrey enjoys his tea and crumpets in the solitude of his library. The name Godfrey calls to mind a distinguished, tea-drinking gentleman who's a bookish loner. People picture him as tall, thin, and dark.

Famous Namesakes: Comedian Godfrey; radio personality Arthur Godfrey

Gomer

(Hebrew) completed, finished. (English) famous battle.

Image: *Shazam!* TV character Gomer Pyle can't be separated from this name's image. Gomer is imagined as a clumsy and goofy hick. People feel he's shy and timid—perhaps even foolish.

Famous Namesakes: Character Gomer Pyle (*The Andy Griffith Show* and *Gomer Pyle, U.S.M.C.*)

Gordon

(English) triangular-shaped hill.

Image: There's a thin line between being *childlike* and *childish*, and Gordon crosses it. People describe Gordon as a goofy, skinny computer geek who sometimes acts lighthearted and sometimes acts immature. He's probably smart and talkative, but he can also be an annoying know-it-all.

Famous Namesakes: Comic book character Flash Gordon; radio personality G. Gordon Liddy; singer Gordon Lightfoot; racecar driver Jeff Gordon

Grady

(Irish) noble; illustrious.

Image: Grady exemplifies simple country life. People see Grady as a sincere, kind, and easygoing farm boy. Thanks to his work on the farm, he's muscular and often wears dirty clothing.

Famous Namesakes: Baseball player Grady Sizemore

Graham

(English) grand home.

Image: Graham may be a refined intellectual, but he's not stuffy. The name Graham reminds people of a bookish but friendly Brit who's classy and gentle. He's pictured as tall, handsome, and clean-cut.

Famous Namesakes: Writer Graham Greene; actor Graham Greene; inventor Alexander Graham Bell; singer Graham Nash

Grant

(English) a short form of Grantland.

Image: Grant knows when to take charge, on or off the sports field. He's thought to be a natural leader who gets things done. People imagine he's charming and popular, and as an athlete, he's a generous team player. As for his appearance, he's probably attractive with brown hair and eyes.

Famous Namesakes: Actor Hugh Grant; actor Cary Grant; football player Grant Wistrom; president Ulysses S. Grant

Grayson

(English) bailiff's son.

Image: Like any gentleman, Grayson has politeness and charm. People describe him as a refined man who's polite and caring. At times, he can be shy, but when he loosens up, he has a dry sense of humor that's quite charming. He probably has blond hair.

Famous Namesakes: Character Dick Grayson (*Batman*); actor Grayson McCouch

Greg

(Latin) a short form of Gregory.

Image: Greg kids around, especially with girls, but he's always a nice guy. He's thought to be flirty and impish, but he has a big heart. People imagine he's intelligent and attractive with strong, broad shoulders.

Famous Namesakes: Actor Greg Kinnear; golfer Greg Norman; diver Greg Louganis; character Greg Montgomery (*Dharma & Greg*); cyclist Greg LeMonde

Gregory

(Latin) vigilant watchman.

Image: Actor Gregory Peck is a classy role model for this name. People think Gregory is a wise, compassionate, and respected man who's tall and handsome with dark hair. He's imagined to be warmhearted as well as witty.

Famous Namesakes: Actor Gregory Peck; actor Gregory Hines; character Gregory House (*House, M.D.*); several popes named Gregory

Griffin

(Latin) hooked nose.

Image: People can't help but find Griffin interesting. He's pictured as a cool guy with deep intelligence, an easygoing attitude, and a magnetic personality. Everyone loves to hear stories about his interesting experiences. He's also tall and handsome with flaxen hair.

Famous Namesakes: Actor Griffin Dunne; talk show host Merv Griffin; actor Eddie Griffin; the Griffin family (*Family Guy*)

Grimshaw

(English) dark woods.

Image: Perhaps it's the *grim* in Grimshaw that gives this image its pallid gloom. Most people suspect Grimshaw is a miserly, moody, and depressed outcast. He may be crazy, suicidal, or even homicidal. He's pictured as an old, white-haired man who's ugly and bony. Then again, those who aren't so morbid think he's a sweet foreigner who's shy and a tad bit eccentric.

Famous Namesakes: Chess expert Walter Grimshaw

Grover

(English) grove.

Image: Grover is downright unlikable. He's viewed as a grumpy, grouchy guy who's also nerdy. It's no wonder people imagine he doesn't receive any valentines on Valentine's Day.

Famous Namesakes: President Grover Cleveland; musician Grover Washington; character Grover (*Sesame Street*)

Gunther

(Scandinavian) battle army; warrior.

Image: Gunther has two distinctly different images. Some people see Gunther as a burly German who's methodical, aggressive, and a hunter. Other people see Gunther as a dorky but sensitive nerd.

Famous Namesakes: Character Gunther (*Friends*); football coach Gunther Cunningham

Guy

(Hebrew) valley. (German) warrior. (French) guide.

Image: Despite the simplicity of the name, Guy is more than your everyday, average guy. He's imagined as a clever, if not brilliant, man with a caring and helpful heart. People also think he's witty, adventurous, and sexy.

Famous Namesakes: Actor Guy Pierce; musician Guy Lombardo; director Guy Ritchie; conspirator Guy Fawkes

Gwidon

(Polish) life.

Image: Gwidon doesn't have any friends, which is no a surprise. He's described as a rude and mean loner. He may be smart, but he's strange—perhaps even creepy. People imagine he's overweight.

Famous Namesakes: None

Habib

(Arabic) beloved.

Image: Habib is a sweet man who knows when to be strong. He's perceived as a caring and responsible people pleaser. He's typically shy and soft-spoken, but he can be quite strict and single-minded when it comes to meeting his goals. Although Habib is an Arabic name, people picture him as an Indian with brown eyes, dark hair, and a strong build.

Famous Namesakes: Diplomat Philip Habib

Hakim

(Arabic) wise. (Ethiopian) doctor.

Image: Don't mess with Hakim. He's described as a thug with an attitude. People think he's distant and cold, but it's his way of dealing with his shyness. He's pictured as tall, thin, and dark-skinned.

Famous Namesakes: Allah title al-Hakim; basketball players Hakeem Olajuwon and Hakim Warrick

Ham

(Hebrew) hot.

Image: Be honest—what else can you expect when you hear the name Ham? It's not surprising that people describe Ham as a piggish, rude, and dorky man. They also claim he's sloppy, ignorant, and totally unappealing to women.

Famous Namesakes: Biblical figure Ham

Hank

(American) a familiar form of Henry.

Image: Hank is a good ol' boy. Many people see Hank as a simple-minded fellow in a small, rural town. He may be a farmer or a football coach, but he likes his beer—and has the round physique to prove it.

Famous Namesakes: Baseball player Hank Aaron; actor Hank Azaria; singers Hank Williams, Sr. and Hank Williams, Jr.; baseball player Hank Blalock

Hans

(Scandinavian) a form of John.

Image: Hans could be a Viking. He's imagined as a Nordic or German man who's caring and generous but not very bright. People imagine he's big, tall, and blond with a heroic sense of adventure.

Famous Namesakes: Composer Hans Zimmer; author Hans Christian Andersen; character Hans Moleman (*The Simpsons*); character Han Solo (*Star Wars*)

Harley

(English) hare's meadow; army meadow.

Image: Harley-Davidson motorcycles are known for their rough 'n' tough image, and this name is no different. Harley is described as gruff, nasty, and rebellious biker. People say he's even reckless. Physically, he's pictured as burly and greasy.

Famous Namesakes: Motorcycle manufacturer Harley-Davidson

Harmon

(English) a form of Herman.

Image: Mark Harmon stars in the TV drama *NCIS*, which may explain this name's military image. People describe Harmon as a loyal, strong-hearted, and very good-looking military man.

Famous Namesakes: Actor Mark Harmon; baseball player Harmon Killebrew

Harold

(Scandinavian) army ruler.

Image: Harold's job is his entire existence. He's thought to be a quiet nerd who keeps to himself and keeps his mind on his work. People envision him as a gangly and balding man who's intelligent, punctual, and always hardworking.

Famous Namesakes: Character Harold Chasen (*Harold and Maude*); director Harold Ramis; actor Harold Perrineau; character Harold Lee (*Harold and Kumar Go to White Castle*)

Harrison

(English) son of Harry.

Image: Perhaps action hero Harrison Ford has made an impression on this name's image. People see Harrison as a hardworking and stoic man who's rugged and masculine. He's thought to be confident and heroic.

Famous Namesakes: Actor Harrison Ford; musician George Harrison; presidents William Henry Harrison and Benjamin Harrison

Harry

(English) a familiar form of Harold, Henry.

Image: Harry is that older gentleman who's quick with a joke and a smile. Most people think of Harry as a smart and funny older man with a kind heart. He may not say much, but when he does speak, his words are honest and sweet.

Famous Namesakes: Film and book character Harry Potter; magician Harry Houdini; president Harry S. Truman; British prince Harry; film character "Dirty" Harry Callahan

Harvey

(German) army warrior.

Image: Harvey harkens back to a simpler, sweeter time. People picture Harvey as an awkward nerd who's smart but quiet. He's considered old-fashioned in a sweet way.

Famous Namesakes: Producer Harvey Weinstein; actor Harvey Keitel; play and film *Harvey*; radio personality Paul Harvey

Hayden

(English) hedged valley.

Image: *Star Wars* star Hayden Christensen's striking good looks play a part in this name's image. Hayden is thought to be a charming and cheerful man who's tall, chiseled, and beautiful. People also consider him easygoing, smart, and kind.

Famous Namesakes: Actor Hayden Christensen; character Hayden Fox (*Coach*); activist Tom Hayden

Heath

(English) heath.

Image: It's easy to let actor Heath Ledger come to mind for this name's image. Most people say Heath is strong, masculine, and thoughtful. They also say he's tall, blond, and stoic, perhaps to the point of being stern.

Famous Namesakes: Actor Heath Ledger; football player Heath Miller

Hector

(Greek) steadfast.

Image: Hector's family loves his big heart. Most people say Hector is a manly Latino who's caring, kindhearted, and dedicated to his family. People suspect he's a bit absent-minded, but he's also silly. A few people, however, say he's brutish and rude.

Famous Namesakes: Greek mythological figure Hector; actor Hector Elizondo

Henry

(German) ruler of the household.

Image: Wise and gracious, Henry is a wonderful man. He reminds people of a scholarly professor—perhaps a reference to Henry Higgins of *My Fair Lady*. He's thought to be responsible, conscientious, and kind.

Famous Namesakes: British king Henry VIII; actor Henry Fonda; industrialist Henry Ford; secretary of state Henry Kissinger; author Henry Miller

Boys

Herbert

(German) glorious soldier.

Image: Herbert looks to books to keep him company. People think Herbert is a generally nice and respectful man who can't overcome his shyness. People imagine he's highly intelligent, and he turns to books to abate his loneliness.

Famous Namesakes: President Herbert Hoover

Herman

(Latin) noble. (German) soldier.

Image: There's a reason why Herman always glances over his shoulder. People feel Herman is fearful and nervous because he gets picked on so often. That's most likely because he's smart and quiet as well as plump and bespectacled.

Famous Namesakes: Author Herman Melville; character Herman Munster (*The Munsters*); band Herman's Hermits

Herschel

(Hebrew) a form of Hershel.

Image: There are two clearly different images of Herschel. Some view Herschel as a mild-mannered and dorky outcast who's scrawny and slight. Thinking of football player Herschel Walker, other people feel he's athletic and strong.

Famous Namesakes: Football player Herschel Walker

Hilario

(Spanish) a form of Hilary.

Image: Perhaps people think the name Hilario sounds like *hilarious*. That may explain why they say Hilario is a funny clown with a big mouth, an amusing laugh, a lot of confidence. He's usually supernice, although he can be a bit hot-tempered. Physically, Hilario is most likely dark and chubby with full lips and odd features.

Famous Namesakes: Basketball player Nene Hilario

Holden

(English) hollow in the valley.

Image: Holden Caulfield, the protagonist of *The Catcher in the Rye*, has affected most people's perceptions of this name. They say Holden is a nervous, increasingly crazy man who's smart and wealthy but mostly an outcast.

Famous Namesakes: Character Holden Caulfield (*The Catcher in the Rye*); actor William Holden

Homer

(Greek) hostage; pledge; security.

Image: People seem to associate this name with TV cartoon character Homer Simpson. They picture him as a beer-guzzling, donut-eating simpleton who is, for the most part, funny and nice. Other people go as far as to call him a worthless loser.

Famous Namesakes: Philosopher Homer; character Homer Simpson (*The Simpsons*)

Horace

(Latin) keeper of the hours.

Image: Kids mean the world to Horace. He's said to be a supportive and friendly dad who loves children and is a great role model. He's described as intelligent and quiet, and children respond to his soft, gentle ways.

Famous Namesakes: Poet Horace; basketball player Horace Grant; politician Horace Greeley

Houston

(English) hill town.

Image: If you share a name with a Texas town, you may just have a little cowboy in you. Houston is pictured as a rancher who's masculine and sexy in his Stetson hat and Wrangler jeans. People feel he's spontaneous and maybe even arrogant.

Famous Namesakes: Statesman Sam Houston; basketball player Allan Houston

Howard

(English) watchman.

Image: Howard loves to regale his clients with endless anecdotes. People think of Howard as a tall, middle-aged salesman who's friendly and talkative, but unfortunately, his stories go nowhere. Luckily for him, people believe he means well.

Famous Namesakes: Radio personality Howard Stern; tycoon Howard Hughes; sportscaster Howard Cosell; comic book character Howard the Duck

Hubert

(German) bright mind; bright spirit.

Image: Hubert is just a bit strange. He's imagined as a quiet genius with great love for *Star Trek* and comic books, which means he has a great big imagination. Physically, he's said to be overweight and unattractive with glasses.

Famous Namesakes: Vice president Hubert H. Humphrey

Hugh

(English) a short form of Hubert.

Image: British film star Hugh Grant's suave style is all over this name's image. People say Hugh is a self-assured and friendly man who's tall and thin. He's thought to be wealthy and smart, but he's perhaps a womanizer.

Famous Namesakes: Actor Hugh Grant; *Playboy* founder Hugh Hefner; actor Hugh Jackman

Hugo

(Latin) a form of Hugh.

Image: Hugo is a goofball with a large personality. He's thought to be funny and goofy, boisterous and outspoken—but not overly intelligent. People picture him with a chubby and stubby body.

Famous Namesakes: Actor Hugo Weaving; designer Hugo Boss; author Victor Hugo

Humphrey

(German) peaceful strength.

Image: Humphrey Bogart gives this name a cool, manly image. People say Humphrey is a smart aleck but also a man's man with a stocky build. He's thought to have a good heart and a sharp mind.

Famous Namesakes: Actor Humphrey Bogart; vice president Hubert H. Humphrey

Hunter

(English) hunter.

Image: While many see Hunter as a kind, laid-back guy, others beg to differ. Most people imagine Hunter as compassionate and loyal with rugged, manly looks. Sometimes he can be outgoing, and other times he can be quiet, but he's always down to earth. In contrast, others say Hunter is a stuck-up rich kid who needs to be the class clown.

Famous Namesakes: Writer Hunter S. Thompson; wrestler "Triple H" Hunter Hearst Helmsley; baseball player Jim "Catfish" Hunter

Hussein

(Arabic) little; handsome.

Image: The name Hussein undeniably evokes images of former dictator Saddam Hussein. People describe Hussein as a corrupt and remorseless man of Arabic descent who's evil and untrustworthy.

Famous Namesakes: Iraqi president Saddam Hussein; senator Barack Hussein Obama

Ian

(Scottish) a form of John.

Image: Ian is two-faced. Sometimes he can be quick-witted and friendly, but he can also be conceited and smug. People describe him as tall, thin, and handsome.

Famous Namesakes: Author Ian Fleming; actor Ian McKellan; actor Ian Ziering; actor Ian Somerhalder

★ Star Kids

Indiana August

Forget Indiana August—when people hear this name, all they can think of is Indiana Jones. For this reason, they describe Indiana August as a brave, smart, and tough archaeology professor who travels the world on daring adventures. He's pictured as a tall man with rugged, weathered looks. It makes you wonder if actors Casey Affleck and Summer Phoenix were watching *Raiders of the Lost Ark* when they chose the name Indiana August for their son.

Ignatius

(Latin) fiery, ardent.

Image: Ignatius knows all about wizards and magic spells, but nothing about hanging out with friends. He's imagined as a brainy geek who spends too much time obsessing over school and fantasy books, and his feeble social life shows it. Physically, he's pale and frail.

Famous Namesakes: Saint Ignatius of Loyola

Ike

(Hebrew) a familiar form of Isaac.

Image: There's a distinct difference between the two images of Ike. Many people think Ike is a quiet guy who lacks friends as well as confidence. He's most likely smart, but his laziness garners him barely average grades in school. Others think Ike is streetwise and tough, perhaps thinking of rock 'n' roll artist Ike Turner.

Famous Namesakes: Singer Ike Turner; president Dwight "Ike" Eisenhower; football player Ike Taylor; football player Ike Hilliard

Ira

(Hebrew) watchful.

Image: Ira is a good person who sometimes has bad days. He's pictured as a caring and reserved man with plain looks. Every now and then, his quiet nature can lead to brooding grumpiness.

Famous Namesakes: Lyricist Ira Gershwin; author Ira Levin

Irving

(Irish) handsome. (Welsh) white river. (English) sea friend.

Image: People think Irving is the smart, studious, and shy type. He wears glasses and may be elderly and wrinkled. He may even be a tad bit eccentric.

Famous Namesakes: Songwriter Irving Berlin; football player Michael Irving; writer Washington Irving

Isaac

(Hebrew) he will laugh.

Image: You can't help but to like Isaac. He's imagined as a very smart and caring gentleman. People say he's full of smiles and laughs, which make him so well liked. In addition, he's pictured as fit and handsome with a larger nose.

Famous Namesakes: Biblical figure Isaac; singer and actor Isaac Hayes; scientist Isaac Newton; designer Isaac Mizrahi; author Isaac Asminov

Isaiah

(Hebrew) God is my salvation.

Image: Isaiah is best described as an all-around good person. People think of him as a caring and tenderhearted man who's insightful and spiritual. He's most likely a tall and strong African American.

Famous Namesakes: Biblical figure Isaiah; basketball player Isaiah Thomas; movie *Losing Isaiah*

Israel

(Hebrew) prince of God; wrestled with God.

Image: Ironically, Israel's peaceful nature is what makes him so fearless. People imagine Israel as a laid-back, crunchy hippie who has bold moments of risk taking. He's probably quiet and a loner, and he may come from the country of the same name.

Famous Namesakes: Rabbi Menasseh Ben Israel; football player Israel Idonije

Ittamar

(Hebrew) island of palms.

Image: People usually leave Ittamar and his money alone. He's seen as a Middle Eastern recluse with swarthy features and a short frame. Some people suspect he's ignorant and untrustworthy, and he may be rich and spoiled as well.

Famous Namesakes: Biblical figure Aaron's son Ithamar

Ivan

(Russian) a form of John.

Image: Ivan is a bear of a man, but a gentle bear. Most people think Ivan is a very polite man who's big and burly. He's thought to be quiet and serious—perhaps even dull. In contrast, some people imagine Ivan as scary and mean—likely a reference to Russian czar Ivan the Terrible.

Famous Namesakes: Russian czar Ivan the Terrible; baseball player Ivan Rodriguez

Jack

(American) a familiar form of Jacob, John.

Image: Jack is a joker. People picture him as a jovial and funny guy who loves to create mischief. He's known to be as smart as he is cool. Physically, he's described as lean with an athletic build and brown hair.

Famous Namesakes: Actor Jack Nicholson; golfer Jack Nicklaus; actor Jack Black; president John "Jack" Kennedy; character Captain Jack Sparrow (*Pirates of the Caribbean*)

Jackson

(English) son of Jack.

Image: Jackson is a cutie, but friends adore him for his personality. Jackson is thought to be good-looking, kind, and smart. People imagine he's outgoing and popular as well as musically gifted.

Famous Namesakes: Artist Jackson Pollock; singer Jackson Browne; president Andrew Jackson; singer Michael Jackson

Jacob

(Hebrew) supplanter, substitute.

Image: Jacob is the boy next door. He's pictured as a nice suburban kid who gets along with everybody. He probably gets good grades and has a good sense of humor, and he's also strong and easy on the eyes.

Famous Namesakes: Biblical figure Jacob; singer Jakob Dylan; character Jacob Marley (*A Christmas Carol*)

Jacques

(French) a form of Jacob, James.

Image: *Ooh la la*, Jacques is *trés chic*! People think Jacques is a Frenchman who's seductive, intriguing, and arty. He's pictured as a well-groomed and snappy dresser. Some people, however, tap into a common stereotype, saying Jacques is snobby and arrogant.

Famous Namesakes: Explorer Jacques Cousteau; character Jacques Clouseau (*The Pink Panther*); chef Jacques Pépin; French president Jacques Chirac

Jaden

(Hebrew) a form of Jadon.

Image: Jaden is a work of art. People see him as a stylish and creative designer and art teacher. With his tall physique and multiethnic features, he's said to be as attractive as any of his art pieces. People find Jaden to be ambitious, confident, and outgoing, but they say he can be stubborn at times.

Famous Namesakes: Star kid Jaden Smith

Jagger

(English) carter.

Image: Half this name's image comes straight from Rolling Stones legend Mick Jagger. The name Jagger makes people think of a rebellious and untrustworthy brute with Mick's looks: a thin body, full lips, and wild clothes.

Famous Namesakes: Singer Mick Jagger

Jake

(Hebrew) a short form of Jacob.

Image: Jake is a strong character in many ways. He's viewed by most as a fun, popular, and strong-willed guy. His confidence can make him come across as stubborn and self-centered at times, but it also makes him seem independent, rugged, and smart. In addition, he's thought to be strong with masculine good looks.

Famous Namesakes: Actor Jake Gyllenhaal; football player Jake Plummer; football player Jake Delhomme; baseball player Jake Peavy

Jamal

(Arabic) handsome.

Image: With several athletes sharing this name (for example, Jamal Mashburn, and Jamal Lewis), it's no surprise Jamal has a sporty edge. He's thought of as an African American athlete who's extroverted and popular, but he can also have an attitude.

Famous Namesakes: Football player Jamal Lewis; basketball player Jamal Mashburn

James

(Hebrew) supplanter, substitute. (English) a form of Jacob.

Image: James is a pleasant person and ever a gentleman. He's pictured as a warmhearted and approachable brown-haired man who's studious and respectful. He's thought to be trustworthy, serious, and handsome.

Famous Namesakes: Biblical figure James; actor James Woods; actor James Earl Jones; singer James Taylor; film and book character James Bond

Jamie

(English) a familiar form of James.

Image: Jamie is thought to have an ugly face and an ugly personality to match. People say he's heartless, rude, and argumentative. Physically, people don't find him attractive in the least. At times, however, he does seem to have a good sense of humor.

Famous Namesakes: Actor Jamie Foxx; comedian Jamie Kennedy; chef Jamie Oliver; poker player Jamie Gold

Jamison

(English) son of James.

Image: Jamison expresses his kindness in creative ways. People think Jamison is an honest and well-educated romantic who writes thoughtful poems and songs. He's also imagined to be good-looking with a charming smile.

Famous Namesakes: Basketball player Antawn Jamison

Jan

(Dutch, Slavic) a form of John.

Image: How do you like Jan—loud or quiet? Some people think Jan is loud, talkative, and full of energy. Others imagine the complete opposite, picturing him as a quiet and shy wallflower. Either way, he's probably scrawny and plain.

Famous Namesakes: Composer Jan Hammer; artist Jan Vermeer; football player Jan Stenerud

Jared

(Hebrew) a form of Jordan.

Image: Jared has a complicated image: He's pictured as a thin, tall, and dark-haired kid who can't harness his intelligence and is thus dropping out of school. People suspect the problem is that he's either the class clown, always joking and trying to please, or he's too mousy and introverted to cope well with school.

Famous Namesakes: Subway spokesperson Jared Fogel; actor Jared Leto; basketball player Jared Jeffries

Jarl

(Scandinavian) earl, nobleman.

Image: Jarl probably works during the summer as hired help on a ranch. People agree he's a burly, scruffy, and rugged country boy. He's said to be hardworking and powerful, and perhaps he can be considered handsome. But folks aren't sure if Jarl is helpful and nice or mean and brutal.

Famous Namesakes: None

Jason

(Greek) healer.

Image: Jason has everything going for him: He's described as handsome, popular, caring, funny, bright, and confident. It's no wonder he's always smiling.

Famous Namesakes: Actor Jason Priestly; basketball player Jason Kidd; baseball player Jason Giambi; singer Jason Mraz; actor Jason Alexander

Jasper

(French) brown, red, or yellow ornamental stone. (English) a form of Casper.

Image: Jasper stands out. He's personable, goofy, extraordinarily gifted, and downright odd. He may draw attention for being quite tall with jet-black hair. Perhaps in reference to artist Jasper Johns, people also sense a creative side to Jasper.

Famous Namesakes: Character Jasper Beardley (*The Simpsons*); artist Jasper Johns

Javier

(Spanish) owner of a new house.

Image: Javier has plenty of self-esteem and pride to go around. People view Javier as a Latino fellow who's headstrong, macho, and fun-loving. At times he may come across as cocky and aloof, but others feel he's only proud of who he is.

Famous Namesakes: Baseball player Javier Vázquez; actor Javier Bardem; baseball player Javier Valentín

 **★ Star Kids**

Jayden James

In athletics or academics, Jayden James exudes charm. People imagine he's a confident, cheerful, and charismatic man. They suspect he's a sports star who's well dressed and sophisticated, but he may also be a scholar or professor. Perhaps it worked out well that Jayden James, son of pop star Britney Spears and backup dancer Kevin Federline, wasn't named Sutton Pierce after all, as early reports alleged.

Jay

(French) blue jay. (English) a short form of James, Jason.

Image: Most people think Jay is a nice guy, but a few disagree. Jay is seen by most as a kindhearted and loving fellow who's friendly to all. He's most likely playful, talkative, and even a little mischievous. He's also pictured as a good-looking African American with cute dimples. A few people, however, say he's a mean loner without many friends.

Famous Namesakes: Talk show host Jay Leno; actor Jay Mohr; actor Jay Hernandez; rapper Jay-Z; character Jay (*Jay and Silent Bob Strike Back*)

Jayden

(Hebrew) a form of Jadon. (American) a form of Jayde.

Image: Jayden has magnetic charm that pulls everyone in. Most people consider Jayden to be a popular, confident, and spunky guy to whom girls flock. His humor, spontaneity, and energy seem to make him the center of attention. It also helps that he's pictured as cute, thin, and olive-skinned.

Famous Namesakes: Star kid Jayden James Federline

Jed

(Hebrew) a short form of Jedidiah. (Arabic) hand.

Image: Ever since Jed Clampett found black gold on *The Beverly Hillbillies*, this name's image has never been the same. Most people say Jed is a hillbilly who does things in his own scatterbrained way. But others think of Jed as a fearless and ambitious man who gets things done.

Famous Namesakes: Character Jed Bartlet (*West Wing*); character Jed Clampett (*The Beverly Hillbillies*)

Jedidiah

(Hebrew) friend of God, beloved of God.

Image: Jedidiah is a biblical name whose image doesn't directly allude to wealthy and wise King Solomon, the biblical Jedidiah. People say Jedidiah is a strict, withdrawn, and deeply religious old man who shies away from society. He's likely tall with a long, white beard.

Famous Namesakes: Alternate name for biblical figure King Solomon; explorer Jedidiah Smith

Jeff

(English) a short form of Jefferson, Jeffrey.

Image: Jeff is full of boyish charm. People think he's mischievous, funny, and always original. At the same time, people also find him caring, helpful, and wise. He's described as lanky with brown hair.

Famous Namesakes: Actor Jeff Bridges; racecar driver Jeff Gordon; comedian Jeff Foxworthy; actor Jeff Goldblum; rapper DJ Jazzy Jeff

Jefferson

(English) son of Jeff.

Image: In a strange way, this name's image combines references to former American presidents Thomas Jefferson and William Jefferson (Bill) Clinton with TV character George Jefferson. People say Jefferson is an intellectual and logical African American, but they aren't sure whether he's slick talking and womanizing or straight-laced and stuffy.

Famous Namesakes: President Thomas Jefferson; Confederate president Jefferson Davis; character George Jefferson (*The Jeffersons*)

Jeffrey

(English) divinely peaceful.

Image: One image of Jeffrey is of someone to admire—the other isn't. Most people think of Jeffrey as a congenial and honest man who makes a great role model, although others imagine him as a self-centered and bratty liar who's insecure and domineering. Physically, he's thought to be sexy and muscular.

Famous Namesakes: Actor Jeffrey Tambor

Jeremiah

(Hebrew) God will uplift.

Image: Jeremiah is both smart and kind. The name Jeremiah creates the image of a lanky and loving egghead. People find him to be sincere, self-assured, and spiritual—no doubt a reference to the Old Testament prophet who shares this name.

Famous Namesakes: Film character Jeremiah Johnson; biblical figure Jeremiah

Jeremy

(English) a form of Jeremiah.

Image: It seems there's a good Jeremy and a bad Jeremy. Jeremy is seen by many as a popular and charming guy who's honest and sweet. Others think he's quick-tempered and cruel, perhaps a nod to actor Jeremy Irons and his villainous roles or to the disturbing song "Jeremy" by rock group Pearl Jam.

Famous Namesakes: Actor Jeremy Irons; actor Jeremy Piven; football player Jeremy Shockey; supercross racer Jeremy McGrath

Jeriah

(Hebrew) Jehovah has seen.

Image: Jeriah proves that not all brainiacs are socially awkward. People believe Jeriah is a caring, happy, and considerate man who's good at listening and big on smiling. At the same time, he's also said to be a focused, motivated, and self-sufficient genius. As for his looks, he's described as handsome with olive skin and dark features.

Famous Namesakes: Biblical figure Jeriah

Jermaine

(French) a form of Germain. (English) sprout, bud.

Image: People speculate about Jermaine's line of work. Some emphasize this African American man is funny and cocky, which means he may be a singer, comedian, or rap artist. Others point out that he's buff and tall, making him a perfect basketball player. No matter what his profession, everyone agrees Jermaine is handsome, friendly, and intelligent.

Famous Namesakes: Singer Jermaine Jackson; boxer Jermain Taylor; singer Jermaine Dupri; basketball player Jermaine O'Neal

Jerome

(Latin) holy.

Image: There's agreement and disagreement about Jerome. People agree Jerome is an athletic African American man—perhaps a reference to former NFL running back Jerome Bettis—who's scholarly and friendly. What people can't agree on is whether Jerome is loud and flirty or quiet and gentle.

Famous Namesakes: Football player Jerome Bettis

Jerry

(German) mighty spearman. (English) a familiar form of Gerald, Gerard.

Image: The images of Jerry range from unpopular rube to well-loved comic. Jerry is imagined as an annoying, gossipy pest who's cloddish and homely. A few people see comedian Jerry Seinfeld, saying Jerry is a comical and witty entertainer who's a good buddy.

Famous Namesakes: Comedian Jerry Lewis; comedian Jerry Seinfeld; singer Jerry Garcia; football player Jerry Rice; talk show host Jerry Springer

Jesse

(Hebrew) wealthy.

Image: Jesse has his wild side, but he also has a good head and heart. People find him to be energetic, fun, and daring—although he's smart enough to exercise caution when necessary. People imagine he's very outgoing and likable as well as generous and loving.

Famous Namesakes: Activist Jesse Jackson; outlaw Jesse James; athlete Jesse Owens; governor and wrestler Jesse Ventura

Jesus

(Hebrew) a form of Joshua.

Image: People cannot separate this name from Jesus Christ: They say Jesus is a forgiving, gentle, and holy bearded man who sacrifices himself. A few people acknowledge the most current use of the name Jesus, saying it belongs to a man of Spanish or Latino heritage.

Famous Namesakes: Biblical figure Jesus Christ; baseball player Jesús Alou; band Jesus Jones

Jibril

(Arabic) archangel of Allah.

Image: Do people revolve around Jibril or does he revolve around others? People aren't sure if Jibril is loud and glad to be the center of attention, or if he's quiet and glad to be a loner. Either way, they say this dark-skinned, curly-haired fellow is typically happy, quick thinking, and kind.

Famous Namesakes: Islamic archangel Jibril

Jim

(Hebrew, English) a short form of James.

Image: Jim is stoic. The image people have of Jim is one of an unhappy and harsh man who doesn't speak much. He's considered brave, having served in the military, but he's also dull.

Famous Namesakes: Actor Jim Carrey; actor Jim Belushi; football player Jim Kelly; singer Jim Morrison

Jimmy

(English) a familiar form of Jim.

Image: People conjure up two opposing images of Jimmy. For some, Jimmy is a kind but timid fellow who hides in his own world, safe from bullies. He's said to be smart, creative, and hardworking, but without friends. Others imagine he's a wild, goofy, and fun-loving guy who's up for anything. Quick witted and funny, his addictive personality may make him a troublemaker. In either case, he's pictured as a gangly, freckle-faced looker.

Famous Namesakes: Actor Jimmy Smits; football coach Jimmy Johnson; actor Jimmy Stewart; singer Jimmy Buffett; president Jimmy Carter

Jock

(American) a familiar form of Jacob.

Image: When most people hear the name Jock, they understandably think of a husky athlete with big muscles. Beyond that, some people imagine Jock as egotistical, immature, and rude—most likely due to an inferiority complex he developed after being teased so much as a child. A few people, however, see a sweeter, more respectful side to him.

Famous Namesakes: None

Joe

(Hebrew) a short form of Joseph.

Image: Joe may be an ordinary guy, but every guy wishes he were like Joe. People imagine Joe as kindhearted, fun, and lovable—which, coupled with his handsome good looks, makes him popular with girls. People also picture Joe as an athlete—not surprising when you consider such famous athletes as Joe DiMaggio, Joe Montana, and Joe Namath.

Famous Namesakes: Football player Joe Namath; football player Joe Montana; baseball player Joe DiMaggio; singer Joe Cocker; actor Joe Pesci

Joel

(Hebrew) God is willing.

Image: Joel has resolve and charm. This name reminds people of a caring, loyal man who makes his own decisions and never takes the easy way out. He's thought to be charming and clever with an easy laugh. People also say he's tall, dark, and handsome.

Famous Namesakes: Biblical figure Joel; singer Joel Madden; singer Billy Joel; director Joel Schumacher

Joey

(Hebrew) a familiar form of Joe, Joseph.

Image: Joey's looks may be dark, but his personality is bright. The name Joey evokes an image of a dark-featured, handsome man who's fun-loving, bright, and sweet. It's easy to see why he's an outgoing, popular guy.

Famous Namesakes: Singer Joey Ramone; actor Joey Bishop; character Joey Tribbiani (*Friends*); football player Joey Harrington

Johann

(German) a form of John.

Image: The great composer Johann Sebastian Bach has left his legacy on this name's image. Johann is said to be a gentlemanly and traditional man who may very well be a genius, especially when it comes to music. He's pictured as tall and big boned with blond hair.

Famous Namesakes: Composer Johann Strauss; composer Johann Sebastian Bach; baseball player Johan Santana

John

(Hebrew) God is gracious.

Image: John is what every man aspires to be. He's described as a levelheaded and hardworking all-American guy. People consider him to be kind, genial, and fun. In addition, he's pictured as tall and strong.

Famous Namesakes: Biblical figure John the Baptist; president John F. Kennedy; actor John Wayne; singer John Lennon; presidents John Adams and John Quincy Adams

Johnny

(Hebrew) a familiar form of John.

Image: Johnny is just one of the guys. People think Johnny is a fun-loving partier who can be too irresponsible and immature. Women may find him faithful and sweet, but he still fears commitment.

Famous Namesakes: Singer Johnny Cash; actor Johnny Depp; lawyer Johnny Cochrane; talk show host Johnny Carson; baseball player Johnny Damon

Jonah

(Hebrew) dove.

Image: Jonah, a biblical name, is a model of good morals. Jonah is thought to be a compassionate and perceptive churchgoer who's quiet and polite. Physically, he may be a tall, big-boned man.

Famous Namesakes: Biblical figure Jonah

Jonas

(Hebrew) he accomplishes. (Lithuanian) a form of John.

Image: Jonas has found his true calling. He's thought to be a religious minister or youth counselor with exceptional interpersonal skills. He's most likely a hardworking go-getter, but he's also considerate, trustworthy, and creative. He may be skinny and tall with curly, black hair.

Famous Namesakes: Researcher Jonas Salk

Jonathan

(Hebrew) gift of God.

Image: It's easy to picture Jonathan as the second-string quarterback of his high-school football team. People imagine Jonathan as a considerate and clever jock with a great smile. He's most likely popular and fun, and he comes from a nice suburban home.

Famous Namesakes: Author Jonathan Swift; actor Jonathan Winters; actor Jonathan Taylor Thomas; book character Jonathan Livingston Seagull

Jordan

(Hebrew) descending.

Image: Jordan's appeal isn't superficial. At first, Jordan may seem carefree because of his cool, playful personality and good sense of humor. But people soon realize he's wise, sensitive, and kind. He's said to be a lanky but attractive brunette.

Famous Namesakes: Basketball player Michael Jordan; singer Jordan Knight

Jorge

(Spanish) a form of George.

Image: Jorge brings joy to any family get-together. He's seen as a loving family man who's Latino with dark hair and eyes. People imagine he loves to laugh, loves to drink and smoke, and loves to have mischievous fun. A few people, however, see a quieter, shier side to Jorge.

Famous Namesakes: Author Jorge Luis Borges; baseball player Jorge Posada; actor Jorge Garcia

Jose

(Spanish) a form of Joseph.

Image: Friends love to be with Jose. He's described as a Latino man who's lighthearted, happy, and fun to be around. People say he's hardworking and easily amused.

Famous Namesakes: Singer José Feliciano; singer José Carreras; baseball player José Canseco; baseball player José Vizcaíno

Joseph

(Hebrew) God will add, God will increase.

Image: Joseph has strong character. People picture him as a dependable, honest, and hard-working man. He's thought to be caring and handsome with a warm smile, and he enjoys a good book.

Famous Namesakes: Biblical figure Joseph; religious leader Joseph Smith; actor Joseph Fiennes; Nez Perce leader Chief Joseph; Soviet leader Joseph Stalin

Josh

(Hebrew) a short form of Joshua.

Image: Josh is one cool dude that everyone wants to be with. People say Josh is a gorgeous guy who's outgoing, cool, and always fun. He's thought to have a competitive streak, which he channels into sports, but he also has a smart, sensitive side. With a nice car and great clothes, it's easy to see why Josh is so popular.

Famous Namesakes: Actor Josh Hartnett; actor Josh Duhamel; actor Josh Brolin; singer Josh Groban; actor Josh Lucas

Joshua

(Hebrew) God is my salvation.

Image: Joshua has quiet strength and leadership. People say Joshua is a patient, soft-spoken man who loves to help others. Like Joshua in the Bible, he's thought to be a leader who stands up for his beliefs. People also imagine he's tall, dark, and handsome.

Famous Namesakes: Biblical figure Joshua; actor Joshua Jackson

Josiah

(Hebrew) fire of the Lord.

Image: Josiah is a biblical name, and the image reflects as such. People imagine Josiah as a God-fearing, caring, and patient man. He may be quiet, but always hardworking. He's likely handsome with dark hair and a thin frame.

Famous Namesakes: Biblical figure Josiah

Juan

(Spanish) a form of John.

Image: Juan knows how to lay on the charm. Juan is regarded as a smooth-talking Latino who some people say is sweet and loving and other people see as a womanizer. People agree he's a hard worker, but he unfortunately isn't so bright.

Famous Namesakes: Singer Juan Gabriel; Spanish king Juan Carlos; racecar driver Juan Pablo Montoya; legendary character Don Juan; baseball player Juan González

Judd

(Hebrew) a short form of Judah.

Image: Although Judd is rough around the edges, he's a stand-up guy. People may think Judd is a slow, gullible hillbilly, but he's friendly and he puts others first. He's most likely rugged and rough with lots of hair all over his face and body.

Famous Namesakes: Actor Judd Nelson; actor Judd Hirsch

Jude

(Latin) a short form of Judah, Judas.

Image: You'll find Jude quietly working on a painting or a new song. Jude is pictured as an introspective and introverted man with a creative flair for music and art. People find him to be respectful and relaxed as well as slender, blue-eyed, and blond.

Famous Namesakes: Biblical figure Jude; actor Jude Law; song "Hey Jude"; character Jude Fawley (*Jude the Obscure*)

Jules

(French) a form of Julius.

Image: Jules is either outgoing or meditative. Some people see Jules as bubbly and friendly, but others see him as articulate and reserved. Either way, his appearance is best described as handsome and slim.

Famous Namesakes: Author Jules Verne; character Jules Winnfield (*Pulp Fiction*)

Julian

(Greek, Latin) a form of Julius.

Image: If you were charming and rich like Julian, you may be a little stuck on yourself, too. People think Julian is a charismatic, classy, and clever aristocrat who at times can be self-absorbed. Physically, he's imagined as handsome with black hair.

Famous Namesakes: Singer Julian Lennon; actor Julian McMahon; musician Julian Marley

Julio

(Hispanic) a form of Julius.

Image: Julio is smooth—maybe too much so. He's regarded as a dark and handsome flirt who can be a little too confident and slick at times. Still, he's most likely kind, romantic, and adventurous.

Famous Namesakes: Singer Julio Iglesias; winemaker Julio Gallo; boxer Julio César Chávez; baseball player Julio Franco

Julius

(Greek, Latin) youthful, downy bearded.

Image: Julius is described as an individualistic and jovial rich boy who loves a glass of wine— or two—and loves to have fun. He's thought to be buff and handsome, and he's self-assured to the point of being conceited.

Famous Namesakes: Emperor Julius Caesar; basketball player Julius "Dr. J" Irving; character Dr. Julius Hibbert (*The Simpsons*)

Justin

(Latin) just, righteous.

Image: Justin is a pretty great guy. Justin strikes people as sweet, personable, and handsome. He's pictured as tall and muscular, and he may be an athlete. People are divided as to whether he's arrogant or ego free, but he's definitely honest and loyal.

Famous Namesakes: Singer Justin Timberlake; singer Justin Guarini; actor Justin Long; baseball player Justin Morneau

Kadar

(Arabic) powerful.

Image: Kadar's intelligence sets him apart from others—in more ways than one. He's seen as a brilliant but quiet intellectual who's logical, serious, and humorless. People imagine he's a tall Arab with a beard and dark, weathered skin. Kadar most likely has a tendency to keep to himself, although some may say he can be empathetic.

Famous Namesakes: Hungarian prime minister János Kádár

 **Star Kids**

Kal-el

Kal-el doesn't do locker room interviews after the game. People perceive him as a professional athlete who's private and quiet. Although it's hard to get to know him, he seems to be a smart, studious observer of life. He's also said to be tall and attractive with dark skin. As it turns out, Kal-el is Superman's birth name, which is a reason why actor (and Superman superfan) Nicolas Cage gave it to his son.

Kale

(Arabic) a short form of Kahlil. (Hawaiian) a familiar form of Carl.

Image: Kale embodies the Hawaiian roots of this name quite well. He's overwhelmingly imagined as a dark-skinned islander who loves the water, loves the beach, and loves to ride the big waves. He's said to be generous and sweet, and his handsome smile seems to say he's up for anything.

Famous Namesakes: Kasey Kahne's brother Kale Kahne

Kane

(Welsh) beautiful. (Irish) tribute. (Japanese) golden. (Hawaiian) eastern sky. (English) a form of Keene.

Image: Charles Foster Kane, the title character from the classic film *Citizen Kane*, may provide some context for this name's image. Kane strikes people as a smart and hardworking businessman. They can't decide, however, if he and his business practices are coldhearted and nasty or kind and noble. He's described as a muscular and tall man.

Famous Namesakes: Character Charles Foster Kane (*Citizen Kane*); wrestler Kane

Kareem

(Arabic) noble; distinguished.

Image: Basketball legend Kareem Abdul-Jabbar casts his tall shadow on this name. Most people describe Kareem as a lanky, African American basketball player who is fun to be around. Others, however, think Kareem could be a secretive and unapproachable religious man who borders on zealotry.

Famous Namesakes: Basketball player Kareem Abdul-Jabbar; skater Kareem Campbell

Karl

(German) a form of Carl.

Image: Karl is usually on the outside, looking in. People say Karl is a gangly geek whose intelligence and formal manners make him an outsider. On the rare occasions when he lets loose, he can be goofy.

Famous Namesakes: Philosopher Karl Marx; basketball player Karl Malone; political advisor Karl Rove; actor Karl Urban

Keaton

(English) where hawks fly.

Image: Keaton's outer appearance says a lot about his inner personality. He's pictured to be neat, clean, and conservatively dressed. People also believe this well-mannered Englishman has a charming side.

Famous Namesakes: Actor Buster Keaton; actor Michael Keaton; the Keaton family (*Family Ties*)

Keelan

(Irish) little; slender. A form of Kellen.

Image: People have as many questions about Keelan as they have answers. Everyone asserts Keelan is a smart, studious achiever. But from there, people wonder if he's loving and kind or strange and different. They also speculate if he's serious and humorless or witty and spirited. At least people have a good grasp on his appearance: a dark-skinned, dark-haired, and lanky looker.

Famous Namesakes: None

Keenan

(Irish) little Keene.

Image: This name's image owes a lot to comedian Keenen Ivory Wayans. People imagine Keenan as an outgoing, polite, and funny African American with a nice smile. Happy and hyper, he's known to be quite likable.

Famous Namesakes: Actor Keenan Ivory Wayans; actor Kenan Thompson; football player Keenan McCardell; singer Maynard James Keenan

Keene

(German) bold; sharp. (English) smart.

Image: Picture Keene at his desk—is he working on the company budget, or is he working on his multiplication tables? Most people say Keene is a hardworking businessman with a sharp, serious focus. There's some debate, though, whether this good-looking blond is snooty or kind. Others see Keene as a schoolboy who's a quiet and nerdy teacher's pet with a penchant for tattling.

Famous Namesakes: Band Keane

Keith

(Welsh) forest. (Scottish) battle place.

Image: Whether quiet or full of spirit, Keith is a good person to know. The name Keith makes some people think of a reliable, caring, and spirited fellow with a fun sense of humor. Others imagine he's stoic and thoughtful. Either way, he's most likely buffed up and well built.

Famous Namesakes: Musician Keith Richards; musician Keith Moon; sportscaster Keith Jackson; singer Keith Urban; TV personality Keith Olbermann

Kellan

(Irish) a form of Kellen.

Image: Kellan's friends take every opportunity to hang out with him. He's said to be an all-around great person who's loving, helpful, friendly, and smart. Being adorable doesn't seem to hurt his image, either. People say Kellan is a lot of fun, whether he's playing a pickup game in the backyard or dancing the night away at a club.

Famous Namesakes: Actor Kellan Lutz

Kelly

(Irish) warrior.

Image: Kelly loves life, and everyone loves Kelly. (Well, almost everyone.) People say he's an overwhelmingly cheerful and fun-loving fellow. He's seen as a caring people pleaser with many friends, but he may be too upbeat for some people's tastes. Physically, Kelly is pictured as sexy and slender.

Famous Namesakes: Surfer Kelly Slater; actor Gene Kelly; gangster George "Machine Gun" Kelly; singer R. Kelly; Australian outlaw Ned Kelly

Kelsey

(Scandinavian) island of ships.

Image: Don't let your guard down around Kelsey. Many people think of him as an unruly, hyper guy who's self-centered and untrustworthy. He's probably smart enough to take advantage of unsuspecting folks. Physically, he's pictured as frail and unattractive.

Famous Namesakes: Actor Kelsey Grammer

Kelvin

(Irish, English) narrow river.

Image: Kelvin's success gives him the opportunity to help those around him. People imagine he's generous, caring, and strong spirited. He's most likely a wealthy, stylish, and successful businessman, but he gives back to his community. People describe him physically as a handsome and fit African American.

Famous Namesakes: Scientist William Thomson, First Baron Kelvin

Ken

(Japanese) one's own kind. (Scottish) a short form of Kendall, Kendrick, Kenneth.

Image: Imagine if the Ken doll suddenly came alive. People picture him with sandy blond hair and a superfriendly and bubbly personality. They also say he's sweet and self-assured. In addition, Ken is imagined as an all-American guy who enjoys surfing and other activities that give him a golden tan.

Famous Namesakes: Doll character Ken Carson; baseball player Ken Griffey, Jr.; *Jeopardy!* champion Ken Jennings; actor Ken Watanabe; producer Ken Burns

Kendall

(English) valley of the river Kent.

Image: Kendall's personality has some kick. People believe Kendall is feisty and spunky—perhaps even bossy. They also imagine he's bright, fun, and attractive to the point of being pretty.

Famous Namesakes: Basketball player Kendall Gill

Kenley

(English) royal meadow.

Image: With his happy-go-lucky personality, Kenley is harmless—or is he? Most people say he's a friendly, fun, and cheerful fellow who's always talking and munching on candy. He's pictured to be short, cute, and plump. Then again, some people suspect there's something secretive and sneaky about Kenley. They believe he may be the type who steals despite his chummy exterior.

Famous Namesakes: None

Kenneth

(Irish) handsome. (English) royal oath.

Image: Kenneth is a wonderful guy with a wonderful life. People say he's friendly, attentive, funny, smart, energetic, well-to-do, and even lucky. On top of it all, he's also thought to be very attractive, tall, and strong.

Famous Namesakes: Actor Kenneth Branagh; lawyer Kenneth Starr; designer Kenneth Cole

Kenny

(Scottish) a familiar form of Kenneth.

Image: Sure, Kenny likes school, but he still knows how to have a good time. People picture him as a geek who loves schoolwork, especially his computer science classes. But he's also known to be a funny and fun-loving guy. He's imagined as short and stocky, and some will even say he's cute.

Famous Namesakes: Sportscaster Kenny Mayne; singer Kenny Rogers; musician Kenny G; singer Kenny Loggins; singer Kenny Chesney

Kent

(Welsh) white; bright. (English) a short form of Kenton.

Image: Kent is an impressive figure. People think he's a strong and in-charge community leader who's part of the country club set. He's said to be smart, respectful, and responsible, but he's always quick with a laugh and a handsome smile.

Famous Namesakes: Character Clark Kent (*Superman*); character Kent Brockman (*The Simpsons*); baseball player Jeff Kent; baseball player Kent Hrbek

Kermit

(Irish) a form of Dermot.

Image: It's so easy to look past Kermit's shortcomings. Most people think he's short and scrawny—but huggable. They say he's shy and bookish—but comical. Overall, he seems to be a lovable guy.

Famous Namesakes: Character Kermit the Frog (*Sesame Street* and *The Muppet Show*); basketball player Kermit Washington; Theodore Roosevelt's son Kermit Roosevelt

Kerry

(Irish) dark; dark-haired.

Image: Kerry is a fun guy with a good head on his shoulders. People describe him as a sociable and popular fellow who's perceptive and levelheaded. He's pictured to be attractive with Irish features.

Famous Namesakes: Senator John Kerry; football player Kerry Collins; baseball player Kerry Wood

Kevin

(Irish) handsome.

Image: Kevin has a good sense of humor but good character as well. He comes across as an easygoing and popular guy who's always joking and having fun. But people also say he's polite and thoughtful, so he never takes his jokes too far. Kevin is imagined to be tall and handsome with a nice smile and beautiful eyes.

Famous Namesakes: Actor Kevin Costner; actor Kevin Spacey; actor Kevin Bacon; basketball player Kevin Garnett; basketball player Kevin McHale

Kieran

(Irish) little and dark; little Keir.

Image: Although Kieran loves to have fun and play games, he's never one to make his teammates feel bad. People picture Kieran as a fun, competitive guy, but he's also thoughtful, intelligent, and sensitive to others. He's imagined as handsome with red hair.

Famous Namesakes: Actor Kieran Culkin

Kim

(English) a short form of Kimball.

Image: Kim is generally a demure soul. Most people see him as quiet, shy, thoughtful, and quite kind—but a few people think of him as active and popular. He's described as having a slender, athletic build.

Famous Namesakes: North Korean leaders Kim Il Sung and Kim Jong Il; South Korean president Kim Dae Jung

King

(English) king.

Image: King is as rough and mean as his music. People see King as a popular and hip punk rocker who usually acts like a tough jerk. They will give him this: He's not short on confidence—he knows how to get what he wants.

Famous Namesakes: Activist Dr. Martin Luther King, Jr.; musician B. B. King; author Stephen King

Kipp

(English) pointed hill.

Image: If you can tolerate Kipp's snobby attitude long enough, you may see a flash of friendliness from time to time. Most people view him as a snobby and self-centered preppy, but he somehow manages to be friendly and happy every now and then. He's pictured with a short, athletic physique.

Famous Namesakes: Singer Kip Winger; character Kip Dynamite (*Napoleon Dynamite*); baseball player Kip Wells

Kirk

(Scandinavian) church.

Image: Kirk is a happy fellow who shares his joy with others. The name Kirk calls to mind an optimistic and excitable guy with a generous heart and sweet intentions. He's described as a cute charmer with brown hair and brown eyes.

Famous Namesakes: Character Captain James T. Kirk (*Star Trek*); actor Kirk Cameron; actor Kirk Douglas; basketball player Kirk Hinrich

Kiros

(Greek) a form of Kyros.

Image: Kiros creates a vivid physical image, but his personality is somewhat hazy. When people hear this name, they first focus on his appearance: They picture Kiros as a strong, physically fit man with dark skin, hair, and eyes. Most people also imagine he's stubborn and proud as well as smart and sophisticated. A few people, though, claim he's naïve and pure of heart.

Famous Namesakes: None

 **Star Kids**

Kingston James McGregor

Kingston James McGregor is clearly an important man with important decisions to make. This name conjures up the image of a snobby, arrogant, and dignified man from a wealthy family. He may be a financial advisor, CEO, or stockbroker, or he may be a scholar or writer. Although the son of rockers Gwen Stefani and Gavin Rossdale was born wealthy, no one yet knows if Kingston James McGregor will join the corporate world or will rock out like his parents.

Kohana

(Lakota) swift.

Image: Kohana has a strong character. He strikes most as a nice, polite, and upstanding boy with tan skin, Hawaiian ancestry, and a dazzling smile. Focused and inwardly strong, Kohana is known to be very responsible, but he likes to unwind with activities like swimming, daydreaming, and writing poetry.

Famous Namesakes: None

Kris

(Greek) a form of Chris.

Image: Kris is nice guy, but he does have his drawbacks. Most people say he's considerate and sweet, as well as charming and artistic. But sometimes he seems to be self-centered and secretive. He's described as lean with blue eyes.

Famous Namesakes: Singer Kris Kristofferson; legendary character Kriss Kringle; football player Kris Jenkins

Boys

Kurt

(Latin, German, French) a short form of Kurtis.

Image: Kurt is a shrinking violet eager to bloom. People think of him as a dopey bookworm who's very sweet underneath his shyness. He can even be hyper and supersmiley when he comes out of his shell.

Famous Namesakes: Actor Kurt Russell; singer Kurt Cobain; author Kurt Vonnegut; racecar driver Kurt Busch; football player Kurt Warner

Kyle

(Irish) narrow piece of land; place where cattle graze. (Yiddish) crowned with laurels.

Image: He's no genius, but Kyle's party-down attitude makes him popular with girls and guys alike. People imagine him as a gorgeous but dumb jock who's rowdy with his frat brothers and charming with the ladies. He's also described as blond and lanky with blue eyes.

Famous Namesakes: Actor Kyle Chandler; actor Kyle MacLachlan; racecar driver Kyle Petty; football player Kyle Boller

Lamar

(German) famous throughout the land. (French) sea, ocean.

Image: Lamar's prickly chin matches his prickly personality. He's pictured as a driven and successful guy, but he's too abrasive to be popular. People imagine he's tall and striking, with a scruffy beard.

Famous Namesakes: Basketball player Lamar Odom; football player Lamar Gordon

Lance

(German) a short form of Lancelot.

Image: As one of the most prominent athletes of our time, cyclist Lance Armstrong is hard to separate from this name. People describe Lance as a noble, caring, and outgoing athlete. To complete the image, they also picture him as blond, tall, and wiry.

Famous Namesakes: Cyclist Lance Armstrong; singer Lance Bass; baseball player Lance Johnson; magician Lance Burton

Landon

(English) open, grassy meadow.

Image: Landon has a lot to tell his therapist. People imagine he's an only child with over-achieving parents who push him too hard, which makes him an obsessive workaholic. Although he's generous and lovable with his many friends, he's very hard on himself.

Famous Namesakes: Actor Michael Landon; soccer player Landon Donovan

Lane

(English) narrow road.

Image: Lane is a total chick magnet. People envision him as a driven, powerful guy with a perfect body and perfect face. He's known to party and flirt with the ladies, but he's always caring and never out of control. People say he even smells good.

Famous Namesakes: Actor Nathan Lane

Laramie

(French) tears of love.

Image: Sharing a name with a town in Wyoming, Laramie has a rugged spirit. People think Laramie is a cowboy who lives out West and enjoys long horse rides. He's said to be stoic, manly, and both mentally and physically strong.

Famous Namesakes: None

Larry

(Latin) a familiar form of Lawrence.

Image: You can call Larry a lot of things, but "stylish" is not one of them. He's imagined as a nerdy, goofy fellow who's tall, heavy, and not very attractive with a unibrow and glasses. People say he's quiet and shy, but he's also sweet.

Famous Namesakes: Character Larry Sanders (*The Larry Sanders Show*); TV personality Larry King; comedian Larry the Cable Guy; basketball player Larry Bird

Lars

(Scandinavian) a form of Lawrence.

Image: Lars is physically imposing, and sometimes his personality can seem the same way. When people think of Lars, they imagine a big, burly, and pale-skinned German. He generally comes across as kind and old-fashioned, but sometimes he can be angry and bitter.

Famous Namesakes: Musician Lars Ulrich

Lawrence

(Latin) crowned with laurel.

Image: Lawrence has a high opinion about himself. People say he's a shrewd and snooty man who's quite pompous and tries to impress others with little-known facts. They also imagine he's wealthy from his job as a lawyer or other high-powered professional, which is a perfect fit for his forceful and intense personality.

Famous Namesakes: Soldier T. E. Lawrence, known as Lawrence of Arabia; actor Martin Lawrence; author D. H. Lawrence; TV personality Lawrence Welk

Lee

(English) a short form of Farley, Leonard, and names containing "lee."

Image: Need a Dungeon Master for your next D&D night? People say Lee is an imaginative geek who loves role-playing games and writes fantasy stories. He's thought to be scrawny, tall, and bespectacled. While some say he's friendly and nice, others just call him a sissy boy.

Famous Namesakes: Actor Lee Marvin; CEO Lee Iacocca; general Robert E. Lee; golfer Lee Trevino

Leif

(Scandinavian) beloved.

Image: There's no question why Leif is so popular. He's a funny, easygoing guy whom everyone wants to be around. People picture him with Nordic features—blond hair and light-colored eyes. Smart and compassionate, he might be a political activist.

Famous Namesakes: Explorer Leif Ericson; singer Leif Garrett

Lenny

(German) a familiar form of Leonard.

Image: Not many people agree about Lenny. The majority thinks he's an awkwardly shy bookworm who has no friends. Others imagine he's goofy and slow witted—perhaps a reference to Lennie in John Steinbeck's *Of Mice and Men*. A few say he's a handyman, and some even say he's obnoxious and rude.

Famous Namesakes: Singer Lenny Kravitz; character Lenny Leonard (*The Simpsons*); character Lennie Small (*Of Mice and Men*); comedian Lenny Bruce; basketball player Lenny Wilkens

Leo

(Latin) lion. (German) a short form of Leon, Leopold.

Image: Leo is passionate, but perhaps too much so. People say Leo is a good-humored, attractive man who enjoys drinking and women—but shouldn't necessarily be trusted with either. Trouble seems to arise when Leo's relaxed, warm demeanor turns into a fiery temper.

Famous Namesakes: Author Leo Tolstoy; actor Leonardo "Leo" DiCaprio

Leon

(Greek, German) a short form of Leonard, Napoleon.

Image: Leon is a master of conversation. People think Leon is a friendly, talkative fellow who's very smart and very funny. He's probably slim, tall, and African American.

Famous Namesakes: Boxer Leon Spinks; revolutionary Leon Trotsky; singer Leon Russell

Leonard

(German) brave as a lion.

Image: It's hard to get to know Leonard—so much of him is a mystery. He comes across as a socially awkward introvert. Some say he's boring, but others understand his dry sense of humor. A few people suspect this mysterious man has amazing intelligence and hidden talents.

Famous Namesakes: Composer Leonard Bernstein; actor Leonard Nimoy; poet and singer Leonard Cohen

Leroy

(French) king.

Image: The name Leroy conjures up contrasting images. He could be cranky, mean, and intimidating, or he could be poised, polite, and articulate. People also can't agree on his physical appearance: He could be either overweight or well defined.

Famous Namesakes: Song "Bad, Bad Leroy Brown"; football player LeRoy Bulter

Leslie

(Scottish) gray fortress.

Image: Leslie is easily misunderstood. He's known to be a selfless, kind man who's polite and quiet. But it's not hard to see how his refined manners can come across as snobbish or stern to some people.

Famous Namesakes: Actor Leslie Howard; actor Leslie Nielsen

Lester

(Latin) chosen camp. (English) from Leicester, England.

Image: Lester is a soft-spoken geek—or a bully who terrorizes geeks. Some say he's a meek, sweet sci-fi fan who likes to read and play computer games. But others say he's an angry, mean bully—if not an evil criminal mind. In either case, Lester most likely has fair skin and hair.

Famous Namesakes: Musician Lester Young; character Lester Burnham (*American Beauty*)

Levi

(Hebrew) joined in harmony.

Image: Luckily for Levi, most people see him hangin' ten—the alternatives aren't nearly as attractive. People primarily imagine he's a Californian surfer who's blond, tan, and handsome. They believe he's easygoing and true to his word. Still, a few people think of Levi as an introverted techie or a hillbilly with missing teeth.

Famous Namesakes: Clothing manufacturer Levi Strauss; biblical figure Levi

Lewis

(Welsh) a form of Llewellyn. (English) a form of Louis.

Image: Lewis is normally mild and meek, but brace yourself when he takes a turn for the worst. People say Lewis is a studious bookworm who's almost always kind, gentle, and compassionate. Every now and then, however, he's known to be rude, grumpy, arrogant, and sarcastic.

Famous Namesakes: Explorer Meriwether Lewis; comedian Lewis Black; author Lewis Carroll; author C. S. Lewis; boxer Lennox Lewis

Lex

(English) a short form of Alexander.

Image: Superman's nemesis, Lex Luthor, is hard to forget. For that reason, people say Lex is a criminal genius who's rich, sneaky, and worldly. Of course, people also describe him as bald and sharply dressed.

Famous Namesakes: Character Lex Luther (*Superman*); wrestler Lex Luger

Liam

(Irish) a form of William.

Image: Liam is a kind soul. He's thought to be a worldly and well-read Irishman who's strong and handsome with green eyes and dimples. Although he may be reserved and conservative, he's also good-humored, friendly, and caring.

Famous Namesakes: Actor Liam Neeson; singer Liam Gallagher

Lincoln

(English) settlement by the pool.

Image: Lincoln may resemble a certain legendary president, but the likeness is only skin deep. He's described as an old, tall, and bearded man, just like Abraham Lincoln. But unlike Honest Abe, he's thought to be an unfortunate blend of arrogance, power, wealth, and rudeness.

Famous Namesakes: President Abraham Lincoln; character Lincoln Burrows (*Prison Break*); football player Lincoln Kennedy

Lionel

(French) lion cub.

Image: Lionel is typically a quiet guy, but a little confidence can make a big difference. People say he's an intelligent and caring man who's usually the silent type. Every now and then, he's known to have a boost of confidence that makes him charming and even bold. It's unclear whether he's lean or burly, but he's most likely African American.

Famous Namesakes: Singer Lionel Ritchie; actor Lionel Barrymore; soccer player Lionel Messi

Lister

(English) dyer.

Image: Lister doesn't have enough oomph to win folks over. He comes across as a quiet and gentle loner. Everyone admits this pale beanpole is a smart academic, and a few will even say he's kind. But unfortunately, most people find Lister to be just too boring, clumsy, and odd.

Famous Namesakes: Surgeon Joseph Lister

Llewellyn

(Welsh) lionlike.

Image: Bold or stuffy, Llewellyn is an odd duck. People say he's a loony eccentric who's either chock-full of attitude or conservative and reserved. Whichever it may be, he's probably unattractive and lanky.

Famous Namesakes: Actor Desmond Llewelyn; several Welsh kings named Llewelyn

Lloyd

(Welsh) gray-haired; holy.

Image: Lloyd is a classic ADHD case. He's imagined as a highly intelligent guy whose indecisiveness prevents him from staying in one place for very long. People say he's hyper-sensitive as well as hyperactive. Although he's most likely in a prestigious profession like law, he's so flighty, he can't get ahead.

Famous Namesakes: Actor Lloyd Bridges; character Lloyd Christmas (*Dumb and Dumber*)

Logan

(Irish) meadow.

Image: Logan is a bonafide surfer dude. People say he's adventurous and daring when it comes to surfing, but he's laid-back and relaxed when it comes to life. He's also thought to be clever, warm, and always charming. Logan is pictured with a muscular tanned body, blue eyes, and sandy hair.

Famous Namesakes: Character Logan Echolls (*Veronica Mars*); character Logan, also known as Wolverine (*X-Men*)

Lonnie

(German, Spanish) a familiar form of Alonso.

Image: Lonnie is easy breezy. He's thought to be extremely friendly, laid-back, and cool. Blond, tall, thin, and young, maybe he's an athlete—or maybe he's just a beach bum.

Famous Namesakes: Basketball player Lonny Baxter; musician Lonny Mack

Lorenzo

(Italian, Spanish) a form of Lawrence.

Image: Soap opera star Lorenzo Lamas gives this name its dashing, dramatic flair. People describe Lorenzo as a strong and confident man who tends to be smarmy and melodramatic. This handsome and muscular Latino may be charming and loving, but others say he's a tacky womanizer.

Famous Namesakes: Actor Lorenzo Lamas; football player Lorenzo Neal; ALD patient Lorenzo Odone and movie *Lorenzo's Oil*

Lorne

(Latin) a short form of Lawrence.

Image: People say Lorne is unusual, but in actuality, he seems to be a normal, nice guy. He's kind, good natured, and dependable, and he has a presence that makes him a popular leader. Maybe it's just his long hair that creates the offbeat impression.

Famous Namesakes: Producer Lorne Michaels; actor Lorne Green

Louis

(German) famous warrior.

Image: Louis has a strong heritage as well as strong values. People believe Louis has a prominent ethnic background, but they can't decide whether he's French, Greek, Italian, or even Welsh. He's thought to be masculine and hard working, but he's also polite, good natured, and dedicated to his family. With respect to looks, he's considered to be handsome with dark hair and eyes and a big smile.

Famous Namesakes: Several kings named Louis; designer Louis Vuitton; musician Louis Armstrong; author Louis L'Amour; actor Louis Gosset, Jr.

Lowell

(French) young wolf. (English) beloved.

Image: Many picture Lowell working in his shop down on Main Street. He's imagined as a mechanic, electrician, or some other laborer who works with his hands. People say Lowell is thoughtful and perhaps a little eccentric with his quiet, small-town ways. He's most likely lanky with glasses and a receding hairline.

Famous Namesakes: Decorator Christopher Lowell; baseball player Mike Lowell

Luc

(French) a form of Luke.

Image: Luc is certainly not ready to settle down. He comes across as a suave, sophisticated, and sexy Frenchman. People suspect he's a wild partier and a generous soul—but perhaps not the marrying type.

Famous Namesakes: Basketball player Luc Longley; hockey player Luc Robitaille; director Luc Besson

Lucas

(German, Irish, Danish, Dutch) a form of Lucius.

Image: Lucas is sneaky—but in a good way. Some people see him as a mischievous joker who's tall, dark, and smart. They say he loves to have fun, but he's also honest and kind. Other people, however, believe he's a quiet and brooding artist.

Famous Namesakes: Director George Lucas; actor Lucas Black; actor Josh Lucas

Luis

(Spanish) a form of Louis.

Image: Luis is a character, and that can be either a good thing or a bad thing. People describe him as a goofy, clumsy Latino who can be colorful and lively in one light and sly, sneaky, and loud mouthed in another. He also may be on the chubby side.

Famous Namesakes: Director Luis Valdez; baseball player Luis Gonzalez; singer Luis Miguel; baseball player Luis Castillo

Luke

(Latin) a form of Lucius.

Image: Luke can't say no to a wild party. He's pictured as a muscular and tall athlete who's personable and always ready to party down. People say he's funny and nice, but with his good looks, he also can have a big ego and be a player.

Famous Namesakes: Biblical figure Luke; actor Luke Perry; actor Luke Wilson; character Luke Skywalker (*Star Wars*)

Luther

(German) famous warrior.

Image: Luther hears more than he speaks. He comes across as a sweet and shy fellow who'd rather listen to a conversation than participate in one. When he's not being so shy, people say he can be charming and even playful.

Famous Namesakes: Theologian Martin Luther; singer Luther Vandross; activist Martin Luther King, Jr.; entertainer Dean Martin

Lyle

(French) island.

Image: It's hard to forget someone as unique as country singer Lyle Lovett. People say Lyle is a friendly Southern country singer with a gangly body and plain looks. He's known to have old-fashioned, good morals.

Famous Namesakes: Singer Lyle Lovett; football player Lyle Alzado

Lyndon

(English) linden hill.

Image: To make it in the business world, Lyndon knows how to temper his emotions. He's seen as a powerful, straightforward professional. Usually, people say he's pleasant, sweet, and even bashful, but he also knows when it pays to be cocky and standoffish.

Famous Namesakes: President Lyndon B. Johnson; political thinker Lyndon LaRouche

Mack

(Scottish) a short form of names beginning with "Mac" and "Mc."

Image: People not only imagine Mack driving a Mack Truck, but they also picture him looking like one. Mack is described as a burly, stocky trucker with a beer belly, big arms, and a bald head. He's most likely tough and hardworking. In addition, he may be crude and disagreeable, or he may be everybody's pal.

Famous Namesakes: Song "Mack the Knife"; baseball player Connie Mack; football player Mack Strong

Malcolm

(Scottish) follower of Saint Columba who Christianized North Scotland. (Arabic) dove.

Image: This name is inextricably tied to civil rights leader Malcolm X. People believe Malcolm is a strong activist leader with passionate purposefulness. He's said to be educated and dignified with a good character. He's also good looking and fit with dark hair.

Famous Namesakes: Activist Malcolm X; actor Malcolm-Jamal Warner; actor Malcolm McDowell; character Malcolm Wilkerson (*Malcolm in the Middle*)

Malik

(Punjabi) lord, master. (Arabic) a form of Malachi.

Image: Malik inspires a dizzying array of images. He's imagined as a courageous African American who could be an intimidating tough guy, a perfectionist student at the top of his class, an earthy tree-hugger, an arty introvert, or a dynamic athlete.

Famous Namesakes: Actor Malik Yoba; basketball player Malik Rose; Allah title al-Malik

Mandek

(Polish) a form of Herman.

Image: It's easier for Mandek to keep to himself than to try fitting in with the others. He's said to be a quiet loner whose unusual and somewhat geeky ways make him socially inept and unpopular. Mandek most likely is of Indian heritage, and he's described as gangly and acne-prone.

Famous Namesakes: None

Manuel

(Hebrew) a short form of Emmanuel.

Image: Manuel gets along with everyone. Above all, people find Manuel to be a caring and loving Latino who's a wonderful friend. In addition, he's said to be smart and handsome with a great sense of humor and good manners.

Famous Namesakes: Panamanian leader Manuel Noriega; makeup artist Jay Manuel

Marc

(French) a form of Mark. (Latin) a short form of Marcus.

Image: Marc is a fine example of the male form. People say Marc is sexy with a muscular, masculine body. He's thought to be a jovial and good-humored party animal, but he can also be a loving family man.

Famous Namesakes: Singer Marc Anthony; designer Marc Jacobs; football player Marc Bulger

Marcel

(French) a form of Marcellus.

Image: You'll find Marcel holed up in his room, working on his sketches. People think of Marcel as a shy guy who's small, plain, and insecure. Underneath it all, he seems to have a creative and inventive flair—perhaps for clothing design—and he's most likely French.

Famous Namesakes: Mime Marcel Marceau; writer Marcel Proust; artist Marcel Duchamp

Marco

(Italian) a form of Marcus.

Image: Marco never gives up until he gets what he wants—and he usually wants women. People think he's a strong-minded, ambitious man who achieves his goals. Those goals seem to be flirting with women and having a fun time. Luckily for Marco, his pretty-boy Italian looks make him quite charming.

Famous Namesakes: Explorer Marco Polo; racecar driver Marco Andretti

Marcus

(Latin) martial, warlike.

Image: Marcus is someone you can rely on. People think he's talented, intelligent, and trustworthy. He's seen as tall, strong, and handsome with dark hair. People can't agree whether he's outgoing or reclusive.

Famous Namesakes: Emperor Marcus Aurelius; Roman statesman Marcus Brutus; football player Marcus Allen; model Marcus Schenkenberg

Mario

(Italian) a form of Marino.

Image: Nintendo gamers will recognize their pint-size hero Mario in this image. People think of Mario as an adventurous, brave, and hyperactive Italian man. He's likely funny and jolly, and he has dark hair and a bushy mustache.

Famous Namesakes: Video game character Mario; actor Mario Lopez; racecar driver Mario Andretti; mayor Mario Cuomo; football player Mario Williams

Marion

(French) bitter; sea of bitterness.

Image: Marion has got it all figured out. He's seen as an intelligent and eloquent African American man who's funny, caring, and a big flirt. He's most likely successful, and some will even say he's livin' large.

Famous Namesakes: Mayor Marion Barry; basketball player Shawn Marion

Mark

(Latin) a form of Marcus.

Image: You'll find one Mark laughing at the dinner table and another Mark praying in a church pew. Many people think Mark is a helpful, caring guy who's perfect to bring home to Mom and perfect family-man material. Perhaps thinking of the Gospel of Mark, others say he's a self-righteous, self-absorbed Holy Roller.

Famous Namesakes: Biblical figure Mark; actor Mark Wahlberg; baseball player Mark McGwire; author Mark Twain; Roman statesman Mark Anthony

Marlon

(French) a form of Merlin.

Image: Marlon is a catch. People imagine him as a deep-sea fisherman—most likely because *Marlon* and *marlin* sound the same. He's said to be confident, strong willed, and self-assured, and he also has a tall, athletic build.

Famous Namesakes: Actor Marlon Brando; actor Marlon Wayans; singer Marlon Jackson

Marshall

(French) caretaker of the horses; military title.

Image: Even though he goes by Eminem, Marshall Mathers influences this name in a big way. People say Marshall is a talented and successful rapper who has gone far in life. However, he's also thought to be arrogant and angry.

Famous Namesakes: Singer Marshall Crenshaw; Supreme Court justice Thurgood Marshall; rapper Marshall Mathers, also known as Eminem; football player Marshall Faulk

Martin

(Latin, French) a form of Martinus.

Image: Martin is the guy you trust to do your taxes. He's imagined as a reliable and mild-mannered man who's polite and well liked by his peers. He's most likely an accountant or a number cruncher who's slightly geeky.

Famous Namesakes: Actor Martin Sheen; director Martin Scorsese; actor Martin Short; actor Martin Lawrence

Marty

(Latin) a familiar form of Martin.

Image: Marty tries to be funniest one in class, but most kids aren't laughing. People say he's a chubby class clown who can be childish, annoying, and dimwitted. He's most likely unattractive, and he's plagued by low self-esteem.

Famous Namesakes: Character Marty McFly (*Back to the Future*); actor Marty Feldman; character Marty Piletti (*Marty*)

Marvin

(English) lover of the sea.

Image: Marvin is a picture-perfect nerd. He's seen as a whiny, dorky guy who's smart but boring. He seems to fit the physical stereotype of a nerd, too: He's imagined as a pipsqueak with glasses and a pocket protector.

Famous Namesakes: Actor Lee Marvin; singer Marvin Gaye; character Marvin the Martian (*Looney Tunes*); boxer Marvin Hagler; football player Marvin Harrison

Mason

(French) stone worker.

Image: Unless you're worth millions, you're worthless to Mason. He's seen as a rich, aloof man who has time only for other rich people and throws lavish parties simply because he can. A few see him in a not-so-harsh view, saying Mason is inquisitive, sensitive, and shy.

Famous Namesakes: Book and TV character Perry Mason; surveyor Charles Mason of the Mason-Dixon Line; comedian Jackie Mason

Mateo

(Spanish) a form of Matthew.

Image: Mateo is a truly good soul. People imagine he's kindhearted, noble, and generous. He's also thought to be handsome and muscular as well as gifted with a quick wit and sharp mind.

Famous Namesakes: Character Mateo Santos (*All My Children*)

Mathias

(German, Swedish) a form of Matthew.

Image: Despite his highly specialized career, Mathias is still a mama's boy. People imagine he's an intellectual medical researcher, doctor, or pharmacist. He may be jolly and friendly, but he's also thought to be a bespectacled, curly-haired nerd who still lives at home with his mother.

Famous Namesakes: Biblical figure Matthias

Matt

(Hebrew) a short form of Matthew.

Image: Matt is seen in many different ways. Most people say he's softhearted, considerate, and cheery. Some think he may be a liar and a cheat. Still others say he's an unpopular and shy outcast. Physically, Matt is thought to be quite attractive with nice eyes.

Famous Namesakes: Actor Matt Damon; actor Matt LeBlanc; football player Matt Hasselbeck; cartoonist Matt Groening; TV personality Matt Lauer

Matthew

(Hebrew) gift of God.

Image: It's hard not to like Matthew. He's described as a caring and friendly guy who's tall and fit. He's a quick learner and has a quick wit, which makes him popular. He's also thought to be trustworthy and honest.

Famous Namesakes: Actor Matthew Perry; biblical figure Matthew; actor Matthew Broderick; actor Matthew McConaughey

Maurice

(Latin) dark-skinned; moor; marshland.

Image: Maurice may be getting on in years, but he still has lots of life. People say he's an old Frenchman who's fun loving, goodhearted, and extroverted. Quick, clever, and good with calculations, he might be an inventor or even a magician.

Famous Namesakes: Singer Maurice Gibb; writer Maurice Sendak; hockey player Maurice Richard

Max

(Latin) a short form of Maximilian, Maxwell.

Image: The name Max makes people think of a rough bad boy who has no manners, but is very popular with women—probably because he's masculine and handsome. He also can be something of a comedian.

Famous Namesakes: TV character Max Headroom; movie character Mad Max; sportscaster Max Kellerman; actor Max von Sydow; boxer Max Schmeling

Maximilian

(Latin) greatest.

Image: If it sounds as though *million* is part of your name, people can't help but think you're rich. People say Maximilian is a powerful, wealthy, and arrogant man. He's most likely a power-hungry leader, which could mean he's a CEO or even an emperor.

Famous Namesakes: Actor Maximilian Schell; character Professor Maximilian P. Arturo (*Sliders*)

Maxwell

(English) great spring.

Image: Maxwell's personality and tongue are as sharp as his looks. He's pictured as an intelligent man who's rich, dapper, and confident, not to mention tall, dark, and handsome. He's most likely a high-powered professional, and he can be opinionated, arrogant, and smarmy.

Famous Namesakes: Character Maxwell Smart (*Get Smart*)

Maynard

(English) powerful; brave.

Image: Maynard isn't a big fan of socializing. Most people see Maynard as an unsure and shy bookworm. He's said to be withdrawn, if not antisocial. In contrast, a few think of him as friendly, funny, and strong-minded.

Famous Namesakes: Singer Maynard James Keenan; character Maynard G. Krebs (*The Many Loves of Dobie Gillis*)

Melvin

(Irish) armored chief. (English) mill friend; council friend.

Image: Melvin doesn't have any friends, let alone a *girl*friend. Overwhelmingly, Melvin strikes people as a nerdy and awkward fellow with a nonexistent social life. He can be kind and smart, but he's puny and odd looking.

Famous Namesakes: Chemist Melvin Calvin; director Melvin Van Peebles; baseball player Melvin Mora

Merlin

(English) falcon.

Image: It's not magic—people associate Merlin with the magician from the King Arthur legend. They describe him as a powerful, mysterious, and, of course, magical old mentor.

Famous Namesakes: Arthurian figure Merlin; football player Merlin Olson

Mervin

(Irish) a form of Marvin.

Image: Mervin doesn't comprehend the art of *conversation*. People imagine he's a smart but socially awkward nerd who's shy and quiet most of the time. When he does speak, it's most likely to expound useless trivia and facts. He's described as a scrawny guy with thick glasses.

Famous Namesakes: Talk show host Mervyn "Merv" Griffin

Michael

(Hebrew) who is like God?

Image: Like the archangel Michael in the Bible, this Michael is an angel—for the most part. People describe him as a sweet, caring, loyal, and trusting family man. He's known to be humorous and a good friend. His one downside may be too much ego and not enough patience.

Famous Namesakes: Biblical figure Michael; basketball player Michael Jordan; singer Michael Jackson; actor Michael J. Fox; filmmaker Michael Moore

Miguel

(Portuguese, Spanish) a form of Michael.

Image: Miguel is resourceful—he knows how to get what he wants. He's imagined as a Latino man who's smooth talking and street-smart. People say he's usually kind and loving, but he can often be self-centered and cocky.

Famous Namesakes: Baseball player Miguel Tejada; author Miguel de Cervantes; baseball player Miguel Cabrera; boxer Miguel Cotto

Mike

(Hebrew) a short form of Michael.

Image: Everybody likes Mike, and Mike likes everybody. People tend to think of Mike as a popular guy who's smart and sweet. He seems to be your average, all-American suburbanite. Physically, people describe him as good-looking, tall, and strong.

Famous Namesakes: Boxer Mike Tyson; actor Mike Myers; TV personality Mike Wallace; baseball player Mike Piazza; rapper Mike Jones

Mikhail

(Greek, Russian) a form of Michael.

Image: This name's image clearly relies on last Soviet leader Mikhail Gorbachev and Russian dancer Mikhail Baryshnikov. People say Mikhail is a Russian man who's interesting, confident, and intense. Like his namesakes, he might be a two-faced Communist or an artistic dancer.

Famous Namesakes: Dancer Mikhail Baryshnikov; Soviet leader Mikhail Gorbachev

Miles

(Greek) millstone. (Latin) soldier. (German) merciful. (English) a short form of Michael.

Image: The image of this name draws a lot from Miles Davis, the cool king of jazz. People think Miles is a debonair and stylish fellow. He's described as handsome, pleasant, smart, and laid-back. To complete the image, he's most likely a talented African American musician.

Famous Namesakes: Musician Miles Davis; Pilgrim Miles Standish

Milt

(English) a short form of Milton.

Image: With these two Milts, it's brain versus brawn. Some people see Milt as a brainy and awkward loner who has a hard time coordinating his enormous feet. Others have a completely different view, seeing Milt as a macho man who's showy and full of himself, like a weightlifter or a bouncer.

Famous Namesakes: Musician Milt Hinton; basketball player Milt Palacio

Milton

(English) mill town.

Image: There are two views of Milton, and one points straight to Milton Berle. Some people say Milton is a bookish, lonely geek who's always sad. Others say he's a hilarious comedian, like Uncle Miltie, who's flirty and outgoing with a twinkle in his eye.

Famous Namesakes: Comedian Milton Berle; poet John Milton; baseball player Milton Bradley; game designer Milton Bradley

Mitch

(English) a short form of Mitchell.

Image: Mitch's image is multiple choice, so take your pick. Everyone sees Mitch as a beefy and bulky guy. From there, he could be any of the following: a jerk who bullies others because of his low self-esteem, a charming and wild ladies' man, a dependable and hardworking athlete, or a smug preppy.

Famous Namesakes: Comedian Mitch Hedberg; sportswriter Mitch Albom; singer Mitch Miller

Mitchell

(English) a form of Michael.

Image: All work and no play make Mitchell a dull boy. Mitchell is thought to be a serious, boring fellow. Sometimes he may appear to be friendly, but he can also be cold and stern. People imagine he's either an athlete or a businessman, but either way, he's not much fun.

Famous Namesakes: Hairstylist Paul Mitchell; musician Mitch Mitchell

Montgomery

(English) rich man's mountain.

Image: With sources like Montgomery, Alabama, and country duo Montgomery Gentry in mind, this name definitely has Southern charm. People describe Montgomery as a studious Southern gent. He's said to be a wonderful, caring man who's quiet and shy, and he lives in a big, beautiful house.

Famous Namesakes: Band Montgomery Gentry; actor Montgomery Cliff; character C. Montgomery Burns (*The Simpsons*); character Montgomery Montgomery (*Lemony Snickett*)

Monty

(English) a familiar form of Montgomery.

Image: A good portion of this image comes from the legendary Monty Python comedy troupe. Most people picture Monty as a hilarious and quirky British cutup. A few imagine he's a snooty, upper-class snob.

Famous Namesakes: Comedy troupe Monty Python; game show host Monty Hall; golfer Colin "Monty" Montgomerie; film *The Full Monty*

Morgan

(Scottish) sea warrior.

Image: There's a sparkle in Morgan's eyes and a sparkle in his personality as well. He's thought to be a vibrant and popular fellow who loves life. People consider him to be caring, friendly, and exciting. In addition, he's most likely well read.

Famous Namesakes: Actor Morgan Freeman; filmmaker Morgan Spurlock; financier J. P. Morgan; baseball player Joe Morgan

Morris

(Latin) dark-skinned; moor; marshland. (English) a form of Maurice.

Image: The only thing to remark about Morris is that he's unremarkable. He's imagined as an ordinary older man who's fairly kind, fairly meek, fairly smart, and thoroughly dull. He most likely wears glasses and a hairpiece, and his gut has a spare tire.

Famous Namesakes: Artist William Morris; cat-food mascot Morris the Cat

Morton

(English) town near the moor.

Image: Morton isn't one to roll the dice. People think of Morton as a reserved guy who's quite intelligent but afraid of taking any risks. On top of that, he comes across as morose, whiny, and anal-retentive. He's also thought to be frail and sickly.

Famous Namesakes: Football player Johnnie Morton; composer Morton Feldman; musician Jelly Roll Morton

Moses

(Hebrew) drawn out of the water. (Egyptian) son, child.

Image: As one would expect, the biblical Moses gives this name moral strength. People think of Moses as a generous and respectful man with strong values. He's said to be wise, gentle, and holy. People believe he's a strong and brave leader.

Famous Namesakes: Biblical figure Moses; basketball player Moses Malone; star kid Moses Martin

Muhammed

(Arabic) a form of Muhammad.

Image: The Islamic prophet Muhammad overwhelmingly influences this name's image. Muhammed is described as a faithful Muslim who's compassionate and strong-minded. Physically, he's thought to be dark skinned with strong facial features.

Famous Namesakes: Islamic figure Muhammad; boxer Muhammad Ali; football player Mushin Muhammad

Murray

(Scottish) sailor.

Image: Murray's slide rule and beakers keep him company. He's said to be a loner with a knack for science and math but absolutely no social skills. He's pictured as an old, stooped man with glasses. When he manages to interact with others, people find him thoughtful and nice.

Famous Namesakes: Actor Bill Murray; baseball player Eddie Murray; character Murray Slaughter (*The Mary Tyler Moore Show*); actor F. Murray Abraham

Myles

(Latin) soldier. (German) a form of Miles.

Image: Myles is urbane in every way. People say he's a brilliant booklover as well as a kind, true friend. As if that weren't enough, he's also a refined gentleman with proper etiquette and a clean-cut style.

Famous Namesakes: NCAA president Myles Brand

Myron

(Greek) fragrant ointment. (Polish) a form of Miron.

Image: Look up *nerd* in the dictionary, and you'll see a picture of Myron. He's imagined as an awkward, bespectacled brainiac who loves chess and role-playing games. People think he's a gangly guy who snorts when he laughs.

Famous Namesakes: Sculptor Myron

Nathan

(Hebrew) a short form of Nathaniel.

Image: There's a lot to say about Nathan, and some of it is inspired by jovial actor Nathan Lane. Most people feel Nathan is a funny, happy, and off-the-wall guy who's kindhearted and clever. He's imagined to be strong and tall with broad shoulders. A few people, however, see Nathan as a dishonest and devious loner.

Famous Namesakes: Actor Nathan Lane; patriot Nathan Hale; biblical figure Nathan; actor Nathan Fillion

Nathaniel

(Hebrew) a form of Nathanael.

Image: Nathaniel is a goodhearted man. People think he's faithful, loving, and wise. While some say Nathaniel is a mellow couch potato, others say he's a hardworking leader. In addition, he's probably tall and skinny with glasses.

Famous Namesakes: Biblical figure Nathanael; writer Nathaniel Hawthorne

Navin

(Hindi) new, novel.

Image: Navin quietly exudes confidence and carriage. He's perceived to be a mild-mannered and pleasant fellow with lots of creativity. People may describe him as calm, quiet, or even introverted, but they also sense he has great inner strength. Physically, Navin is pictured to have a tall build and dark skin.

Famous Namesakes: Character Navin R. Johnson (*The Jerk*)

Neal

(Irish) a form of Neil.

Image: Neal has a high-maintenance personality but low-maintenance appearance. He's perceived as a very smart but stubborn man who borders on fussiness. Some people consider him shy and quiet, while others say he's batty and neurotic. Physically, he's most likely handsome but messy and careless about his looks.

Famous Namesakes: Singer Neal McCoy; astronaut Neil Armstrong; playwright Neil Simon; radio personality Neal Boortz

Nelson

(English) son of Neil.

Image: Do you think Nelson is the one who gets bullied, or the one who does the bullying? Most people say the name Nelson calls to mind a skinny nerd who's a mama's boy. Others say he's an antagonistic ruffian who lacks empathy, much like the character Nelson from *The Simpsons*.

Famous Namesakes: Politician Nelson Rockefeller; activist Nelson Mandela; character Nelson Muntz (*The Simpsons*); the Ozzie and Harriet Nelson family

Nicholas

(Greek) victorious people.

Image: Nicholas's charisma seem to manifest itself in many ways. People say he's charming, personable, and attractive. He's a popular friend, a passionate leader, and an amorous flirt.

Famous Namesakes: Actor Nicholas Cage; author Nicholas Sparks; saint Nicholas; czar Nicholas I

Nick

(English) a short form of Dominic, Nicholas.

Image: Everyone likes Nick—and that includes kids and pets. People say Nick is a good-looking and goofy guy who loves sports, animals, and children. Strong, tall, and tan, Nick seems to be an easygoing, popular fellow.

Famous Namesakes: Singer Nick Carter; singer Nick Lachey; actor Nick Nolte; golfer Nick Faldo

Nigel

(Latin) dark night.

Image: Nigel sure seems to be a pantywaist. People imagine he's an attractive but wimpy Brit. He's most likely brilliant and well mannered, but his gutless insecurities make him appear nerdy and snooty.

Famous Namesakes: Actor Nigel Bruce; musician Nigel Kennedy

Noah

(Hebrew) peaceful, restful.

Image: The biblical figure Noah seems to flood people's minds when they hear this name. Noah is believed to be a noble, hardworking, and godly man. Physically, Noah may be older with a white beard or strong and healthy.

Famous Namesakes: Biblical figure Noah; lexicographer Noah Webster; actor Noah Wyle; basketball player Joakim Noah

Nodin

(Native American) wind.

Image: Nodin doesn't think of himself as a geek. (But everyone else does.) This name makes people picture a quiet, introverted dork with a nasally voice, a chubby body, and Norwegian heritage. Nodin is most likely smart, and he's probably egotistical, refusing to admit he's a complete dweeb.

Famous Namesakes: None

Noel

(French) day of Christ's birth

Image: Noel is both an intellectual and an artist. He's imagined as an intelligent chap with a talent for music, poetry, and art. People consider him to be shy but sweet, and he's easy to get along with.

Famous Namesakes: Writer Noel Coward; musician Noel Gallagher

Nolan

(Irish) famous; noble.

Image: This name's image has a hard-nosed attitude, thanks to famed pitcher Nolan Ryan. People say Nolan has a tough, stubborn competitive streak, which he most likely channels into sports. Overall, though, he's thought to be goodhearted and well liked.

Famous Namesakes: Baseball player Nolan Ryan; director Christopher Nolan; hockey player Owen Nolan

Norman

(French) Norseman.

Image: There are a trio of images for Norman: Most people think Norman is a chess-club nerd who's bashful but kind. Some remember Norman Bates from *Psycho* and consider him a creepy serial killer with strange quirks. And still others turn Norman into *normal* and imagine him as a straight-laced all-American who doesn't stand out in a crowd.

Famous Namesakes: Artist Norman Rockwell; character Norman Bates (*Psycho*); writer Norman Mailer; general Norman Schwarzkopf; golfer Greg Norman

Norton

(English) northern town.

Image: Some names just scream *geek*, and Norton is one of them. People imagine Norton as a brainy dweeb with glasses and a penchant for science. Not surprisingly, he's viewed as a withdrawn loner. Some say he's goofy underneath it all, but others say he's an obnoxious goody-goody.

Famous Namesakes: Actor Edward Norton; character Ed Norton (*The Honeymooners*)

Obert

(German) wealthy; bright.

Image: Obert has his supporters and his detractors. Everyone acknowledges that Obert is an overweight fellow with glasses. Some people claim he's a genius, but others call him a geeky know-it-all. Some believe he's mellow and silly, but others insist he's goofy, odd, and a little creepy. Some gush that he's a freewheeling, open-minded guy. But others point out that he's the shiftless type who bounces from career to career every few years.

Famous Namesakes: None

Octavius

(Latin) a form of Octavio.

Image: This powerful image is inspired by Octavius, the legendary king of the Britons, or perhaps even Octavian, the Roman emperor. People imagine Octavius is a masterful leader who's strong-willed, serious, and confident. At times he can be short-tempered and standoffish or even greedy and spoiled. Physically, he's described as strong and fit.

Famous Namesakes: Legendary Briton king Octavius; character Doctor Otto Octavius (*Spider-Man*)

Og

(Aramaic) king.

Image: Og inspires about as much agreement as disagreement. People agree Og is thick, tall, ugly, and bald. As for his personality, people disagree on whether he's wise and crafty or dumb and uneducated. But they do agree that he's a wealthy and successful gangster who's tough and angry.

Famous Namesakes: Biblical figure Og; inspirational figure Og Mandino; Celtic mythological figure Angus Og

Oliver

(Latin) olive tree. (Scandinavian) kind; affectionate.

Image: Most people see Oliver in an upbeat light. Many say he's charming, fun, smart, and attractive. Some believe he's depressed with low self-esteem—perhaps a sad reference to Oliver Twist—but others feel he's loving and kind. Physically, he's believed to be blond and thin.

Famous Namesakes: Book and play character Oliver Twist; director Oliver Stone; general Oliver North; British lord protector Oliver Cromwell; comedian Oliver Hardy

Boys

Ollie

(English) a familiar form of Oliver.

Image: You'll never catch Ollie feeling down or blue. He's perceived as a silly, happy, and upbeat fellow. He's most likely clever and friendly, but sometimes he can be shy. People imagine he has a small frame and cute face.

Famous Namesakes: Skateboarder Alan "Ollie" Gelfand; basketball player Kevin Ollie

Omar

(Arabic) highest; follower of the Prophet. (Hebrew) reverent.

Image: Omar has a charm people can't resist. He's thought to be a charismatic and popular dark-skinned man. Most people believe he's kind and nice, but a few imagine he's sneaky and selfish. He's most likely strong and athletic.

Famous Namesakes: Actor Omar Sharif; poet Omar Khayyám; actor Omar Epps; baseball player Omar Vizquel

Orien

(Latin) visitor from the east.

Image: Some folks like Orien; some folks don't. Many people think Orien is moody, mean, and hard to like. But others say he's caring, happy, funny, and well liked. Either way, he's pictured as a heavyset gent with dark features, and he's most likely smart.

Famous Namesakes: Basketball player Orien Greene

Orlando

(German) famous throughout the land. (Spanish) a form of Roland.

Image: Orlando Bloom plays memorable roles in movies, and he plays a major role in the image of this name. People imagine Orlando is courteous and kind but also an intense actor who's talented and creative. A few people even transfer his talent to sports, saying he's an athlete. Either way, he's thought to be beautiful and lean.

Famous Namesakes: Actor Orlando Bloom; comedian Orlando Jones; singer Tony Orlando; book character Orlando

Orson

(Latin) bearlike.

Image: Everyone wishes for a grandpa like Orson. He's seen as an old grandfather who's stocky and balding. He's believed to be intelligent, softhearted, and eloquent.

Famous Namesakes: Director and actor Orson Welles; TV personality Orson Bean

Oscar

(Scandinavian) divine spearman.

Image: Oscar is initially described as grouchy, likely thanks to Oscar the Grouch from *Sesame Street*. But people's views take different directions from there: Some say he's whiny, some say he's shy, some say he's old, and some say he's just plain weird.

Famous Namesakes: Character Oscar the Grouch (*Sesame Street*); writer Oscar Wilde; boxer Oscar de la Hoya; businessman Oscar Mayer

Oswald

(English) God's power; God's crest.

Image: Oswald is a weirdo rejected by society, despite his riches and fame. Nearly everyone describes Oswald as a nerdy loner who's introverted and odd. He may be wealthy and famous, but he's still a social outcast. He's pictured with greasy hair, big ears, and a long nose.

Famous Namesakes: Assassin Lee Harvey Oswald; character Oswald Lee Harvey (*The Drew Carey Show*)

Otis

(Greek) keen of hearing. (German) son of Otto.

Image: What's your preference—grumpy Otis or kind Otis? People see Otis as an old, overweight man, but that's where the consensus ends. Some believe he's a no-good meanie, but others uphold that he's sweet, gentle, and likable.

Famous Namesakes: Singer Otis Redding; inventor Elisha Otis

Otto

(German) rich.

Image: Otto may be slow when it comes to book smarts, but he's quick when it comes to jokes. He's said to be a chubby German who's dumb but funny. Some suspect he's shifty and untrustworthy, but others maintain he's innocent and kind.

Famous Namesakes: German statesman Otto von Bismark; director Otto Preminger; character Otto Mann (*The Simpsons*)

Ottokar

(German) happy warrior.

Image: Many conflicting images come to mind for this name. Some people think Ottokar is a helpful, moral, and heroic fellow who's always looking to do the right thing. Others believe he's an introverted loner who's shy around strangers—perhaps he's even creepy or crazy. A few people suspect he's a strong-willed, hard-working, and dominant man who likes to boss his family and friends around. Whatever the case, he's pictured with a burly build, dark skin, and a scraggly beard.

Famous Namesakes: Bohemian king Ottokar I

Owen

(Irish) born to nobility; young warrior. (Welsh) a form of Evan.

Image: You can't describe Owen without using a lot of superlatives. People think of Owen as a very intelligent, very nice, and very entertaining guy. In addition, he most likely has very blond hair and a very round physique. People disagree whether he's a workaholic or a couch potato, but he's still a very popular fellow.

Famous Namesakes: Actor Owen Wilson; actor Clive Owen; hockey player Owen Nolan; Welsh hero Owen Glendower

Oz

(Hebrew) a short form of Osborn, Oswald.

Image: Thanks to L. Frank Baum's books and the beloved film about the Wizard of Oz, this name's image is a bit strange and magical. People think Oz is a one-of-a-kind man who's quirky, creative, and funky. He's said to be fun-loving, smart, and confident, but he also seems to have a kind, shy side. As for his looks, people picture him as a pale redhead.

Famous Namesakes: Director Frank Oz; book and movie character Wizard of Oz

Pablo

(Spanish) a form of Paul.

Image: Pablo Picasso is one of the most influential artists of all time, so it's natural he figures into the image for this name. People think Pablo is a Latino artist who's a creative free spirit. He's said to be jaunty but kindhearted.

Famous Namesakes: Artist Pablo Picasso; drug lord Pablo Escobar; writer Pablo Neruda; baseball player Pablo Ozuna; actor Pablo Montero

Paddy

(Irish) a familiar form of Padraic, Patrick.

Image: Paddy is an easygoing guy, and he finds it easy to go along with what others say. People see him as a good-natured and mild-mannered chap who's more of a follower than a leader. He most likely follows laws to the letter. Perhaps thinking of Paddington Bear, people also imagine Paddy is cuddly and soft, like a big teddy bear.

Famous Namesakes: Writer Paddy Chayefsky; musician Paddy Moloney

Palmer

(English) palm-bearing pilgrim.

Image: Palmer is an elitist who looks and acts the part. People say Palmer is a snobby, smarmy, and materialistic yuppie, but, boy, is he well dressed. Under the designer clothes, however, he's described as wimpy and self-conscious with a tall, slim frame.

Famous Namesakes: Golfer Arnold Palmer; football player Carson Palmer; character David Palmer (*24*)

Paolo

(Italian) a form of Paul.

Image: Paolo may be a ladies' man, but he's always a gentleman. Paolo is pictured as a sexy Italian smooth talker. People believe he has a sweet and gentle demeanor and an old-fashioned romantic appeal.

Famous Namesakes: Artist Paolo Veronese

Park

(Chinese) cypress tree. (English) a short form of Parker.

Image: It's a good thing Park will inherit a load of money, because he probably can't make it on his own. He's imagined as a wealthy heir who's spoiled, snobby, and self-centered. Lean and perfectly handsome, Park seems to be an introvert, thanks to his sheltered life. He's also said to be lazy and impatient, thanks to being waited on hand and foot.

Famous Namesakes: Baseball player Chan-ho Park

Parker

(English) park keeper.

Image: Parker seems to have an exaggerated sense of self-worth. People imagine Parker as a rich, flaxen-haired WASP who's smart, dry humored, and sociable. But at times, his spoiled nature can make him arrogant, snobbish, jaded, and lazy.

Famous Namesakes: Character Parker Lewis (*Parker Lewis Can't Lose*); game makers Parker Brothers; actor Parker Stevenson; character Peter Parker (*Spider-Man*)

Pascale

(French) born on Easter or Passover.

Image: Artists are often difficult to understand, and Pascale is a good example. People say he's a talented artist who's either loud and talkative or solemn and quiet. Whichever the case, he may be a tad weird.

Famous Namesakes: Thinker Blaise Pascal

Pat

(Native American) fish. (English) a short form of Patrick.

Image: Pat is a nice enough guy, but he's pretty boring. The name Pat evokes the image of a sincere and reliable fellow with a plump physique. People say he's typically friendly, but when you get down to it, he's a dull and oafish computer nerd.

Famous Namesakes: Singer Pat Boone; actor Pat Morita; politician Pat Buchanan; sportscaster Pat Summerall; game show host Pat Sajak

Patrick

(Latin) nobleman.

Image: Either Patrick is a sparkling personality, or he's as dull as they come. Most people think Patrick is a merry, flirty, and bright guy who's full of laughter. Yet some think of him as snobbish, quiet, and dull. Physically, he's thought to be athletic and tall.

Famous Namesakes: Actor Patrick Stewart; saint Patrick; basketball player Patrick Ewing; actor Patrick Swayze; hockey player Patrick Roy

Paul

(Latin) small.

Image: Sweet, smart, and funny—Paul is a terrific guy. He's described as kind, compassionate, dependable, and humble. People also think he's highly intelligent and goofy with his practical jokes.

Famous Namesakes: Biblical figure Paul; singer Paul McCartney; actor Paul Newman; singer Paul Simon; patriot Paul Revere

Payton

(English) a form of Patton.

Image: Peyton Manning is one of the hardest-working players in the NFL; although the spelling is different, this name's image reflects that drive. Payton gives the impression of a football player who's resourceful, driven, and businesslike. People also imagine he's outgoing and polite.

Famous Namesakes: Football player Walter Payton; football player Peyton Manning

Pedro

(Spanish) a form of Peter.

Image: Pedro is a friendly fellow—especially with the ladies. He's described as a short Latino who's entertaining, generous, and kind. People imagine he's a flirt, and a few even say he's a cheating womanizer.

Famous Namesakes: Director Pedro Almodóvar; character Pedro Sanchez (*Napoleon Dynamite*); baseball player Pedro Martínez

Percy

(French) a familiar form of Percival.

Image: Percy is a blend of qualities, and they're all bad. People think Percy is snobby, fussy, bossy, spoiled, wimpy, whiny, and dorky. People also don't have good vibes about his looks, saying he's either a frail waif or a pudge.

Famous Namesakes: Poet Percy Bysshe Shelley; singer Percy Sledge

Perry

(English) a familiar form of Peregrine, Peter.

Image: One portrait shows Perry as a snob, but his other snapshots are more positive. Most people think Perry is an articulate but pretentious chap who's too intense. In addition, others say he's a sports nut; a whimsical joker; an introverted wallflower; or even an average, unassuming guy. Whichever the case may be, he's most likely lanky with dark hair and glasses.

Famous Namesakes: Singer Perry Como; football player William "The Refrigerator" Perry; book and TV character Perry Mason; designer Perry Ellis; actor Matthew Perry

Pete

(English) a short form of Peter.

Image: Popular opinion suggests Pete is a nerd, but there are grounds for other views, too. Most people think Pete is a scrawny, nerdy, and obnoxious teacher's pet. Others see him as outgoing and loyal to family and friends. Still others believe he's aloof and strongly determined.

Famous Namesakes: Baseball player Pete Rose; musician Pete Townshend

 **★ Star Kids**

Phinnaeus Walter

Phinnaeus Walter clings to the comforts of academia. People say this history professor is strong-willed, determined, and dignified within his field. They also say he's completely and utterly inept in social situations. Although he's a recluse, he probably never leaves the house without a stuffy bowtie and an old-fashioned hat. All in all, it's not exactly the lifestyle anyone expects Phinnaeus Walter, son of actress Julia Roberts and cinematographer Danny Moder, will lead when he's older.

Peter

(Greek, Latin) small rock.

Image: Is Peter dry or dashing? People describe him as one or the other. Some say he's a quiet, bookish dud, but just as many others say he's a romantic sophisticate. Either way, he's most likely gentle, caring, and loyal.

Famous Namesakes: Biblical figure Peter; news anchor Peter Jennings; book and movie character Peter Pan; character Peter Parker (*Spider-Man*); actor Peter O'Toole

Philip

(Greek) lover of horses.

Image: Philip may be a rude snob, but his determination can't be ignored. He's pictured as a rude, egomaniacal, and spoiled aristocrat. People also admit he's intelligent and focused as well as handsome.

Famous Namesakes: Biblical figure Philip; British prince Philip; football player Philip Rivers

★ Star Kids

Pilot Inspektor

Do you expect someone named Pilot Inspektor to be normal? Many people sense he's an unsociable and even unapproachable recluse. Others say he's a friendly but goofy guy who barely has enough motivation to hold down a fast-food job. He's probably tall, unshaven, and messy-haired. In a way, this image sounds a bit like that of Earl Hickey, the TV character played by Jason Lee—who happens to be Pilot Inspecktor's dad.

★ Star Kids

Pirate Howsmon

Arr! A salty swashbuckler may Pirate Howsmon be. People imagine he's a devilish and rebellious pirate who loves to gamble and con landlubbers when he comes to shore. He's most likely an old and weathered seadog with black eyes and a gravelly voice. In truth, Pirate Howsmon, son of Korn frontman Jonathan Davis and former adult-film star Devon Davis, is more likely to grow up on a tour bus than on a pirate ship.

Phineas

(English) a form of Pinchas.

Image: Phineas's skin is as pale as it is thin. He's thought to be quite intelligent and thoughtful, but perhaps he's too sensitive for most people's tastes. Pasty and skinny, it's no wonder he's pictured as a quiet loner.

Famous Namesakes: Greek mythological figure Phineas; showman Phineas Taylor "P. T." Barnum; star kid Phinnaeus Moder

Pierce

(English) a form of Peter.

Image: It's hard to tell what Pierce loves most—his money or himself. People say he's a snob who flaunts his money and is quite full of himself. Most imagine he looks like actor Pierce Brosnan: tall, dark, handsome, and well groomed. A few disagree with the snob image, believing he's sweet, charming, and romantic instead.

Famous Namesakes: President Franklin Pierce; actor Pierce Brosnan; character "Hawkeye" Pierce (*M*A*S*H*); actor David Hyde Pierce

Pierre

(French) a form of Peter.

Image: Despite all his sophistication, Pierre doesn't know how to treat people equally. He's thought of as a French sophisticate who's worldly and elegant. The drawback is, he seems to be personable and charming with his friends but snobbish and self-centered with others.

Famous Namesakes: Canadian prime minister Pierre Trudeau; designer Pierre Cardin; baseball player Juan Pierre

Pin

(Vietnamese) faithful boy.

Image: People aren't sure how Pin will handle social situations. Some say he's timid, nervous, and withdrawn; others see him as lighthearted, easygoing, and strong. Either way, he's most likely a talented writer with a sharp mind. People describe him as a frail, skinny fellow who's pretty in an almost feminine way.

Famous Namesakes: None

Poni

(Scottish) a form of Pony.

Image: Can you take someone named Poni seriously? He's seen as a strange goofball who loves silly jokes. People suspect he's high strung and maybe even wild because he has a difficult time sitting still.

Famous Namesakes: None

Porter

(Latin) gatekeeper.

Image: Porter is a good pal, despite the fact that he's a little dull. Most people see Porter as an accommodating and loyal friend. He seems to be a smart thinker as well as a smart dresser, but sometimes he can be conventional and kind of boring.

Famous Namesakes: Singer Porter Wagoner; character Porter (*Payback*); composer Cole Porter

Preston

(English) priest's estate.

Image: Preston is both nerdy and snobby. He seems to be a geek who's as pretentious and snooty as he is studious. To make matters worse, people also consider him to be an uptight overachiever.

Famous Namesakes: Character Preston Burke (*Grey's Anatomy*); singer Billy Preston

Prince

(Latin) chief; prince.

Image: Prince is an unforgettable rock icon, so of course his image lends itself to this name's image. People imagine Prince is a raunchy and arrogant singer whose sexually explicit manner seems sleazy and perverted to some. He's also described as a tiny guy with a short, frail frame.

Famous Namesakes: Singer Prince; star kid Prince Michael Joseph Jackson

 **Star Kids**

Prince Michael Joseph

Prince Michael Joseph is hard to read and even harder to trust. He's imagined as a withdrawn and reserved man with shifty eyes. People suspect he's a compulsive liar, and they certainly believe he's weird. As for his appearance, he's likely a thin, short, and light-skinned African American. All in all, it's easy to see how Michael Jackson, the "King of Pop" and father of Prince Michael Joseph, shaped this name's dubious image.

Pryor

(Latin) head of the monastery; prior.

Image: If it weren't for his arrogance, Pryor would have no personality at all. This name creates an image of a stuffy, pompous preppy. He's said to be smart and rudely opinionated, but for the most part, people find this lanky bloke to be dreadfully dull.

Famous Namesakes: Comedian Richard Pryor; baseball player Mark Prior

Purdy

(Hindi) recluse.

Image: For being a country boy, Purdy sure is wound tightly. People believe this hillbilly is anal-retentive, prudish, and overly sensitive. His uneasy state makes him seem bratty to other folks. It's unclear whether Purdy is dumb or smart, but people agree he's a looker with dark hair and clear skin.

Famous Namesakes: None

Quentin

(Latin) fifth. (English) queen's town.

Image: Quentin doesn't just think outside the box—he lives outside it. People think Quentin's a lanky academic with quirky creativity and overachieving discipline. He seems to be outgoing, but he can be loud, overwhelming, and goofy at times.

Famous Namesakes: Director Quentin Tarantino; author Quentin Crisp; football player Quentin Jammer

Quincy

(French) fifth son's estate.

Image: John Quincy Adams was the sixth American president, but he's the first person who comes to mind when people hear the name Quincy. People say Quincy is a dedicated and high-achieving man who's educated, prudent, and patriotic. He's also thought to be religious and proper.

Famous Namesakes: President John Quincy Adams; music producer Quincy Jones; character Dr. Quincy (*Quincy, M.E.*); football player Quincy Morgan

Quinlan

(Irish) strong; well shaped.

Image: Quinlan feels the world around him is just too fast. People picture him as a tiny man with dark features and a gentle, calm manner. At times, he's so calm, he seems to move slowly. Quinlan is most likely kind, and some people imagine he's earthy and arty as well.

Famous Namesakes: Baseball player Robb Quinlan; star kid Quinlin Stiller

Quinn

(Irish) a short form of Quincy, Quinlan, Quinten.

Image: Quinn has a lovely demeanor. People imagine he's well mannered, sweet, and sincere. A handsome Irishman, he's known to be a thoughtful and loyal fellow.

Famous Namesakes: Basketball coach Quin Snyder; actor Aidan Quinn; actor Anthony Quin

Quintin

(Latin) a form of Quentin.

Image: Many years later, Quintin still loves the science kit he received for his tenth birthday. Most people call Quintin a nerdy science guy who's shy, wimpy, and boyish. Others see him as an aggressive and stern brooder. Either way, he's tall and pasty with glasses.

Famous Namesakes: Football player Quintin Mikell

Raheem

(Punjabi) compassionate God.

Image: Raheem is a bold, take-charge man. Many people find him to be an ambitious, daring, and confident leader. A few, however, sense he may be a deceptive troublemaker or untrustworthy in some way. Nevertheless, he's likely a gifted scholar and perhaps even an athlete. Raheem is often depicted as African or Middle Eastern with strong muscles.

Famous Namesakes: Character Radio Raheem (*Do the Right Thing*)

Ralph

(English) wolf counselor.

Image: Most people laugh *with* Ralph, but a few laugh *at* him. People think Ralph is a sweet but goofy nerd who's unintentionally funny and a little on the dumb side. Overall, he's said to be friendly and kind, but he does have a tendency to be bullied.

Famous Namesakes: Activist Ralph Nader; designer Ralph Lauren; character Ralph Wiggum (*The Simpsons*); poet Ralph Waldo Emerson

Ramon

(Spanish) a form of Raymond.

Image: Ramon is always energized, especially when women are around. Ramon is described as a happy and excited ladies' man with a Latin heritage and a big smile. People say he has a good sense of humor and a suave, masculine demeanor.

Famous Namesakes: Baseball player Ramon Hernandez

Randolph

(English) shield wolf.

Image: What could Randolph possibly complain about? He reminds people of an arrogant and spoiled fellow from a well-off family. He seems to be smart and studious, but he annoys everyone with his constant complaining and cynicism.

Famous Namesakes: Actor Randolph Scott; publisher William Randolph Hearst

Randy

(English) a familiar form of Rand, Randall, Randolph.

Image: You'll find Randy livin' it up at the honky-tonk every Saturday night. People imagine he likes to get loud and crazy in a fun, good-natured way. People picture him as a gangly country boy who's never without a pack of smokes and a tin of chew.

Famous Namesakes: TV personality Randy Jackson; actor Randy Quaid; singer Randy Travis; baseball player Randy Johnson; football player Randy Moss

Ranger

(French) forest keeper.

Image: This name evokes the image of a ranch on the open range—and the rugged folks who live there. Ranger is imagined as an adventurous, outdoorsy man who works with horses and other animals. Some say he's loud and outspoken, but others sense he's serious and not much for talking at all. To complete the image, people picture him as ruggedly handsome in a cowboy hat and chaps.

Famous Namesakes: None

Raphael

(Hebrew) God has healed.

Image: Raphael is one of the great Italian masters of art, and part of this name's image reflects his creative genius. People picture Raphael as a handsome Italian painter who's intelligent and unique. Some say he's strong and brave, but others say he's wimpy and effeminate.

Famous Namesakes: Artist Raphael Santi; archangel Raphael; baseball player Rafael Palmeiro

Rashad

(Arabic) wise counselor.

Image: No one sees eye to eye about Rashad. To some, he comes across as an intelligent and visionary man who's an eloquent speaker. But to others, he's shy and reserved, with just a few close friends. People also disagree about his profession, saying he's either a computer tech or a sports star. Lastly, some say he's African American, but others believe he's Middle Eastern.

Famous Namesakes: Football player Ahmad Rashad; basketball player Rashad McCants

Raul

(French) a form of Ralph.

Image: Raul would much rather think of others than himself. People say he's a dark Latino man who's handsome, deep, and not a bit conceited. Helpful and hardworking, he's known to greet everyone with a smile.

Famous Namesakes: Actor Raúl Juliá; Cuban political figure Raúl Castro; baseball player Raúl Ibáñez

Ray

(French) kingly, royal. (English) a short form of Rayburn, Raymond.

Image: Come take a test drive with Ray—*he wants to see you go home in that new car today!* People think Ray is a used-car salesman with a pretty persuasive sales pitch. He seems to be gregarious, funny, and all smiles with some customers, but sometimes his sales tactics are rude and mean spirited.

Famous Namesakes: Actor Ray Romano; singer Ray Charles; boxers Sugar Ray Leonard and Sugar Ray Robinson; businessman Ray Kroc; author Ray Bradbury

Boys

Raymond

(English) mighty; wise protector.

Image: Raymond runs his mouth a lot, but most folks don't mind. People think of Raymond as a high-strung, loud-mouthed goof. Most say he's nice, generous, and loyal under all that talk, but some can't help but find him annoying.

Famous Namesakes: Actor Raymond Burr; sitcom *Everybody Loves Raymond*; author Raymond Chandler; character Raymond Babbitt (*Rain Man*)

Reese

(Welsh) a form of Reece.

Image: Reese can chase the clouds away. He's believed to be a fun-loving guy who's nice and always happy. People say he has blond hair to match his sunny disposition.

Famous Namesakes: Character Reese Wilkerson (*Malcolm in the Middle*); baseball player Pee Wee Reese

Reggie

(English) a familiar form of Reginald.

Image: This name has a sporty image, thanks to great athletes like Reggie Jackson. Reggie is said to be a kind and loving African American athlete who works hard and has a stable life.

Famous Namesakes: Baseball player Reggie Jackson; basketball player Reggie Miller; football player Reggie Bush

Reginald

(English) king's advisor.

Image: Reginald takes his formal, high-class lifestyle too far. He's imagined as an upper-crust Brit who's sophisticated and intelligent but also stuffy, snobby, and spoiled. He's physically described as tall, thin, and pale.

Famous Namesakes: Truck driver Reginald Denny

Regis

(Latin) regal.

Image: Talk show host Regis Philbin is on everyone's TV and on everyone's mind for this name's image. People see Regis as a loud gabber who's good-natured and outgoing. He's also pictured as old and short.

Famous Namesakes: TV personality Regis Philbin

Rei

(Japanese) rule, law.

Image: Rei has phases during which he doesn't feel or act like himself. Most of the time, Rei is said to be a nice, thoughtful African American man with a big smile. Sometimes, however, he can be moody and perplexing. When he's not in one of his moods, people describe him as a soft-spoken intellectual.

Famous Namesakes: None

Reid

(English) redhead.

Image: Reid is well heeled and well groomed. He's believed to be a preppy, professional WASP. His private education seems to have groomed him to be knowledgeable, articulate, and confident in his career as a lawyer, doctor, or executive. Outside of work, this tall blond is known to enjoy playing tennis and competing in triathlons.

Famous Namesakes: Senator Harry Reid; football coach Andy Reid; actor Tim Reid

Reilly

(Irish) a form of Riley.

Image: People aren't sure if Reilly is a name for a girl or a boy, and they also aren't sure what image this name inspires. Most people imagine Reilly as a polite and sensitive person with a kind face. Others say Reilly is smart, outgoing, and popular—a regular boy or girl next door. Still others picture a cocky cowboy or cowgirl out on the rodeo circuit. In any case, Reilly is most likely tall, skinny, and attractive.

Famous Namesakes: Actor Charles Nelson Reilly; writer Rick Reilly; actor John C. Reilly

Rex

(Latin) king.

Image: Naughty or nice, Rex works a lot. Some say Rex is rude, hot tempered, and uptight. Others say he's talkative, sweet, and charming. Either way, he's most likely a successful workaholic.

Famous Namesakes: Actor Rex Harrison; critic Rex Reed; football player Rex Grossman

Reynard

(French) wise; bold, courageous.

Image: Reynard is the type of guy who has no desire or ability to live on his own. People suspect he's never been married and still lives with his mother. Not surprisingly, he's said to be a withdrawn bookworm who's quite learned but unable to do much for himself except pour a bowl of cereal. Unattractive, pimply, and scrawny, he seems to need his mom at all times.

Famous Namesakes: Fable character Reynard the Fox

Reynold

(English) king's advisor.

Image: You'll find Reynold either on a firing range or in his parents' basement. People agree Reynold is cold and uptight. But they aren't sure if he's a bold and manly soldier or a nerdy and quiet homebody.

Famous Namesakes: Actor Burt Reynolds; actor Ryan Reynolds

Rhett

(Welsh) a form of Rhys.

Image: Who can forget *Gone with the Wind*'s Rhett Butler—one of the best-loved characters of all time? Rhett is pictured as a charming and kind man who's handsome, romantic, and not afraid to take risks. He may come across as a sheltered and elitist snob, but others describe him as extravagant.

Famous Namesakes: Character Rhett Bulter (*Gone with the Wind*); singer Rhett Akins; singer Rhett Miller

Rhys

(Welsh) a form of Reece.

Image: However you slice it, Rhys is an off-beat guy. He's said to be one of the following: a dorky computer nerd, a wealthy and weird Welshman, or an antisocial loner who's often picked on by bullies. People picture him as slim, unattractive, and sickly.

Famous Namesakes: Writer Rhys Davies; actor Jonathan Rhys-Meyers; actor John Rhys-Davies

Ricardo

(Portuguese, Spanish) a form of Richard.

Image: Ricardo has a cool style everyone loves. Whether he's Cuban, Spanish, or Italian, he's imagined to be suave, cool, and popular. People say he's good-looking and always a gentleman.

Famous Namesakes: Actor Ricardo Montalbán; character Ricky Ricardo (*I Love Lucy*)

Richard

(English) a form of Richart.

Image: It's been years since Watergate, but people still associate this name with former president Richard Nixon. They say Richard is a man with bad judgment and a tendency to lie. He's a no-nonsense authoritarian and an arrogant conservative.

Famous Namesakes: President Richard Nixon; king Richard the Lionheart; actor Richard Gere; racecar driver Richard Petty; singer Little Richard

Rick

(German, English) a short form of Cedric, Frederick, Richard.

Image: Rick is a positive guy—but he tries not to be *too* positive. Rick is described as a smart, friendly, and talented man. Some call him happy and others call him cautiously optimistic. On the downside, he may be a bit clingy.

Famous Namesakes: Singer Rick James; actor Rick Schroder; singer Rick Springfield

Boys

Ricky

(English) a familiar form of Richard, Rick.

Image: When others fall, Ricky reaches out and lifts them up. People say Ricky is a good-natured, smiling, and deeply empathetic man. He's thought to be a social worker or someone who gives willingly and lovingly to others.

Famous Namesakes: Singer Ricky Martin; character Ricky Ricardo (*I Love Lucy*); football player Ricky Williams; racecar driver Ricky Rudd; actor Ricky Gervais

Rico

(Italian) a short form of Enrico. (Spanish) a familiar form of Richard.

Image: Latin rapper Gerardo had a hit with "Rico Suave" in the early '90s, and this name's image has that same steamy swagger. Rico is thought of as a self-confident and flirtatious slickster, but many say he's arrogant, promiscuous, and even chauvinistic. With dark good looks and a Latin or Italian heritage, Rico is truly suave.

Famous Namesakes: Song "Rico Suave"; character Uncle Rico (*Napoleon Dynamite*)

Riley

(Irish) valiant.

Image: There's a thin line between Riley's confidence and his self-centeredness. He's thought to be a carefree, happy, and rambunctious free spirit. But beneath Riley's playful exterior, people believe he's a competitive, annoying, and demanding attention-hog. He's most likely quite attractive and muscular, which only gains him more attention.

Famous Namesakes: Character Chester A. Riley (*The Life of Riley*)

Ringo

(Japanese) apple. (English) a familiar form of Ring.

Image: With such a ubiquitous namesake as former Beatle Ringo Starr, it's surprising to see other images for this name. Naturally, many think Ringo is fun-loving and musically inclined with a big nose and weird teeth. But just as many others describe him as mean, hateful, and mysterious, perhaps a connection to The Ring series of horror films.

Famous Namesakes: Singer Ringo Starr

Robbie

(English) a familiar form of Robert.

Image: Robbie is well rounded in every way. People describe him as a Renaissance man who's observant and intelligent enough to excel in everything. He's also imagined to be generous, kindhearted, and fun-loving. Physically, people see him as tall, athletic, and handsome.

Famous Namesakes: Singer Robbie Williams; stuntman Robbie Knievel; singer Robbie Robertson; racecar driver Robbie Gordon; character Robbie Hart (*The Wedding Singer*)

Robert

(English) famous brilliance.

Image: Robert is a golden boy. People say he's kind, conscientious, and popular as well as successful, attractive, and smart. In addition, he's thought to have an easygoing demeanor and a talent for sports.

Famous Namesakes: Actor Robert Redford; actor Robert De Niro; singer Robert Plant; general Robert E. Lee

Roberto

(Italian, Portuguese, Spanish) a form of Robert.

Image: Roberto has a strong heart. People think of him as a dark-featured man who's loyal, sweet, and romantic. Those with a bleaker view say he's poor and illiterate, but confident and not afraid to challenge authority.

Famous Namesakes: Director Roberto Benigni; designer Roberto Cavalli; baseball player Roberto Clemente; boxer Roberto Durán

 **Star Kids**

Rocco John

Don't be messin' with Rocco John, *capice*? He's said to be a tough guy who's always looking for a fight. Maybe he's a boxer, maybe he's a Mafioso, and maybe he's both. In any case, he's described as a bulky Italian with handsome dark features. Megastar Madonna and director Guy Ritchie's son is named Rocco John, but the only fights he may pick are with the paparazzi who watch his every move.

Robin

(English) a short form of Robert.

Image: Most people think Robin is a good person, but others feel quite differently. He's primarily described as a patient, loving, and trustworthy guy. Some people, however, see him as ugly, rude, and mean—not a good person at all.

Famous Namesakes: Legendary character Robin Hood; actor Robin Williams; singer Robin Gibb

Rocco

(Italian) rock.

Image: Rocco fits the stereotypical image of a Mafioso. People believe he's violent, crude, street-smart, and fierce. They also feel he's not very intelligent. Completing the image, he's pictured as a big and hairy Italian.

Famous Namesakes: Actor Alex Rocco; chef Rocco DiSpirito; star kid Rocco Ritchie

Rock

(English) a short form of Rockwell.

Image: *Dumb as a rock. Strong as a rock.* How can you argue with that? Rock is pictured as a big, muscular wrestler who's tough, bullish, and not too smart. Some say he's generous and sweet under it all, but others say he's self-absorbed.

Famous Namesakes: Actor and wrestler Dwayne "The Rock" Johnson; actor Rock Hudson; comedian Chris Rock; singer Kid Rock

Rocky

(American) a familiar form of Rocco, Rock.

Image: When people hear the name Rocky, they immediately think of a boxer, be it Rocky Balboa or Rocky Marciano. They describe him as macho, stubborn, cocky, and powerful. People also say Rocky is strong and stocky with dark hair and an attractive face.

Famous Namesakes: Movie character Rocky Balboa; boxer Rocky Marciano; character Rocky the Flying Squirrel (*The Rocky and Bullwinkle Show*)

Rodney

(English) island clearing.

Image: Rodney is a nice fellow, but a lot of folks still can't stand him. People say he's a kind and friendly guy who's outgoing to the point of being rowdy and hyper. Some however, find his antics obnoxious, especially considering he's also sloppy, smelly, and rotund.

Famous Namesakes: Comedian Rodney Dangerfield; taxi driver Rodney King; football player Rodney Peete

Rodrigo

(Italian, Spanish) a form of Roderick.

Image: Rodrigo is overwhelmingly pictured as a Latino who's lively, carefree, and always ready to party. Not surprisingly, he's also imagined to be a charming, flirty ladies' man with a clever wit and sexy smile. In addition, some people find him to be athletic.

Famous Namesakes: Baseball player Rodrigo López; actor Rodrigo Santoro

Roger

(German) famous spearman.

Image: Throughout the years, Roger is quiet but kind. People think he's an older fellow with a few wrinkles, a receding hairline, and a shy demeanor. He might be a farmer, and he's as caring as he is dependable.

Famous Namesakes: Critic Roger Ebert; tennis player Roger Federer; baseball player Roger Clemens; runner Roger Bannister

Roland

(German) famous throughout the land.

Image: Roland's knowledge is as impressive as his girth. He's pictured as a respectful and caring man with a big belly and Nordic looks. People believe this intellectual is well read and well traveled.

Famous Namesakes: Legendary character Roland

Rolando

(Portuguese, Spanish) a form of Roland.

Image: Rolando is a wild and crazy guy. People think he's a flashy partier with a loud voice and even louder clothes. He's also said to be a hysterical cutup. Under all the fun, though, people believe this heartthrob is a friendly, caring soul.

Famous Namesakes: Singer Rolando Villazón

Rollo

(English) a familiar form of Roland.

Image: Rollo is a barrel of fun. People say he's a bawdy but likable joker who loves to make others as jolly as he is. He also loves eating and drinking, making him a roly-poly Rollo.

Famous Namesakes: Viking ruler Rollo of Normandy

Roman

(Latin) from Rome, Italy. (Gypsy) gypsy; wanderer.

Image: Roman is not someone to trifle with. He's described as a tall and muscular warrior. He's also a vengeful, strict, and powerful leader.

Famous Namesakes: Director Roman Polanski; actor Roman Coppola; character Roman Brady (*Days of Our Lives*)

Ron

(Hebrew) a short form of Aaron, Ronald.

Image: Ron is a sunny guy. He reminds people of a witty and upbeat people pleaser. He's imagined to be sincere and generous, but sometimes he can be lazy when it comes to his own life.

Famous Namesakes: Actor and director Ron Howard; radio personality Ron Reagan; basketball player Ron Artest; comedian Ron White

Ronald

(Scottish) a form of Reginald. (English) a form of Reynold.

Image: Ronald is strong in character, mind, and body. He's said to be self-sufficient, decisive, and determined. Physically, he's portrayed as chiseled with an athletic build. People also believe he's intelligent, pleasant, and a loyal friend.

Famous Namesakes: President Ronald Reagan; mascot Ronald McDonald

Ronnie

(Scottish) a familiar form of Ronald.

Image: You wouldn't think a hick could be a snob, but somehow Ronnie is. People think he's a pudgy country boy who's obnoxious, slow, and snobby after being spoiled most of his life. Some say he can be a goofball, but others just find him annoying.

Famous Namesakes: Singer Ronnie Van Zant; football player Ronnie Lott; football player Ronnie Brown; singer Ronnie James Dio

Roosevelt

(Dutch) rose field.

Image: People associate the name Roosevelt with a meld of former presidents Theodore and Franklin D. Roosevelt. They describe Roosevelt as a successful and powerful leader who's charismatic, intelligent, and handsome. He most likely comes from old money.

Famous Namesakes: Presidents Theodore Roosevelt and Franklin Roosevelt; character Roosevelt Franklin (*Sesame Street*); football player Roosevelt Brown

Roscoe

(Scandinavian) deer forest.

Image: Roscoe likes rowdy fun. Roscoe is pictured as a tough guy who's strong-willed and rugged. He's probably not the sharpest tool in the shed, but he likes to have a good time. People imagine him with dark hair and a stocky, muscular build.

Famous Namesakes: Character Roscoe P. Coltrane (*The Dukes of Hazzard*)

Ross

(Latin) rose. (Scottish) peninsula. (French) red.

Image: Ross Gellar is one of those memorable *Friends*. This name makes people think of a geeky and sensible guy who's friendly and funny in a goofy way. With dark hair and a cute smile, Ross seems to be quirky but cool.

Famous Namesakes: Politician Ross Perot; character Ross Geller (*Friends*); character Dr. Doug Ross (*ER*)

Roy

(French) king. A short form of Royal, Royce.

Image: Like Roy Rogers, this name has a Western ruggedness. Roy reminds people of a caring, devoted, and lanky cowboy. He most likely works with his hands and doesn't say a lot.

Famous Namesakes: Cowboy Roy Rogers; singer Roy Orbison; magician Roy Horn; baseball player Roy Campanella

Royce

(English) son of Roy.

Image: Royce has two contrasting images. People agree Royce is book smart, but their views bisect from there. He could be a popular and friendly leader with a strong focus, or an antisocial and uppity snob with few friends.

Famous Namesakes: Businessman Henry Royce

Ruben

(Hebrew) a form of Reuben.

Image: *American Idol* winner Ruben Studdard is nicknamed the "Velvet Teddy Bear," and this image bears his soulful style. People imagine Ruben as a heavyset African American who's friendly, caring, and generous. Of course, he's also known to be a fantastic singer.

Famous Namesakes: Singer Ruben Studdard; basketball player Ruben Patterson

Rudolph

(German) famous wolf.

Image: There are two very different pictures of Rudolph: He's thought to be a suave and stately ladies' man or an annoying and dweeby know-it-all. People say he could be British or Italian.

Famous Namesakes: Actor Rudolph Valentino; character Rudolph the Red-Nosed Reindeer

Rudy

(English) a familiar form of Rudolph.

Image: Rudy is dedicated to his family, which sometimes means the Mafia. Many people think of Rudy as a hardworking and helpful family man, leader, and role model. Others think of him as a shifty mobster.

Famous Namesakes: Singer Rudy Vallee; inspirational figure Daniel "Rudy" Ruettiger; mayor Rudy Giuliani

Rufus

(Latin) redhead.

Image: Rufus is an outcast for a reason. People picture Rufus as a loner and introvert with a dull personality and a dull wit, though some argue he's intelligent. He may be Southern or rural.

Famous Namesakes: Singer Rufus Wainwright

Rush

(French) redhead. (English) a short form of Russell.

Image: Left or right, right or wrong—most people think of radio show host Rush Limbaugh when they hear this name. They describe Rush as a blowhard who's very outspoken, pushy, and cynical. Those not familiar with talk radio take a literal approach, saying he's energetic, swift, and always in a rush.

Famous Namesakes: Radio personality Rush Limbaugh; actor Geoffrey Rush

Ruskin

(French) redhead.

Image: "Rough" is the general theme of this name's image. People say Ruskin is a rough and tough, rude and crude country boy with dirty, ruddy skin. He most likely vents his aggression through brutal pickup sports, where he's been known to growl at his opponents.

Famous Namesakes: Critic John Ruskin

Russell

(French) redhead; fox colored.

Image: Russell sure is full of himself. He's pictured as a rude jerk who's competitive, cocky, and bossy. People can't decide if he's skinny or burly, but he's most likely tall.

Famous Namesakes: Actor Russell Crowe; basketball player Bill Russell; music mogul Russell Simons; actor Kurt Russell

Rusty

(French) a familiar form of Russell.

Image: These two images of Rusty reflect very different cultures. Some people say Rusty is a laid-back and cool surfer who loves to joke around. Others believe he's a blue-collar worker who didn't do well in school and now has a hard time providing for his family. In either case, people picture Rusty with red hair and freckles.

Famous Namesakes: Racecar driver Rusty Wallace

Ryan

(Irish) little king.

Image: Ryan is either totally ordinary or absolutely extraordinary. Most people say he's an average guy who's funny, caring, and cute, but somewhat bland. In contrast, others think he's a gifted athlete and label him a sports star.

Famous Namesakes: Actor Ryan O'Neal; TV personality Ryan Seacrest; character Jack Ryan (*The Hunt for Red October*); actor Ryan Phillippe

Saburo

(Japanese) third-born son.

Image: Saburo is a good person with a bad temper. He seems to be an outspoken and opinionated Latino whose anger sometimes gets in the way of his nicer qualities. When he's not so wound up, people say he's friendly, kind, and well meaning. Strong and athletic, he may be a runner or a bodybuilder.

Famous Namesakes: Japanese pilot Saburo Sakai

Sadler

(English) saddle maker.

Image: Sometimes word association shapes an image; for example, with the name Sadler and the word *saddle*. People describe Sadler as a Western cowboy who's tall and muscular. Although he mostly tends to keep to himself, he's known to be a smart, easygoing, and even goofy guy.

Famous Namesakes: Racecar driver Elliott Sadler

Salvador

(Spanish) savior.

Image: Like many powerful men, Salvador is a complex character. He's seen as a dark-featured Spanish man with great wealth and power. Some describe him as confident and vibrant, but others say he's sly and sleazy.

Famous Namesakes: Artist Salvador Dalí

Sam

(Hebrew) a short form of Samuel.

Image: Sam lives a good, clean life. People think he's a happy and likable guy who's open-minded and full of helpful advice. He seems to be athletic, religious, wise, and hardworking.

Famous Namesakes: Actor Sam Elliot; playwright Sam Shepard; patriotic figure Uncle Sam; character Samwise "Sam" Gamgee (*The Lord of the Rings*)

Sammy

(Hebrew) a familiar form of Samuel.

Image: Sammy is hilarious and quirky, but he's no Einstein. People think he's a silly goofball who's likable and confident, but a little brainless. He's pictured as short, pale, and boyish.

Famous Namesakes: Entertainer Sammy Davis, Jr.; baseball player Sammy Sosa; singer Sammy Hagar; singer Sammy Kershaw

Samson

(Hebrew) like the sun.

Image: Like the mighty Samson from the Bible, this Samson is a complicated figure. First and foremost, people picture him as a muscular man with broad shoulders. From there, some say he's rough, crude, and dumb, but others say he's loyal, honest, and goodhearted.

Famous Namesakes: Biblical figure Samson

Samuel

(Hebrew) heard God; asked of God.

Image: Samuel is an upstanding gent who likes to unwind at the club. He's described as a respectful and thoughtful upper-class man. He most likely enjoys cigars and belongs to a stodgy gentlemen's club, but he's a healthy, virile fellow.

Famous Namesakes: Biblical figure Samuel; patriot Samuel Adams; author Samuel Clemmons, also known as Mark Twain; actor Samuel L. Jackson

Santiago

(Spanish) a form of James.

Image: On the dance floor or with women, Santiago has the right rhythm. He's imagined as a Latino who loves dancing, playing drums, and wooing ladies. With his long hair and attractive features, Santiago is said to be quite charismatic and passionate. He may have a short fuse, though.

Famous Namesakes: Character Santiago (*Old Man and the Sea*); baseball player Benito Santiago

Santos

(Spanish) saint.

Image: Snap your fingers—that's how fast Santos can "snap" from one personality to the next. He's thought to be a dark-haired Latino with sudden and intense mood swings: Sometimes he's happy-go-lucky and friendly, and other times he's angry and rude.

Famous Namesakes: Character Matthew Santos (*The West Wing*); baseball player Victor Santos

Sarngin

(Hindi) archer; protector.

Image: Sarngin's image could go two ways. Most people describe him as a mousy, secretive man who's often serious and brooding. Then again, a few people say he's funny, festive, and feisty. Physically, Sarngin probably has curly hair and a prominent nose.

Famous Namesakes: None

Saul

(Hebrew) asked for, borrowed.

Image: Saul loves to entertain with his jokes and tales. People say he's a wisecracking retiree who's full of wisdom and stories. He's most likely Jewish and a bit eccentric.

Famous Namesakes: Biblical figure Saul; writer Saul Bellow; musician Saul Hudson, also known as Slash; author John Saul

Boys

Sawyer

(English) wood worker.

Image: Gals, Sawyer likes holding hands and stargazing on the porch swing. People imagine Sawyer is an old-fashioned and sensitive romantic. This countrified Southern gentleman is also said to be handsome, well spoken, and boyish.

Famous Namesakes: Book character Tom Sawyer; character Sawyer Ford (*Lost*); band Sawyer Brown

Schuyler

(Dutch) sheltering.

Image: Schuyler is the first to raise his hand in class. He's imagined as a brainy, blond boy who most likely reads up on all kinds of subjects even when he's out of school. People suspect Schuyler has been coddled by his upper-crust family, which may explain why he's a little know-it-all with a big ego.

Famous Namesakes: Vice president Schuyler Colfax

Scott

(English) from Scotland. A familiar form of Prescott.

Image: Scott can smooth talk anyone, but beware of his "sales pitch." He reminds people of a popular and charming playboy who's the life of the party. People say he's sexy, slender, and sporty. He comes across as smart and sweet, but some recognize he's a conceited fibber who sells himself higher than he should.

Famous Namesakes: Actor Scott Baio; singer Scott Weiland; writer F. Scott Fitzgerald; skater Scott Hamilton

Scotty

(English) a familiar form of Scott.

Image: What can a person say? *Scotty* rhymes with *snotty*. Most people see Scotty as snobby, snotty, sassy, and sissy. But a few people think he's friendly, pleasant, and well meaning. Physically, Scotty is pictured with fair hair and a fair complexion.

Famous Namesakes: Character Montgomery "Scotty" Scott (*Star Trek*); basketball player Scottie Pippen

 **Star Kids**

Sean Preston

Sean Preston has a winning personality and a well-to-do upbringing. He's said to be a handsome man with a great smile and lean physique. He's most likely bright, well spoken, confident, charming, and athletic—traits that come naturally to this pampered trust-fund baby. As the son of pop star Britney Spears and back-up dancer Kevin Federline, Sean Preston will grow up in the lap of luxury. But considering his parents, it's difficult to say just how *polished* he'll be....

Seamus

(Irish) a form of James.

Image: Somewhere under that gruff exterior, Seamus is quite a character. On the outside, Seamus is an Irishman who's crabby, odd, and not well liked. Those who aren't afraid of his mean demeanor and grizzled appearance find him to have a great sense of humor.

Famous Namesakes: Character Seamus Finnigan (*Harry Potter*); poet Seamus Heaney

Sean

(Irish) a form of John.

Image: Sean is a puzzle. Some people think he's an easily distracted, energetic guy who loves life. Others think he's quiet, serious, and considerate. Then there are those who see him as moody and demanding.

Famous Namesakes: Actor Sean Connery; actor Sean Penn; singer Sean Paul; rapper Sean Combs, also known as Diddy; football player Sean Salisbury

Sebastian

(Greek) venerable. (Latin) revered.

Image: People say Sebastian is an intelligent and hardworking guy who wants to succeed. Some imagine he's arrogant, cocky, and perhaps even mean; but others say the opposite, that he's a laid-back pushover. Either way, he's probably tall, slim, and dark.

Famous Namesakes: Character Sebastian (*The Little Mermaid*); explorer Sebastian Cabot

Senior

(French) lord.

Image: It's not surprising how people came up with this name's image. When people hear the name Senior, they imagine an old, gray man who's hunched over, frail, and hard of hearing. They suspect he moves at a slow, gentle pace, and at times he can be stubborn and rough around the edges.

Famous Namesakes: None

Serge

(Latin) attendant.

Image: Serge's personality hits you like a surge. He's imagined as a willful foreigner whose determination has the ability to sway others. Others, however, would call those qualities demanding, arrogant, and macho. In calmer moments, he's thought to be witty, fun, and outgoing.

Famous Namesakes: Poet and songwriter Serge Gainsbourg; singer Serj Tankian

Sergio

(Italian) a form of Serge.

Image: The only thing people can agree on is Sergio's ethnicity. When people hear the name Sergio, they think of a dark-haired Italian man with an accent. He's said to be either macho, arrogant, and aggressive or quiet, caring, and hardworking.

Famous Namesakes: Composer Sérgio Mendes; director Sergio Leone; golfer Sergio García

 ★ **Star Kids**

Seven Sirius

Seven Sirius marches to his own beat. He's believed to be a daring hip-hop musician, movie director, or basketball player who keeps to himself and doesn't always follow the rules. Some find him to be intimidating and wild. He's pictured as an African American with a scruffy beard. In some ways this image may fit Seven Sirius, son of OutKast rapper André 3000 and soul singer Erykah Badu—both of whom are famous for their groundbreaking music.

Seth

(Hebrew) appointed.

Image: Seth is like an iceberg, and his brains are just the tip. Most people think of Seth as a logical intellectual, even though he's perfectly built for athletics. He seems quiet, withdrawn, and a bit nerdy, but those who know him say he's patient, gentlemanly, and smiley. A few people feel there's a strong-willed leader deep inside Seth, or perhaps a funny prankster.

Famous Namesakes: Biblical figure Seth; actor Seth Green; character Seth Cohen (*The OC*); cartoon creator Seth MacFarlane

Shakir

(Arabic) thankful.

Image: Shakir is the guy to call if you need to kick-start your party. He's seen as a witty, outgoing, and personable African American man. People seem to enjoy his sense of humor and his fun-loving attitude—especially at parties. Most of the time, Shakir is said to be happy and easy to please, but sometimes he can be a bit intense and commanding.

Famous Namesakes: Muslim scholar Zaid Shakir

Shane

(Irish) a form of Sean.

Image: Shane is young at heart. This name calls to mind a fun-loving man with a loud laugh, a big smile, and a mischievous twinkle in his eyes. People attest he's as goofy as he is sweet, which makes him great with children. He's also thought to be handsome and tall.

Famous Namesakes: Actor Shane West; movie and book character Shane; boxer Sugar Shane Mosley

Sharif

(Arabic) honest; noble.

Image: Strong or timid, Sharif is a studious, intelligent man. People agree he's a portly Middle Easterner who's well read and serious. Some think he's a powerful and natural-born leader, but others say he's a shy and quiet fellow. As for his looks, he's described as handsome with dark features and olive skin.

Famous Namesakes: Egyptian actor Omar Sharif

Shavar

(Hebrew) comet.

Image: Don't be surprised if Shavar has a far-off look. People view him as a distant, distracted man who always has his head in the clouds. He's probably poetic and a dashing romantic, and most find him to be friendly and silly. Either Indian or Arabic, Shavar may have black hair, tattoos, and piercings.

Famous Namesakes: Actor Shavar Ross

Shawn

(Irish) a form of Sean.

Image: Shawn comes across as a great guy, but he keeps his shady side under wraps. He's pictured as a brown-haired and gorgeous guy who's fun, humorous, and caring. People see why he's so obviously popular. What's not so obvious is that he can be sneaky and cunning as well.

Famous Namesakes: Wrestler Shawn Michaels; actor Shawn Wayans; basketball player Shawn Kemp

Sheldon

(English) farm on the ledge.

Image: Sheldon is a rare combination of preppy *and* nerdy. Smart and bookish, Sheldon is thought to have a wealthy and sheltered upbringing, but it made him a loner who's much too serious and antisocial. Some picture him as pudgy, but others see him as a skinny weakling.

Famous Namesakes: Football player Sheldon Brown; writer Sidney Sheldon

Shepherd

(English) shepherd.

Image: In his own laid-back way, Shepherd is a crusader. People imagine he's an easygoing and quiet suburbanite. An intellectual and an innovator, he seems to love the arts, especially poetry. He's most likely a responsible citizen who drinks fair-trade coffee and supports local conservation efforts. Shepherd is probably handsome with blue eyes and a great head of brown hair.

Famous Namesakes: Character Dr. Derek Shepherd (*Grey's Anatomy*); singer Kenny Wayne Shepherd; playwright Sam Shepard

Sherman

(English) sheep shearer; resident of a shire.

Image: If you were in the bull's-eye like Sherman is, you might stick up for yourself, too. He's said to be a tough but dorky kid who's a popular target for fights. It's no wonder this lanky guy seems so sad and lonely.

Famous Namesakes: Actor Sherman Hemsley; character Sherman McCoy (*Bonfire of the Vanities*); general William Tecumseh Sherman; singer Bobby Sherman

Sherrod

(English) clearer of the land.

Image: People don't know which way to go with Sherrod. Most say he's a bookish dork with thick specs and high-waist pants. Others chime in that he's a good-looking and romantic ladies' man or even a tall, strong basketball player.

Famous Namesakes: Comedian Sherrod Small; senator Sherrod Brown

Sidney

(French) from Saint-Denis, France.

Image: Sidney is unflappable. People say he's cool, collected, and perfectly poised. This cute looker is also known to be happy, smart, and friendly.

Famous Namesakes: Actor Sidney Poitier; writer Sidney Sheldon; hockey player Sidney Crosby

Silas

(Latin) a short form of Silvan.

Image: It doesn't take long to understand why ladies flock to Silas. People think he's a cool, sexy guy who's very popular with women. Adding to his allure, he's also imagined to be generous, funny, and dependable.

Famous Namesakes: Biblical figure Silas; book character Silas Marner; character Silas (*The Da Vinci Code*)

Simba

(Swahili) lion. (Yao) a short form of Lisimba.

Image: Simba has a bright mind, bright personality, and bright eyes. The name Simba creates an image of a confident and determined African man with curious intelligence. He's also thought to be happy, lively, and energetic, and his big eyes show his emotions.

Famous Namesakes: Character Simba (*The Lion King*)

Simon

(Hebrew) he heard.

Image: They don't mean to be rude, but… people associate this name with *American Idol* judge Simon Cowell. Simon is imagined as an arrogant, mean, and overpowering Brit who's quite successful, despite his bad attitude.

Famous Namesakes: Biblical figure Simon; character Simon (*Alvin and the Chipmunks*); singer Simon LeBon; TV personality Simon Cowell; singer Paul Simon

Sinclair

(French) prayer.

Image: Sinclair has a proper air about him, but it's just that—air. People think of him as a wealthy, stuffy, and pretentious bookworm. (Perhaps a distant reference to author Sinclair Lewis.) He's known to be a well-mannered gentleman for appearances' sake, but it doesn't do much to hide the fact that he's an unfriendly loner.

Famous Namesakes: Writer Sinclair Lewis; writer Upton Sinclair

Skipper

(Scandinavian) shipmaster.

Image: Nerd or jock—you pick. Skipper is either a shy nerd who's awkward with women or an all-American jock who's well liked and preppy.

Famous Namesakes: Character Skipper Jonas Grumby (*Gilligan's Island*)

Skyler

(Dutch) a form of Schuyler.

Image: Skyler is bursting with positive energy. People describe him as having Nordic looks and a bright, beautiful smile. He's said to be loving, cheery, and energetic. In addition, people believe he's a creative and hip freethinker.

Famous Namesakes: Football player Skyler Green

Slade

(English) a short form of Sladen.

Image: Slade is ambitious, but most question how far he'll go to get what he wants. He's perceived as a bold and daring go-getter who's calm under pressure. He's said to be strong both physically and mentally. Slade may be a little too strong, because some people say he's boastful and pompous. He may be deceitful and sly as well.

Famous Namesakes: Musician Chris Slade; singer Isaac Slade

Slater

(English) roof slater.

Image: If you run into Slater on or off the sports field, you'll be sorry. Slater appears to be a violent, mean, and stubborn man with whom people no doubt have a hard time communicating. With his big muscles, hardworking attitude, and aggression, he might be an athlete.

Famous Namesakes: Actor Christian Slater; character A. C. Slater (*Saved by the Bell*); surfer Kelly Slater

Soloman

(Hebrew) a form of Solomon.

Image: In the Bible, King Solomon's wisdom and power were legendary. Although spelled differently, this Soloman is also said to be intelligent, introspective, and strong-willed. People picture him as muscular, protective, and stern.

Famous Namesakes: Biblical figure Solomon

Spencer

(English) dispenser of provisions.

Image: Spencer is the kind of guy you'd want your daughter to marry: He's said to be an upstanding, caring, and well-versed Ivy Leaguer with striking blond looks and good manners. Distinguished yet humble, he's also known as a determined leader.

Famous Namesakes: Actor Spencer Tracy; poet Edmund Spenser; racecar driver Jimmy Spencer

Stanislav

(Slavic) a form of Stanislaus.

Image: Stanislav is a good provider. This name gives the impression of a responsible, honest, and hardworking man. He clearly loves his family, and he smiles a lot to show it. He also seems to be full of jokes. Physically, Stanislav is depicted as a large, strong man who's ready to put in a long day of work.

Famous Namesakes: Actor Stanislav Ianevski; hockey player Stanislav Chistov

Stanley

(English) stony meadow.

Image: Stanley may share more of his knowledge than his personality. He's described as an authoritative academic who's kind yet serious. People say he's quiet and polite, but he does have a sense of humor. In addition, he's pictured as skinny with thinning hair and glasses.

Famous Namesakes: Director Stanley Kubrick; actor Stanley Tucci; character Stanley Kowalski (*A Streetcar Named Desire*); musician Ralph Stanley

Steel

(English) like steel.

Image: You can't have a tough name like Steel and not live up to the image. People say Steel is as macho, mean, and strong as his name suggests. He may be a bodybuilder or the leader of a motorcycle gang. Either way, he's most likely loud, angry, and uncompromising.

Famous Namesakes: TV character Remington Steele

Stefan

(German, Polish, Swedish) a form of Stephen.

Image: Stefan's brilliant mind is full of dark schemes. People think he's an arrogant and intelligent brooder who quietly conjures up conniving thoughts that shouldn't be trusted. Strong and blond, he's perhaps German or Norwegian.

Famous Namesakes: Tennis player Stefan Edberg

Stefano

(Italian) a form of Stephen.

Image: Stefano suggests a Chianti to complement your chicken cacciatore. This tall, curly-haired Italian is imagined to be a sommelier in a gourmet restaurant. He's most likely confident, proud, and compassionate, as well as attractive. But as soon as the conversation progresses beyond wine, he's considered to be something of an airhead.

Famous Namesakes: Character Stefano DiMera (*Days of Our Lives*); singer Giuseppe Di Stefano

Stephen

(Greek) crowned.

Image: Stephen has a sincere bedside manner. He's pictured as an educated professional, like a doctor or surgeon. People believe he's kind, quiet, and dedicated as well as tall and handsome.

Famous Namesakes: Author Stephen King; actor Stephen Baldwin; saint Stephen

Sterling

(English) valuable; silver penny. A form of Starling.

Image: Sterling is an international man of mystery. He strikes people as a cunning and elusive spy who's smart, sophisticated, and smooth. He's most likely wealthy and well traveled, and he's always cool.

Famous Namesakes: Actor Sterling Hayden; racecar driver Sterling Martin; football player Sterling Sharpe

Steve

(Greek) a short form of Stephen, Steven.

Image: With two images of Steve, you'd invite one to your Saturday night poker game, but you'd be smart to leave the other one alone. Some people think Steve is a loud, funny, and gregarious guy who's quirky and sweet. Others say he's a mean and stubborn misfit who thinks only of himself. Whatever his personality may be, he's described as fit, tall, and plain.

Famous Namesakes: Actor Steve McQueen; actor Steve Martin; actor Steve Harvey; basketball player Steve Nash; talk show host Steve Allen

Steven

(Greek) a form of Stephen.

Image: Steven proves that social skills are the difference between having nerdy characteristics and being a full-blown nerd. Steven is seen as a charming, easygoing guy with a good heart. People imagine he's smart, studious, and into books and computers, but he's too well liked to get the "nerd" label.

Famous Namesakes: Director Steven Spielberg; singer Steven Tyler; football player Steven Jackson; actor Steven Segal

Stevie

(English) a familiar form of Stephen, Steven.

Image: Stevie is cool, but he's not too cool to give to his community. People say he's a kind and considerate guy who loves to volunteer. Blond and slender, Stevie is thought to be trendy, cool, and a creative thinker. He can be loud and hyper at times, which some find obnoxious but most find joyful.

Famous Namesakes: Singer Stevie Wonder; singer Stevie Ray Vaughan; skateboarder Stevie Williams

Stuart

(English) caretaker, steward.

Image: Stuart is captain of the Math League, but he won't be let near the football field. He's seen as a socially challenged nerd whose intellect makes him great at studies, but whose scrawny frame makes him terrible at sports. When people get to know this wallflower, they say he's considerate and dependable.

Famous Namesakes: Sportscaster Stuart Scott; book and movie character Stuart Little; actor Stuart Townsend; character Stuart Smalley (*Staurday Night Live*)

Sullivan

(Irish) black-eyed.

Image: Describing Sullivan is a "glass-half-full" versus "glass-half-empty" experiment. Optimists say he's quiet, well mannered, and book smart. Pessimists say he's timid, dull, and naïve. Both picture him to be tall, blond, and slim.

Famous Namesakes: Variety show host Ed Sullivan; composer Arthur Sullivan

Sundeep

(Punjabi) light; enlightened.

Image: Sundeep changes as his moods dictate, but he never loses sight of his kindness. He's described as a warm, affectionate, and philosophical man. At times, he can be intense and serious, and at others, radiant and carefree. People picture Sundeep with dark skin and hair.

Famous Namesakes: Bollywood composer Sandeep Chowta

Boys

Sutherland

(Scandinavian) southern land.

Image: Sutherland is as classy and gracious as you'd imagine a Southern gentleman to be. People picture him as a wealthy, polite, and distinguished Southern professional. He's imagined to be charming, intriguing, and handsome.

Famous Namesakes: Actors Donald Sutherland and Kiefer Sutherland

Sylvester

(Latin) forest dweller.

Image: Sylvester is a boisterous fellow. People say he's a caring man with a loud voice and a friendly smile. Perhaps of Italian or some other Mediterranean descent, he's pictured with dark hair and eyes, but he may not be very attractive. He's known to be smart but naïve.

Famous Namesakes: Actor Sylvester Stallone; character Sylvester J. Pussycat (*Looney Tunes*)

Tad

(Welsh) father. (Greek, Latin) a short form of Thaddeus.

Image: No wonder Tad can live it up at wild parties—his daddy takes care of everything else. People imagine Tad as a fun partier with boyish charm and a rich father who bought his son's way into a prestigious college. The silver spoon lifestyle has most likely made Tad arrogant and snooty to anyone but country clubbers. He's also said to be good-looking and athletic.

Famous Namesakes: Character Tad Hamilton (*Win a Date with Tad Hamilton!*); Abraham Lincoln's son Tad Lincoln; author Tad Williams

Tan

(Burmese) million. (Vietnamese) new.

Image: Maybe Tan is a nice guy—or maybe not. Some say Tan is an easygoing, relaxed fellow who's likable and cool. Others contend he's a selfish, jerky know-it-all who's secretly insecure. Either way, he's probably rich.

Famous Namesakes: Composer Tan Dun

Tanner

(English) leather worker; tanner.

Image: Tanner is the boy next door if you live in the 'burbs with the soccer moms and minivans. He's pictured as a happy and boyish suburban kid who's friendly and caring. He's most likely athletic and active, but he can also be a bookworm. People imagine him with blond hair and blue eyes.

Famous Namesakes: Artist Henry Ossawa Tanner; character Danny Tanner (*Full House*)

Tariq

(Arabic) conqueror.

Image: Without saying a word, Tariq makes an impression. He's envisioned as a quiet observer who may be shy but is more likely laconic. Despite his silent nature, he's still said to be a commanding presence as a strong-willed, confident, and even stern man. Dark-skinned, Tariq may be African American or Arabic.

Famous Namesakes: Iraqi official Tariq Aziz; football player Tarik Glenn

Tate

(Scandinavian, English) cheerful. (Native American) long-winded talker.

Image: Just because Tate believes everything he hears doesn't mean he's dumb. He's thought of as a naïve and easily manipulated guy with an athletic lifestyle and lots of charm. Some have a more positive view, saying he's actually quite intelligent despite his gullibility.

Famous Namesakes: Poet Allen Tate; actor Tate Donavan; actor Larenz Tate; commercial character Terry Tate

Taylor

(English) tailor.

Image: Taylor's upper-class background either made him an upstanding gentleman or a rebellious snob. He's seen as a handsome blond who's wealthy and spoiled. Some say he's kind, intelligent, and popular. Others say he's stuck-up and unmannerly despite his proper upbringing.

Famous Namesakes: President Zachary Taylor; singer Taylor Hicks; football player Fred Taylor; singer James Taylor

Ted

(English) a short form of Edward, Edwin, Theodore.

Image: With a name like Ted, you may as well change your name to Ted E. Bear. Ted is considered a jolly, outgoing, and sometimes boisterous man. He's most likely strong and tall, and people think he's a big, cuddly teddy bear.

Famous Namesakes: Actor Ted Danson; tycoon Ted Turner; senator Ted Kennedy; singer Ted Nugent; baseball player Ted Williams

Teddy

(English) a familiar form of Edward, Theodore.

Image: Here's an easy one: Teddy makes people think of a teddy bear. He's described as a huggable, squeezable, and lovable guy who's chubby with dark hair and a big smile. Like any good teddy bear, he's a sweet friend who's nice to be around.

Famous Namesakes: President Theodore "Teddy" Roosevelt; singer Teddy Pendergrass; singer Teddy Geiger; boxing trainer Teddy Atlas

Terrell

(German) thunder ruler.

Image: Wide receiver Terrell Owens and running back Terrell Davis are two prime reasons why this image has a sporty appeal. People say Terrell is an African American athlete—most likely a football player—who's tough mentally as well as physically. He's imagined to be focused, consistent, intelligent, and perhaps even arrogant.

Famous Namesakes: Football player Terrell Owens; football player Terrell Davis

Terrence

(Latin) smooth.

Image: Terrence is a lot like the weather: If you don't like his mood, wait a few minutes. He's perceived as an African American who's tall, powerful, and handsome. People say he's moody, ranging from fun-loving to clingy to arrogant to angry in an instant.

Famous Namesakes: Actor Terrence Howard; singer Terence Trent D'Arby; actor Terrence Mann

Terry

(English) a familiar form of Terrence.

Image: Sometimes Terry cares more about getting a laugh than about other people. He's described as a funny, boisterous man whom many see as a clown or a free spirit. People believe he's friendly and caring for the most part, but he can be selfish and immature at times.

Famous Namesakes: Writer Terry Brooks; wrestler Terry Bollea, also known as Hulk Hogan; football player Terry Bradshaw; football coach Terry Bowden

Tevin

(American) a combination of the prefix Te + Kevin.

Image: Tevin's pranks are all in good fun, but you still need to keep a close eye on him. He's mostly seen as a playful and impish practical joker with an attractive smile. He's known to be so mischievous that you can't really trust him, but deep down, he's a friendly and decent person. Some people have a different view, saying he may be a timid and shy mama's boy.

Famous Namesakes: Singer Tevin Campbell

Thaddeus

(Greek) courageous. (Latin) praiser.

Image: Thaddeus is a great combination of qualities. He's regarded as a charming and suave gentleman with a winning personality. People suspect he's well educated and confident, and he may even be playful and funny in his more devilish moments.

Famous Namesakes: Biblical figure Thaddeus

Thanos

(Greek) nobleman; bear-man.

Image: Thanos's hot temper gets him into hot water. He's described as a troublemaker who's quick to anger. Of Greek ancestry, he's most likely smart, serious, and strong-willed to boot. No matter how he treats everyone else, at least he seems to dote on his mother.

Famous Namesakes: None

Boys

Theo

(English) a short form of Theodore.

Image: Theo Huxtable from *The Cosby Show* influences this name's image. People think Theo is a responsible and sensible African American who comes from a good family and has a good head on his shoulders. He's known to be determined and popular, and he's also attractive.

Famous Namesakes: Art dealer Theo van Gogh; character Theo Huxtable (*The Cosby Show*); baseball executive Theo Epstein; hockey player Theo Fleury

Theodore

(Greek) gift of God.

Image: Theodore Roosevelt was a memorable American president, and this name's image bears resemblance to him. Theodore strikes people as a name for an intelligent and savvy politician who reads people well and is a natural leader. He's most likely pleasantly plump, attractive, and from an upper-class family.

Famous Namesakes: President Theodore Roosevelt; character Theodore (*Alvin and the Chipmunks*); poet Theodore Roethke; hockey player José Theodore

Thomas

(Greek, Aramaic) twin.

Image: Thomas is as sophisticated and refined as the handcrafted leather chair in which he loves to read. He's imagined to be mature, distinguished, and scholarly. Because he's so quiet, some people say he's snobbish, but others believe he has a good sense of humor and a positive outlook.

Famous Namesakes: President Thomas Jefferson; revolutionary Thomas Paine; biblical figure Thomas; inventor Thomas Edison; saint Thomas Aquinas

Thornton

(English) thorny town.

Image: If you're afraid of the world, you can always try hiding behind your money, like Thornton does. People think of him as a snooty, rich preppy who's skinny, lanky, and pale. Under the façade, however, he's really just shy and scared.

Famous Namesakes: Actor Billy Bob Thornton; playwright Thornton Wilder; hockey player Joe Thornton

Tim

(Greek) a short form of Timothy.

Image: Most folks love Tim, but a few aren't won over by his goofy ways. People think he's a sweet and caring man who can be a goofball. Skinny and short, he's said to be a wonderful person most of the time, but some people argue he's an annoying and loud know-it-all.

Famous Namesakes: Actor Tim Allen; singer Tim McGraw; basketball player Tim Duncan; actor Tim Robbins; character Tiny Tim Cratchit (*A Christmas Carol*)

Timmy

(Greek) a familiar form of Timothy.

Image: Timmy's weak appearance and meek personality hide his more endearing qualities. He's thought of as a scrawny, fragile boy who's quiet, timid, and happy to stay out of the spotlight. When he's not so shy, people discover he's kind, lovable, smart, and fun-loving.

Famous Namesakes: Character Timmy (*Lassie*); character Timmy (*South Park*)

Timothy

(Greek) honoring God.

Image: Timothy puts on an exciting show with nothing more than impromptu creativity and sharp wit. People think he's creative, spontaneous, smart, and outgoing. Some people say he's well mannered and giving, but others say he's bratty and manipulating. Either way, most people describe Timothy as a blue-eyed blond.

Famous Namesakes: Biblical figure Timothy; actor Timothy Hutton; actor Timothy Dalton; psychologist Timothy Leary

Titus

(Greek) giant. (Latin) hero. A form of Tatius.

Image: If you're as physically impressive as Titus, you don't need to be intelligent to lead others. He's imagined as a muscular, manly, and confident leader. But people say he's not very bright, despite being so powerful a figure.

Famous Namesakes: Biblical figure Titus; play character Titus Andronicus; Roman emperor Titus; comedian Christopher Titus

Tobias

(Hebrew) God is good.

Image: Tobias is both soft and hard. He's described as a loyal, friendly guy who's innocent and perhaps even naïve. Some people also say he's muscular, rugged, and hardworking, but a few people imagine he's a quiet geek.

Famous Namesakes: Biblical figure Tobias; character Tobias Fünke (*Arrested Development*); actor Tobias Menzies

Toby

(Hebrew) a familiar form of Tobias.

Image: Toby is a sweet, spunky guy who may or may not be gainfully employed. He's imagined to be loving, compassionate, and fun, especially when he can cut loose and get loud. Even though he's a little pudgy, he's said to be sexy. Most people believe he's hardworking and strong-willed, but some say he's an unmotivated bum.

Famous Namesakes: Singer Toby Keith; actor Tobey Maguire; skiier Toby Dawson

Todd

(English) fox.

Image: If a ten-page paper is due on Thursday, Todd will turn in a twenty-page paper on Tuesday. He's imagined as an incredibly smart preppy who's tall and lean. He's said to be sensitive yet spunky, and he's a classic overachiever.

Famous Namesakes: Actor Todd Bridges; hockey player Todd Bertuzzi; designer Todd Oldham; singer Todd Rundgren; football player Todd Heap

Tom

(English) a short form of Thomas, Tomas.

Image: Tom is a funny guy, but different people react to him in different ways. Everyone agrees Tom is loud, silly, and famous for laughing too much. Some people find his silliness pleasant, others think he's annoying and rude, and a few just call him a dork.

Famous Namesakes: Actor Tom Hanks; actor Tom Cruise; football player Tom Brady; actor Tom Selleck; singer Tom Petty

Tomlin

(English) little Tom.

Image: Tomlin is certainly kind, but he can be a little unexciting. He comes across as a sweet fellow who's soft-spoken, conservative, passive, and, unfortunately, dull. He's said to be smart, however, so every now and then he shows some wit. People tend to picture Tomlin as attractive, clean-cut, and strong.

Famous Namesakes: Singer Chris Tomlin

Tommy

(Hebrew) a familiar form of Thomas.

Image: Tommy could be just about anyone. People say he's a hyper jock, a rude snob who likes only the popular crowd, or a wholesome kid next door. With a diminutive name like Tommy, he's most likely a young, small boy.

Famous Namesakes: Musician Tommy Lee; designer Tommy Hilfiger; actor Tommy Lee Jones; character Tommy Pickles (*Rugrats*)

Tony

(Greek) flourishing. (Latin) praiseworthy. (English) a short form of Anthony. A familiar form of Remington.

Image: Tony is a wallflower? *Fughet about it!* People think of Tony as an Italian who's friendly, charismatic, and popular. Although he's said to be kind and honest, he's also macho and headstrong.

Famous Namesakes: Character Tony Soprano (*The Sopranos*); racecar driver Tony Stewart; singer Tony Bennett; skateboarder Tony Hawk; British prime minister Tony Blair

Tracy

(Greek) harvester. (Latin) courageous. (Irish) battler.

Image: As contradictory as it may seem, Tracy is either the center of attention or lost in the crowd. Many people think Tracy is a spunky and funny comedian (perhaps like former *Saturday Night Live* cast member Tracy Morgan) who's energetic, daring, and loud. In quite a contrast, other people imagine he's meek, quiet, and unremarkable.

Famous Namesakes: Actor Tracy Morgan; singer Tracy Lawrence; basketball player Tracy McGrady; comic character Dick Tracy

Travis

(English) a form of Travers.

Image: Some of Travis's image might come from country singer Travis Tritt. When people hear the name, they think of a rowdy cowboy or country hick who's loud, mean, and laid-back. In addition, he's described as a heavyset guy.

Famous Namesakes: Singer Travis Tritt; character Travis Bickle (*Taxi Driver*); musician Travis Barker; baseball player Travis Hafner; singer Randy Travis

Trayton

(English) town full of trees.

Image: For the life of him, Trayton can't settle on a major at college. He's described as an intellectual, geeky young man who could master any subject—which is precisely why he's so confused. People say this lanky looker is friendly and compassionate, but he'd benefit from a little direction.

Famous Namesakes: None

Tremaine

(Scottish) house of stone.

Image: Tremaine is the player the other teammates look up to. People picture him as a tall African American man with tremendous athletic talent. They also find him to be mature, kind, and smart. His open mind and easy nature seem to make Tremaine a natural leader.

Famous Namesakes: Basketball player Tremaine Fowlkes; book character Johnny Tremain; director Jeff Tremaine

Trent

(Latin) torrent, rapid stream. (French) thirty.

Image: Trent is the It Boy, and there's no question why. He's goodhearted, buff, handsome, sporty, wealthy, outgoing, funny, popular, and good at just about everything he does. A few people (most likely detractors) say he's short-tempered and stuck-up.

Famous Namesakes: Singer Trent Reznor; senator Trent Lott; football player Trent Green; character Trent Walker (*Swingers*)

Trenton

(Latin) town by the rapid stream.

Image: The only way Trenton can handle his shyness is to lash out against others. The name Trenton calls to mind a quiet loner who overcompensates for his shyness by acting like a bully and a punk. People describe him as tall and slight, but he can be a real menacing figure.

Famous Namesakes: Basketball player Trenton Hassell

Trevor

(Irish) prudent. (Welsh) homestead.

Image: Trevor is nice enough, but he's a mess in many ways. He's said to be a kind, likable guy who's unkempt and lazy. Some describe him as easygoing, which may be an understatement, because others call him a bum. Physically, he's pictured as short with a small frame.

Famous Namesakes: Basketball player Trevor Ariza; boxer Trevor Berbick; baseball player Trevor Hoffman

Trey

(English) three; third.

Image: Trey is tough in body and character, but that may just lead him into trouble. He's pictured as a large, buff athlete who's strong-willed to the point of being obstinate and rough edged to the point of being criminal. On the positive side, some believe he's protective and caring.

Famous Namesakes: Singer Trey Anastasio; cartoon creator Trey Parker; sportscaster Trey Wingo

Tristan

(Welsh) bold.

Image: This name embodies a romantic, noble spirit due to the legend of Tristan and Iseult and the protagonist Tristan from *Legends of the Fall*. Tristan reminds people of a very handsome blond man who's compassionate, well loved, and charming. He seems to be intelligent, confident, and always willing to stand up for what he believes.

Famous Namesakes: Arthurian figure Tristan of Cornwall; character Tristan Ludlow (*Legends of the Fall*)

Troy

(Irish) foot soldier. (French) curly-haired. (English) water.

Image: Troy's Lamborghini says it all. People picture him as a toned, model-like pretty boy who's smarmy, snobby, and egotistical. He's said to be an aggressive and domineering businessman with an oceanfront home, yacht, sailboat, and foreign sports car. Supposedly, ladies love him, but he may be just a womanizer. A few sympathetic people describe him as kind-hearted and sweet.

Famous Namesakes: Football player Troy Aikman; singer Cowboy Troy; football player Troy Polamalu; character Troy McClure (*The Simpsons*)

Tucker

(English) fuller, tucker of cloth.

Image: Tucker is either slow as an ox or smart as a fox. This name makes most people think of a sweet and gentle country bumpkin who's not too bright. Other people imagine he's a whiny nerd with intelligence to spare. Either way, he's probably a short guy with sandy blond hair.

Famous Namesakes: Actor Chris Tucker; TV personality Tucker Carlson; entrepreneur Preston Tucker

Ty

(English) a short form of Tyler, Tyrone, Tyrus.

Image: Ty either wears his emotions on his sleeve or locks them inside. Most people think of him as a friendly, likable guy who's outgoing, vivacious, and carefree. Other people think he's serious and emotionless.

Famous Namesakes: Baseball player Ty Cobb; singer Ty Herndon; football player Ty Law; TV personality Ty Pennington

Tyler

(English) tile maker.

Image: Does Tyler have two faces—one for his inner circle and one for those not as popular as he? He's thought to be a blond, fit cutie who's playful, friendly, and outgoing. People say he's quite lovable and charming. But some people think this upper-middle-class preppy is snobby, self-centered, and childish.

Famous Namesakes: President John Tyler; character Tyler Durden (*Fight Club*); singer Steven Tyler

Tymon

(Polish) a form of Timothy. (Greek) a form of Timon.

Image: People quarrel over Tymon's image. Some find him to be shy, quiet, and passive. Others describe him as stubborn and proud. Then there are those who claim he's a dumb airhead, while others say he's a smart nerd. The only point people seem to agree on is that Tymon is African American.

Famous Namesakes: Musician Tymon Dogg; play *Timon of Athens*; character Timon (*The Lion King*)

Tyree

(Scottish) island dweller.

Image: Tyree is a natural role model to those around him. He comes across as an African American man who's hardworking, competitive, and assertive. People likely look to him for leadership. He's also said to be charismatic and spunky. Tyree may apply his leadership skills on a football field, or he may apply them in the executive boardroom.

Famous Namesakes: Author Omar Tyree; football player David Tyree

Tyrel

(American) a form of Terrell.

Image: Tyrel's athletic skills aren't in question, but his interpersonal skills are. People picture him as a basketball or football player who's African American, tall, and solidly built. They say Tyrel may be a fun-loving, likable prankster, but he may also be an angry, untrustworthy bully.

Famous Namesakes: Boxer Tyrell Biggs; singer Steve Tyrell

Tyrone

(Greek) sovereign. (Irish) land of Owen.

Image: If what they say is true, you don't want to cross Tyrone. He reminds people of a muscular guy who's arrogant, insensitive, and thuggish. Others have a much more positive view, saying he's comical, outgoing, and popular. He may be African American.

Famous Namesakes: Singer Tyrone Davis; football player Tryone Williams; football player Tyrone Carter

Tyson

(French) son of Ty.

Image: People have strong feelings about this name, simply because it belongs to notorious boxer Mike Tyson. Tyson is described as a physically formidable African American heavyweight boxer who's mentally slow and tormented by anger, insecurity, and maybe even insanity.

Famous Namesakes: Boxer Mike Tyson; model Tyson Beckford; basketball player Tyson Chandler

Ulysses

(Latin) wrathful. A form of Odysseus.

Image: Ulysses is as fascinating as the many adventures he's encountered over the years. He's imagined as a wise and bold man who's fond of travel and adventure. An older fellow, he's thought to be interesting and witty.

Famous Namesakes: Character Ulysses, Latinized name for Odysseus (*The Odyssey*); novel *Ulysses*; president Ulysses S. Grant

Upton

(English) upper town.

Image: Upton sounds likes *uppity*, and most people think he's just that. They describe him as a snooty and pretentious spoiled brat who's geeky and boring. He's imagined to be bony, unattractive, and pale.

Famous Namesakes: Author Upton Sinclair

Vance

(English) thresher.

Image: You wouldn't think someone as self-centered as Vance could be a good teammate, but he is. He's thought to be a self-absorbed and high-maintenance jock who's tall, muscular, and dumb. People are amazed that he can somehow set his vanity aside and be a helpful team player.

Famous Namesakes: Actor Courtney B. Vance; baseball player Dazzy Vance

Vaughn

(Welsh) small.

Image: The images of Vaughn are plentiful: People think he's a funny, outgoing prankster; a pushy go-getter; a cultured aristocrat; a sweet gentleman; a deep thinker; or a moody narcissist. With any of these options, he's most likely handsome, strong, and tall.

Famous Namesakes: Golfer Vaughn Taylor; actor Vince Vaughn; baseball player Mo Vaughn; singer Stevie Ray Vaughan

Vernon

(Latin) springlike; youthful.

Image: Where's Vernon? In the library or out in the fields? People agree Vernon is skinny and lanky, but they can't decide if he's a shy bookworm or a backwoods farmer. In either case, he's most likely steadfast, trustworthy, and a bit goofy at times.

Famous Namesakes: Businessman Vernon Jordan; baseball player Vernon Wells; football player Vernon Davis

Vic

(Latin) a short form of Victor.

Image: Vic has no friends, which is no surprise. People think he's a rude, arrogant, and grouchy guy who keeps to himself. They also say Vic is grungy and dark haired with a big nose.

Famous Namesakes: Singer Vic Damone; actor Vic Morrow

Victor

(Latin) victor, conqueror.

Image: To the victor go the spoils, and Victor is a powerful man. He's pictured as a commanding leader who's masculine, worldly, and strong-willed. Some imagine he's stern and some imagine he's amiable, but he's always in control.

Famous Namesakes: Author Victor Hugo; actor Victor Garber; musician Victor Borge; book and movie character Victor Frankenstein

Vijay

(Hindi) victorious.

Image: No one doubts that Vijay is confident in his abilities. Either an Indian or Asian man, he's said to be a tech-savvy computer programmer. People believe he's quite intelligent and driven, but that means he can sometimes be a boastful know-it-all. More often than not, though, Vijay is known to be friendly and engaging.

Famous Namesakes: Golfer Vijay Singh; tennis player Vijay Amritraj

Vince

(English) a short form of Vincent.

Image: Vince is a genial guy with his ups and downs. He's described as a dark-haired Italian who's warm, witty, and driven. He may be plagued by a short temper and a big ego, but most people say he's a generally happy and caring man.

Famous Namesakes: Actor Vince Vaughn; football coach Vince Lombardi; character Vince Chase (*Entourage*); football player Vince Young; singer Vince Neil

Vincent

(Latin) victor, conqueror.

Image: The name Vincent elicits so many images, some based on famous namesakes. Some people imagine Vincent as a tender parent or friend. Some think of horror-film actor Vincent Price and say he's creepy. Others recall Vincent van Gogh and picture him as an artist. And still others say he's smart and shy.

Famous Namesakes: Artist Vincent van Gogh; actor Vincent Price; character Vincent Vega (*Pulp Fiction*); hockey player Vincent Lecavalier

Vinny

(English) a familiar form of Calvin, Melvin, Vincent.

Image: People see Vinny in two completely different ways: Most people think Vinny is tough, pig-headed, and possibly abusive. Others think he's quiet and shy with a mild temperament. In either case, he's pictured as a dark-featured Italian.

Famous Namesakes: Football player Vinny Testaverde; character Vinny LaGuardia Gambini (*My Cousin Vinny*); baseball player Vinny Castilla

Virgil

(Latin) rod bearer, staff bearer.

Image: Virgil may be literary like the ancient Roman poet of the same name, but he's quite a character in his own right. He's imagined as literate, contemplative, poetic—and downright nerdy. A frail and thin fellow, he's known to be introverted, quirky, and clumsy.

Famous Namesakes: Roman poet Virgil; lawman Virgil Earp

Vito

(Latin) a short form of Vittorio.

Image: This name's image certainly reflects *The Godfather* Vito Corleone, but not perfectly. People imagine Vito is a powerful Italian mob boss who's dangerous yet businesslike. But unlike Vito Corleone, this Vito is thought to be dimwitted, cranky, and rude.

Famous Namesakes: Character Vito Corleone (*The Godfather*); mobster Vito Rizzuto

Vladimir

(Russian) famous prince.

Image: For this name's image, people perhaps meld qualities of the current Russian president, Vladimir Putin, and the former Soviet leader Vladimir Lenin. People see Vladimir as a determined and confident Russian leader who ranges from dominant to militant to tyrannical to evil. Others have a completely different view, saying Vladimir is a name for a ghoulish vampire.

Famous Namesakes: Russian president Vladimir Putin; Soviet leader Vladimir Lenin; author Vladimir Nabokov; baseball player Vladimir Guerrero

Wade

(English) ford; river crossing.

Image: The images of Wade are contradictory. Some say he's a defiant, rude troublemaker. Others say he's a dependable, honest friend. Still others say he's smart and unique, but a few say he's uneducated and dull. Physically, Wade is thought to be a redhead with fair skin and freckles.

Famous Namesakes: Baseball player Wade Boggs; basketball player Dwayne Wade

Wallace

(English) from Wales.

Image: Meek or assertive, Wallace is an intelligent fellow. People believe he's studious, articulate, and thoughtful as well as skinny, tall, and bespectacled. He could be powerful and commanding or meek and quiet.

Famous Namesakes: Racecar driver Rusty Wallace; character Wallace (*Wallace and Gromit*); Scottish patriot William Wallace; basketball player Ben Wallace

Walter

(German) army ruler, general. (English) woodsman.

Image: Walter's pursuits are as traditional and upstanding as he is. He's described as an inquisitive thinker who loves reading, chess, bird watching, and other old-fashioned activities. Pictured with glasses, a skinny build, and a clean-cut style, he's also thought to be hardworking, trustworthy, and bighearted.

Famous Namesakes: News anchor Walter Cronkite; football player Walter Payton; actor Walter Matthau; vice president Walter Mondale; explorer Walter Raleigh

Warren

(German) general; warden; rabbit hutch.

Image: Young or old, Warren is a bore. As a kid, he's most likely a nerdy, mousy bookworm who's always on the honor roll. As an older man, he's probably an uptight fuddy-duddy who's snobbish and boring. At either juncture, he's most likely fair, overweight, and four-eyed.

Famous Namesakes: President Warren Harding; actor Warren Beatty; football player Warren Moon; rapper Warren G; singer Warren Zevon

Waylon

(English) land by the road.

Image: Singer Waylon Jennings was a major part of the "outlaw country" music scene of the '60s and '70s. So people imagine this Waylon as a country singer who may be unsophisticated, but is certainly sure of himself. He's said to be assertive, determined, and even self-centered. At the same time, people also find him to be a fun-loving and charming cowboy. Physically, he's depicted as lanky and brown-haired.

Famous Namesakes: Singer Waylon Jennings; character Waylon Smithers (*The Simpsons*); actor Waylon Payne

Wayne

(English) wagon maker.

Image: Wayne is always annoyed. People think he's grumpy and fussy, and he often feels pestered. The pestering most likely stems from the fact that he's a prissy mama's boy with pale skin and a lanky figure.

Famous Namesakes: Hockey player Wayne Gretzky; singer Wayne Newton; actor Wayne Brady; character Wayne Campbell (*Wayne's World*); character Bruce Wayne (*Batman*)

Wendall

(German, English) a form of Wendell.

Image: *Brainiac*, *geek*, *nerd*, or *dork*: No matter which of these words you call him, Wendall is it. He's pictured as a bookish, brainy guy who's frail, antisocial, overly sensitive, and vision impaired.

Famous Namesakes: Poet Oliver Wendell Holmes, Sr., and Supreme Court justice Oliver Wendell Holmes, Jr.

Wesley

(English) western meadow.

Image: Wesley is full of personality, and he likes to share it. He's seen as a vibrant, popular, and amusing guy who's as smart as he is kind. He's most likely lanky with light-brown hair. Some people say this hard worker is eager to please, but others describe him as a bit of a showoff.

Famous Namesakes: Actor Wesley Snipes; theologian John Wesley; actor Wesley Jonathan

Weston

(English) western town.

Image: Weston uses his inheritance to make even more money. People imagine he inherited a great deal of wealth from his grandfather, but he's also a powerful entrepreneur in his own right. Weston is known to be a smart decision maker, but he's also anal-retentive and sometimes ruthless. In relaxed situations, he can be gregarious and funny.

Famous Namesakes: Photographer Edward Weston; actor Michael Weston

Boys

Wilbert

(German) brilliant; resolute.

Image: Wilbert is a goofy guy, no matter what lifestyle he lives. Everyone agrees he's a humorous and gregarious fellow who's rotund and a little clumsy. From there, people disagree as to whether Wilbert is a geeky computer tech or a beer-drinkin' and flag-wavin' backwoods conservative.

Famous Namesakes: Baseball player Wilbert Robinson

Wilbur

(English) wall fortification; bright willows.

Image: Wilbur never outgrew his shy, simple ways. He's pictured as a nerdy older gent who's quiet and easily intimidated. He seems to be a sweet husband and grandfather, but some would say this stout man is boring and slow.

Famous Namesakes: Aviator Wilbur Wright; character Wilbur (*Charlotte's Web*)

Wiley

(English) willow meadow.

Image: Wiley is *wily*, it seems. He comes across as a dirty, sneaky schemer who's always in trouble unless he has constant supervision. He could also be a highly competitive sportsman who's pushy and angry.

Famous Namesakes: Aviator Wiley Post; football player Marcellus Wiley

Wilfred

(German) determined peacemaker.

Image: Wilfred can land a trophy catch but he can't carry a conversation. He's thought to be an outdoorsy guy who loves fishing, hunting, and nature in general. But he can be awkward and quiet in social situations.

Famous Namesakes: Actor Wilford Brimley

Will

(English) a short form of William.

Image: Will is an all-around all-American guy. He's said to be friendly, loving, funny, and handsome. Taking a different approach, some think of Prince William of the United Kingdom and say Will is regal.

Famous Namesakes: Actor Will Smith; actor Will Ferrell; character Will Truman (*Will & Grace*); humorist Will Rogers

Willard

(German) determined and brave.

Image: Willard isn't a fan of new experiences and ideas. People think of him as a meek fellow who's overweight, old, and a bit of a hermit. He's imagined to be kind and wise, but he may also be old-fashioned and narrow-minded.

Famous Namesakes: TV personality Willard Scott; actor Fred Willard

William

(English) a form of Wilhelm.

Image: People associate this name with the United Kingdom's Prince William. They describe him as a royal, noble prince who's kind, altruistic, and a smart college student. He's physically pictured as tall and blond with blue eyes.

Famous Namesakes: Playwright William Shakespeare; legendary hero William Tell; prince William; author William Faulkner; musician will.i.am

Willie

(German) a familiar form of William.

Image: It's not clear whether Willie gets teased *despite* or *because of* his goofy nature. This name evokes the image of a scrawny, mischievous guy who's always smiling and having fun. But people imagine he gets picked on often, which makes him seem like a wimpy mama's boy.

Famous Namesakes: Singer Willie Nelson; baseball player Willie Mays; character Willy Wonka (*Charlie and the Chocolate Factory*); character Willy Loman (*Death of a Salesman*)

Willis

(German) son of Willie.

Image: Times have been tough since Willis retired. People think of him as a gray-haired, short retiree who's shy and quietly funny. He's said to be wise, but he's down on his luck at this late point in his life.

Famous Namesakes: Actor Bruce Willis; character Willis Jackson (*Diff'rent Strokes*); baseball player Dontrelle Willis; football player Willis McGahee

Wilson

(English) son of Will.

Image: This name calls to mind either *Dennis the Menace* neighbor George Wilson or movie star Owen Wilson. Some people describe Wilson as a grouchy and mean old man. Others imagine him as a friendly, intelligent blond with surfer looks and a handsome smile.

Famous Namesakes: President Woodrow Wilson; character George Wilson (*Dennis the Menace*); character "Wilson" the volleyball (*Cast Away*); actors Owen Wilson and Luke Wilson

Winston

(English) friendly town; victory town.

Image: Thank Winston Churchill for this name's image. People associate Winston with a gruff, extremely bright, pipe-smoking British politician. He's seen as a poised speaker as well as a hefty and gray older man.

Famous Namesakes: British prime minister Winston Churchill; jeweler Harry Winston

Wood

(English) a short form of Elwood, Garwood, Woodrow.

Image: Like a great forest, Wood is deep, natural, and silent. He's imagined as an intelligent thinker who loves the outdoors and the solitude it offers. Although he's usually a quiet loner, this tall, muscular blond is also said to be devoted, hardworking, and sometimes even funny.

Famous Namesakes: Actor Elijah Wood; artist Grant Wood; musician Ron Wood

Wyatt

(French) little warrior.

Image: Wyatt Earp became a legend at the O.K. Corral, and his image still lives on. Wyatt is said to be a brave, rugged Westerner who's tough and mean. People believe he's handsome, quiet, and intelligent.

Famous Namesakes: Lawman Wyatt Earp

Xander

(Greek) a short form of Alexander.

Image: Xander's personality seems to contradict his appearance. Most people imagine him as an introspective and complicated thinker. He's known to have profound observations, but he keeps them to himself, thanks to his shyness and passivity. A book lover, he may also be working on the Great American Novel. Despite his bookish personality, Xander is most often pictured as a lanky guy with tattoos, piercings, and spiked hair.

Famous Namesakes: Character Xander Cage (*xxx*); actor Xander Berkeley; character Xander Harris (*Buffy the Vampire Slayer*)

Xavier

(Arabic) bright. (Basque) owner of the new house.

Image: Xavier's muscular body just leads him to trouble. He's pictured as big, manly, and tough. Because he's perfectly built for fighting, he finds himself in scrapes quite a bit. When he's not brawling, people imagine he's funny, take charge, and honest.

Famous Namesakes: Saint Francis Xavier; character Professor Charles Xavier (*X-Men*)

Xerxes

(Persian) ruler.

Image: There's no one quite like Xerxes. He's imagined to be as eccentric as he is physically strong. People say this Greek is obnoxious—although others describe him as an *individual*—but he's self-confident and smart nonetheless.

Famous Namesakes: Persian king Xerxes the Great; opera character Xerxes, also known as Serse

Boys

Yakov

(Russian) a form of Jacob.

Image: It's hard to know if Yakov is upset or just animated. People find him to be a vodka-loving Russian who's high-strung and strong willed. He often seems argumentative and annoying, but perhaps that's just because he can be loud and hard to understand. As for his appearance, he's probably thin and muscular with a big nose.

Famous Namesakes: Comedian Yakov Smirnoff

Yoshi

(Japanese) adopted son.

Image: Yoshi's creative energy is as addictive as his smile. People say Yoshi is a mild-mannered and shy fellow who's kindhearted and smiley. When he breaks out of his shell, he's said to be funky and creative—maybe even one-of-a-kind weird. He's most likely of Asian descent.

Famous Namesakes: Dinosaur character Yoshi (*Super Mario World*); Japanese actor Yoshi Kato

Zachariah

(Hebrew) God remembered.

Image: Zachariah has the intelligence and kindness to lead others. He's said to be a wise, educated man who's also kind and thoughtful. He likely works with people either as a teacher or a minister. Some imagine he's a strong leader, but others sense he's insecure and afraid to take risks. He's described as short and dark-haired, and he may be older.

Famous Namesakes: Biblical figure Zechariah; book *Z for Zachariah*

Zachary

(Hebrew) a familiar form of Zachariah.

Image: Zachary is a popular fellow, especially with the opposite sex. He's described as a warm, considerate guy with blond good looks and a flirty attitude. People also say he's passionate and daring, making him even more fun for the ladies to be around.

Famous Namesakes: President Zachary Taylor

Zane

(English) a form of John.

Image: Zane is either tellin' jokes or bustin' broncos. He seems to be hunky and sweet—on that, people agree. But people aren't sure if he's a loopy and unordinary funny guy or if he's an adventurous and bold cowboy (perhaps a nod to Western novelist Zane Grey).

Famous Namesakes: Actor Billy Zane; baseball player Zane Smith; author Zane Grey

Zedekiah

(Hebrew) God is mighty and just.

Image: In the Bible, Zedekiah is a wicked king. But in this name's image, Zedekiah is quite pious. He's thought to be a quiet, humble, and simple man with great spiritual faith and wisdom. Although he's known to keep to himself, he's also respectful to others. He may be Amish or perhaps Israeli, and he's pictured as tall, lean, and handsome.

Famous Namesakes: Biblical figure Zedekiah

★ Star Kids

Zolten Penn

People bisect this name to create two images. For Zolten, they picture a diabolical and menacing mastermind with an evil grin and a combative persona. But for Penn, they envision a quiet, philosophical poet who keeps to himself. Zolten Penn, son of illusionist Penn Jillette and TV producer Emily Zolten, will probably grow up to be someone with a combination of these two personalities.

Zeke

(Hebrew) a short form of Ezekiel, Zachariah, Zachary, Zechariah.

Image: Surprise—it's Zeke! People believe he's a loud, wild guy who loves surprises and spontaneity. He's thought to be witty and friendly, but he may have a moody side. Physically, Zeke is thought to be fair and skinny, but some imagine he's old and hunched over.

Famous Namesakes: None

Zeno

(Greek) cart; harness.

Image: Most of the time Zeno is a friendly guy, but sometimes his wild side can get out of hand. He gives the impression of a fun-loving and adventurous guy who's outgoing and easy to talk to. He's most likely a class clown, but sometimes he can be bullheaded and quick to fight with his muscular build.

Famous Namesakes: Byzantine emperor Flavius Zeno

Zephyr

(Greek) west wind.

Image: A zephyr is a pleasant wind, and this name's image fits quite nicely—whether it be for a girl or boy. Zephyr is imagined as an outgoing and energetic free spirit. He or she is most likely a caring, gentle friend who likes to have fun. People describe Zephyr as a striking blond.

Famous Namesakes: Song "The Zephyr Song"

Favorite Girls' Names

_____   _____

_____   _____

_____   _____

_____   _____

_____   _____

_____   _____

_____   _____

_____   _____

_____   _____

_____   _____

_____   _____

_____   _____

_____   _____

_____   _____

_____   _____

_____   _____

_____   _____

_____   _____

_____   _____

Favorite Boys' Names

_____   _____

_____   _____

_____   _____

_____   _____

_____   _____

_____   _____

_____   _____

_____   _____

_____   _____

_____   _____

_____   _____

_____   _____

_____   _____

_____   _____

_____   _____

_____   _____

_____   _____

_____   _____

Our Top Ten Names

Girls' Names

1. _____
2. _____
3. _____
4. _____
5. _____
6. _____
7. _____
8. _____
9. _____
10. _____

Boys' Names

1. _____
2. _____
3. _____
4. _____
5. _____
6. _____
7. _____
8. _____
9. _____
10. _____

Also from Meadowbrook Press

Baby Bites combines everything parents need to know about feeding babies and toddlers in one book. Part nutrition guide, part recipe book, this is the most comprehensive baby nutrition book on the market. Informative subjects include breastfeeding, formula-feeding, first-food purêes, and table foods. Facts and practical tips help parents understand their baby's nutritional needs and prepare tasty food that encourages healthy eating habits and avoids health problems.

Breastfeeding with Confidence is a practical guide to breastfeeding that's designed to provide new mothers with the practical skills and confidence they need to have a positive breastfeeding experience. Internationally known lactation expert Sue Cox explains both the art and the method of breastfeeding, and addresses the fact that making milk comes naturally but breastfeeding is a learned skill. She provides invaluable information, advice, resources, and encouragement for new mothers.

100,000+ Baby Names is the #1 baby name book and is the most complete guide for helping you name your baby. It contains over 100,000 popular and unusual names from around the world, complete with origins, meanings, variations, and famous namesakes. It also includes the most recently available top 100 names for girls and boys, as well as over 300 helpful lists of names to consider and avoid.

Feed Me! I'm Yours is an easy-to-use, economical guide to making baby food at home. More than 200 recipes cover everything a parent needs to know about teething foods, nutritious snacks, and quick, pleasing lunches. Now recently revised.

First-Year Baby Care is one of the leading baby-care books to guide you through your baby's first year. It contains complete information on the basics of baby care, including bathing, diapering, medical facts, and feeding your baby. Now recently revised.

The Toddler's Busy Book, *The Preschooler's Busy Book*, *The Arts and Crafts Busy Book*, and *The Wiggle & Giggle Busy Book* each contain 365 activities (one for each day of the year) for your children, using items found around the home. The books offer parents and child-care providers fun reading, math, and science activities that will stimulate a child's natural curiosity. They also provide great activities for indoor play during even the longest stretches of bad weather!

Baby Play and Learn, by child-development expert Penny Warner, offers ideas for games and activities that will provide hours of developmental learning opportunities and fun for babies. The book contains step-by-step instructions, illustrations, and bulleted lists of skills your baby will learn through play activities.

**We offer many more titles written to delight, inform, and entertain.
To order books with a credit card or browse our full
selection of titles, visit our website at:**

www.meadowbrookpress.com

or call toll free to place an order, request a free catalog, or ask a question:

1-800-338-2232

Meadowbrook Press • 5451 Smetana Drive • Minnetonka, MN • 55343